CW00958157

CONTROLLING FRONTIERS

Published by
Ashgate Publishing Limited
Gower House
Croft Road
Aldershot
Hants GU11 3HR
England

Ashgate Publishing Company
Suite 420
101 Cherry Street
Burlington, VT 05401-4405
USA

Ashgate website: http://www.ashgate.com

British Library Cataloguing in Publication Data
Controlling frontiers : free movement into and within
    Europe
    1.Foucault, Michel 2.Bauman, Zygmunt 3.Migration, Internal
    - European Union countries 4.Emigration and immigration law
    - European Union countries 5.National security - European
Union countries 6.Immigrants - Government policy - European
Union countries 7.Discrimination in law enforcement -
European Union countries 8.European Union countries -
Emigration and immigration 9.European Union countries -
Emigration and immigration - Government policy
I.Bigo, Didier II.Guild, Elspeth
325.4

Library of Congress Cataloging-in-Publication Data
Controlling frontiers : free movement into and within Europe / edited by Didier Bigo
and Elspeth Guild.
        p. cm.
    Includes bibliographical references and index.
    ISBN 0 -7546-3011-0
    1. European Union countries--Emigration and immigration. 2. Globalization. I. Bigo,
Didier. II. Guild, Elspeth.

    JV7590.C667 2005
    325.4--dc22

                                                              2004027011

ISBN 0 7546 3011 0

Printed and bound in Great Britain by Antony Rowe Ltd, Chippenham, Wiltshire

Controlling Frontiers
Free Movement Into and Within Europe

Edited by

Didier Bigo
Sciences-Po, France

and

Elspeth Guild
University of Nijmegen, The Netherlands

ASHGATE

Contents

Notes on Contributors

Didier Bigo

Didier Bigo is Professor of International Relations at Sciences-Po, the Institut d'Etudes Politiques, Paris, researcher at the CERI (Centre d'Etudes et de Recherches Internationales) director of the Centre for Conflict Studies, and editor of the journal *Cultures & Conflits,* Paris. Didier Bigo is visiting professor for three years at King's College, department of war studies. He works on the following issues: terrorism, war, internal and external security, conflicts resolution, International Relations theories. He has recently published "Global (in)security: the field of the professionals of unease management and the Ban-opticon", *Traces: a multilingual series of cultural theory*, n° 4, 2004.
His web page is http://www.conflits.org/article.php3?id_article=466
His email address is didier.bigo@conflits.org

Laurent Bonelli

Laurent Bonelli is lecturer in politics at the University of Paris X—Nanterre and member of the Centre for Conflict Studies. He is co-editor with Gilles Sainati (2001) of *La machine à punir. Pratiques et discours sécuritaires*, L'Esprit Frappeur: Paris. He works on the following issues: security policies, police knowledge and practices, and intelligence services.
His web page is http://www.conflits.org/rubrique.php3?id_rubrique=59
His email address is bonelli@conflits.org

Ayse Ceyhan

Dr Ayse Ceyhan is a political scientist graduate from the University of Paris I Panthéon-Sorbonne. She teaches International Relations and Political Science at the Institut d'Etudes Politiques (IEP) of Paris and is affiliated as researcher with the Centre for Conflict Studies. She specializes in issues of security, identity and borders that she analyzes in a comparative approach between the US and France. She has published articles on security, border controls and surveillance in several specialized journals.
Her email address is ayseceyhan@hotmail.com

John Crowley

John Crowley is a Senior Programme Specialist at UNESCO and Executive Director of CIR (Interdisciplinary Research Centre), where he also heads the Research Policy department. He has a PhD in political science from the Institut d'Etudes Politiques de Paris (1995). He is currently editor of the *International Social Science Journal*. His research focuses on the political theory of contemporary democracy in a comparative perspective.
His email address is j.crowley@iccr-international.org

Elspeth Guild

Elspeth Guild is Professor of European Immigration Law at the Centre for Immigration law, Faculty of Law, University of Nijmegen, the Netherlands. She is also research partner at Kingsley Napley, London. She is teaching Conflict Regulation and Security at the Institut d'Etudes Politiques, Paris and at King's College, London. She has recently published with E.R Brouwer, P. Catz, *Immigration, asylum, and terrorism. A changing Dynamic in European Law*, Nijmegen: KU Nijmegen, 2003.
Her email address is elspeth@conflits.org

Anastassia Tsoukala

Anastassia Tsoukala, jurist and criminologist, is Associate Professor at the Paris XI University. She is working on internal security issues in the EU, with particular focus on immigration and football hooliganism. She has published: *Sport et violence* (Athens/Brussels: Sakkoulas/Bruylant, 1995), *Policing Sport Events in Europe* (Athens: Sakkoulas, 1999, in Greek) and *Crime and Migration in Europe* (Athens: Sakkoulas, 2001, in Greek).
Her email address is tsoukala@conflits.org

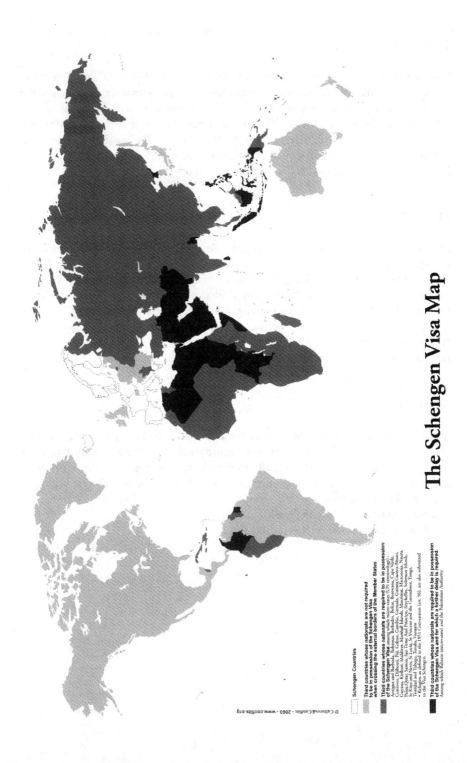

The Schengen Visa Map

Schengen Countries

Third countries whose nationals are not required
to be in possession of the Schengen Visa
when crossing the external borders of the Member States

Third countries whose nationals are required to be in possession
of the Schengen Visa among which major-states (UN terminology):
Antigua and Barbuda, Bahamas, Barbados, Belize, Botswana, Cape Verde,
Comoros, Djibouti, Fiji, Gabon, Gambia, Grenada, Guinea,Guinea-Bissau,
Guyana, Kiribati, Maldives, Marshall Islands, Mauritius, Micronesia , Nauru,
Palau, Qatar, Samoa, Sao Tome and Principe, Seychelles, Solomon Islands,
St Kitts and Nevis, St Lucia, St Vincent and the Grenadines, Tonga,
Trinidad and Tobago, Tuvalu, Vanuatu
• Refugees, as defined in the 1951 Convention (art. 96), are also submitted
to the Visa Schengen

Third countries whose nationals are required to be in possession
of the Schengen Visa and for which a further delay is required.
Among which Pakistan (non-exhaustive) and the Palestinian Authority

Introduction

Policing in the Name of Freedom*

Didier Bigo and Elspeth Guild

Introduction

Inequalities and patterns of domination and exclusion are persistent and changing. They are persistent in that they have been found in all societies and international systems throughout history, and changing, in that their manifestations, sources, consequences and justifications vary in time and space. The eight chapters presented in this book explore dimensions of inequality, domination, exclusion, and their rationalization through the freedom of movement and the control of frontiers in the European Union, in a theoretically explicit, comparative, and empirically grounded fashion. The authors of this book try to understand if there is a link between the current rise of securitization, penalization, and incarceration affecting the Western societies, the decrease of welfare and social support for the poor and the development of discourses concerning freedom of movement of people giving way to a new form of policing: policing at a distance. This policing in the name of freedom moves the locus of the controls and delocalizes them from the borders of the states to create new social frontiers both inside and outside of the territory, which is envisioned as a European territory.

For such authors as Allessandro dal Lago, Salvatore Palidda, David Garland, Loic Waquant and Pierre Bourdieu, liberalism is replacing the welfare state by a kind of social panopticon of surveillance and coercion towards the people who do not hold regular jobs and who are migrants.[1]

For them, it is a general phenomenon in different Western societies despite the specificity to the US because of its focus on young and poor Black people. We have developed this book along these lines because they address directly the central questions of domination and inequalities today, while avoiding at the same moment the discourse of "class war" and sometimes over simplification between the complex relations linking poverty and ethnicity, citizenship and foreignerness. This book examines along these lines the process at work at the level of the European Union and the differences that it is creating, in comparison with the US. There is a special focus on the role of the rhetoric of freedom of movement and how it frames the discourses and practices concerning the "migration problem" in Europe and the fears which have spread through the media, the political discourses of the professionals of politics and the administrative practices of the professionals of security.

The main questions which link all the chapters are: how do globalization and freedom of circulation affect securitization and how far is it connected with poverty? Is freedom of circulation for everybody or only for consumers of the middle and upper classes? Is freedom of circulation endangered by an ethnic bias? Is it a liberty or a new way of controlling and watching people in an age of risk and travel? Which are the categories of people that can travel and which are the categories that are blocked at the borders or have no chance to access travel facilities and are trapped in the local? Who may travel and stay in Europe in the new travel regime institutionalized by the Schengen agreements? What are the forms of policing which emerge from the deterritorialization of surveillance, its digitalization and its move towards controlling abroad and monitoring the future.

A discussion is needed about the relation between inequality, class, ethnicity and liberalism in the age of globalization. A Clausewitzian or Schmittian vision finishes by creating a polarization between the "have" and the "have not", the "rich" and the "poor", the "white" and the "coloured". Very often the leftist criticism of Wacquant and others seeks to show the danger of this war against the poor and the racist agenda, but, by doing so, the authors believe that a polarization takes place and is often a struggle for rights at the border of the territorial state. The hypothesis presented here is thus to deconstruct this belief in the polarization of struggles by analyzing the micro-rationality of the different agencies and the correlation between the social and the security agencies as well as their relationship with political discourses.

In this sense the underpinning reference of all the contributors, independently of their discipline, is the work of Michel Foucault.[2] Not the idealized and sometimes post-modern Americanized vision of Foucault as a French post structuralist, "maître à penser" that is quoted instead to be understood, but the one some of us have known in Paris, at the College de France, whose work is rooted in history and sociology, not literature. Michel Foucault loved nothing more than obscure documents forgotten by everyone else, but which were formative, like the books of Delamarre concerning police as the art of the government, or the research of Jeannine Bordas-Charon and H Tulard. He prefers to analyze directives and administrative circulars rather than the great authors of the time to understand the relations of power. He had a passion for administrative law. In everyday life he always listened to significant anecdotes about concrete practices and could spend hours on this subject but avoiding any great debate about Jean Paul Sartre, or Jacques Lacan's theories of the world. His work with prisoners at the GIP (prisoner information group) was built on this capacity to listen and to understand the political where it lies, in the more obvious complaints about the living conditions lack of space for sleep, lack of food, insults and not in the rhetoric about freedom inside the prison or the rights they had. This work with them was to give them a voice and not to speak for them, i.e., in their place. And if the connection between the GIP and the writing of "Discipline and Punish" was very strong, he always refused to use their voices as "material". As he often said, "don't quote me, use my work and destroy it if you can".

This advice has been followed. This book can be understood as a way to follow some of the main hypotheses of Foucault concerning power relations and as a specific critique of the thesis of the pan-opticon and of the role of police and surveillance in modern societies from the conditions of the present. It seems that Foucault has underestimated the role of technologies such as computerization, and data bases which were only at their beginning, even if he has seen the move from the "territorial" state to the "population" state and the strategies of following and tracing the movement of the people instead of the old discipline to attach them to a territory. Foucault has also overestimated the capacity and the will of control of national governments, their capacity to decide and to affect the life of everybody. He has based his reasoning on the "equality" of all under surveillance, following Bentham, but we note that the social practices of surveillance and control sort out, filter and serialize who needs to be controlled and who is free from that control, because he is "normalized". It is more a Ban than a Pan opticon. Even if Foucault was the first to criticize the sovereign moment, he connects police too much with government and sovereignty because he was still working in a national mindscape. Because he has worked more on punishment than on policing, he has not seen the development of the transnational networks of surveillance, of intelligence which were existent from the beginning of the nineteenth century, but which were restructured and accelerated by the "Europeanization" of the nation states. Interested in international politics, he has not so much connected his theoretical work with these subjects.

On all these points this book tries to give some elements to its readership coming from an analysis of law, implementation of international agreements, the role of the companies in relation to the state and the individual, the analysis of the rhetoric of politicians and of the more undercover narratives of the professionals of security as well as the analysis of what they are doing, who they target, with what kind of techniques are used and where.

The second source of this book is the work of Zygmunt Bauman and his hypothesis than the new dividing criterion of the world is between those who can live globally and those who are anchored in their localities, between freedom to move for some and the incapacity to enjoy it and the fate of being trapped in the local for the others.[3] By analyzing the social consequences of globalization, and the "liquefaction" of society, Bauman has opened a new field of research, concerning the disjuncture of globalization as Apadurai examines, or the emergence of a global society in the making as in David Held.[4] But, except for Thomas Mathiesen, David Lyon, Richard Ericson and James Sheptycki, few people have worked on the connection between globalization and policing.[5] They have mainly analyzed the technologies of control but not the correlation with the imperative of circulation implemented in the European Union as a "freedom". It is in that nexus that this book tries to give a different view, by showing that Bauman is optimistic if he thinks that rich people on the move are not controlled by the transnational networks of agencies following the tracks of the individuals and too pessimistic concerning the poor people trapped in the local. They move nevertheless and by moving they re-structure all the relations of power, both externally, at the global scale between rich and poor countries and internally, at the individual level, by blocking the capacity of anybody to manage the flow of millions of individual decisions, even when all the professionals of politics seek to prevent and negate this structural transformation which endangers their power and the symbolic reassurance that they are in charge of the security in a specific territory. Their resistance, as poor tourists, as people on the move for better jobs, as people fleeing conflicts or bad conditions of life, structure the relations of power and the anxieties of loosing their "privileges" by the professionals of politics, of (in)security, of media and of some segments of the population. The governmentality by fear and unease which emerges from this is then different from the situation which existed before, especially in the European Union where the notion of freedom of movement of persons has been considered as essential for the building of a European identity. Policing in the name of freedom in a global age is organized differently from before and each contributor analyzes in detail some aspects of these transformations.

This book tries then, by discussing Foucault and Bauman concerning the nature of the frontier controls in the European Union and the way policing is carried out in the name of freedom of circulation, to offer a comprehensive vision that permits the reader to understand better the notions of frontiers, security, and identity in the European context.[6] As the focus is more theoretical, the sociological articles are not filled with interviews, but the reader may rest assured that the findings are based on long in-depth research by the sociologists and political scientist contributors comparing the way the security agencies analyze their role and their duties concerning control and surveillance of people crossing the borders.[7] Interviews began in 1992 and every two years, the team of researchers returned to the question of border controls and each time developed new ways of looking at it, using different angles and systematic comparison between the situation inside Europe and between Europe and the US to specify what is the effect of Europeanization and its originality: the fields include the legal framework, the techniques of border controls and surveillance at a distance like the visa policies, the techniques of identification and impact on citizenship, the structuration of an "us"/"them" vision with an (in)securitization of the migrants in the role of the enemies, the criminalization of the poor inside the society and "alienization" of their image as outsiders, the de-differentiation between internal and external security and the construction of a global (in)security field where the different professionals of security agencies structure their vision through a proactive attitude, leading them to believe that they can anticipate and master time as well as space, the development of a "normalization" of free movement and the creation of categories of people under control because they are considered threats to the state and the society they live in, the constitution of a "Ban-opticon".[8]

These hypotheses locate the events of 11 September 2001 in a series of structural transformations where the novelty of the attack is relativized, but where the nature of the answer is seen as an accelerator and a sign of the emergence of a new form of governmentality. We have rejected the option of a specific article about 11 September 2001 as it is not relevant per se, but each article internalizes the post 11 September transformations. So the contributors dismiss the rhetoric about the novelty of terrorism and global crime but emphasize the role of globalization and the tensions between the professionals of politics, who are often sovereignty-bound and -minded, and the professionals of security who are more and more globally oriented and perceive the world (inside and outside the state) as a global insecurity system. In so doing, they try to introduce the question of democracy, of the struggles of civil liberties against unlimited security or an internalization of the way of excluding people from the normal conditions and of obliging them to live in a permanent state of exception, in a quasi state of a permanent emergency. In that sense, the criticism of state and sovereignty is no longer sufficient, even if it is crucial, what is needed, after 11 September, is a criticism of the security focus and of the velocity of the spread of beliefs concerning this globalized (in)securitization of the world. Two steps are needed here.

The first step is to refuse the "cultural" explanations seeking to homogenize large groups of predominantly different people under the same denomination of "civilization", very often only to create the possibility of reconstructing a simple and major clash, easy to define and to combat (Huntington, or Kagan) as was the case during the cold war.[9] These are cultural policy devices, transferred into the field of geopolitics, using the same concept of border as line of demarcation, line of division. The neo Schmittian approach of the "US versus Them" and "Them as enemies to constitute US with a strong identity" has to be abandoned from the beginning as it is not an analytical tool but just a securitarian rhetoric. We should also be cautious concerning some of the "globalist" explanations that exaggerate the strength and the size of the global by confusing it with transnational and cross-border activities. Even baptizing like Hardt and Negri, the situation "Empire", stating the diversity beyond the hegemony or the unilateralism of one state is very often simply an attempt to find (as in the case of Huntington but in the reverse) a simple way of naming a new enemy as it was in class struggles. The dialectic of the Multitude as a singular name, thus homogenizing existing diversity, is a way to dismiss complexity, to name the heterogeneity in order to "master" it, and a strategy to re-create the eschatology of the proletariat instead of dealing with the differences and the heterogeneity.[10] Consequently, there are no "grand narratives" that provide a simple explanation for everything.

The complexity of the situation has to be accepted, as well as the specificity of the European case in comparison with the USA. The book looks at the heterogeneity of concrete situations and analyzes the diagram of forces which gives them their originality and at the same moment allows comparisons. The space and time of globalization are not driven by the tendency towards more homogeneity and unity, but by disjunctures. The debate is not only to determine whether it is for the wealth and the good of humanity or only for the sake of some new forms of bourgeoisie at the global level and against the multitudes that globalization is at work.

The space and time of globalization are compressed, but the application is diverse and fragmented. So, no clear borders can be found along the lines of class or large territories, or even racism. There is a need to insist firstly on the heterogeneity and the transversality of the devices of power and secondly to de-nationalize the vision of the state by looking specifically to the European Union level as a specific and different process from the aggregation of the national elements of it.

The second step is to theorize this emergence of what is not only across, but beyond the state, and to understand the relationship between borders, territory, population and government in this context. How and where is the political located? What are the forms of domination if they are not bound by the nation state and the democratic procedures? Have they changed? Who benefits and who loses? How do the institutions work together, in what framework and with what kind of legitimacy? What are the proto-norms that justify the practices of power at the transnational level? Who has the capacity to re-draw the boundaries between legitimate and illegitimate use of violence? How is the difference between violence and force to be drawn if the idea of using state apparatus as an ultimate force for stopping violence disappears? What if individuals or little groups can threaten the largest states with some chance of success in destroying them at once? What if, in the name of such a threat, the governments destabilize the relationship between democracy and civil liberties? What if they blame some weak groups as being the causes of violence because they are not able to find the real ones and what is the relation to justice? What if, in the name of the promise of unlimited security, they destroy the balance with freedom by their own excesses and become, in the end, the main danger for individuals asking them for protection?

This book could not answer all these questions. But it is important to see that they are related in order to avoid engaging in very old battles with new names. Here, there is a we will focus on the questions of globalized (in)security and frontier controls because they are now at the core of the administrative practices, the public policies, the discussion in international relations, the state of the art in political theory. And to analyze them is to come back to the structuration of power and desire at the global scale.

To analyze people's desire to move, their possibilities to move just to enjoy other places or to work there, opens new venues to understand why, how, and for what reason we have such an emphasis on the "immigration problem" in Europe and why the political class is in each country so tempted by populist arguments and a discourse feeding fears about the "invaders". Each chapter tries to analyze how the differentialist management of the people on the move structures the way policing is now disconnected from the territorial border and mainly done by identification technologies and at a distance. And why the professionals of politics refuse to admit these changes, at the risk of being totally disconnected from the transformation of the social world as they create more and more inadequate labels and descriptions of the world concerning movement of people and use of violence for political reasons. This "desire" to move is not ingrained inside the individual need but is more a Deleuzian desire, an imperative, a transversal flow.[11]

The second desire is the possibility to work and to find better opportunities. The management of work at the global scale seeks to serialize who is entitled to work and to move for work and who is not. Here also the professionals of politics are challenged, as their will to master the situation is less and less credible and the role of the major companies is more and more important. The transnationalization of bureaucracies of labour and industry in competition with the transnational networks of the professionals of (in)security creates a field of struggle which does not obey national logic but rather corporatist one, and different visions of the world linked to the specific doxa of these professional groups.

The third desire is the capacity or not to choose between multiple identities and to have a politics of belonging. The management of this aspect is now to try to dispossess the individual from his or her right to say who he or she is and what are the identities by assigning him or her to a biological identity, stamped by the network of data bases working in relations to the different governments and professionals (private and public) of (in)security. The biopower is technologized and digitalized to reduce the individual to "bare life", to genetic capital, to the tracks he leaves on the spot when he moves.

The connection of these desires or forms of productive relations of power is the way to read each chapter of this book which analyzes the forms of domination and inequalities at the frontiers of Europe. They are organized first to deconstruct the so-called immigration problem in Europe which supposedly can be managed only by the frontiers control and the role of police at the borders, and secondly to show what is really at stake with the control of some specific groups in Europe.

The first chapter deals with the legal framework of the European Union to understand who is and who is not entitled to move. Instead of speaking of migrants in general as an analytical category, Elspeth Guild shows how people on the move have different rights if they are EC nationals or third country nationals. She explains the logic of application for a visa, for entering the territory at the border, for having a work permit and the conditions under which people could be expelled by differentiating the situation regarding if they are tourists and visitors, labour migrants, family members, or asylum seekers. Emergent from her work is the heterogeneity of the rights and of situations that the political and mediatic discourses want to amalgamate. It is not possible for an EC national to be asylum seeker under the "mantra" that all EU member states are by definition democracies and by definition could not persecute their own population or treat them badly, even when they are considered as terrorists. Unfortunately many cases show the contrary. But mainly the situation of EC nationals is largely better than that of third country nationals and it is less problematic for them to travel, to live and to work. What is labelled migrant by the professionals of politics is very often the third country nationals only, but the suspicion that they come to work illegally undermines the categories of visitors for tourism and of asylum seekers. The last one is under suspicion as "bogus" refugees. They are constructed by the media and the professionals of politics as cheating with false narratives of their lives exaggerating the persecution or fear of persecution they have suffered. The first one, tourism for the poor, is just unthinkable in a world of consumption and the visas requirements prevent them leaving their country if they don't have enough money.

The second chapter analyzes what is a frontier, a frontier control and who is in control. Didier Bigo tries to analyze the web of official narratives which struggle between them at the European level but unanimously promise to be "the" solution to the "immigration problem" and to have found the way to manage "really" the frontier controls. This discursive formation structures the debate and makes opaque what is at stake by evoking sovereignty, security, survival, defence of the society as the main topics concerning people on the move. The professionals of politics insist so much that they are in charge there is a need to analyze if it is true or not, if they can have an impact on the flows of people and why they insist so much on frontiers as the locus of control when the professionals of (in)security are dealing with other ways to manage these flows. The third chapter, by Elspeth Guild, continues the demonstration of the weakness of the professionals of politics by analyzing the role of the major companies and their influence inside the policies of the bureaucracies dealing with industry and labour, and the struggles with the professionals of security. She shows that the right for legal persons to move is so powerful and so linked with the interests of major private companies wanting to move their own personnel without difficulties that no government dares to oppose that position. Concerning frontier controls, the different governments of Europe have agreed to expand the freedom of movement in regards to capital, services, and workers, thinking in economic terms of a more efficient allocation of resources. But the movement of workers is also the movement of people, and after many struggles, the idea of the right for all categories of people to move if they want is emerging, and challenging the legitimacy of the state's monopoly on the means of movement. The frontiers in an age of the retreat of the state are then differently located. The question is about who is excluded from freedom of movement and not who is entitled to move in a sealed and divided world of homogeneous states with strong borders. The fourth chapter, by John Crowley, then discusses where are the borders of the welfare state? It seems that the controls "protect" more a multiplicity of points of access to benefits than a "territory". And he analyzes who is suspected of attacking "welfare" and where the boundaries run which were created to exclude or to downsize the possibilities of some people to be citizen in the T.H. Marshall sense. The "territorial state" is an ambiguous notion, not something to be taken for granted, especially in the formation of the European Union. The discussion about identity and politics of belonging is then at the heart of the relation between security and frontiers.

The rest of the book emphasizes some of the main features of domination and inequalities. Anastassia Tsoukala analyzes the social construction of threats by the professionals of politics, of security and of journalists and why they construct a continuum of threat from terrorism, organized crime, petty crime and migration or asylum seekers or even citizens of foreign origins through the notions of illegality and the transformation of action into the building of categories of dangerous "people". She uses mainly Italy and Greece to show that this social construction is not culturally rooted in the past and linked with colonial attitudes. It is a political construct which could emerge even in societies where a large proportion of the population was treated badly as migrants ten years ago. This construct is reinforced by the specific forms of policing the borders chosen by the European Union. In the sixth chapter Laurent Bonelli analyzes, from the French example, how policemen build their institutional knowledge and frame the French citizen whose parents were born in the Maghreb as a danger for the norms of French society. He shows how these strategies are applied to "construct" new areas of danger and to make them visible by designating all the people living nearby these French citizens of foreign origin of the suburban area as the locus of danger. He shows how they construct these young people as a fifth column waiting a sign from abroad to attack the values of republicanism. They consider them as infiltrated enemies, as enemies "within". After this analysis of the logic to control downstream, inside the territory,

Ayse Ceyhan comes back to the locus of the state border to show how the controls have changed nowadays. They are not systematic and egalitarian as well as routinized. They are linked with data bases, with previous knowledge, with profiling and stocks of identification data. They are transnational and not national. They participate to the reduction of the individual to its body and its tracks.

Finally Elspeth Guild and Didier Bigo analyze the logic of control of the border upstream, at distance from the border of the state and how the notion of frontier control is moving. They use the example of the Schengen visas policies to show the dynamics of power struggles between the member states and the Commission, between the logic of border control of the border guards and the logic of proactive policing of the consulates and embassies abroad. Beyond the question of the rights, the question of speed is central. As Virilio has explained, this is the kind of "dromocracy" we live in. The reign of speed and acceleration is linked with technologies, with remote control policies, with virtualization and anticipation through morphing of the future of the persons who are on the move. And against speed, slowness never wins. The judicial apparatus is accused of being responsible for the slowness of the security professionals. He is attacked by the politicians because the time to avoid passion and the time to think is time considered lost or wasted. This argument is used against all controls, even those of customs and police when they slow the flow of merchandise, services or information. Security technologies that stop or slow the flow can not be permitted in our world. The techniques of frontier controls are obliged to change because the old paradigm of the sealing of the border is now meaningless. The surveillance and similar controls are now at a distance, by remote control, by international collaboration, by anticipation of crime before it happens. This policy of remote control, of preventive policing, of preemptive defence or of deterrence is oriented towards a policy of policing in the name of freedom of movement which focusses only on some categories and normalizes others, which tries to monitor the future by the resources of identification and technologies of data bases. The map of the Schengen visa is in that sense a metaphor of the new divides of our world where the globalization of surveillance is now oriented towards the control of the individuals and not only of their states of origin, about the control of the poor on the move, especially if they are third country nationals.

Notes

* This book would never have been possible without the contribution of the European Commission through the ELISE research program (European Liberty and Security/contract n°HPSE-CT-2002-00150). All the contributors to this book are grateful to Miriam Perier and Gulçin Lelandais for their contribution of commented bibliographies for each author, and Colin Steinbach for his typographic reading of the texts.
[1] Bourdieu, P. (2000), 'L'immigrant comme Shebollet', in *Contre-Feux 2. Pour Un Mouvement Social Européen*, Liber-Raisons d'agir, Paris.
Bourdieu, P. (2000), *Propos sur le champ politique*, Presses Universitaires de Lyon, Lyon.

Dal Lago, A. (1999), *Non-Persone: L'esclusione Dei Migranti in Una Società Globale, Interzone*, Feltrinelli, Milano.

Garland, D. (2002), *The Culture of Control*, Oxford University Press, Oxford.

Mariani, P. (2001), 'Law, Order, and Neoliberalism', *Social Justice*, 28(3), pp. 1-152.

Palidda, S. (1999), 'La criminalization des migrants', *Actes de la recherche en sciences sociales*, 129, pp. 39-49.

Palidda, S. (1993), 'L'anamorphose de L'Etat-nation: le cas italien (Anamorphosis of the Nation-State: The Italian Case)', *Cahiers internationaux de Sociologie*, 93, pp. 269-98.

Tournier, P. (1997), 'La Délinquance des étrangers en France. Analyze des statistiques pénales', in *Délit D'immigration, Cost A2 Migrations*, edited by S. Palidda, Commission européenne, pp. 133-62.

Wacquant, L. (1999), 'Des "ennemis commodes"', *Actes de la recherche en sciences sociales*, 129, pp. 63-67.

[2] Foucault, M. (1977), *Discipline and Punish: The Birth of the Prison*, 1st American ed., Pantheon Books, New York.

——— (1994), *Dits et Ecrits: 1954-1988*, Gallimard, Paris.

——— (1997), *Il faut défendre la société. Cours au Collège de France (1975-1976)*, Seuil/Gallimard, Paris.

——— (1989), *Sécurité, Territoire, Population. Résumé des cours*, Julliard, Paris.

——— (1975), *Surveiller et punir: Naissance de la prison*, Gallimard, Paris.

——— (1999), *Les Anormaux. Cours au Collège de France (1974-1975)*, Seuil/Gallimard, Paris.

Foucault, M. and Gordon, C. (1980), *Power/Knowledge: Selected Interviews and Other Writings, 1972-1977*, Harvester Press, Hassocks.

Foucault, M. and Kriegel, B. (1975), *I, Pierre Rivière, Having Slaughtered My Mother, My Sister, and My Brother...: A Case of Parricide in the 19th Century*, 1st American ed. Pantheon Books, New York.

——— (1973), *Moi, Pierre Rivière, ayant égorgé ma mère, ma soeur et mon frère... Un cas de parricide au XIXe siècle*, Gallimard, Paris.

Perrot, M., Foucault M. and Agulhon, M. (1980), *L'impossible prison: recherches sur le système pénitentiaire au XIXe siècle*, Seuil, Paris.

Trombadori, D. and Foucault, M. (1981), *Colloqui Con Foucault, Discorsi; 1*, Salerno: 10/17.

[3] Bauman, Z. (1988), *Freedom, Concepts in Social Thought*, University of Minnesota Press, Minneapolis.

——— (1998), *Globalization: The Human Consequences*, Polity Press, Cambridge.

——— (2000), *Liquid Modernity*, Polity Press/Blackwell, Cambridge, Malden, MA.

——— (1982), *Memories of Class: The Pre-History and After-Life of Class, International Library of Sociology*, Routledge & Kegan Paul, London/Boston.

——— (1976), *Towards a Critical Sociology: An Essay on Common Sense and Emancipation*, Routledge & Kegan Paul, London/Boston.

——— (2001), 'Wars of the Globalization Era', *European Journal of Social Theory*, 4(1), pp. 11-28.

[4] Appadurai, A. (2001), *Globalization*, Duke University Press, Durham, NC.

——— (1996), *Modernity at Large: Cultural Dimensions of Globalization, Public Worlds; V. 1.*, University of Minnesota Press, Minneapolis.

Held, D. (1996), 'Cosmopolitan Democracy and the Global Order: Reflections on the 200th Anniversary of Kant's Perpetual Peace', *Alternatives*, 20(4), pp. 415-29.

——— (1992), 'Democracy and Globalization', *Alternatives*, 16(2), pp. 201-8.

―――― (1991), 'Democracy, the Nation-State and the Global System', *Economy and Society*, 20(2), pp. 138-72.

―――― (2002), 'Globalization, Corporate Practice and Cosmopolitan Social Standards', *Contemporary Political Theory*, 1(1), pp. 59-78.

[5] Ericson, R. V. and Haggerty, K. D. (1997), *Policing the Risk Society*, University of Toronto Press, Toronto.

Ericson, R. V. and Stehr, N. (2000), *Governing Modern Societies, The Green College Thematic Lecture Series*, University of Toronto Press, Toronto.

Lyon, D. (1994), *The Electronic Eye*, Polity Press, Cambridge.

Mathiesen, T. (1997), '"The Viewer Society: Michel Foucault's Panopticon Revisited", ½', *Theoretical Criminology*, pp. 215-34.

Sheptycki, J. W. E. (2002), *In Search of Transnational Policing: Towards a Sociology of Global Policing, Advances in Criminology*, Ashgate, Aldershot.

Sheptycki, J. W. E. (ed.) (2000), *Issues in Transnational Policing*, Routledge, London.

[6] The style is certainly surprising for an Anglo-American audience which is accustomed to understanding theory as an equivalent of abstraction and history as case studies which are examples of an abstract argument. Here theory is grounded in the historical events, not in abstraction, and the singularities of the events are recognized as such, but from them emerge alternative visions of the world. So theory is embedded inside historical narratives and not summarized as a 'finding' after an analysis of different patterns and variables at the end of each chapter. Style is more than accuracy in writing. It shows the dominant pattern of thinking. Too often the normalization of style is in fact a surrender to behaviourist and positivist agenda which does not really recognize what theory is.

[7] Albert, M., Jacobson, D. and Lapid, Y. (2001), *Identities, Borders, Orders: Rethinking International Relations Theory*, University of Minnesota Press, Minneapolis.

Bigo, D. (1992), 'Les attentats de 1986 en France: un cas de violence transnationale et ses implications (The 1986 Terrorist Actions in France: A Case of Transnational Violence and Its Implications)', *Cultures & Conflits*, 4, pp. 123-73.

―――― (2001), 'The Mobius Ribbon of Internal and External Security', in Albert M., Jacobson D. and Lapid Y. (eds) (2001), *Identities, Borders, Orders*, University of Minnesota Press, Minneapolis, pp. 91-116.

―――― (1996), *Polices en réseaux. L'expérience Européenne*, Presses de la FNSP, Paris.

―――― (1998), 'Sécurité et immigration: vers une gouvernementalité par l'inquiétude?' *Cultures & Conflits*, 31/32, pp. 13-38.

―――― (2002), 'Security and Immigration: Towards a Governmentality of Unease', *Alternatives/Cultures & Conflits*, 27, pp. 63-92.

―――― (1995), 'Terrorisme, drogue, immigration: les nouvelles figures de l'insécurité en Europe (Terrorism, Drugs and Immigration: The New Faces of Insecurity in Europe)', *Revue Internationale d'Action Communautaire*, 70, pp. 43-59.

Bigo, D. and Guild, E. (2002), 'De Tampere à Séville: bilan de la sécurité européenne', *Cultures & Conflits*, 45/46, pp. 5-18.

Bigo, D. (2000), 'Polices post-communistes. Une transformation inachevée?', *Les Cahiers de la Sécurité Intérieure*, 41, IHESI, Paris.

Ceyhan, A. (1994), 'Le communautarisme et la question de la reconnaissance (Communitarianism and the Problem of Recognition)', *Cultures & Conflits*, 12, pp. 169-84.

Ceyhan, A. and Tsoukala, A. (1997), 'Contrôle de l'immigration: mythes et réalités', *Cultures & Conflits*, 26/27, pp. 9-14.

―――― (2002), 'The Securitization of Migration in Western Countries', *Alternatives*, 27, pp. 21-33.

Ceyhan, A. and Périès, G. (2001), 'L'ennemi intérieur: une construction politique et discursive, *Cultures & Conflits*, 43, pp. 3-11.
Crowley, J. (2001), 'Differential Free Movement and the Sociology of the "Internal Border"', in Guild, E. and Harlow, C., *Implementing Amsterdam. Immigration and Asylum Rights in EC Law*, Hart, Oxford, pp. 13-33.
——— (2002). 'Locating Europe', in Guild, E., Gronedijk, C. and Miderhoud, P. (eds), *In Search of Europe's Borders*, Kluwer, Dordrecht.
——— (1999), 'The Politics of Belonging: Some Theoretical Considerations', in Favell, A. and Geddes, A. (eds), *The Politics of Belonging. Migrants and Minorities in Contemporary Europe*, Ashgate, Aldershot, Brookfield USA, Singapore, Sydney, pp. 15-41.
Groenendijk, C. A., Guild, E. and Minderhoud, P. E. (2003), *In Search of Europe's Borders, Immigration and Asylum Law and Policy in Europe*, Kluwer Law International, The Hague/New York.
Guild, E. (2000), 'Entry into the UK: The Changing Nature of National Borders', *I&NL&P* pp. 227-38.
——— (2000), 'Adjudicating Schengen: National Judicial Control in France', *European Journal of Migration and Law*, 1(4), pp. 419-39.
Guild, E. and Minderhoud, P. E. (2001), *Security of Residence and Expulsion: Protection of Aliens in Europe, Immigration and Asylum Law and Policy in Europe*, Kluwer Law International, The Hague/Boston.
Tsoukala, A. (1997), 'Le contrôle de l'immigration en Grèce dans les années 90', *Cultures & Conflits*, 27, pp. 51-72.
——— (1999), 'The Perception of the "Other" and the Integration of Immigrants in Greece', in Geddes, A. and Favell, A. (eds), *The Politics of Belonging: Migrants and Minorities in Contemporary Europe*, Ashgate, Aldershot, Brookfield USA, Singapore, Sydney, pp. 109-24.
[8] Different reports for the French ministries of research, of defense and of interior have been published including some of the interviews: Bigo, D., Smith, A. and Guittet, E. (2002), '*La participation des militaires aux questions de sécurité intérieure: Royaume Uni, Irlande du Nord*', rapport établi pour la DAS (Ministry of Defense), Centre d'études sur les conflits, Paris, 120 p.
Bigo, D., Hanon, J. P., Tsoukala, A. and Bonelli, L. (2001), *La fonction de protection*, rapport établi pour le Centre de prospective de la gendarmerie, Centre d'études sur les Conflits, Paris, 182 p.
Bigo, D., Hanon, J. P. and Tsoukala, A. (1999), *La participation des militaires aux questions de sécurité intérieure*, rapport établi pour la DAS, Centre d'études sur les conflits, Paris, 180 p.
Bigo, D. (1998), *Sécurité intérieure, implications pour la défense*, rapport établi pour la DAS, 207 p.
'Security, Borders and the state', in Sweedler, A. and Scott, J. (eds) (1996), *Border regions in functional transition*, (for Europe) Institute for Regional Development (IRS), Berlin; 1997 (for the US), SDSU Press, San Diego. [Abstract of the report of 1993].
Bigo, D. (1994), *Controlling the Border: a Comparative Approach Europe (Schengen, Maastricht) North America (NAFTA)*, Conference 'Bridge and Barriers: Immigration', USD, San Diego.
Bigo, D. (1993), *Interpénétration sécurité intérieure sécurité extérieure: enjeux américains et européens*, rapport établi pour la FEDN, Centre d'études sur les conflits, Paris, 180 p.
Different issues of the journal *Cultures & Conflits* have summarized these various reports. They are all available online (http://www.conflits.org). Concerning the notion of Ban opticon see Bigo, D. (2004), *Policing Insecurity Today*, forthcoming, Palgrave.

[9] Huntington, S. P. (1993) 'The Clash of Civilizations?', *Foreign Affairs*, 72(3), pp. 22-49.

Kagan, R. (2003), *Of Paradise and Power: America and Europe in the New World Order*, Knopf, New York.

[10] Hardt, M. and Negri, A. (2001), *Empire*, Harvard University Press, Cambridge.

[11] Deleuze, G. (1986), *Foucault*, Editions de Minuit, Paris.

Deleuze, G. and Guattari, F. (1972), *L'anti-Oedipe*, Editions de minuit, Paris.

———— (1980), *Mille Plateaux*, Editions de Minuit, Paris.

———— (1986), *Nomadology: The War Machine, Foreign Agents Series*. Semiotext(e), New York.

Chapter 1

The Legal Framework:
Who is Entitled to Move?

Elspeth Guild

Introduction

One of fundamental characteristics of globalization is the elevation of the interest in movement in search of economic gain above that of the nation state to exercise controls across and within its borders. The transnational corporation uses its economic power to ensure the best possible conditions for its economic activities irrespective of national borders. Border controls which offend against the interests of the beneficiaries of globalization are the subject of attack by them. This simplicity of formulation masks much more complex processes which Beck describes as those "through which sovereign national states are criss-crossed and undermined by transnational actors with varying prospects of power, orientations, identities and networks".[1]

The right to move for economic gain, however, whether in the form of goods, capital, services or persons, in a globalising world is increasingly limited to those who are already economically advantaged. "As the national framework loses its binding force, the winners and the losers of globalization cease to sit at the same table. The new rich no longer 'need' the new poor."[2] One of the constant features of the "globalising" world is the exclusion from the possibility of movement of the poor and those in search of international protection – refugees. So while on the one hand, the discussion about globalization focuses on the increasing power of legal persons to move (transnational corporations in particular) in relation to the state and their interests the other side of the coin is the increasingly draconian legal regime of the state to exclude from movement persons who are poor. This exclusion takes the form of legal measures by states in respect of persons defined as poor and by definition then unwanted (and unneeded) and thus to be excluded. However, this is not simply a question of blind exclusion. Andre Gorz states:

> The social security system must be reorganized, and new foundations put in place. But we must also ask why it seems to have become impossible to finance this reconstruction. Over the past twenty years, the EU countries have become 50 to 70 percent richer. The economy has grown much faster than the population. Yet the EU now has twenty million unemployed, fifty million below the poverty line and five million homeless. What has happened to the extra wealth? From the case of the

United States, we know that economic growth has enriched only the best off 10 percent of the population. This 10 percent has garnered 96 percent of the additional wealth. Things are not quite as bad in Europe, but they are not much better.

He goes on to stress that the rich are now virtual taxpayers denying the state the funds for social welfare programmes.[3] Thus the exclusion of persons feared to be a potential burden to the social welfare system becomes a priority for the state.

In a globalising world where the rich do not need the new poor, the state which cannot afford the new poor takes ever more severe measures to ensure that they are excluded from the possibility to move across borders. The national legal measures excluding the poor are set against the economic interest of transnational corporations in the transport industry to reduce the costs of travel in order to increase their profits. So while the cost of international bus, train and air travel tickets is reduced, so compensatory measures are adopted by the state (and in this study I will look only at the European "state") to make sure that the world's poor cannot move but remain locked in their country of origin irrespective of international commitments, including human rights obligations which require them to provide protection to persons fearing persecution.

In this chapter legal mechanisms will be looked at whereby exclusion of the poor from movement into and within the European Union is achieved. The reason for this is because the Union itself can be compared with a form of "mini" globalization. It was based on the laisser-faire principle of free movement of goods, persons services and capital within the territory of the Member States. The abolition of national controls on movement was and continues to be the most important principle of Community law. The strength of European Community law to override national law within the areas of competence of the Union is no longer disputed. Thus globalization within the EU's Europe is capable of completion. Within this context, the right and limitations of natural persons to move will be examined, as will the relationship between the right to move and economic strength for individuals within the Union and of those seeking to come to the Union. Conclusions will then be drawn about the right to move for individuals and economic power in the light of the globalization discussion. This chapter builds on the work of Bommes and Geddes (2000) on immigration and the welfare state, while their focus was different, their research has enriched this work.[4]

Immigration and Poverty: The European Union Legal Framework

Four different categories of migration in European Union law and policy will be looked at: visitors/tourists; labour migrants; family members and asylum seekers. In each category, the tests which are applied on financial means will be looked at, along with the consequences of failure to fulfil them at four stages in the migration process:

1.   Application for a visa;
2.   At the border;
3.   Application for a residence permit;
4.   Expulsion.

Within each category, there are two separate sets of measures: those which apply to Community nationals[5] who are moving within the Union and those which apply to third country nationals.[6] The differences between the treatment of the two groups is pronounced. Each group will be considered within each category.

The treatment of persons in European Community law varies depending on the nationality of the individual and whether or not a free movement right has been exercised. Thus there is one regime for Community nationals and their third country national family members migrating within the Union, another for Community nationals who do not move and a third regime which applies to third country nationals either seeking to come into or residing in the Union. For nationals of the Member States, the introduction of citizenship of the Union in 1993 was intended to create a single framework for all nationals of the Member States and bring about an approximation of their rights in Community law. Citizens of the Union moving to and living in a Member State other than that of their underlying nationality were promised the same rights as nationals of the host state. This promise will be examined in the light of the economic means of the individual: does Community law, at least in principle, achieve equality between its citizens in this field?

This chapter will not examine the legislative structure of the Union, however a few words of explanation are required for the non-expert reader. First, the European Union is made up of three principal parts – the European Community (established and regulated by the EC Treaty) which is the only part entitled to adopt binding EC law. The second part, the Common Foreign and Security Policy is outside the scope of this investigation. The third part, now entitled Provisions on Police and Judicial Cooperation in Criminal Matters, is important here, but only because before 1 May 1999 and the entry into force of the Amsterdam Treaty it included cooperation on Justice and Home Affairs: including the fields of immigration and asylum. This third part, commonly called the Third Pillar does not adopt "law" but rather sets out policy. For the period of interest to this chapter of the Third Pillar, from November 1993 when the Maastricht Treaty created it until the move out of its areas of concern of the fields of immigration and asylum, the venue was intergovernmental in format, and its products in these fields were primarily Resolutions, Recommendations and Decisions[7] – statements of common policy among the Member States rather than law on which individuals could rely.[8] In this chapter, references to Directives and Regulations are references to binding law of the European Community (ie Community law). References to Resolutions and Recommendations are to measures adopted in the intergovernmental fora which set out policy only.

As regards third country nationals, a welter of EU measures apply. Before 1 May 1999, only third country nationals with a family relationship with a Community national or as employees of a Community based company were encompassed in Community law on movement of persons. However, a series of measures which did not give rights to individuals was adopted in the intergovernmental forum of the Union, the former Third Pillar on the movement, economic activity and expulsion of third country nationals. With the entry into force of the Amsterdam Treaty, a new Part II Title IV has been inserted into the EC

Treaty which gives the European Community the power and duty to regulate most forms of migration by third country nationals. The Community is in the process of exercising these duties; a series of measures (Directives and Regulations) on migration by third country nationals to the Member States have been proposed and some have now been adopted.[9] The extent to which the treatment of third country nationals in these Union measures varies depending on the economic strength of the individual will be examined, along with the main differences between that treatment and the treatment of Community nationals.

The Categories

1. Tourists – Visitors

Tourists or visitors, for the purposes of EU immigration law, are persons who move from one state to another without exercising economic activities as employed or self employed or acquiring infrastructure. For migrant Community nationals a visit is not defined in terms of permitted length. Rather it is defined in terms of its purpose: service provision or receipt.[10] Thus the important characteristic is not a specific length of time but whether the individual is acquiring infrastructure in the host state, how periodical his or her movement and visits are and what his or her intentions are.[11]

The right to move is defined by the economic capacity of the individual – he or she is providing or receiving services. These must be services for which the individual is paid or paying: for instance the intention to use publicly funded education does not entitle a Community national to a right of movement as a service recipient.[12] Thus an economic definition is the basis of the right of travel within the Union. Although it covers all types of economic activity it is limited to economic activity. It includes whatever is necessary to achieve economic activity but no more. For instance a service provider based in one Member State seeking to send a third country national employee to provide services for it in another Member State has a right to do so without the host Member State being entitled to place work permit obstacles in the service provider's way.[13] The third country national who is sent, however, has no right to move or remain except as an employee of an entity with such a right. He or she remains the instrument of the service provision of his or her employer.

For *third country nationals*[14] a short stay is defined as three months[15] though for three Member States who are outside the Community border control regime (Denmark, Ireland and the UK) slightly different rules apply.[16] There is no specific restriction on the acquisition of infrastructure, for instance property, but there is a general prohibition on employment, work or exercise of a profession. The development of a Community law regime for short stay visits by third country nationals has had a complicated history. The right to cross the internal borders of the EU was included in the EC Treaty in 1987 by what is now Article 14. The deadline for abolishing intra-Member State border controls was set for 31.12.91. However, there was disagreement among the Member States about the legal requirement. The European Commission proposed a Regulation on border crossing in 1993 combined with a proposal for a convention on the crossing of the external borders.[17] This was not adopted. Five of the original six Member States[18] adopted an intergovernmental convention for the abolition of intra-state border controls known as the Schengen Convention 1985. This was followed by an Implementing Convention in 1990 and the abolition of controls on persons crossing intra-state borders on 25 March 1995 (but with many exceptions). It was in this context that the rules on short stay visits by third country nationals were developed. By a protocol to the Amsterdam Treaty, provision was made for the Schengen Conventions and the implementing decisions of the executive committee to be inserted either into the EC Treaty or the Treaty on European Union. The necessary decisions to effect the transfer were taken in May 1999. These rules are now part of Community law though Denmark, Ireland and the UK have opted out of this part of the law.

Visas

Community nationals: Member States are not permitted to require visas of Community nationals who move for visits from one Member State to another.[19] They may require visas of third country national family members of Community nationals when family members are accompanying the Community national.[20] However, such visas must be issued free of charge and every facility must be provided for their issue.[21] Under the regime of the Schengen Agreements even border controls at the internal frontiers among the Member States were in theory abolished.

Third country nationals: By a series of Regulations adopted in Community law, the list of countries whose nationals must have a visa in order to enter the territory of the Member States is common to all Member States (except the three which have opted out).[22] It similarly includes a standard list of those countries whose nationals do not require a visa to enter a Member State. According to the explanatory memorandum to the most recent proposal for amendment of the Regulation, the reason for the inclusion and exclusion of certain countries from the list is as follows:

> To determine whether nationals of a third country are subject to the visa requirement or exempted from it, regard should be had to a set of criteria that can be grouped under three main headings:
>
> • illegal immigration: the visas rules constitute an essential instrument for controlling migratory flows. Here, reference can be made to a number of relevant sources of statistical information and indicators to assess the risk of illegal migratory flows (such as information and/or statistics on illegal residence, cases of refusal of admission to the territory, expulsion measures, and clandestine immigration and labour networks), to assess the reliability of travel documents issued by the relevant third country and to consider the impact of readmission agreements with those countries;

- public policy: conclusions reached in the police cooperation context among others may highlight specific salient features of certain types of crime. Depending on the seriousness, regularity and territorial extent of the relevant forms of crime, imposing the visa requirement could be a possible response worth considering. Threats to public order may in some cases be so serious as even to jeopardise domestic security in one or more Member States. If the visa requirement was imposed in a show of solidarity by the other Member States, this could again be an appropriate response;

- international relations: the option for or against imposing the visa requirement in respect of a given third country can be a means of underlining the type of relations which the Union is intending to establish or maintain with it. But the Union's relations with a single country in isolation are rarely at stake here. Most commonly it is the relationship with a group of countries, and the option in favour of a given visa regime also has implications in terms of regional coherence. The choice of visa regime can also reflect the specific position of a Member State in relation to a third country, to which the other Member States adhere in a spirit of solidarity. The reciprocity criterion, applied by States individually and separately in the traditional form of relations under public international law, now has to be used by reason of the constraints of the Union's external relations with third countries. Given the extreme diversity of situations in third countries and their relations with the European Union and the Member States, the criteria set out here cannot be applied automatically, by means of coefficients fixed in advance. They must be seen as decision-making instruments to be used flexibly and pragmatically, being weighted variably on a case-by-case basis.[23]

The lists themselves do not discriminate directly on the basis of the GDP of the countries whose nationals do or do not have to get visas. For example, nationals of Saudi Arabia, Brunei and the UAE must always get visas to travel to the Union. These are countries which are in general wealthy. Similarly, on the list of countries whose nationals are not required to obtain visas to travel for short stays are most South American countries (Colombia is one notable exception), not all of which can be considered particularly wealthy. However, the white list contains almost exclusively countries which are rich.[24]

Instead, the list indicates that traditional prejudices of the Member States in respect of race and religion ensure that almost all countries, the majority of whose population is either black or Muslim are on the list. However, those prejudices are supplemented by a second level of privilege or discrimination: wealth. An example of the power of economic wealth of some countries over others as regards the treatment of visitors is particularly well demonstrated by a proposal put forward by the Portuguese Presidency of the Union in February 2000.[25] The proposal would permit the Community to enter into agreements with third countries to extend beyond three months the period for travel within the territory of the Union for nationals of the contracting parties.[26] The political history of the proposal is instructive: US nationals were unhappy that whereas before the commencement of the Schengen arrangements they were entitled to travel for three months within each of the Member States separately, after the entry into force of the arrangements they are restricted to three months in the combined territory of all the Member

States.[27] Presumably US nationals were finding themselves overstaying their visas. Pressure was brought to bear on the US government which in turn sought a special arrangement for its nationals so that they would have more time lawfully as visitors within the Member States without becoming illegally present. The fact that sufficient pressure was brought to bear on the Portuguese government that it proposed the adoption of measures which would permit such bilateral changes to the meaning of "visitor" evidences the difference of perspective on who should and who should not be allowed to remain in the Union.

The rules surrounding obtaining a visa are contained in the Common Consular Instructions made under the Schengen Implementing Convention and now part of Community law under Article 62 EC. The rules indicate clearly that the financial capacity of the individual is a very important consideration. First, there are common rules for the cost of visas.[28] Secondly, there are specific rules on the amount of money which the individual must have calculated by amount per day of visit intended.[29] Thirdly in the Instructions, there is very clear guidance to the officials of the risk of granting visas to the economically challenged:

> The diplomatic mission or consular post shall assume full responsibility in assessing whether there is an immigration risk. The purpose of examining applications is to detect those applicants who are seeking to immigrate to the territory of the Contracting Parties and set themselves up there, using grounds such as tourism, studies, business or family visits as a pretext. Therefore, it is necessary to be particularly vigilant when dealing with 'risk categories', in other words unemployed persons, and those with irregular income etc.[30]

At the Border

Community nationals: Where a Community national moves from one Member State to another he or she cannot be required to answer questions at the border itself regarding the amount of money which he or she has.[31]

Third country nationals: Where a visa national is entering the combined territory of the Union, it is open to the Member States to check the underlying reasons why an individual has been granted a visa. Entry can be refused on grounds of public policy which includes the risk that the individual will fall a charge on public funds. Where a non-visa national seeks entry at the external border it is open to the border official to make such inquiries as he or she thinks appropriate. This includes questions whether the individual has the funds required per day to sustain a visit.

Residence Permits

It is not normal for persons coming for short stays to require residence permits. In the case of Community nationals, where their stay is intended to exceed three months they may be required to notify the authorities of their presence on the territory. There is no requirement that they provide further information about their economic means. For third country nationals the rules only permit visits of not more than three months. Further only one such visit is permitted every six months – that means third country nationals are only permitted to remain in the territory of the Union (excluding the three states which have opted out) for a maximum of three months out of every six months irrespective of how many times they have entered and exited the territory. Once within the territory of the Union, they are entitled to move without checks at the borders. Member States are permitted, however, to put in place internal controls. These rules remain national. In general, third country nationals who are visiting the Union are either excluded from access to public benefits or the use of such benefits is, under national law, a reason for their expulsion.

Expulsion

Community nationals who are exercising EC free movement rights are protected from expulsion to a fairly high degree. They may not be expelled on economic grounds.[32] However, it has been argued that where a migrant Community national ceases to exercise an economic activity or otherwise to qualify, he or she ceases to have a right of residence and may be expelled. Service providers and recipients appear to be the most vulnerable. There is substantial discussion in different Member States about the need to prevent "benefits" tourism (for example the UK in 1995/6)[33] or "medical" tourism (for example Germany in 1998/9) by Community nationals from other Member States.

Where Community nationals are clearly exercising a free movement right, they may only be expelled on the grounds of public policy, public security or public health.[34] This does not include expulsion for lack of means.[35] There has been much discussion whether the right to move and reside granted by citizenship of the Union can be limited on grounds of destitution. The first indications are that it cannot be – Mrs Sala, a Spanish national living in Germany had been a worker but was no longer. She sought a public benefit on the birth of a child which benefit was only available to Germany nationals or nationals of other Member States who were in possession of residence permits. The German government claimed she was not entitled to a residence permit as she did not come within any of the categories of persons entitled to residence. The Court held that she was entitled to residence and as a result to non-discriminatory access to the benefit. The case, unfortunately, is vague on the source of the residence right.[36]

Third country national visitors are in principle liable for expulsion if they become destitute in the territory of the Member States.

2. Labour Migrants

Labour migration holds a particularly important position in Community law. Labour migration constitutes one of the fundamental freedoms of the Union: the right to move from one Member State to another to seek employment. Article 39 EC which consecrates the right is not worded in terms of nationals of the Member States. It provides that: "Freedom of movement for workers shall be secured within the Community by the end of the transitional period at the latest."[37] As a result there has been much academic discussion about the possibility of including within the concept of a "worker" for Community law purposes third country nationals who are within the Union.[38] The matter has, however, been resolved against the wide interpretation of the concept by the European Court of Justice.[39]

For *Community nationals*, then, in the subsidiary legislation of Article 39, the right to move for employment is recognized as of great importance to the individual; the preamble to Regulation 1612/68, which provides the detail for important rights of workers, states: "Whereas freedom of movement constitutes a fundamental right of workers and their families; whereas mobility of labour within the Community must be one of the means by which the worker is guaranteed the possibility of improving his living and working conditions and promoting his social advancement, while helping to satisfy the requirements of the economies of the Member States..." Thus in principle the Community is particularly concerned about enabling the worker, whatever his or her status, to move to enjoy better living conditions. However, it was not until 1991 that the Court of Justice confirmed that work seekers were also entitled to the right to move to seek employment. As the right to move as a worker was limited in Article 39 to movement to take up employment some Member States had argued that there was no right to go to seek employment if the individual was unemployed.[40]

Further, in giving effect to the right of free movement of workers, Regulation 1612/68 excludes persons moving in search of employment from the right of equal treatment in social and tax advantages.[41] This means that a work seeker, national of another Member State, has no right to seek social benefits which are available to nationals of the State.[42] Only after he or she gets a job and is thus transformed into a "worker" does he or she get the right to equal treatment in this field. In other words the right only accrues to those who no longer need it. While provision is made in the Community's Regulation on co-ordination of social security systems for a work seeker to receive his or her benefits in another Member State for a maximum period of three months the rules surrounding the arrangements are so arcane and difficult that it is little used.[43]

Thus for the Community national who is taking a job in another Member State, the legal controls which prevent him or her doing so are limited. But similarly there is little assistance for those who do not have financial means to make the move. However, once a migrant has found a job, under Community law he or she is entitled to all social benefits which are available to own nationals of the host state. Thus where the job is part time and the migrant qualifies on economic grounds under national law for social benefits to top up his or her salary to the minimum guaranteed by the state, the state cannot exclude the person from the benefit only because of his or her nationality (provided, of course, that the person is a national of a Member State or the family member of such a person).[44]

For *third country nationals* labour migration is intended to be more limited. First, for third country nationals already resident within the Union, there is no free movement for employment. If, however, their employer requires them to go to another Member State to carry out service provision or receipt for the employer then their right to move for economic purposes is limited to that action for the employer. There is no individual right for the employee.[45] This situation mirrors that contained in the General Agreement on Trade in Services attached to the WTO agreement in some important respects. In both cases, the right to move is granted to the company (the service provider). The individual is treated only as the means for carrying out the economic activity. The individual's right to enter, stay and engage in economic activities is completely dependent on the company for which he or she works. The state no longer acts as intermediary in the relationship, controlling the entry, presence and activities of the individual. Thus the power of the company over the individual is intensified greatly. Any lack of loyalty by the individual to the company may now be punished by the withdrawal by the company of the individual's right of presence on the territory of the state.

In 1994 the Member States agreed a resolution on limitations on admission of third country nationals to the Member States for employment[46] and in 1996 on limitations on admission as self employed persons.[47] As regards access to the territory for employment, the Resolution provides that "Member States will refuse entry to their territories of third country nationals for the purpose of employment".[48] As an exception to that rule, Member States will "consider requests for admission to their territories for the purpose of employment only where vacancies in a Member State cannot be filled by national or Community manpower or by non-Community manpower lawfully resident on a permanent basis in that Member State and already forming part of the Member State's regular labour market." In addition, the exception of admission on a temporary basis may be taken in the light of the specialist qualifications of the third country national and "initial authorization for employment will normally be restricted to employment in a specific job with a specified employer."[49] Thus the intention is that third country nationals will only be allowed to enter the Union for employment where there is a job already available for them in a skilled occupation. Such persons are not likely to be unemployed in their home state.

Visas

Community nationals cannot be required to have visas in order to enter a Member State other than that of their nationality (see above section 1). As regards their third country national family members, the same rules as set out in section 1 apply, visas can be required but their issue must be facilitated and free.

Third country nationals are, in principle, required to have visas before they travel to a Member State for employment according to the Resolution, though there is some latitude to the Member States to dispense with this requirement: "A third country national will not be admitted for employment unless prior authorization has been given for him to take up employment in the territory of the Member State concerned. Such prior authorization may be in the form of a work permit issued either to the employer or to the employee. In addition third country nationals must also be in possession of any necessary visa or, if the Member States concerned so requires, of a residence permit."[50]

At the Border

Community nationals: again the situation is as described above at section 1.

Third country nationals: In principle, according to the Resolution, the individual must have a visa or at least prior authorization before arriving at the border. This cannot be granted at the border. This means that the individual must have a job to which he or she is going, the employer must have completed all the formalities in order to obtain the authorization before the individual leaves his or her country of origin. Thus only workers who are in high demand will gain admission. The employer must be aware of their existence without necessarily having interviewed them and have invested the time and effort to satisfy the authorities of the host state that the individual is the only one who can do the job and that there is no one else in the Community labour market (including third country nationals already residence lawfully in that Member State) who is able and willing to take the job.

For the third country national this means that he or she will usually be accepting a job without having seen the place of work or met his or her colleagues. Thus a substantial obstacle is placed in the way of a third country national seeking to take up employment in a Member State – he or she must have sufficient confidence in the level of the work and the employer as well as in the opportunities open to him or her at home should the job not work out, to take the risk of moving.

Residence Permits

Community nationals are entitled to a residence permit provided they have a job in the host Member State. The residence permit, while only declaratory of the right of the worker to be employed is often in practice important for establishing the individual's right to social benefits. The duty on the state is to grant a residence permit free of charge or on payment of an amount not exceeding the dues and taxes charged for the issue of identity cards to nationals.[51] The residence permit must be valid for five years from the date of issue and automatically renewable.[52] However, only persons with a job lasting more than one year are entitled to a residence permit. Where a worker will be undertaking an activity expected to last less than three months then he or she is not entitled to a residence permit at all.[53] This means that if the individual seeks social benefits he or she will usually be refused by the authorities because a residence permit is necessary to access the benefit (see for instance the case of Mrs Sala above). The fact that this is contrary to the individual's right to equal treatment in social benefits does not change the administrative practices. Only an individual who has good legal advice and threatens court action is likely to succeed in obtaining social benefits in the absence of a residence permit. Both legal advice and threats of court action are more easily available to the educated and affluent migrant.

Further, where the migrant has a job which lasts more than three months but less than a year "the host state shall issue him with a temporary residence permit, the validity of which may be limited to the expected period of the employment".[54] In many Member States it is not possible or very difficult for migrants to access social benefits with a temporary permit. Additionally, administrative delay means that the migrant is unlikely to get a residence permit immediately. The only constraint on the authorities to issue a residence permit is to be found in Article 5(1) Directive 64/221: "A decision to grant or to refuse a first residence permit shall be taken as soon as possible and in any event not later than six months from the date of application for the permit." It is unfortunately common for Member States' authorities to take longer than six months to issue a permit. Not only that, but the authorities usually require evidence that the job will last more than one year at the time when they come to process the residence permit application, which may be up to six months after it has been made. So for a person who would have qualified for a five year permit at the time the application was made may well no longer so qualify by the time the application is processed. Short contracts and temporary work are most common in bottom end jobs with low pay and insecure working conditions, thus persons in these positions are placed in the most precarious position.

Finally, even once a worker has a permit, if he or she is unemployed for more than 12 months when the permit comes up for renewal the host state is entitled to limit the renewed permit to 12 months or more.[55]

Thus migrants who have casual or temporary jobs have great difficulty ever getting residence permits. This then has consequences for their ability in practice to access social benefits where production of a full five year residence permit is usually required. It is often those with insecure jobs who are most likely to need social benefits.

Third country nationals, according to the Employment Resolution, are only given the right of admission and residence on the basis of their employment. While the issue of their residence status if the job ends or they lose their jobs is not addressed directly, all the provisions relating to their residence status presuppose continuing employment. The Resolution does not touch upon the question of access to social benefits. Indeed, there is no provision guaranteeing a right to equal treatment in working conditions in the Resolution at all.

In 1996 the European Union adopted a Resolution on the status of third country nationals residing on a long term basis in the territory of the Member States.[56] This Resolution addressed the issue of residence permits for third country nationals. In order to be recognized as "long resident" under the Resolution, a third country national must be able to "provide proof that they have resided legally and without interruption in the territory of the Member State concerned for a period specified in the legislation of that Member State and, in any event, after 10 years' legal residence".[57] The long stop for a third country national to qualify for the rights contained in the Resolution is proof of ten years lawful residence. Where a third country national makes an application for such an authorization, "it should be possible for the factors determining whether the authorization is to be granted to include the level and stability of the means of existence which the applicant demonstrates, in particular whether he has health insurance, and the conditions for exercising an occupation."[58]

Once the individual has acquired the status, he or she is to be granted equal treatment in working conditions, membership of trade unions, public policy in the sector of housing, social security, emergency health care and compulsory schooling. Thus in order to gain access to benefits, and it is worth noting that these do *not* include social assistance benefits or normal health care, the individual may be required to have resided lawfully for ten years and to show a stable means of support and health insurance. It is the poor who are less likely to be able to satisfy the authorities of these requirements. They are less likely to have a stable job or other means of support. If they are required to have private health insurance, they are less likely to be able to prove this. Those migrants most likely to be able to satisfy the requirements in order to get access to further benefits are those least likely to need the further benefits – they are the migrants with stable, well paid jobs or spouses with such jobs. Again, the poor who are most in need of security and support are those most likely to be excluded from the benefits of the Resolution.

Expulsion

Community nationals cannot be expelled for economic reasons alone. Measures taken by Member States regarding issue or renewal of residence permits, or expulsion for the territory of Community nationals and their family members may be taken on grounds of public policy, public security or public health but "such grounds shall not be invoked to service economic ends."[59] It remains an open question when and under what circumstances a Community national loses the protection of Community free movement rights when resident in the territory of another Member State. In the *Sala* case (supra) the Court of Justice indicated that the rights of migrant workers under Community law might no longer apply after a long period of economic inactivity. In practice, however, in many Member States the passport to benefits is a five year residence permit. As mentioned above, the renewal of the first permit can be limited to not less than 12 months if the individual has been unemployed for more than 12 months before the request for renewal. Thus the limitation on expulsion of Community nationals on the basis of poverty is substantially limited provided they have acquired and can evidence their status as workers.

   Third country nationals are not protected from expulsion on grounds of poverty. As discussed above under residence permits, as regards measures adopted at the European Union level, there is a linkage between permission to reside, work access to benefits and vulnerability to expulsion.

   The treatment of third country nationals who are no longer working lawfully or whose work has never been authorized was dealt with in the Recommendation concerning checks on and expulsion of third country nationals residing or working without authorization 1993.[60] Here, the Member States agree that in principle migrants without authorization to work but who are working irregularly should be expelled.[61] In order to identify these persons: "Checks, should, in particular be carried out in respect of persons who are known or suspected of staying or working without authority, including persons whose request for asylum has been rejected."[62]

   Member States are encouraged to undertake checks on (a) persons who have received authorization for residence but not for employment; (b) persons who have received a residence permit, but whose work permit is of a limited nature (in other words persons admitted in accordance with the Employment Resolution which in time post-dated the expulsion recommendation) (c) persons who work without authorization after being admitted as short term visitors or tourists. The consequences of this Recommendation, if actually put into effect are wide. This would require substantial internal checks on persons throughout the period of their residence. The Recommendation encourages checks in particular on persons who have been authorized to be reunited with their family with a view to living together and persons whose residence/work permit is on the basis of their marriage to a resident of the host state.[63] It would appear that expelling family members working without authorization of lawful residents is an objective of the Recommendation.

A subsequent measure, a Recommendation on harmonising means of combating illegal immigration and illegal employment and improving the relevant means of control[64] provides further clarification on these checks and their relationship with the poor:

> Where national law regards the residence or employment situations as a prerequisite for foreign nationals to qualify for benefits provided by a public service of a Member State in particular in the area of health, retirement, family or work, that conditions cannot be met until it has been verified that the residence and employment situation of the person concerned and his or her family does not disqualify them from the benefit. Verification of residence or employment status is not required where intervention by a public authority is necessary on overriding humanitarian grounds. Such verifications are carried out by the services providing the benefits, with the assistance if necessary, of other authorities responsible in particular for issuing residence or work permits, in accordance with nationals law relating, in particular to data protection.[65]

Thus the link between authorization to work, benefits and expulsion is clarified through different documents. Where the migrant is no longer authorized to work the state should carry out checks on whether he or she is in fact still working. This is the case even if the individual has a continuing right of residence. If the individual is found to be working without authorization, even if he or she is a close family member or spouse of a person lawfully resident in the host state, the individual should in principle be subject to expulsion. The checks to find persons unlawfully working or resident should be carried out by the authorities responsible for providing social benefits such as health or family benefits. Thus, for example, a doctor's surgery or a hospital is charged with carrying out checks on the individual and according to the Recommendation should be charged with revealing and exchanging information with whichever other authorities are they consider appropriate. The checks are intended to be carried out before the service is provided though there is an exception on humanitarian grounds. Thus the migrant is likely to be faced with delay, intrusive questioning, data exchange and humiliation whenever he or she comes in contact with authorities providing social benefits. Of course the poor, by definition, have greater need of and contact with social services authorities than the rich. Further, for them, seeking private services is not an option. Each contact with the social benefits authorities carries with it the possibility that it will lead to expulsion from the state, even where the individual is a spouse or close family member of a lawful resident of the host state.

3. Family Members

The right to family life is a constant theme in human rights conventions.[66] Following the trend, the EU Charter of Fundamental Rights states that "every person has the right to respect for his or her private and family life..."[67] The Community regulation giving effect to the free movement right of workers states: "Whereas the right of freedom of movement, in order that it may be exercised, by objective standards, in freedom and dignity, requires that equality of treatment shall be ensured in fact and in law in respect of all matters relating to the actual pursuit of activities as employed persons and to eligibility for housing, and also that obstacles to the mobility of workers shall be eliminated, in particular as regards the worker's right to be joined by his family and the conditions for the integration of that family into the host country."[68]

These statements in support of family life are, however, rather vague. They do not spell out what a family is or which members of a family should have the right to live together and in which state.[69] Recognising the fundamental importance of family life for migrants is only a first step. As in the other aspects of migration law and policy in the EU, the definition of family members who are permitted or may be permitted to join a migrant depends on the nationality of the migrant. A generous Community law regime applies for Community nationals and their family members. A soft law Resolution applies a common EU policy to family reunion for third country nationals in the Union. However, this is an area of law where the new powers of the Community to adopt binding measures under Title IV EC have already been exercised. The European Commission has proposed a Directive on family reunification which sets out the rules for third country nationals.[70]

Before considering the requirements for movement to join a principal in a Member State, the categories of family members who are eligible for family reunion in each of the two categories will be set out, starting with Community nationals.

The definition of family members of any nationality who are eligible to join a *Community national* who has exercised a free movement right to go and live in another Member State is generous. The same definition is used for family members of migrant workers, the self employed and service providers and recipients. There is a right of admission and residence for the following family members of any nationality of a Community law principal:

- spouses (the Commission has proposed the extension of this concept to unmarried partners in relationships which are akin to marriage provided that such relationships give rise to immigration rights for nationals of the host state);
- children of both or either party to the marriage who are under 21; or if they are over 21 who are dependent on the principal;
- all dependent relatives in the ascending and descending lines of the principal and his or her spouse.[71]

In addition, Member States are under a duty to facilitate (or favour[72]) the admission of any member of the family not coming within the above provisions if dependent on the principal or living under his or her roof in the country whence he or she comes.[73] This provision has never been interpreted by the Court of Justice. There is a slight variation on permitted family members for the purposes of the economically inactive, pensioners and students. Where the principal comes within the first two categories all children must be dependent on the principal.[74] For students only spouses and children under 21 are entitled to accompany the principal to the host state.[75] All family members are entitled to take employment or to enter into self employment.[76]

In the event of divorce (but not separation only), the right of residence of a third country national spouse ceases as does it if the principal leaves the host state.[77] The rights of children are not necessarily extinguished by either event.[78] However, if the Community national principal is resident in his or her home state and has not exercised a free movement right then the Community rules do not apply to him or her and family reunification is subject only to the national law of the state.[79]

Thus as regards Community nationals, the possibility to enjoy a right to family reunification with children over 21 and other family members in ascending and descending lines requires the individual to be so poor as to be dependent on the principal. This then presupposes that the principal is sufficiently wealthy to be able to support the family member. The Court of Justice has not yet been asked to clarify whether a principal who is in receipt of social benefits but who nonetheless provides support for his or her family members abroad is entitled to enjoy family reunion in the host state with those family members. In any event, where the principal is economically inactive, for a pensioner or a student to exercise a free movement right on that basis, he or she must prove or, at least, in the case of students declare, that he or she has sufficient income not to be a burden on the social welfare scheme. Thus poverty determines, for these persons, the right to move and the right to family reunification. Once family reunification has been completed, there are indications from the Court of Justice that it will not permit, at least as regards the family members of Community nationals, an interference with family life merely on the grounds that a dependent family member has become economically active and thus is no longer dependent on the principal.[80] It would appear that, for instance, dependent children do not have to remain dependent for life on their parents or else risk losing their residence right.

Where the principal is a *third country national* a rather different regime applies. First, according to the soft law Resolution on the harmonization of national policies on family reunification[81] Member States may admit:

- spouses (only in a marriage which is recognized in the host state);
- children under 18 (though Member States are allowed to set a lower threshold of 16) other than adopted children of the resident and his or her spouse;
- children (subject to the same age limit) adopted by both the resident and his or her spouse by an order recognized by the host state.

Member States are expressly permitted to apply waiting periods for admission. Further, third country nationals who are present in a Member State on a short term basis are excluded from the Resolution.

According to the Commission's proposal under Article 63 EC, for a Directive on family reunification (primarily dealing with resident third country nationals) a different group of persons are included as family members:

- spouses (and unmarried partners if the national legislation of the host state gives an immigration right to such partners of own nationals);
- minor children of either party to the marriage and minor children adopted by a recognized order provided the parents have custody of the child and the child is dependent on them;
- other relatives in the ascending line of either party to the marriage provided they are dependent on the principal and have no other family support in the country of origin;
- children of the principal or his or her spouse who are no longer minors but who are objectively unable to satisfy their needs by reason of their state of health.

Here the criteria of support are much more widespread. Only spouses escape the requirement of being financially dependent on the principal in order to enjoy a right of reunification. There is no clarification of what happens to the other family members should they become economically independent after exercising the family reunification right. Thus lack of funds for the family members, coupled with the concomitant necessity of financial solvency for the principal is necessary for third country nationals to enjoy family reunification in the Union.

Visas

Community nationals' family members of any nationality can be required to obtain visas in order to join their principal in a host Member State.[82] However, as mentioned above in section 1, these visas must be granted quickly and no charge can be made for them. It is unclear what the family members must produce to obtain visas. The question is not covered in the implementing legislation. However, it can certainly be no more than is required in order to obtain a residence permit once within the territory and those requirements are fully spelt out in the implementing legislation.[83] As regards proof of dependency, the only document which can be required by a host Member State as proof of this is "a document issued by the competent authority of the state of origin or the State whence they came, testifying that they are dependent on the worker or that they live under his roof in such country."[84] Thus the host State is obliged to accept the evidence produced by the state of origin as regards the dependency of family members on their Community principal. Problems do arise in practice where the country of origin has no system of making such documents or holding such information.

So long as the principal is either self employed or a worker in the host State, the fact that he or she is in receipt of social assistance is not relevant to his or her right to be joined by family members, even if they are dependent on him or her. However, the principal is required to "have available for his family housing which is considered as normal for national workers in the region where he is employed".[85] However, the Court of Justice has held that the requirement to have available housing considered as normal applies solely as a condition under which each member of the worker's family is permitted to come to live with him or her and that once the family has been brought together, the position of the migrant worker cannot be different in regard to housing requirements from that of a worker who is a national of the Member State concerned. Consequently, if the housing regarded as normal at the time of the arrival of members of the migrant worker's family no longer fulfils that requirement as a result of a new event, such as the birth or arrival at the age of majority of a child, the measures which may be adopted in regard to the members of the worker's family cannot be different from those required in regard to nationals of that Member State and cannot lead to discrimination between those nationals and nationals of other Member States.[86]

It would seem that a check on available housing may be made at the time the visa is issued, but provided arrangements have been made for the requirement to be met when the family members arrive this must be sufficient. Further, the principal's right to equal treatment as regards social advantages means that he or she is entitled to social housing and re-housing if this is available for own nationals.

The situation as regards work seekers, however, is different. The right to family reunification only arises in Part II of the Regulation and thus applies to persons who have jobs (or have started self employment).

Third country nationals' family members are subject to a different policy. According to the Resolution these family members will not normally be admitted to the territory without a visa.[87] Further the Member States reserved the right "to make entry and stay of family members conditional upon the availability of adequate accommodation and of sufficient resources to avoid a burden being placed on the public funds of the Member State, and on the existence of sickness insurance."[88] Thus the Member States did not commit themselves to requiring either housing or sufficient funds for issuing visas for family members to join a third country national principal.

According to the Commission's proposal for a Directive, the application is to be made by the principal within the Member State but at a time when the family members are outside the Union.[89] Exceptions are possible on humanitarian grounds. At the time the application is made (ie normally while the family members are still abroad) the principal is required to provide evidence that he or she has adequate housing for the family members, sickness insurance for him or herself and for the family members; stable and sufficient resources which are higher than or equal to the level of resources below which the Member State concerned may grant social assistance or higher than the level of the minimum social security pension paid by the Member State.[90] Thus the standard of financial means for the migrant in order to enjoy family reunification means that he or she cannot be reliant on social assistance in the state. Further the principal must have enough money to secure sickness insurance for the family, a requirement which may well exclude any family members who are disabled or have long term illnesses.

For third country nationals, family reunification is conditional on financial standing. Poor immigrants will not be able to enjoy the right to family life. All the solemn declarations and articles in international conventions about the right to family life appear to be qualified. The right to family life only exists where the principal is sufficiently wealthy to support all the family members without cost to the state.

At the Border

Community nationals' family members may not be subject to additional checks at the border. Once they have obtained the visas which the Member State is entitled to apply the next step is the application for a residence permit.

Third country nationals' family members under the Resolution are supposed to have visas or other prior authorization but Member States are entitled to waive the requirement. No further clarification is given as to procedures at the border. Similarly the proposal for a Directive is silent.

Residence Permits

Community nationals' family members are entitled to residence documents (the term used for the document given to third country national family members) on production of the document on which they entered the territory and the document issued by a competent authority in the country of origin (or whence they came) proving the relationship.[91] At this point as well, the Member State can check the availability of housing, but only once, when the family is united. No other financial requirement can be placed on the issue of the residence document. As in respect of the permit of the principal, only fees consistent with those for national identity cards can be charged. As regards the practical problems of obtaining the residence document, in particular delays and access to benefits, these are the same for third country national family members as for Community nationals themselves (see above section 2).

Third country nationals' family members, according to the Resolution, may be authorized to stay for such period as the Member State concerned determines and may be conditional upon the continued fulfilment of the criteria for admission.[92] This means that the continued enjoyment of family life may be subject to the principal continuing to hold down his or her job and to have enough income and accommodation not to qualify for social assistance. The Resolution does provide that Member States may authorize family members to stay on a personal basis "within a reasonable period of time" and if appropriate be authorized to work. Thus dependent relatives may eventually be permitted to become independent. However as noted in section 2 above, according to the Resolution on lawfully resident third country nationals, under the Union policy only after ten years lawful residence does a presumption in favour of an independent residence permit take effect.

The Commission's proposal for a Directive subsumes the application for a visa and a residence permit into one application, made while the family members are abroad. If the application is successful then the family may be reunited. The proposal provides that renewal of a residence permit "may not be withheld and removal from the territory may not be ordered by the competent authorities of the Member State concerned on the sole ground of illness or disability suffered after the issue of the residence permit."[93] It would then appear that a renewal can be refused (and indeed removal from the territory ordered) if the principal is no longer able to support and accommodate the family without social assistance so long as the reason for that reliance is not solely illness or disability.

Expulsion

Community nationals' family members may only be subject to expulsion on the same grounds as the Community principal him or herself (see section 2 above). However this only holds true for spouses so long as the marriage is intact (even if the couple is living apart) and the principal is still resident in the host state.[94] If either of these two requirements are not meet, the third country national spouse becomes liable to national law.[95]

Third country nationals' family members both under the Resolution and under the proposal for a Directive remain subject to the continuing requirement that their principal supports them. If he or she fails to be able to do that then they are liable for expulsion. However, after a period of not more than four years residence and provided that the family relationship continues to exist, the spouse, unmarried partner or child who has reached majority shall be entitled to an autonomous residence permit independent of that of the applicant.[96] A shorter period of one year applies in the case of widowhood, divorce, separation or death of the principal.[97]

4. Asylum Seekers

This category of persons has a particularly tenuous position in EU law and policy. In considering the economic consequences of being an asylum seeker, a number of initial clarifications need to be made. First, the differentiation between Community nationals and third country nationals is no longer helpful. The European Union has attempted to define out of existence asylum seekers who are nationals of a Member State. The (infamous) Protocol on Asylum for Nationals of the Member States attached to the EC Treaty by virtue of the Amsterdam Treaty[98] provides that taking into account the special status and protection which EU citizens have under the Treaty and "respecting the finality and the objectives of the Geneva Convention" each Member State shall be regarded as a safe country of origin by the other Member States as regards applications for asylum made by their nationals. Although exceptions to the bar on consideration of asylum applications by nationals of the other Member States have been incorporated, the general policy and law of the Union presumes that there is no such thing as an asylum seeker who is a national of a Member State.

The political history of this protocol, commonly known as the Aznar Protocol after the Spanish President who initiated and pressed for it, bears repeating. At the time of the negotiation of the Amsterdam Treaty, a number of claims for political asylum had been made by Basques of Spanish nationality to the authorities in Belgium. While the authorities had refused the applications, the Belgian courts were considering the cases and the claims by the individuals that they would be persecuted in Spain on the basis of the political beliefs if forced to return there. In view of the public and judicial concern being expressed in Spain at that time about the activities of the authorities in respect of Basques (which resulted in the condemnation of a number of political and police officials by the Spanish courts) the Belgian courts considered that a full review of the claims was appropriate. The political response from Spain was to press for a protocol which would prevent such applications being received or considered in any Member State.[99]

The concept of a safe country of origin as a presumption (either rebuttable or not depending on the circumstances) for rejecting or indeed refusing to receive an application for asylum within the EU has a longer history than this. It dates to the Conclusions on countries in which there is generally no serious risk of persecution adopted by the Member States intergovernmentally in 1992.[100] The concept was gradually adopted into the national law of many Member States, Germany being one of the first.[101] The first step in the implementation of the policy was to pass legislation declaring that the other Member States of the EU were by definition safe countries of origin.

Thus this section will focus on asylum seekers who are nationals of third countries as it is this group which is the subject of the growing EU law and policy. The EU Member States have three principle international commitments to the protection of persons fleeing persecution or torture. The best known is that contained in the UN Convention relating to the status of refugees 1951 and its 1967 protocol (the Geneva Convention).[102] Article 1A of the convention defines a refugee as a person who is outside his or her country of origin (or habitual residence) and has a well founded fear of persecution there on the grounds of race, religion, membership of a social group or political opinion.[103] The duty, contained in Articles 32 and 33 is not to return such a person to a country where he or she would be persecuted. Secondly, there is the obligation contained in Article 3 of the UN Convention against torture 1984 which prohibits the return or extradition of a person to a state where there are substantial grounds for believing that he or she would be in danger of being subject to torture.[104] Thirdly, there is the regional obligation contained in the European Convention on Human Rights as interpreted by the European Court of Human Rights at Article 3 prohibiting return of a person to a country where there is a substantial risk that he or she would suffer torture, inhuman or degrading treatment.

The duty to give protection to persons fearing persecution and torture has been held to be absolute. States which are parties to the international conventions are not entitled to make their protection conditional on the economic ability of the individual to support him or herself, or even to refuse protection on national security grounds.[105] So, with asylum seekers arrives the duty of support, accommodation and the maintenance of a system for the determination of their claims. The Geneva Convention explicitly requires states parties to provide support for refugees. Thus for states increasingly seeking to limit expenditure as the new prosperity results in shrinking revenues through the processes of globalization[106] asylum seekers are increasingly unwelcome. Because of the problems of international obligations of the Member States, the primary focus of attention is to seek ways of ensuring that asylum seekers to not arrive at the border. Once they have arrived at the border they are particularly difficult to get rid of, and once they have gained access to the territory the problems and expense for the Member States in terms of sending them back to other countries becomes substantial.

The first mechanisms which the Member States have put in place are designed to prevent arrival at the border.

Visas

The reasons given by the UK government for the imposition of visas on nationals of countries added to the national mandatory visa list over the past five years have been analyzed elsewhere.[107] In all cases except one, the imposition of a visa requirement was justified in the official press releases which accompanied the announcements of the measure on the grounds that there were rising numbers of asylum seekers arriving in the UK from that country. Thus the objective of the visa regime is specifically and expressly to prevent asylum seekers from arriving in the UK.

This is not an isolated case of one Member State. If one returns to the reasons given in the Commission's explanatory memorandum to the Visa Regulation (section 1) while the term "asylum seekers" is not actually used, the euphemisms of controlling migratory flows, illegal migratory flows etc. point to the practiced eye to asylum seekers.

In any event, as noted above, in the Common Consular Manual, the criteria for a visa for a short stay excludes the possibility that an asylum seeker might qualify not least as the person must intend to leave the territory before the end of his or her three month stay. This will never be the case for an asylum seeker. The intention that the visa regime should apply specifically to exclude the possibility that asylum seekers reach the European Union is well demonstrated in the list of countries whose nationals are under an even more stringent visa regime than the others: that is to say whose nationals must get visas even if they are only transiting through a Member State en route to a third country. This list is short: in the proposal of the Finnish Presidency of the Union for a Regulation on airport transit arrangements (Autumn 1999) the countries included are: Afghanistan; Iran, Iraq, Democratic Republic of the Congo, Nigeria, Ethiopia, Eritrea, Somalia, Ghana and Sri Lanka. They are also the principal countries of origin of the majority of asylum applicants in the European Union.

Thus the visa system is designed, *inter alia*, to prevent asylum seekers from getting to the territory of the Member States lawfully so that they can apply for asylum. This system is enforced through the private sector. The Schengen Implementing Agreement provides at Article 26 that "if an alien is refused entry into the territory of one of the Contracting Parties the carrier which brought him to the external border by air, sea or land shall be obliged to assume responsibility for him again without delay. At the request of the border surveillance authorities the carrier must return the alien to the Third State from which he was transported..." and "The carrier shall be obliged to take all necessary measures to ensure that an alien carried by air or sea is in possession of the travel documents required for entry into the territory of the Contracting parties...The Contracting parties undertake...to impose penalties on carries who transport aliens who do not possess the necessary travel documents by air or sea from a Third State to their territories."

This creates three mechanisms for preventing asylum seekers who by definition will normally be visa nationals, from arriving: the air and sea carriers are first placed under an obligation to check that the individual has the necessary travel documents (including visas where required). If the carrier carries a person who has not got the right travel documents and visas it will be required to return the person to the country of origin (at its own cost) and it will be subject to penalties. During the French Presidency of the European Union in the second half of 2000 a proposal was put forward for harmonization of the fines on carriers at a minimum of Euro 2,000 for transporting persons without documents.[108]

Two further considerations arise as to refugees: first under the Geneva Convention, a refugee is a person already outside his or her country of origin or habitual residence. Thus someone who has not yet escaped is not covered by the convention. This then means that there is no international obligation arising from the Geneva Convention to provide for a system for issuing visas to asylum seekers so they can leave their country of origin to become refugees in the host State. The only international obligation on the Member States which relates to seeking asylum is contained in Article 14(1) Universal Declaration of Human Rights.[109] As a Declaration its force is limited. Secondly, the duties in respect of asylum seekers are state duties. As yet there is no clear indication that they devolve on private parties. As most carriers are private parties they are not self evidently bound by the Geneva Convention or other international human rights instruments. Thus, the decision of an airline not to carry a passenger who does not have a visa where one is required is not by law influenced by the consideration whether the individual is seeking to flee persecution.

At the Border

The legal mechanisms to avoid responsibility for asylum seekers at the border are nuanced. At the European level, the first substantial effort to limit responsibility for asylum seekers is found in the Dublin Convention determining the State responsible for examining applications for asylum lodged in one of the Member States of the European Communities 1990 which finally entered into force on 1 September 1997.[110] The Convention is based on two principles: first that the Member States are entitled to pool their responsibility for asylum seekers. Even though each Member State is separately a signatory to the Geneva Convention (and the other two relevant conventions) a decision on an asylum application by one of them absolves all the others from any duty to consider an asylum application by the same individual.[111] This position, particularly in the absence of a consistent interpretation of the term "refugee" among the Member States, has been challenged by the European Court of Human Rights.[112]

Secondly, a mechanism is created for determining which Member State is responsible for considering an asylum application. In the absence of unusual factors (such as the possession of a visa or residence permit or a first degree family member recognized as a refugee in one Member State) responsibility lies with the first Member State through which the asylum seeker arrived in the Union.[113] In the light of the increasingly stringent provisions regarding visas and carriers sanctions, the idea was that asylum seekers would only be entering the Union over the land borders. Thus, at the time of the negotiation of the agreement though less so at the time of its signature, the responsibility for caring for asylum seekers was intended to fall on the Southern European countries – Greece, Spain, and Italy whose border controls were considered suspect in any event.[114] Of course the changes to Central and Eastern Europe meant the opening up of Germany's Eastern border and a flood of asylum seekers appearing there, much to the chagrin of the German government.[115]

This policy was refined two years later with the adoption of a Resolution on manifestly unfounded applications for asylum[116] and a Resolution on a harmonized approach to questions concerning host third countries.[117] Together with the Conclusions on countries in which there is generally no serious risk of persecution (see above) these two Resolutions were interlocking. First, the Member States announced jointly their policy and interpretation of the Geneva Convention that an asylum seeker does not have a choice of which state to address his or her asylum claim. The Member States considered that the Geneva Convention only prohibits return to the country of persecution, not to any other country. Accordingly, the Member States took the view that there is a duty on an asylum seeker to seek protection in the *first* safe country through which he or she passes. In light of the obstacles placed in the way of an asylum seeker ever getting to a Member State in the first instance, the chances appeared fairly good that the person would have to travel through some other country on the way. Having thus placed the duty on an asylum seeker to seek protection in the first safe state he or she came to when in flight, the secondly policy could be introduced: any asylum seeker arriving in a Member State who had passed through such a safe third country would have his or her asylum application categorized as manifestly unfounded (as the person did not need asylum in the Member State but could seek it elsewhere) and no substantive determination of the case was required. Further the procedural guarantees could be truncated as in theory at least the individual would be returned to the safe third country and would have all the necessary guarantees there.[118]

Therefore the Member States agreed a definition of what a safe country is – by reference primarily to the states on the borders of the Member States (states far away were not particularly relevant) in the Conclusions and adopted a Resolution on manifestly unfounded applications so that persons seeking asylum at the borders of the Union could be rejected immediately and pushed back into the adjacent state.[119] To make the system operational in the light of possible objections from border states on the Union a system of readmission agreements was embarked upon whereby neighbouring states were induced to enter into agreements undertaking to take back persons who had travelled through their state to the Union.[120] The whole system, of course, came unstuck rapidly as asylum seekers began to appear without any travel documents or any credible story about how they had arrived in the Member State where they applied for asylum.[121] However, the lack of an explanation on the travel route was particularly unfortunate for the asylum seeker as the conviction of the authorities that the asylum seeker was lying about the means of arrival inevitably tainted the consideration of the substantive case of the individual to credibility as regards his or her claim to a well founded fear of persecution or torture.

The system for which the legislative foundations were laid was one where arrival by air or sea was patrolled by the visa system and enforced by the carriers. Arrival by land was dealt with at the border by the immediate rejection of the asylum claim at the border itself without suspenseful remedies and the return of the asylum seeker across the border to which ever country was on the other side. The problem however, which increasingly arose was the appearance of asylum seekers within the territory of the Member States without records of travel routes.

Residence Permits

The responsibility for caring for asylum seekers did not go away with the regime which the Member States set into place in the early 1990s. Instead, asylum seekers continued to arrive and make asylum applications, but increasingly this took place within the state itself. Some Member States sought to place limits on the period of time within which an asylum seeker had to make his or her claim after arriving in the Member State.[122] Other Member States adopted legislation which provides for a preliminary check on whether an asylum seeker has been staying in a safe third country before being admitted to the asylum determination procedure.[123] Access to social benefits for asylum seekers was the subject of public discussion and legislation in many Member States.[124] There was no longer a consensus that asylum seekers' physical needs should be treated in the same way as those of nationals of the state.

In the UK a series of measures were adopted which made seeking asylum increasingly difficult for the poor.[125] One rather pernicious example which gives an indication of the way in which poverty becomes a reason for rejection of an asylum claim is the procedure which was introduced whereby an asylum seeker has two weeks from making his or her claim to complete and return a standard form to the authorities. The asylum seeker must include with the form a statement explaining all the grounds and events on account of which he or she seeks asylum. The applicant is given the form and told to go away and complete it.[126] Underlined on the first page of the form it is stated that the form "*must be completed in English*". On the last page of the form the applicant is advised: "A number of private translator services are available within the United Kingdom and will usually advertise in telephone directories such as *Yellow Pages*. You should be aware that such translators will not provide their services freely and charges could be considerable..." As support for destitute asylum seekers takes the form of accommodation and vouchers exchangeable for food with only a tiny sum of cash for travel expenses[127] the suggestion that the asylum seeker will have the wherewithal to pay for commercial translations of their statements is risible. However, failure to do so, as the applicant is warned in large print in bold on the from of the form, means that "his application may be refused in accordance with paragraphs [ ]...and his benefits may be stopped". In other words, the asylum seeker's failure to find enough money in two weeks to pay for translation into English of his or her statement of persecution in itself constitutes a ground to cease providing the asylum seeker with any benefits at all.[128]

An increasing number of Member States reduced the benefits available to asylum seekers in order to dissuade them from coming to that Member State.[129] Germany and the UK in particular lead the way. Even serious disquiet from the UK courts[130] about the plight of asylum seekers left without resources did not prevent additional legislation being adopted limiting asylum seekers access to benefits.[131]

Attempts to reach agreement at a European level on reception of asylum seekers did not succeed. A Spanish proposal in 1995 never made much progress.[132] However, since the entry into force of the Amsterdam Treaty, there is a duty to adopt a measure on reception conditions.[133] The Commission committed itself in its Scoreboard to presenting a proposal on definition of common minimum conditions for reception of asylum seekers by April 2001.[134] The concerns of the Member States regarding reception standards is reflected in the unusual step taken by the French Government in June 2000 to propose a discussion paper on conditions for the reception of asylum seekers which was acknowledged by the Council as a basis for a Commission proposal.[135] The discussion paper states that the host Member State "should ensure decent living conditions throughout the procedure for asylum applicants and accompanying family members. To this end, either an allowance should be paid, supplemented if need be, depending on the composition of the family, or accommodation should be provided by the competent authorities in the host Member State to include lodging, food and basic daily expenses." However, the assessment of what is needed to achieve decent living conditions is left to each Member State "depending on the cost of living and minimum social standards, if any, applied in its territory. Similarly, determination of arrangements for housing asylum must come within the competence of Member States". The discussion paper very strongly objects to asylum seekers being given the right to work. Only if the asylum claim has been outstanding for more than a year should this prohibition be reconsidered. However, these principles are specifically excluded as regards request for asylum at border posts. Instead the document proposes a system like the French system of *zones d'attente* – confinement to former cheap hotel rooms near the airport/border post instead.

Expulsion

As mentioned above, expulsion on grounds of poverty is not possible as regards asylum seekers. International commitments require Member States to care for asylum seekers and determine their claims. However, once a claim has been rejected the asylum seeker can be expelled. While the Member States have frequently confirmed their commitment to the expulsion of rejected asylum seekers the indications are that this does not take place on any particularly systematic scale. One of the main difficulties is that in view of the length of time which the asylum procedures can take (in the UK an amnesty had to be declared in 1999/2000 for asylum seekers whose applications had been pending for more than 7 years without even an initial decision being reach[136]) that the carriers cannot reasonably be held liable for returning the asylum seeker to the country of origin, that is even if a carrier can be identified as responsible. Thus the cost of returning asylum seekers to countries of origin falls on the host Member State. There is evidence that Member States are particularly reluctant to undertake these costs and continue to push rejected asylum seekers across their land borders into one another's territory as a cheaper option.[137]

The numbers of persons involved is not insignificant. If the UK is taken as an example, in 1998, 22,315 asylum applications were refused, in 1999, 11,025 and in 2000, 76,850. The rate of success on appeal was 27 percent in 1999 and 17 percent in 2000. However, the total number of asylum seekers leaving the UK as a result of enforcement action (ie removal/deportation etc.) was 3,430 in 1998 and for the first two quarters of 1999, 2,840.[138] What happens to the rest of them? They are no longer eligible for social assistance, most of them have no travel documents, nor means to obtain travel documents from their embassies. Least of all have they means to purchase tickets to travel elsewhere, even if they could get the travel documents necessary to be permitted to board a carrier moving across European borders. If the UK figures are indicative of the larger Member States at least,[139] well might one ask where are the rejected asylum seekers?

At Sangatte, France, the Red Cross is providing support for refugees seeking to get out of France and into the UK.[140] Hundreds of persons whose asylum claims are not accepted in France shelter in the centre near Calais near the Eurotunnel entrance trying to get out of France. According to the press "Calais has become the new destination of choice for thousands of refugees from Eastern Europe and the Middle East ..."[141] The fact that over 3,500 persons had registered there between the establishment of the Centre at the end of September 1999[142] and February 2000 but only 500 are present at any given time indicates that the camp is a staging post but again one must ask where do these people go? These are persons who have not been admitted to the asylum procedure or have been rejected in France. They are no longer eligible (if they ever were) to social benefits. They are required to leave the territory of France and the Schengen states (ie all the EU states with the exception of the UK and Ireland). However, they have no money and no documents. They are excluded from any form of legal transport.

The vulnerability of these refugees is hard to exaggerate. According to a BBC report, a 16 year old Sudanese girl was raped by a French border policeman while he was taking her to the Sangatte camp. According to the TV report the man said "it was a kind of agreement between them, in exchange for her crossing to Britain, in other words she was willing..."[143] The only chance for these people to leave France lawfully is to travel unlawfully to the UK. Their presence at a Red Cross camp in France is the result of the unwillingness or inability of the French authorities to return them to their countries of origin and the application by the UK authorities of the policy of keeping asylum seekers away from the territory.[144] The unwillingness or inability to carry out expulsions decisions is a characteristic of the EU policy. Rejected asylum seekers are expected to find their own way out of the country which has rejected them. If they are poor and cannot leave lawfully, which is the case for the vast majority, that is their problem – it appears that only the Red Cross is willing to show any compassion towards these victims of poverty.

Conclusions

Bauman brings together many of the strands of both thinking (including Bourdieu and Wacquant) and practice which are the subject of this chapter regarding the poor in his book *Globalization:*

> In the United States, says Pierre Bourdieu, referring to the study of French sociologist Loïc Wacquant, 'the Charitable State, founded on the moralizing conception of poverty, tends to bifurcate into a Social State which assures minimal guarantees of security for the middle classes, and an increasingly repressive state counteracting the effects of violence which results from the increasingly precarious condition of the large mass of the population, notably the black.'[145] This is but one example – though admittedly a particularly blatant and spectacular one, like most American versions of wider, also global phenomena – of a much more general trend to limit the remnants of the original political initiative still held in the fast weakening hands of the nation-state to the issue of law and order; an issue which inevitably translates in practice as orderly – safe – existence for some, all the awesome and threatening force of the law for the others.[146]

The specific area under examination is that of migrants, both voluntary and forced. Even within the legal framework of free movement of persons of the European Union, migrants are advantaged and disadvantaged by reference to their economic means when they leave home. Indeed, whether they can leave home at all will depend on them having the security of resources to be able to support themselves and return to their state of origin in the event of destitution.

For third country nationals the situation is much more extreme. Unless they are well off they will have no chance of getting short stay visas, work or residence permits. If they lose their employment and have no means to fall back on, their right of residence will be at risk. Their possibility of enjoying family reunification is dependent on their means: the poor are not entitled to family life, they must earn enough to support their family members before they can make a claim to it.[147] Finally those seeking international protection are ever more excluded because they are poor. Their ability to flee persecution depends on having the financial means to bribe officials and traffickers and purchase good quality travel documents in order to thwart the policy of the European Union to keep them trapped in the region or country of persecution and to manage to get to a country where they can seek asylum. Assuming that they have succeeded in this, once they arrive, their asylum applications are delayed and delayed, and the majority are rejected. Whatever amounts of public assistance have been made available to them while their applications are under consideration ceases on the refusal except in exceptional circumstances. But they are not necessarily expelled. Expulsion is expensive for the state. So they are trapped in a limbo of poverty and vulnerability outside the edges of society.

Notes

[1] U. Beck, *What is Globalization?*, Polity Press: Cambridge, 2000, p. 11.
[2] U. Beck, *What is Globalization?*, Polity Press: Cambridge, 2000, p. 7.
[3] An interview with Andre Gorz, Frankfurter Allgemeine Zeitung, Frankfurt/Main 1997, p. 377 ff, quoted in U. Beck, *What is Globalization?*, Polity Press: Cambridge 2000, p. 6.
[4] M. Bommes and A. Geddes, *Immigration and Welfare: Challenging the Borders of the Welfare State*, Routledge: London 2000.
[5] I.e. nationals of any one of the fifteen Member States. I will not deal separately with nationals of the non-EC EEA Agreement states – i.e. of Norway, Iceland and Liechtenstein. Their rights are the same as those of Community nationals even though they are in law third country nationals as their states of origin have not joined the European Union.
[6] Third country national is the term which I am applying to nationals of any country which is not a Member State of the European Union or the European Economic Area Agreement.
[7] This is notwithstanding the fact that under the wording of the then Third Pillar the titles of measures which were available were Common Positions, Joint Actions and Conventions.
[8] In this regards the Third Pillar of the time continued the completely intergovernmental policy setting which the Member States were engaged in the fields from about 1990.
[9] For the first five years following the entry into force of the Amsterdam Treaty, the Member States also have a right of initiative in this area, which they have exercised substantially. I will consider, therefore, these proposals of the Member States as well.
[10] Article 49 EC, 286/82, *Luisi and Carbone* [1984] ECR 377.
[11] C-55/94, *Gebhard* [1995] ECR I-4165.
[12] The consideration (enrollment fees) provided by a student in order to benefit from a service made available by a State in the form of courses provided under the national education system is not sufficient to make this a service within the meaning of Article 450 as the State, in establishing and maintaining the system, is not seeking to engage in gainful activity but is fulfilling its duties towards its own population in the social, cultural and educational fields. 263/86, *Humbel* [1988] ECR 5365.
[13] C-43/93, *Vander Elst* [1994] ECR I-3803.
[14] Here I am leaving aside the case of third country nationals who are family members of a Community national. Such persons are included in the Community law regime.
[15] Article 62 EC as and to the extent it is given effect by the incorporated Schengen *acquis*.
[16] In Ireland and the UK the period of a visit is currently six months or less.
[17] COM(93) 684 final.
[18] Belgium, France, Germany, Luxembourg, the Netherlands participated in the original Schengen Convention. The sixth original Member State is Italy.
[19] Article 3 Directive 68/360.
[20] Article 3(1) Directive 68/360.
[21] Article 9(2) Directive 68/360.

22 I will refer here exclusively to the Regulation which is about to be adopted by the Community. Document 14191/00 in the EC Council's register of documents which is expected to be adopted at the March/April 2001 Council meeting.

23 Document 500PC0027: Commission Proposal – COM (2000) 027 final.

24 For example, South Korea, Singapore and Malaysia are on the white list while Laos, Vietnam and Cambodia are on the black list.

25 OJ 2000 C 164/6.

26 It is questionable whether this is even actually possible in view of the fact that the three month period is now stated in Article 62(2)(b) EC.

27 S. Peers, 'Legislative Update', *European Journal of Migration and Law*, vol. 3, n° 1, 2001.

28 Airport transit visas: EUR10; Very short stay visas: EUR 15-25; Short stay visa: Eur 30 + Eur 5 from the second entry where there are multiple entries; multiple entry visas EUR 50; etc. Annex 12 CCI.

29 This has only recently been harmonised: Draft Initiative of the French Republic with a view to the adoption of a Council Decision on the conditions for issuing visas by Member States Doc 8297/1/00 Rev 1, Brussels, 29 May 2000.

30 Section V, CCI.

31 C-68/89, *Commission v Netherlands* [1993] ECR I-2637.

32 Article 3 Directive 64/221.

33 E. Remedios, 'Benefits, immigrants and asylum seekers – a review', *I&NL&P*, vol. 12, n° 1, 1998, p. 19.

34 Directive 64/221.

35 316/85, *Lebon* [1987] ECR 2811.

36 C-85/96, *Martinez Sala* [1998] ECR I-2691.

37 1968.

38 R. Plender, ICLQ 1996.

39 C-416/96, *Awoyemi* [1998] ECR I-6781.

40 C-292/89, *Antonissen* [1991] ECR I-745.

41 Article 7(2) Regulation 1612/68 on social and tax advantages is found in Title II which relates to workers. Title I relating to persons moving to take up employment is silent on this point.

42 316/85, *Lebon* [1987] ECR 2811.

43 Regulation 1408/71: for a discussion on this see F.J.L. Pennings and G. Essers, *Het Voorstel van de Europeese Commissie tot Vereenvoudiging van Verordening 1408/71*, Sociaal Maandblad Arbeid, November/December 2000, n° 11/12, pp. 512-525. The useful Guide produced by the European Commission entitled *"The Community Provisions on Social Security – Your rights when moving within the European Union"*, seeks to simplify as far as possible the rules. It states: "You must have remained available to the unemployment services of the State which pays your unemployment benefit for at least four weeks after becoming unemployed...within seven days after departing, you have to register with the unemployment services of the country in which you are looking for work...you have to comply with the control procedures organized by the unemployment services of that country. You will then retain your unemployment benefit for a maximum period of three months...If you are not able to find a new job within this period you will continue to receive unemployment benefits in the country where you were last employed only if you return before the end of the three month period. If you return later than this, without the explicit permission of the employment services of that country, you will lose all entitlement to benefits. You are entitled to the three month payment only once between two periods of employment." p. 30.

[44] 53/81, *Levin* [1982] ECR 1035.

[45] C-43/93, *Vander Elst* [1993] ECR I-3803.

[46] OJ 1996 C 274/3.

[47] OJ 1996 C 274/7.

[48] Resolution on limitations on admission of third country nationals to the Member States for employment C(i).

[49] Resolution C(iii).

[50] Resolution C(ii).

[51] Article 9(1) Directive 68/360.

[52] Article 6(1)(b) Directive 68/360.

[53] Article 8(1)(a) Directive 68/360.

[54] Article 6(3) Directive 68/360.

[55] Article 7(2) Directive 68/360.

[56] OJ 1996 C 80/2.

[57] Resolution Article III(1).

[58] Resolution Article IV(2).

[59] Article 3(2) Directive 64/221.

[60] E. Guild and J. Niessen, *The Developing Immigration and Asylum Policies of the European Union*, Kluwer Law International, The Hague/London, 1996, pp. 219-230.

[61] Article 2 Recommendation.

[62] Article 3 Recommendation.

[63] Article 4 Recommendation.

[64] OJ 1996 C 5/1.

[65] Article 4 Recommendation.

[66] Ryszard Cholewinski, *Migrant Workers in International Human Rights Law: Their Protection in Countries of Employment*, Oxford: Clarendon Press, 1997.

[67] Article 7.

[68] Preamble, Regulation 1612/68.

[69] For a general discussion on the variety of definitions given to the concept of a family depending on the purposes for which they are used see L. Hantrais, *What is a Family or Family Life in the European Union?*, in E. Guild, *The Legal Framework and Social Consequences of Free Movement of Persons in the European Union*, Kluwer Law International, The Hague/London, 1999, pp. 19-30.

[70] Proposal for a Council Directive on the right to family reunification: Document delivered on: 27/12/2000 http://www.europa.eu.int/eur-lex/en/com/dat/1999/en_599PC0638.html.

[71] Article 10 Regulation 1612/68 and Article 1 Directive 73/148.

[72] This is the term used in the English version of Directive 73/148.

[73] Article 10(2) Regulation 1612/68.

[74] Article 1 Directive 90/364 and 90/365.

[75] Article 1 Directive 93/96.

[76] Article 11 Regulation 1612/68.

[77] 267/83, *Diatta* [1985] ECR 567; C-370/90, *Singh* [1992] ECR I-4265.

[78] 389, 390/87, *Echternach* [1989] ECR 723.

[79] C-370/90, *Singh* [1992] ECR I-4265.

[80] 316/85, *Lebon* [1987] ECR 2811.

[81] E. Guild and J. Niessen, *The Developing Immigration and Asylum Policies of the European Union*, Kluwer Law International, The Hague/London, 1996, pp. 251-257.

[82] Article 3(2) Directive 68/360.

[83] Directive 68/360.

[84] Article 4(3)(e) Directive 68/360.

[85] Article 10(3) Regulation 1612/68.

[86] 249/86, *Commission v Germany* [1989] ECR 1263.

[87] Article 13 Resolution.

[88] Article 16 Resolution.

[89] Article 7(1) Proposal for a Directive.

[90] Article 9(1) Proposal for a Directive.

[91] Article 4 Directive 68/360.

[92] Article 11 Resolution.

[93] Article 8(3) Proposal for a Directive.

[94] In the Commission's proposal for amendment to Regulation 1612/68 a right of residence for such spouses would be created.

[95] An exception is made for the widows of Community national workers where the worker has worked in the Member State for more than two years: Article 3(2) Regulation 1251/70.

[96] Article 12(1) Proposal for a Directive.

[97] Article 12(3) Proposal for a Directive.

[98] Protocol 6 to that Treaty.

[99] S. Peers, *EU Justice and Home Affairs Law*, Longman: Harlow, 2000, p. 129.

[100] E. Guild and J. Niessen, *The Developing Immigration and Asylum Policies of the European Union*, Kluwer Law International, 1996, pp. 177-180.

[101] G. Noll, The Non-Admission and Return of Protection Seekers in Germany, *International Journal of Refugee Law*, vol. 9, 1997, pp. 415-452.

[102] The protocol lifts the territorial and temporal limitation of the original convention.

[103] G. Goodwin-Gill, *The Refugee in International Law*, OUP: Oxford, 1978; J. Hathaway, *The Law of Refugee Status*, Butterworths: Toronto, 1997; J.-Y. Carlier, *Who is a Refugee?*, Kluwer Law International: The Hague/London, 1997.

[104] There has been substantial interpretation of the Convention by the Committee established to adjudicate individual claims under it.

[105] *Chahal*, European Court of Human Rights reports 1996-I.

[106] U. Beck, supra.

[107] E. Guild, 'Entry into the UK: The Changing Nature of National Borders', *I&NL&P*, vol. 14, n° 4, 2000, pp. 227-238.

[108] S. Peers, 'Legislative Update', *EJML* (2001), vol. 3, n° 1.

[109] "Everyone has the right to seek and to enjoy in other countries asylum from persecution".

[110] For a review of the Dublin Convention see G. Noll, 'Formalism vs. Empiricism: Some Reflections on the Dublin Convention on the Occasion of Recent European Case Law', *Nordic Journal of International Law*, vol. 70, n° 1, (2001); A. Hurwitz, 'The 1990 Dublin Convention: A Comprehensive Assessment', *International Journal of Refugee Law*, vol. 11, 1999, pp. 646-677.

[111] Article 3(2) Dublin Convention OJ 1997 C 254/1.

[112] *TI v UK*, European Court of Human Rights reports 2000 – I.

[113] Article 4 and 5 Dublin Convention.

[114] J. van der Klaauw, *The Dublin Convention: A Difficult Start*, in M. den Boer, *Schengen's Final Days?*, EIPA: Maastricht 1998, pp. 77-92.

[115] For a discussion of this see G. Noll, supra.

[116] E. Guild and J. Niessen, *The Developing Immigration and Asylum Policies of the European Union*, Kluwer Law International: The Hague/London, 1996, pp. 141-147.

[117] E. Guild and J. Niessen, *The Developing Immigration and Asylum Policies of the European Union*, Kluwer Law International: The Hague/London, 1996, pp. 161-165.

[118] E. Guild, 'The impetus to harmonise: asylum policy in the European Union', in F. Nicholson and P. Twomey, *Refugee Rights and Realities*, CUP: Cambridge, 1999, pp. 313-335; D. Winterbourne, P. Shah and C. Doebbler, 'Refugees and safe countries of origin: appeals, judicial review and human rights', *I&NL&P*, vol. 10, n° 4, 1996, pp. 123-135.

[119] For a discussion of the issues for Central and Eastern European countries see M. Fullerton, E. Sik and J. Toth (eds), *Refugees and Migrants: Hungary at a Crossroads*, Institute for Political Sciences of the Hungarian Academy of Sciences: Budapest, 1995.

[120] Recommendation concerning a specimen bilateral readmission agreement between a Member State of the European Union and a third country OJ 1996 C 274/21.

[121] G. Noll and J. Vedsted-Hansen, *Non-Communitarians: Refugee and Asylum Policies*, in P. Alston, *The EU and Human Rights*, OUP: Oxford, 1999, pp. 359-410.

[122] *Asylum Procedures in the European Union*, Trentham: London, 1999.

[123] For example, the Netherlands.

[124] P. Minderhoud, *Asylum seekers and access to social security: recent developments in the Netherlands, United Kingdom, Germany and Belgium*, in A. Bloch and C. Levy (eds), *Refugees, Citizenship and Social Policy in Europe*, MacMillan: Houndmills, 1999, pp. 132-148.

[125] For a full examination of the link see A. Geddes, *Denying access: asylum seekers and welfare benefits in the UK*, in M. Bommes and A. Geddes, *Immigration and Welfare Challenging the Borders of the Welfare State*, Routledge: London, 2000, pp. 134-147.

[126] Home Office form SEF.

[127] Indeed, it is not even enough to cover the bus costs for asylum seekers to attend at their interviews.

[128] Home Office form SEF.

[129] R. Bank, in M. Bommes and A. Geddes, *Immigration and Welfare: Challenging the Borders of the Welfare State*, Routledge: London, 2000, p. 148.

[130] See E. Remedios, 'Benefits, Immigrants and Asylum Seekers – a Review', *I&NL&P*, vol. 12, n° 1, 1998, pp. 19-22; in particular *R v Secretary of State for the Home Department ex parte JCWI & An* The Times, 27 June 1996.

[131] A. Geddes, *Denying Access: asylum seekers and welfare benefits in the UK*, in M. Bommes and A. Geddes (eds), *Immigration and Welfare: Challenging the Borders of the Welfare State*, Routledge: London, 2000, pp. 134-147.

[132] See S. Peers, *EU Justice and Home Affairs law*, Longman: Harlow, 2000, pp. 120-121.

[133] Article 63(1)(b) EC Treaty.

[134] European Commission, Communication: Scoreboard to Review Progress on the Creation of an Area of "Freedom, Security and Justice" in the European Union COM (2000) 167 final, 24.03.00.

[135] 9703100 Limi – Asile 28, 23 June 2000.

[136] In 1999, 11,140 persons benefited from the amnesty; in 2000 a further 10,330 received residence rights on the amnesty basis; Home Office, *Asylum Statistics: December 2000*, United Kingdom.

[137] French Television report on the French gendarmes in Belgium, Autumn 2000.

[138] Home Office, *Control of Immigration: Statistics United Kingdom Second Half and Year 1998*.

[139] Comparable statistical information on asylum seekers is not available in most other Member States.

[140] *Hundreds Queue for British "Eldorado"*, Agence France Presse, Feb 1, 2000; *Refugees set their Sights on Britain*, The Independent, August 21, 1999.

[141] *Calais one step from Heaven for refugees*, The Scotsman, April 1, 2000.

[142] Agence Press, February 1, 2000, supra.

[143] BBC Monitoring Service July 22, 2000. According to the report the French border policeman was arrested and held in custody. Charges were being brought.

[144] In the case of Sangatte this policy is reinforced by the Protocol between the UK and France concerning frontier controls and policing, co-operation in criminal justice, public safety and mutual assistance relating to the Channel fixed link 1991 and its Additional Protocol 2000 whereby the policing of the UK border is the duty of the French border guards.

[145] P. Bourdieu, *L'architect de l'euro passé aux aveux*, Le monde diplomatique, September 1997, p. 19.

[146] Z. Bauman, *Globalization: The Human Consequences*, Columbia University Press: NY 1998 p. 103.

[147] A notable exception to this principle is France where economic criteria are not applied to family reunification.

References

Bank, R. (2000), in Bommes, M. and Geddes, A. (eds), *Immigration and Welfare: Challenging the Borders of the Welfare State*, Routledge: London, pp. 148.

Bauman, Z. (1998), *Globalization: The Human Consequences*, Columbia University Press: NY.

Beck, U. (2000), *What is Globalization?*, Polity Press: Cambridge.

Bommes, M. and Geddes, A. (2000), *Immigration and Welfare: Challenging the Borders of the Welfare State*, Routledge: London.

Bourdieu, P. (1997), 'L'architect de l'euro passé aux aveux', *Le monde diplomatique*, September 1997, p. 19.

Carlier, J.-Y. (1997), *Who is a Refugee?*, Kluwer Law International: The Hague/London.

Cholewinski, R. (1997), *Migrant Workers in International Human Rights Law: Their Protection in Countries of Employment*, Clarendon Press: Oxford.

Fullerton, M., Sik, E. and Toth, J. (1995), 'Refugees and Migrants: Hungary at a Crossroads', Institute for Political Sciences of the Hungarian Academy of Sciences: Budapest.

Geddes, A. (2000), 'Denying Access: Asylum Seekers and Welfare Benefits in the UK', in Bommes, M. and Geddes, A. (eds), *Immigration and Welfare Challenging the Borders of the Welfare State*, Routledge: London, pp. 134-147.

Goodwin-Gil, G. (1978), *The Refugee in International Law*, OUP: Oxford.

Guild, E. (1999), 'The Impetus to Harmonise: Asylum Policy in the European Union', in Nicholson, F. and Twomey, P. (eds), *Refugee Rights and Realities*, CUP: Cambridge, pp. 313-335.

Guild, E. (2000), 'Entry into the UK: The Changing Nature of National Borders', *I&NL&P*, vol. 14, n° 4, pp. 227-238.

Guild, E. and Niessen, J. (1996), *The Developing Immigration and Asylum Policies of the European Union*, Kluwer Law International: The Hague/London.

Hantrais, L. (1999), 'What is a Family or Family Life in the European Union?' in Guild, E. (ed.), *The Legal Framework and Social Consequences of Free Movement of Persons in the European Union*, Kluwer Law International: The Hague/London.

Hathaway, J. (1991), *The Law of Refugee Status*, Butterworths: Toronto.

Hurwitz, A. (1999), 'The 1990 Dublin Convention: A Comprehensive Assessment', *International Journal of Refugee Law*, vol. 11, n° 4, pp. 646-677.

Minderhoud, P. (1999), 'Asylum Seekers and Access to Social Security: Recent Developments in the Netherlands, United Kingdom, Germany and Belgium', in Bloch, A. and Levy, C. (eds), *Refugees, Citizenship and Social Policy in Europe*, MacMillan: Houndmills, pp. 132-148.

Noll, G. (1997), 'The Non-Admission and Return of Protection Seekers in Germany', *International Journal of Refugee Law*, vol. 9, n° 3, pp. 415-452.

Noll, G. (2001), 'Formalism vs Empiricism: Some Reflections on the Dublin Convention on the Occasion of Recent European Case Law', *Nordic Journal of International Law*, vol. 70, n° 1/2, pp. 161-182.

Noll, G. and Vedsted-Hansen, J. (1999), 'Non-Communitarians: Refugee and Asylum Policies', in Alston, P. (ed.), *The EU and Human Rights*, OUP: Oxford, pp. 359-410.

Peers, S. (2000), *EU Justice and Home Affairs Law*, Longman: Harlow.

Peers, S. (2001), 'Key Legislative Developments on Migration in the European Union', *EJML*, vol. 3, n° 2, pp. 231-255.

Remedios, E. (1998), 'Benefits, Immigrants and Asylum Seekers – a Review', *I&NL&P*, vol. 12, n° 3, pp. 188-196.

van der Klaauw, J. (1998), 'The Dublin Convention: A Difficult Start', in den Boer, M. (ed.), *Schengen's Final Days?*, EIPA: Maastricht, pp. 77-92.

Winterbourne, D., Shah, P. and Doebbler, C. (1996), 'Refugees and Safe Countries of Origin: Appeals, Judicial Review and Human Rights', in *I&NL&P*, vol. 10, n° 4, pp. 123-135.

Chapter 2

Frontier Controls in the European Union: Who is in Control?

Didier Bigo

Introduction: Frontier and Controls What Relations?

This chapter seeks to deconstruct one of the strongest myths of political discourses: the statement that controls are linked with the place where the borders of the European Union run.[1] The genealogy of the different narratives will be traced which forge the link between frontiers and especially European frontiers on the one hand, and the public rhetoric of politicians concerning border controls in relation to the social practices of the controls by security professionals on the other hand. The chapter will come back to the very first moment of the discussion of the 1980s, and particularly to the so-called debate between the dangers of Sieve Europe or Fortress Europe and the invention of the differentiation between internal and external frontiers of the EU. It has structured our view for more than twenty years now. But it is still difficult to get out of it and to think alternatively.

The effort of this chapter is to reveal the connection between the state and the frontier and to analyze the different actors playing a role in controlling the movements of people inside the EU but across the borders of its member States and beyond the EU, especially when people want to enter. It is not an easy task. The relation between frontiers and control is so naturalized that it is often difficult to analyze it. It is taken for granted that the state has the right to control its borders and to differentiate between its citizens and foreigners, and to treat them differently. The definition of State through territory, population and administration captures our political imagination. The monopolization of the regulation of movement of people by the state is considered its right, opposed and superior to the right of the individual to move freely. Thus, everything is already said. Frontier controls are a technical measure which needs to be enforced, not a political choice. State and European laws can rightfully deal differently with citizens and foreigners, citizens and immigrants.[2]

A second naturalization derived from the first one and the conception of the State in the West, is the idea that politicians pass laws that are enforced afterwards by bureaucracies (customs, police, border guards...) – the so-called US labeling of law enforcement agencies – and that the politicians are in charge of the border controls, that they can act upon the flow of people crossing borders by changing laws. It is only a question of will to act, not a question of capacity. In fact, the professionals of politics, at the national level, or even at the level of the European Council, cannot channel the millions of individual decisions of border crossing. The impossibility in liberal regimes to seal borders, the practical management of very long borders, as well as the autonomy of bureaucracies charged with controlling them counter the politicians' will to master the flows, even when they invoke a permanent state of emergency or exception to justify the tightening of controls. They surf on the wave of the flows and try to mask it by tough discourses. They follow the technologies of controls proposed by the professionals of security and often legitimate afterwards what has already become common practice before, and try to hide that fact behind rhetoric concerning the "new" balance between security and freedom.

The real structural factors of managing flows of people are, on the one hand, linked with the transformations of the possibility to travel and with the development of the individuals' increasing desire and imperative to move. On the other hand, they are determined by the technologies of identification, the policing at distance and the collaboration between the different internal security agencies on a global level attempting to control more efficiently how people move by trying to block some of them, by sorting out those who are welcome and those who are undesirable. The problem is that these elements are obscured by the so-called solutions adopted by the professionals of politics (concerning border controls, migration...), which are in fact the main problem because their symbolic politics prevent us from understanding what is at stake.

This chapter will discuss in detail the symbolic politics of the professionals of politics concerning border controls and how the terminology used in political science for describing the relations of frontiers and controls are prisoners of the state of mind behind all these assumptions about the role of the state or the future of the European Union as a quasi-state. The last chapter of this book will discuss the practical logic of controls beyond the frontiers and the delocalization of the institution "frontier", its malleability and its capacity to adapt to the different groups of individuals and not to be the sharp edge of a territory. So my attachment to the central role of discourse will be complemented by the description of the more invisible social practices. This way of thinking challenges the traditional notions of borders, frontiers, boundaries and their relations with facts, with institutions, and with social practices.

The first part will try to disentangle the notion of frontiers from other notions, to understand why state and frontier were so closely related in political theory, and how both globalization and the construction of the European Union change the conceptual link between them. The second part will develop the effects of the uncertainty which is con-substantial to the EU mapping and will not finish with a "completed Europe" embraced by a "real federal state".

The Europeanization has created uncertainty about the notion of frontiers and has reinforced the de-linking between the locus of controls and the locus of the state borders. This has destabilized the differentiation between friends and foes, insiders and outsiders, and opened the door for the possibility to think about friendship and human rights all over the world, but also for the possibility of outsiders inside, of enemies within, of the importation of the chaotic tendencies reigning outside. These narratives oblige us to re-think what a boundary and a frontier are. Evoking the European level implies methodologically rethinking the relations between frontiers and state formation, coercion and security, friendship and enmity, as well as otherness and self-identification. Nothing can be taken for granted as long as Europe is not mistaken for a federal state embryo at the level of the fifteen or twenty-five countries, even if, unfortunately, this is the underlying discourse of so many narratives concerning the European future.

Uncertainty lies at the heart of the European identity. It is a creative heterogeneity but this uncertainty creates strong reactions and calls for more homogeneity, integration, and unity (at the EU level or against it by a revival of the nation state or even at the regional level). Because the question of belonging is not seriously addressed, the professionals of politics have diverted the issue to immigration and how to control it. That was the only way for them to continue to claim that they were in charge of the politics concerning the movement of persons, all the while being perfectly aware of the fact that they do not control these flows (as they know they do not control the bankers and the flow of credits, either). Nevertheless they construct the political spectacle in such a way that everybody believes that it is, first, a key issue of politics, second, that they can manage it, and third, that a real competition among possible solutions to the problem exists. Hence, it is also crucial to understand the way in which the discourses about the impact of Europeanization on national border controls are framed and why they concentrate on immigration controls, with a permanent suspicion in regards to the narratives of the individuals and with an unease concerning their own identity and behaviour which push them to re-draw the lines of otherness differently.

This is not the first book trying to achieve this goal. This chapter will point out the main findings of other researchers who have already tried to gain a better understanding of contemporary politics by de-linking the conditions of existence and functioning of politics from state theory and by discussing the notion of frontier itself.[3] Already, the themes of frontiers, of security (both internal and external) and of identities are the subject of a large number of studies in history, sociology, political science and international relations.[4] But little has been done either using interaction between these fields, or in terms of a general analysis. For example, the theme of identities has been much explored in research on exclusion, but often from a very philosophical or social interactionist perspective.[5] The perceptions of otherness, the relations of otherness, belonging, and discrimination are frequently discussed in this literature but, paradoxically, controls of identity and the production of identity documents (national identity cards, passports, etc.) have been far less examined.[6] Few field studies observing the controls at borders or in those urban areas considered by governments to be at risk have been conducted – still fewer have been carried out since the implementation of the Schengen agreements.[7]

But there does not exist a combination of the different findings coming from political theory, international relations, political sociology, and European studies yet. The sociological research about European police liaison officers has obliged this author to conduct many interviews with officials coming from politics or the security sector and to try to theorize beyond the traditional comparative national approaches. The discourses of these two hundred interviews from the last seven years are not used here, but it is from their voices, their struggles that this chapter tries to reframe the subject. The bibliography is also in that sense quite heterodox, but it constitutes an effort to combine these different findings and to put them into a coherent framework inspired by Michel Foucault's approach. He is not quoted as a way to justify this discourse, but it is the underpinning reference, and his work is used in order to delineate a different frame. This chapter tries to understand at the edge of our time, the genealogy of the discourses concerning border controls as a sign of an ending world that tries to survive as long as possible and to actively forget about its contradiction in order to artificially prolong its life. But as can be seen in the chapter concerning policing at a distance, the disconnection between the national professionals of politics and the transnational professionals of (in)security is drawing new maps and different futures.

Border, Boundary, Frontier and the State

The notion of border is very often considered a materialized line between two spaces. Borders are associated with differentiation between inside and outside, with control of who crosses the line. This is important since the notion of border is embedded, as far as common knowledge is concerned, into a theory of the territorial state that inhibits the capacity to understand the passage of frontier controls beyond the national territory and that is blinded by the juridical perception of embassies and consulates as delocalized parts of the nation-state.[8] Borders, control and state are by definition intertwined.

As Malcolm Anderson has pointed out, the notions of boundaries and frontiers are more complex than border, even if they are often used as synonyms. Boundary is used to refer to the act of drawing a line and not as to the result. It may have a more philosophical meaning and apply to every kind of delimitation, not only the geographical ones. Frontier is used, at least in political science and geography in Europe, to connect space and population. It is the limit of a territory. Frontier is an institution, not a fact, not a result. The underlying concept comprises the possibility to consider a territory a space one belongs to. A frontier describes the relation between forces, between powers that must struggle for delimitation in a competitive way whereas a border is the materialization in space of this struggle through time. Michel Fouché has developed and explained the concept of frontier as a narrow line and a no man's land typically linked with the rise of the nation-states in Europe. It creates confusion between frontiers and borders. But, in other places of the world or in earlier periods, the frontier was not a border and much more of a "line", a front, a symbolic differentiation between people. It was a mark of belonging quite independent of the place they were located. And perhaps the European Union is (re)inventing this kind of belonging and differentiation with the others where the limits of the territory are less and less relevant in terms of identity. That is why the concept of frontier is perhaps more useful in order to discuss the contemporary situation of Europe than the concept of border.

Frontier, when conceived as border, became a symbol of certainty, of clarity and was associated with the truth of one state, with the capacity of control of a state apparatus alongside the development of nationalist ideology. 'Truth on one side of the Pyrenees is a lie on the other side' was a well-known proverb popular both in Spain and in France. And perhaps the main question about frontier control is in fact this question of the truth provided by an institution which considers sacred the materialized line of a *rapport de force* as a divide between truth and lie, good and evil. Law is always reassuring frontiers in that sense. But, now, certainty and clarity disappear to the eyes of everybody and not only for a little group of academics.

The contradictions between the notions of frontier, of territory, of stateness, of construction of the European Union are obvious and produce visible effects. National law and European Law enter into strong competition. The state is struggling with the emerging power of the European Commission and European Courts to assert the truth of marking the frontier. The location of the frontier and its relationship with control becomes thus more complex. Frontiers, and particularly European Union frontiers with their differentiation between internal and external frontiers, create uncertainty about the location, the site of the frontier. But this uncertainty is nothing one should fear, even if governments want to frame the question in such a way. It is an advantage. It allows people to have more practical freedom, even if their right to travel is contested and, hence, critical academic research should frame a different view from the traditional conception of state frontier. This can be done by analyzing where the frontier runs for the individual, what the relationships between state frontier, political authority and collective identity are, and how one can develop a framework that gives rights to the individuals.

Yosef Lapid has encapsulated a complete research agenda in the formula "identities, borders, and orders" thus opening what was sealed by the "State thinking" (*pensée d'Etat*).[9] For him, the three concepts are like a triangle where each one co-determines the two others. No possibility exists to think about the different identities without an analysis of the borders and of the different orders. He invites us, together with the French political sociology (especially the school represented by Bourdieu), to think differently about borders, about who a migrant is and why a migrant defined as an "outsider inside" is breaking the traditional division between citizens and foreigners.[10]

In another article, I have developed the theoretical lines that enhance the possibility to understand the notion of frontier differently, not as a delimitation of "inside" and "outside" but as a Mobbius ribbon where the perception of what is inside and what is outside varies depending on the position of the observer.[11] Here, the consequence of this intersubjective framework of the frontier will be developed in order to show what the implicit statements (or what Bourdieu calls the doxa) are and how the different institutions in charge of controls share the same statements as far as frontiers and their limits are concerned. The transformation of the notion of frontier with the discussion between internal and external frontiers of the European Union facilitates the understanding of the practical implications of the de-linking of frontiers and controls. The key moment was when migration was constructed as a political problem at the very beginning of the eighties by different political discourses differentiated by the right/left and the nationalist/European cleavages, but united in the same broad assumptions about control at frontiers as a way to solve immigration policies.[12] The result did not consist of a comeback of the frontier as a military barrier, but it was not regarded as point of junction either. The novelty was the linkage of freedom and policing, the act of policing in the name of freedom.

In the European context, especially from the main narrative of the four freedoms of the EC internal market including freedom of movement of people, the relationship between border controls and immigration laws on the one side, and politics and social practices of control on the other, is framed differently compared to other regions. If it is compared to NAFTA for instance, in the European Union the "norm", the "imperative" is set up as freedom of movement of people, even if restrictions may occur (for national security or internal security reasons). And the US audience needs to be aware of such a difference rooted in a very different approach of freedom, equality, stateness and belonging. But, simultaneously, in Europe as in the US, the framing of the link between frontiers and control was and still is constructed as a security issue, as a well-balanced organization between freedom of movement and necessary measures to protect the insiders from people entering from the outside. So, the dynamics are different. The framing of this internal security discourse, which, in Europe, remains connected to the 1980s discussion (at the beginning of Schengen) will be discussed later to show that this framing is not an effect of the end of the cold war, as too often assessed. It comes from a different set of norms and ideas on issues of freedom and security.

The end of the cold war has opened up a possibility for the EU to act and to develop positively the uncertainty without resolving the contradictions. Consequently, they still continue to exist, but are reinforced, in the post-September 11 era by the US strategy of imposing its own views concerning the relationship between frontiers and controls through visa requirements, airlines carriers, and a different attitude towards freedom and technologies.

Frontiers: Barriers or Junctions

As we have seen the notions of border or frontier were long seen as unproblematic in political science, geography, and law in Europe. Frontiers were conceived as the outer limits of the power of a sovereign state over a population on a specific territory. And the sovereign state was "a bordered power container".[13] The frontiers were state frontiers and the state was a territorial state before being a population state. The tautological statements between state, frontiers, and sovereignty were accepted as the essence of a polity.[14] The division between political theory and international relations disciplines reinforces the naturality of the frontier by avoiding an open discussion of the contradictions.[15] In this classical approach, borders or frontiers are synonymous with questions of defense, war, citizenship, or the right to punish criminals through collaboration with other states. It is essentially an interstate vision where frontiers delineate natural cultural containers and clear security barriers.

But, now, the meaning of what is a state is changing, sovereignty is being discussed, the meaning of border or frontier is being challenged. Concerning state and sovereignty, the ongoing discussion about the spread of capitalism, the globalization of cultural models and the globalization of the world with the development of resistance against uniformity have changed what was taken for granted. States are conceived as networks of power and no longer as bordered power containers. Sovereignty is conceived as a claim to authorize oneself to act and not as state sovereignty disclaiming liability in front of any other authority.

The first challenge has to do with the military conception of borders. For a long time the enemy – the 'natural' enemy – was the territorial neighbor; the frontier served as a protection against the neighbor. The frontier was in fact a "military zone" more than a barrier even though the term is very frequently used. State making and war making were linked through this territorialization of the State and its capacity to differentiate internal and external zones of control.[16] Fortresses were built on the State borders. They sometimes stopped the enemy but the phenomenon of transnational flows of people is not new and could not be stopped. It was already there. Migration has always been central in the history of mankind, either in the context of peaceful displacements or with "crusades" and "holy wars". They were often slow and contiguous movements. So, the state builders tried to control these flows by organizing military controls at the frontiers in order to take away the possibility for the outsiders to enter without permission, and also to block the possibility for insiders to flee a regime. Borders were seen as containers differentiating inside and outside, at least in the case of the European trajectory of State making. The claim was nevertheless often virtual and, in fact, States adapt to the demographic and economic situations by encouraging what they cannot control. The technology of war making has created this imagery of the frontiers as barriers. But aerial warfare, the disappearance of any distinction between the military frontline and civilian zones, and the development of atomic weapons have destroyed this notion. The States are now less and less "containers" which are clearly defined and only have a thin but tough line between them (a no man's land). The strategic problem is not yet to break through the enemy front lines.

If the border function of security is to survive, it will be more along its second function, the police function. Gérard Noiriel has shown the importance for the creation of "national" state of new means of surveillance. The surveillance of individuals started to rely less on a face to face relationship on a narrow local basis, and more on technologies of identification which mediate the relationship: identity papers, travel authorizations, visas and so forth. The "tyranny of the national" refers to the ability of the state to control individuals at a distance, beyond their place of birth and to the great emphasis on the difference between the national territory, with the notions of nationality and citizenship on the one hand, and the foreign territory with the associated notions of foreigners, aliens, etc. on the other.[17] But, it was not effectively enforced before the nineteenth century and the idea of effective strong controls by national states from the time of Westphalian peace onwards is only a suitable fiction for IR theory specialists.

John Torpey has developed this idea by highlighting the claim of the state to the monopoly on the movement of persons from one state to another, and sometimes even within its own frontiers. As he explains "modern states, and the international state system of which they are a part, have expropriated from individuals and private entities the legitimate means of movement particularly though by no means exclusively across international boundaries. An understanding of the processes whereby states monopolized the legitimate means of movement is thus crucial to an adequate comprehension of how modern states actually work".[18] And John Torpey insists on the fact that the claim by the state was for a very long time symbolic, concerning the "right" of someone to move, and was very far from an effective capacity of control of borders by the state apparatus. The frontier security technologies and their effectiveness only began to expand in the nineteenth century, when customs and gendarmes intensified their efforts to catch smugglers and traffickers, and when it became an obligation to have papers in due form in order to cross the borders. The "crustacean" type of Nation, as he explains, developed only lately, even if it was backed by the discourses of philosophers of the sixteenth century. The first part of the twentieth century was a struggle between economic liberalism and crustacean nationalism. The first wave of globalization was possible, but only "inside" colonial empires, and protectionism as well as the rise of authoritarian regimes in the heart of liberal Europe show the limits of the expansion of liberalism.[19] With the second part of the twentieth century, the contradictions were not resolved but exacerbated. Some regimes tried to have an absolute control of their borders (Berlin wall, Iron curtain of Eastern countries). The idea to construct walls around the frontiers was considered as a serious solution by some of the communist hard-liners. Liberal democracies, on the contrary refused this kind of technology of "protection", alleging that it was the sign of a police state.

The idea to block the people "inside" a state is said to be different from the idea of preventing the people "outside" to come in, even if the frontiers are the locus of these different kinds of controls. The ideological struggle of the cold war allows in principle for liberal regimes to have an "exit" option, to have the right for the people to travel freely, but not to settle.[20] So, during this period and after, the effective sealing of borders, when they took place in liberal regimes, were only for a very short period of time because it too openly contradicts economic and democratic values.[21] They were and are still justified by exceptional circumstances but their legitimacy is undermined if they continue for an extended period of time.[22] The contrast between the discourses concerning the creation of a free movement area and the narratives evoking a sealing, a closure of frontiers needs to be analyzed, especially when these discourses are expressed in specific forms of surveillance, because they always come back, in the name of security, to the boundary between liberal and authoritarian regimes.[23]

The tensions between normative and economic liberalism and fears of public demands for more controls at the borders have always been present in the public discourses. It is not a post September 11 effect, even if some analysts only discover the contradiction now. But the governmentality by fear or unease was "contained" by the norms of liberalism, especially when freedom is associated with equality and when it is not possible to sacrifice the freedom of others for its own security. In that sense, policing in the name of freedom supposes the refusal to differentiate inside between citizens and non-citizens, and to consider the possibility of the emergence of an enemy within or more precisely of an infiltrated enemy. The enemy is in that case infiltrated, coming from outside and alien but nevertheless inside and sometimes for more than one generation but it is still possible to distinguish to the "real" insider. And this difference legitimates a "genuine" racism as a way to "trace" the signs of the enemy within without abandoning the state dowa that inside is associated with friendship or institutional opposition, and outside with enmity.

Policing thus equals controlling the border to check who is entering the territory. It raises the question whether the claim to the monopoly on the circulation of movement by a state apparatus is legitimate or not. But the legitimacy is neither obvious nor "given", and this is one of the weaknesses of a lot of research concerning policing, passports, or means of identification. States do not have the right, but simply the habit to control. They have transformed this habit into Law, but they do not provide the answer as to why. The argumentation about their right is weak, especially if freedom of movement of individuals is recognized at the same moment. Tensions about global individual rights to move and claims of the state to control their movement have developed in the last forty years. If politicians in liberal democracy are obliged to invoke a permanent state of emergency to re-claim their monopoly, they are undermining their own legitimacy, in comparison with authoritarian states.

The problem for the liberal governments is that the security argument itself is always considered a "threat", a danger. It attacks the roots of liberalism and is considered a backlash of history, a reaction of fear against the globalization and its opportunities. It is not only traditional. It is a reactionary argument.[24] The discourse of securitization of the frontier is only receptive if it does not undermine freedom and equality. If it does, it creates a longstanding resistance and transforms the regime. So, the strategy is to play verbally with the limits between inside and outside, but not to act as if the frontiers did not exist. It is here that the power of the professionals of politics is important. The military language used to justify more security and border controls, does not mask that it is, in fact, a police question. The discourse concerning transversal threats, global threats, global terrorism or global organized crime could not overcome the effects of the importation inside a liberal regime of the rules of war and the suspicion of everyone against everyone. The limits are there and it is not possible to claim that war is everywhere, without any frontier. Of course the temptation is strong to mobilize the old military discourse of the frontier as an effective barrier, but it is highly ineffective in practice and in case of real conflict it gives more power to the enemy than a discourse expressing that the military frontiers are now relative.

Securitization also turns against the concept of frontiers as junctions, as economic operators. The well-known argument will not be developed here. The conflict is not directly between security and economy but between two different visions of the world, one where the global is a sign of chaos and threats, and the other where the global is a new stage for humanity as such. The competition for the truth about the world is here very strong. New descriptions and narratives emerge to try to explain the new sets of transborder activities around the world, the role of markets, the role of Diasporas and individuals. And, as soon as the state is not seen as the only actor of International Relations, the picture of the frontiers and the possibility to control them, changes too.

Frontiers and Transnational Activities

The ease of crossing frontiers, of communication of huge quantities of information across frontiers, of establishing trans-frontier economic and social relationships, and of utilizing virtual spaces has definitely altered perceptions and assessments of frontiers as effective barriers to human activity. Now, cross-border flows of people are associated, for better or worse, with economic globalization, with the process of the international division of labor, and with the economic cycle, although the demand for labor is present even during periods of crisis.[25] Practically everybody now uses the term transnational to speak about the cross-border flow of people and especially about migration. But first of all, transnational is not an equivalent of globalism and some transnational flows are very local. They just cross an international frontier but are in the same border region.[26] Second, cross border flows are not reducible to migration, they are more a way of life, the emanation of nomadism repressed by territorial states. Cross border activities cover more than a one way move from one country to another to settle – they are the manifestation of multiple phenomena as differential demographic development, internal migration in Third World countries and, especially in the countries which border the European Union or the United Sates, effects of diffusion of the 'Western model', linguistic policies affecting the major languages – English, French, German – reinforcement of images through television, explosion of the number of television channels via satellite, promotion of the model of 'market democracy' to the countries which border the big blocks, desire by refugees to escape authoritarian state control structures, and violent conflicts.[27]

The catchword globalization is very often used to analyze this move towards economic, liberal norms, idea of individual free movement, right to cultural differences. And even if all these objectives contradict each other, they constitute an alternative to the statist vision of the world. It is thus described either as a "bifurcation of the world",[28] a "global turning point",[29] a "Retreat of the State",[30] or a path to "global transformations".[31] For some it equates to the defeat of the State,[32] or the bypassing of the State,[33] or the emergence of a de-territorialized Empire.[34] For others it shows the emergence of a new form of governmentality beyond the territorial State by transnational bureaucracies and elites.[35] In these latest approaches, the territorial State is admittedly fading but disciplinarization expands. The State is no longer the only apparatus framing the microphysics of power and resistance according to its own boundaries, the scales are changing and the local, national and global levels are increasingly intermingled.

In that picture, immigration, as well as tourism, cross-border circulation, and all kinds of nomadic behavior, seem to undermine the classical conceptions of States as governing entities. Even security is now a structure where the state retreats. Susan Strange has made a mistake in believing that, contrary to wealth credit and information, security continues to be in the hands of the state. Security is affected by the same movement as the other structures. But the "Retreat of the

State" does not signify less control than before, and it is not the triumph of anarchy. In short, markets win and with them domination expands to the global level, destroying the democratic counterparts of the rule of law. Other kinds of polity are in their premises and they have to invent other forms of democratic controls. The European Union is perhaps one of them. As Christian Lequesne and Andy Smith have shown, the national states seem destined to change – and the European Union looks like a confused attempt to find a post-national, post-state form of governmentality where a transnationalization of the bureaucratic systems of control corresponds to (or even anticipates) the transnational flows.[36] So, if transnationality is blurring the distinction between the internal and the external, destabilizing the related concepts of sovereignty, territoriality and security, the governments also play with the transnational in order to continue to hold power. And the main strategy was to transform the original idea of the internal market of the European Community with borders as junctions to the idea of a common strategy for the border controls of the European Union with borders as a means to block immigration.

Uncertain European Frontiers: An Opportunity for a New Technology of Control

Mapping the EU

Europe is not where it is supposed to be as Rob Walker has carefully demonstrated.[37] Europe is not territorial. The naturalization of the European Union as a quasi-state, as an entity assembling territorial states creates a pattern of homogeneity and stability, which is far from the social practices encapsulated in this terminology. Microstates, for instance, are at the very heart of Europe and play a crucial role in finance and, at times, in money laundering. They are also important for the media and for some new information technologies such as Internet sites. Financescape and mediascape play extensively with the discrepancies they introduced in the representation of a single EU border unit.[38] Contrary to widespread perception, the functioning of the European Union is not based on a delimited inside-outside frontier. The territorial framework of the European Union is not stable, even if the frontiers of the member states are not seriously in competition nowadays (with the exception of Gibraltar, some Aegean Sea islands and in the future Kaliningrad…). On the contrary, it is undergoing a profound transformation, which goes further than the completion of a virtual map of all the states inside geographical Europe.

As John Crowley explains, "Europe defies location. Neither geography, nor sociology, nor ideology, offers an unambiguous demarcation between what is and what is not European…Europeaness is more a reflection of the democratic character of the different societies. Maps are to be drawn, and not simply to be read".[39] The transformation affects the notion of what a frontier as an institution is. Concerning the first point, members of the European Union have not yet agreed on a unitary policy to be completed in the future. They do not follow the same ends, do not share the same vision of what a "completed Europe would look like, as shown by the discussion about Turkey between Valery Giscard d'Estaing on one side and Tony Blair as well as Romano Prodi on the other, and they do not even have any idea in common as far as the means, by which frontier management and border control techniques should be harmonized, are concerned. The fights continue between current member states and the future members about the locus of controls in the future. More importantly, Schengenland does not even correspond to the territory of the European Union because of the UK's and Ireland's respective policies of opting out and it creates a multitude of ambiguities and desperate situations such as the Sangatte camp.[40] Schengenland also includes Norway, Iceland as well as, in practice, Switzerland and the gap between what is being said and what is being done is considerable.

This uncertainty about where the frontiers actually run enhances the development of different visions of belonging. UK citizens, for example, still have great difficulty defining themselves as part of "continental" Europe (as they say). Sense of identity is far from being homogeneous. The European Union is more like an empire than a federal nation-state in the making. Heterogeneity is at the heart of European identity and the projects that try to reduce it are no longer sustainable. The myth of the founding fathers of Europe that technocracy will create homogeneity does not survive the contradictions it creates. Yet, without a common project and a sense of a shared identity, it is also difficult to deal in a homogeneous way with foreigners and to accord them a common status for their entry into the fifteen national territories, which do not coincide with a "unified" European territory, even if the discourses concerning the uniform Schengen visa pretend that uniformity exist.[41] And, since it is easier to blame some of them than to address the question of heterogeneity and of the belonging of different groups connected through states and transnational civil societies, the European leaders prefer to focus on foreigners and "migrants". They construct the category of immigrants as a political problem at the European scale and, in so doing, hope that, focusing on the outsiders inside, they will avoid discussing the institution of frontiers for the identity of the European Union. They refuse to deal with the uncertainty of where the frontiers run and what purpose they serve. They try to play the old national games but without believing in them. As uncertainty is present everywhere and is being promoted as a technique of government, it explains in part the rise of fear and unease within the different populations of the EU.

Research of migrations often takes for granted that migration is a political problem coming from demographic disequilibria and differentiation in growth between different areas. It fails to realize the displacement from the questions of belonging and frontiers to the question of immigrants. Thus, researchers tend to underestimate the role of the professionals of politics in the construction of migration as a problem. They address logical flaws of the arguments put forward as if they had discovered something the politicians did not know where, in fact, politicians know perfectly well but nevertheless choose a different agenda. For example, the discussions on illegal immigrants are quite always framed as if they were illegal border crossings. Yet every official knows that agreement has not been reached on the issue of resident foreigners, although according to Europol, 80 percent of "illegal" immigration is due to expiration of tourist visas, while only 20 percent result from illegal frontier crossing. Agreements are also exclusively concerned with short stay visitor status and even on this issue the British are firmly committed to a different position. Denmark was in an uncomfortable position between the European and the Nordic Union at the time of "the Europe of the Twelve". The enlargement of EU member states to fifteen in 1995 introduced another complicated situation by isolating Norway since it chose not to adhere to the European Union while remaining in the Nordic free movement zone. The EU expansion projects favored by the Germans and others in the IGC raised even more questions: membership of Poland, Slovenia and the Czech Republic would push back the EU frontiers a long way East. Germany in particular wants Poland to increase controls of its Eastern border while trying to prevent that it remove its control at the Western border, thus transforming Poland into a "buffer" state for illegal migrants and refused asylum seekers.[42] Poland, on the contrary, tries to keep intact its good relationship with its Eastern neighbors and to ease its Western border.

But in that case internal migration "problems" would become as great as external ones. Would Schengen be 'an EU internal security curtain between the most developed countries and the others – inside the EU'? Paul Masson of the French senate commission, in his 1999 report, envisaged this role for Schengen much more than the introduction of European citizenship and free movement.[43] New fears arise with the arrival on the agenda of Turkey's admission to the EU as well as the issue of the Kaliningrad enclave and the future of the Southern Balkans.

The instability of the framework, of the Union's external frontier is not simply geographic, it is increasingly the instability of "different Europes", differentiated according to policing areas. The single currency would not include the same countries as the common defense policy, which would again be different from the countries participating in 'home affairs' Europe. If there are as many Europes as pillars, it will render the task of defining frontiers very difficult. The maps of these different Europes are analogous to the maps of the Holy Roman Empire, with microstates and overlapping jurisdictions.

The geography of free movement will not follow the European Union boundaries and state-controlled territoriality cannot be managed as before. To understand the relationship between flows of people and territories, we must return to concrete practices and the thinking which informs them. What is at stake is inherently symbolic and involves our conception of the State.

The European Union is in danger of being built solely on fears of imaginary enemies: the immigrants. This neo-schmittian process is not free from analogies with processes of previous state formation, and states built before on strong identities in conflict and structured by enmities still play a part in the construction of the European Union. Some attitudes of Eastern European countries concerning "sovereignty" could be understood by the way they frame their relationship with foreigners and nationalism. But even highly nationalistic countries such as Romania need to understand that a military war against migrants in order to set up a stronger European identity does not make sense. They will not be rewarded for their tough attitudes even if some governments try to convince them to do what they dare not do yet. Nonetheless, they will still be targeted as "barbarians".

Hence, uncertainty cannot be resolved by the creation of an effective war against migrants. It is mainly a symbolic policy nourished by strongly opposed rhetoric. Here lies the heart of the different public policies conducted by the member states, the European Council and the European Commission.

Despite their differences in position and discourses, they have shared the idea that border controls were a solution for migration and that stopping illegal migration was a way of constructing a feeling of a shared identity between Europeans facing the "same" danger. They have (in)securitized the freedom of movement of the individuals and tried to cope with the uncertainty of frontiers by displacing the controls both within and beyond the frontiers. Thus, they entered into competition for responsibility for and legitimization of these controls by means of a general discourse concerning freedom of movement of individuals. At the same time, they have developed technologies of poling at distance and remote controls, made possible by transnational networks of security professionals whose interests may diverge from the national(ist) professionals of politics. As a result, the relations between frontiers, controls and population have been re-articulated. The genealogy of this process can be traced to the beginning of the 1980s. 1974 was symbolic as in different countries, after the petroleum crisis and the rise of unemployment, for the first time the professionals of politics specifically targeted immigrants and wanted them to return their respective countries of origin. They were not useful for the new economy any longer. But the process of migration continues without much trouble in the host societies. In the 1980s the discussion changed its topic. It was not the cost and benefits of migration that were important but the difficulties of integration of these "new" migrants coming from the Third World and the fact that they used their rights, such as the right to family reunion, in order to settle definitively with their wives and children instead of forming a single men working class. From that the discussion developed along the lines of identity and belonging, with a sub-text of invasion that different populist parties promoted.

The Rhetoric of 'Sieve' Europe and 'Fortress' Europe: The Focus on Border Control and the Imperative of Freedom of Movement

As Elspeth Guild explains, free movement has become an imperative for the European Union beyond the traditional idea of free movement of goods, capital, ideas and people, where the understanding of people was associated with "workers". The role of the different European Courts (ECJ and ECHR) was crucial in enlarging the idea of an individual right to move that contradicts the claim to the monopoly of circulation of movement by the states or an interstate regulation. Free movement is not only a right in certain specific conditions, as the right to leave a country if one's individual life is in danger, but also a norm, even an imperative. It is a norm as the "good" way of life nowadays includes travels and tourism. To visit as many countries as possible is now a strategy of distinction among the elites. Zygmunt Bauman has developed this transformation as one of the major human consequences of globalization. Travel and especially speed travels are desirable, enjoyable. The pleasure does not lie in the travel but in the visit and the collection of "things which need to be seen" and photographed. Tourism is a complex industry but it has promoted a life style where speed is linked with leisure and leisure with money. A tourist is not a "vagabond", a nomad without money.

So, what about all those people who are prisoners of the local and cannot benefit from the time-space compression of the world because they are too poor to be good tourists? What about the desire of the so-called third country nationals to visit Europe and the world? They are considered a threat, as potential immigrants, even if they do not envisage staying and have their own life in their country of origin. But the suspicion will remain. They will be considered as "virtual invaders". The Common Consular Instructions of the Schengen visa are in that respect particularly clear and cynical. In the cross border flows rich tourists are allowed to spend their money without too many constraints once they are inside or too many difficulties to enter but the notion of a genuine poor tourist disappears if he does not happen to be the son of a white man travelling the world but a third country national coming from a poor or a Muslim country. In the latter case, he is a migrant and he becomes part of a political problem for Europeans (and US Americans). All the officials of Justice and Home Affairs seem uneasy about the relationship between tourism and migration. They refuse to take into account the type of discrimination, which is embedded inside the difference between tourists and migrants, between North-South roads of tourism and South-North roads of what they want to see only as migration, or organized crime roads. The disconnection between the norm to move freely and quickly and the possibility to move has perhaps never been as large as now, where at the same moment the desire to move is developed through TV satellites, competitive cultural policies between the main languages and powers, and cheap flights for tourists. So if many people expected to enjoy freedom of movement, especially after the end of the cold war, as soon as they wanted to move without possessing sufficient amounts of money to buy goods and services, they were and still are considered a danger, an anonymous threat created by the aggregation of thousands of identical behaviors. The framing of the question of migration and control of cross border flows of people is thus structured towards a "policy of forgetting" in respect of the construction of migration as a political problem and by the difference between the freedom – even if light and private controls exist – for the rich when they travel, and the heavy and coercive control of the poor who want to visit another rich country, or even now want to flee to another country.

In that context, if no one in Europe is ready to stay behind a wall keeping migrants out and if Europeans are not afraid of the "exotic" Third World, because they want to enjoy tourism and vacation in these places, an active minority will disclaim the same possibility for third country nationals in the name of their fear of being invaded, of seeing their society transformed by these changes. It is only a minority who connects its fear of structural changes and its unease about globalization and freedom of movement of people, but this minority has been shaped by different populist parties, very often but not always at the far right of the political spectrum. A paradox emerges when their ultra-liberalism for goods, capitals and their own travels encounters their anxiousness about conserving their own collective identity and their ensuing demand for more controls. This process of securitization of migration along parallel lines has been developed by Didier Bigo, Ole Waever and Jef Huysmans. Now the securitization of migration is well known and Anastassia Tsoukala develops in her chapter this process of securitization and criminalization of migrants. But the connection with the European Union is not often well understood. Comparison with the US seems to show that it is a general process. But as will be seen, this is not the case.

The European Union has specificity by the claim of a large freedom of movement and by the possibility to travel across "internal frontiers" without control. The norms of free movement and the activism of a minority, especially present in the media, which now demand a reinforced barrier role for the state borders against migrants in the name of nationalism, have set up a specific agenda. They have mobilized a reactionary rhetoric from the nineteenth century according to which borders function as bottlenecks and constitute or need to constitute barriers. They believe "that the idea of belonging which is at the root of the concept of citizenship is threatened when people cross borders, leaving spaces where they "belong" and entering those where they do not".[44] And they complain that some migrants are legally in the country but that they still do not belong to the country because they do not share the main values. Therefore, very often the childrens of migrants are considered more dangerous than their parents because they are institutionally inside and often have citizenship but they are still for the professionals of politics and security on the other side of the symbolic frontier of belonging.

The "political spectacle" is then full of arguments for or against borders controls, and tries to avoid both, the question of belonging and the question of the capacity to enforce a severe policy of controls at the borders. The Europeanization will be for all the member states, except for the UK, a strategy to play at a different level and to try, first, police collaboration for border control purposes, and second, to put the blame of the lack of coherence, not at the national level but at the transnational level. Schengen with the invention of the difference between internal and external frontiers of the EU will become the arena where the politicians will put into place a "stock exchange of fears of otherness" between the member states managed by the professionals of security. The original Schengen debate is crucial in that regard.

The Schengen original debate and its fame   Schengen is a small town in Luxembourg but its name has become synonymous with the agreement by that name which abolished border controls between five original parties[45] (Member States of the European Union) and established a system for common conditions of entry and exclusion of third country nationals[46] into the combined territory. The Schengen *acquis*, which has been incorporated into the EC Treaty by the so-named protocol to the Amsterdam Treaty and now published in the Official Journal consists of:

1.   The Agreement signed in Schengen on 14 June 1985, between the Governments of the States of the Benelux Economic Union, the Federal

Republic of Germany and the French Republic on the gradual abolition of checks at their common borders;

2. The Convention, signed in Schengen on 19 June 1990 between the Kingdom of Belgium, the Federal Republic of Germany, the French Republic, the Grand Duchy of Luxembourg and the Kingdom of the Netherlands, implementing the Agreement on the gradual abolition of checks at their common borders, signed in Schengen on 14 June 1985, with related Final Act and common declarations;

3. The Accession Protocols and Agreements to the 1985 Agreement and the 1990 Implementation Convention with Italy (signed in Paris on 27 November 1990), Spain and Portugal (signed in Bonn on 25 June 1991) and Denmark, Finland and Sweden (signed in Luxembourg on 19 December 1996), with related Final Acts and declarations;

4. Decisions and declarations adopted by the Executive Committee established by the 1990 Implementation Convention, as well as acts adopted for the implementation of the Convention by the organs upon which the Executive Committee has conferred decision making powers.

The initial Schengen Agreement of 14 June 1985 created a framework for the abolition of border controls on persons and goods between participating states. It was supplemented by the Schengen Implementing Convention 1990 which set out the detailed provisions on the abolition of border controls between the participating states, the application of controls at the common external border of the participating states, provisions on division of responsibility in respect of asylum[47] and provisions on police co-operation. The creation of the Schengen system arose from an economic pressure not least from the transport industry to remove obstacles to cross-border trade within the European Union.[48] It was foreshadowed by the European Commission's White Paper on the Completion of the Single Market.[49]

The Schengen Convention entered into force in September 1993 but was not applied in any Schengen state until 26 March 1995. Even after that date France maintained border checks on persons moving between France and the other Schengen states. The abolition of border controls was achieved with Greece in March 2000 and the Nordic states in December 2000.

The title of the implementing convention which covers free movement of persons contains seven chapters:

1. crossing internal borders (Article 2);
2. crossing external borders (Articles 3-8);
3. visas (Articles 9-17) and visas for long visits, (Article 18);
4. short term free movement of third country nationals (Articles 19-24);
5. residence permits (Article 25);
6. organized travel (Articles 26-27);
7. responsibility for examining asylum applications (Articles 28-38 – superceded by the Dublin Convention when it entered into force in September 1997).

The legal basis of the Schengen Information System is found in Articles 92-119, creating a data base on objects and persons.

Over the next 12 years all other Member States of the European Union acceded to the Schengen instruments with the exception of the UK and Ireland. While the abolition of intra Member State border controls, *inter alia*, on persons was part of the internal market embodied in Article 14 EC, the priority of Community law was never officially used to impede the Schengen system. Rather it was given legitimacy through the use of the comparison with an "avant garde" or experiment for the Community to adopt later. The argument was that the Schengen arrangement was legitimate as it would enable the difficulties with the system to be dealt with in a controlled environment. It could then be used as the blueprint for the whole of the Community.[50] In fact the incorporation into Community law could hardly be messier or more difficult. The Commission has suggested that in its opinion all the so-called *acquis* must be replaced by Community legislation adopted in accordance with the Treaty rules in Title IV EC.[51]

The operation of Schengen was the responsibility of the Executive Committee established by the instruments. The Executive Committee was assisted by a small secretariat based at the Benelux Secretariat. Like the EU's Third Pillar, the Executive was aided by working groups on specific areas. Like the Third Pillar, the lack of a strong institutional structure meant there was only limited coordination on implementation and interpretation of the agreement.

The Amsterdam Treaty which came into force on 1 May 1999 attaches a Protocol on Schengen to the EC and EU Treaties which in effect provides for the insertion of the Schengen Agreement 1985, the Schengen Implementing Convention 1990 and the decisions of the Executive Committee made under the two agreements into the EC Treaty insofar as they involve borders and third country nationals. The same Protocol provides for moving into the Third Pillar of the Treaty on European Union those provisions on Schengen relating to policing and criminal judicial co-operation. The UK, Ireland and Denmark all negotiated protocols which permit them to remain outside of the new European Community rules on borders and third country nationals. Ireland and the UK may decide in each instance whether they wish to participate or not case by case in the new regime.[52]

By decisions of the Council of 12 May 1999, the Council allocated a legal base within the new EC Treaty as amended by the Amsterdam Treaty for the Schengen *acquis* as identified in its decision.[53] Accordingly, the European Community has inherited the Schengen *acquis* which has been transferred in a somewhat less than systematic manner into new Title IV of the EC Treaty: visas, asylum, immigration and other policies related to free movement of persons. The legal base for most of the Schengen *acquis* which has been transferred into the EC Treaty is Articles 62(1)[54] Article 62(2)(a) and (b),[55] Article 62(3)[56] Article 63(3)[57] while having respect to Article 64(1) the internal security reserve of the Member States.[58]

So Schengen *acquis* is still with "us" and embedded in the Freedom Security and Justice idea of the EU. But, nobody has clearly discussed what was the debate of the eighties and how all these norms were set up. Very often the propaganda of a

Schengen laboratory in advance, in regards to the natural evolution of the EU, was considered as sufficient, but a more critical look shows that Schengen logic was clearly against freedom of movement of people and was conducted not only by fears about criminals but also migrants, foreigners from third world countries.

Sieve Europe: from the eighties to 11 September 2001, an anti-third country nationals agenda? The content of the public debate in France, but also in other countries, is conditioned by the way its terms were set up at the beginning of the eighties, and in the present case, the terms took the form of a confrontation between those who found the content of the agreements insufficient (sieve Europe/*Europe passoire*) and those who found them excessive (fortress Europe/*Europe forteresse*). The terminology sieve Europe is not well known in Anglo American literature because they use the same formula "fortress Europe" to describe the discourses for more controls and the discourses against this reinforcement of controls. But it was mainly because English media and people were excluded from the first debates concerning Schengen. From the Schengen documents in 1985 and 1990, and from the analysis of all the intermediary stages of the intergovernmental discussions, we can see that a strong opposition developed between the governments who wanted more controls at the borders because they feared a security deficit and the ones who believed that it was possible to remove the controls at the national borders. The former immediately spoke of a sieve Europe where terrorists, criminals, Mafiosi, immigrants would enter freely if border controls were to be removed. And the success of this discourse was immediately important in all the administrations. Other works have analyzed the reason of this success, explaining that there was nothing necessary about its triumph, but it is worth remembering this period as a period still structuring the current debates. It was the period where the notions of fear of violence, feeling of insecurity, reports on crime and migration appeared to transform the beliefs of people as well as their voting patterns and motivations.

The notion of continuum of (in)security has been developed to explain how the transfer of legitimacy of the struggle against crime and clandestine organizations was used for control of petty crime, incivilities, illegal migration and even asylum seekers. The different professionals of security joined together and gave credentials to these political discourses about the connection between the different dangers. It came mainly from four reasons: the first was the real transformation of the practices of political violence in the eighties with the killing, by clandestine organizations (revolutionary, nationalist or coming from abroad), of more third parties not directly involved in the conflict; the second was the transnationalization of these conflicts exporting them visibly to Western Europe and showing some involvements of the foreign affairs of these governments, which were not acknowledged, with the effect to mixed foreign affairs, defense matters and police matters; the third was the tactic of some media and political parties to connect migrants with potential terrorists and to link their arrival with a governmental project of infiltration of the country by their government of origin, even if they were opponents and fleeing this country; the fourth one is more mundane but not less important: the fears of the professionals of internal security to lose their jobs at the borders (especially customs and border police), and their influence as a lobby in the framing of migration policies. These arguments favored more control and disregarded the advantages of free movement of people. They did not create a more realistic discourse than the fortress Europe rhetoric but they benefited from the legitimacy of the people who announced it, that is to say the professionals of the management of unease and especially the bureaucracies dealing with internal security, which, at that time, were more and more connected through police liaison officers abroad. This rhetoric became the actual basis of the legal provisions in the most recent texts and converted an extremist rhetoric into a symbolic power engaging the authority of the State.

The change of paradigm also results from the end of the security/freedom and right/left opposition of the seventies, which has been replaced by the "new" debate on free movement and the necessary compensatory security measures. This change, undermining the notion of freedom to the benefit of (in)security or safety remained largely unnoticed, due to the tensions which arose, and opposed, not those advocating freedom of movement and those wanting safeguard measures, but between those who accepted the principle of free movement and extension of border controls beyond the limits of their own sovereignty (which implies a minimal trust in neighboring countries) and those who totally refused giving up controls. The NGOs were left apart in the intergovernmental discussions and it was only the different positions of the governments which constituted the debate. The British government immediately affirmed that it would maintain border checks, which, in its view, assured an "essential element in the fight against criminality and immigration" and refused to give up the "privilege" of the insularity. This 'extreme' position allowed partisans advocating border control reductions in order to favor economic prosperity and, in particular, to increase the transborder traffic, and, to a lesser extent, to implement the principle of free movement, to expose the "compensatory measures position" as progressivist, reasonable and positioned at the right level. The pro-Schengen group composed of the Belgian, Dutch, Luxembourg, German, and French governments could thus, according to the moment, insist either on free movement or compensatory measures, as the international situation, and opinion trends allowed. The structuring of the debate by the governments and some rare media as a conflict between the British and Europeans progressivists for Schengen was extremely successful in masking the fact that the left in France more or less followed the right in developing arguments in favor of tough measures concerning immigration, even though the left rhetoric put more emphasis on freedom of movement inside the EU as one big territory. It also disguised that the debate was by no means a question of disagreement with the British about control of immigration and struggle against terrorism, but instead a divergence between European governments concerning the means, technologies, and the credibility of police co-operation, especially the efficiency of border checks. From the eighties on, before the end of the cold war, the idea of free movement increasingly turned into a pretext; a justification for security measures and measures to fight against clandestine immigration and fraud asylum cases rather than a real objective to implement at a global level. The idea of a security deficit if border controls were removed was considered a truth unchallenged and unchallengeable.

For five years, nothing came out in the media, even if most of the more important decisions were set up at that time (especially the Palma document in 1988 which provided the main lines and the road map for what is still on the agenda). It is only when the Schengen agreement needed to be ratified by the Parliament that public opinion came to know these agreements. The discussion reached a considerable level only in France and the Netherlands, where the Parliaments discussed the beneficial aspects of these agreements in some detail.[59] But, in France, the public debate was largely connected with the positioning towards the themes of the Front National and it explained why the notion of Sieve Europe became so popular so soon (while emerging much later in Germany, and the Netherlands, and only now in the UK). The end of bipolarity created a new impetus for the discourses of border control and fear of migrants. Germany changed its discourse and argued also for more border control. The mass media played with the fear of an invasion by Eastern European migrants leaving their home countries to come in large numbers into Western Europe.

In the context of the 1990s, by reading only the main article in the Schengen document concerning free movement (article 2.1) without reading the other articles, some members of the right (and not only the far right) accused Schengen and Maastricht of increasing the risk of international criminality and immigration, despite the compensatory measures. In France, Pierre Mazeaud emphasized in the National Assembly the risks of an influx of immigrants from Central Europe and Africa by, for example, taking advantage of the breach in Schengen external frontiers created by the German-Austrian agreement allowing East Europeans to enter Germany and from there to go on to other EU countries. Immigration from the Maghreb was likely, Mazeaud alleged, to pass through Italy or Spain whose lax frontier controls are notorious. Europe would be destabilized, Francois d'Aubert argued, by the infiltration of the Italian mafia into France; drugs would come from the Netherlands, argued Gerard Larcher; Turkish immigrants, asserted Charles Pasqua, a theme later taken up by Jean-Louis Debré, driven out from Germany by the arrival of the Eastern immigrants, would invade France. Based upon forecasts by Lesourne and Chesnais of potential immigration from the Maghreb countries into Europe in the next millennium, some members of Parliament now in government spoke, at that time, of "an immigration explosion from the Maghreb countries". The same narratives full of fears about the "invaders" continue again and again for more than ten years and are taken for granted even if there is no evidence to sustain them and if they were proved to be wrong during the two decades which have now passed. But it is nevertheless useful to understand the diverse arguments inside the sieve Europe narrative to have a chance to deconstruct their logic.

The argumentation *is often rooted by reference to invasion and inassimilability.* It raises identity questions in an essentialist manner and opposes block against block, cultures and civilizations whose values are seen as antagonistic.[60] It claims at the same time that globalization and unequal distribution of wealth in the world push the poor to immigrate towards the prosperous countries and to remain there. It considers that this presence ruins the national homogeneity, splits up the nation and puts the security of the State in danger. It thus sees immigration as a simultaneous attack on the security of society, because it affects coherence of national identity, and on State security, because it favors terrorism, drug trafficking, urban riots, and delinquency.

Some people refuse this argumentation of inassimilability. Immigrants can be assimilated. They can be integrated under specific conditions: through a loyalty statement to the host country, socialization through language, institutions (schools, army...), work, and duration of their exposure to the country. This argument is strongly structured by *the idea of Sovereignty and the relationship with the Law.* The republic needs to be a strong regime. Its borders must be controlled by the national state only. Debré but also Chevènement are not so far from this nationalist position and fear a European opening up.

A third argument concerning the limits of sieve Europe was put forward with greater success than the two others, which were too extremist. It is indeed necessary *to block clandestine immigrants*, but the best strategy is to control them at the borders of the Community, through European police cooperation. It could *ensure some free movement of people* and goods but a *freedom under surveillance.* Paul Masson, President of the Schengen Control Commission in the Senate says: "Each weakness, each act of clumsiness in implementing the agreements (of Schengen) will lead, I am sure, to many French people contesting the idea of Europe itself, which would become, for them, a Europe of insecurity and dubious activities." Xavier de Villepin and Masson particularly emphasized both, the limited but recurrent problems of refugees from conflicts such as Yugoslavia and the necessity for "burden sharing". They noted: "It is likely that the abolition of controls at internal frontiers will be interpreted as a signal to all the poverty-stricken of the world, in particular those in the South and the East" – reviving the specter of an immigration invasion and, in a manner repeated by some members of the European Parliament, justifying their position by promoting the necessity of firmness now in order to avoid the need tó be repressive later. They ended their argument as follows: "neither fortress Europe nor sieve Europe, the Europe of the Schengen agreement must be a Europe of freedom because it must be a Europe of firmness".

If one analyzes the reports on immigration, police, immigrants' foyers, realized by members of the French Parliament, if one looks at the directives implementing law, if one examines the few available documents concerning the Trevi groups and then the Third pillar, one always finds a mix of these three arguments. They do not strictly correspond to political tendencies or bureaucratic positions. But they all ask for new technologies and new loci of controls in addition or in replacement of internal border controls. They all ask for visas in the name of prevention of terrorism, and the right of refusal without explanation, the computerization of consulates, the harmonization of Schengen procedures, and penalties on airline companies. They ask for police cooperation with the establishment of a frontier zone (a zone of 20 km as in Schengen with joint police stations) and through SIS, Interpol and Europol. Since people are still getting inside, because it is too difficult to seal the borders, it is argued that illegal immigrants already in the country must be located, marriages of convenience prevented, people pretending to be students or tourists identified, and search and detection of illegal immigrants facilitated by checks in schools, social security offices, workplaces, and places of residence. Thus, the welfare agencies are turned into the places to check the people.[61]

Whatever variant forms it may have, the discourse on Sieve Europe and the securitization of immigration is based on debatable beliefs concerning a certain reading of History (as a permanent war between people, civilizations, races), the relationship between man and the territory he occupies (feeling of ownership of the first occupant and fear of invasion), the mechanism of constitution of identities (which would presuppose the existence of an enemy to structure a "we"), the perception of law (positive law, not natural law) as sacred, and State prerogatives (State reason just as much as sovereignty, pre-eminence of national interest on all other criteria) administrations' border control capacities (control of migratory flows, fights against the illegal entries, discovering frauds and misuse of procedures). It also relies upon statistics from administrations with only security responsibilities (constitution of statistics on immigration and delinquency, irregular foreigners and unemployment.). It is the doxa of almost all police and customs officers and a considerable number of politicians, thus providing an authoritative character, a strong social legitimacy that the media, and in particular television, largely diffuse. It is a discursive formation sufficiently large to provide many variants and to give to the social actors the impression that they are very different, even all these actors are prisoners of the maximalist statements emanating from the extreme right wing parties because they are positioning themselves in front of these statements.[62]

Following this vision, new legislation in France, under Pasqua, Debré and even Chevènement, have created and reinforced a category of unauthorized persons who are not strictly illegal immigrants and who have been living in France for many years: the so called "*sans papiers*" (undocumented).[63] The legal position of every person of foreign origin thus becomes a matter of permanent suspicion. Immigration control has become analogous to enemy infiltration, against which we must be protected by systematic control at frontiers or elsewhere, by a sort of electronic Maginot line. The minister of Interior JP Chevènement has tried, first, to avoid this suspicion, and the law for the *sans papiers* and for the asylum seekers was changed but the practices of the agencies are not so different from those under conservative governments and the Minister came to justify them later on. In the name of secularity and moral order, Islam continues to be seen as a threat in general. Illegality, even created by the state itself, is seen as a reason to be expelled. Youth is seen in the suburbs as people without morality, without sense of justice and fairness. The idea that urban violence could come from a sense of injustice and not from anomie is simply refused.

More than ten years of the same "story telling" by the media, the right-wing parties and some politicians of the left, by a lot of people inside the security agencies have created a "structuration" of the present time. This discourse does not need to be explained. It is seen as self-evident, as a truth (in the Foucault sense).

This form of rhetoric is not confined to France – it closely corresponds to the discourse of German, Belgian and even Dutch conservatives. Political milieus throughout the EU share a belief that controls at external frontiers must be seriously reinforced, and that the co-operation between frontier police forces is necessary to avoid the growth in crime and to support the policy of "controlling immigration".[64]

September 11 2001, in this sense, has by no means created a new agenda. The policies after September 11 remain along the exact same lines of the previous twenty years of active anti-immigrant rhetoric and its connection with terrorism and crime. But the politicians and the professionals of security have used these events and the emotive impact of sympathy for the victims to overcome the resistance concerning rights of foreigners and to try to create a "state of exception".[65]

Fear of reinforced controls: 'fortress Europe': a form of resistance? Humanitarian organizations rejected the idea of sieve Europe since they saw reinforced controls and new levels of policing as involving a harmonization by the fifteen at the most repressive end of the spectrum. In France, Amnesty International, the Human Rights League, *France Terre d'Asile* (pro-asylum organization) criticized Schengen, in the late eighties, when its provisions were discussed in parliament, by pointing out that these agreements were attacking the right of asylum and providing reminders that this was against the Geneva Convention. Yet, they did not succeed either at the level of governments or at the level of public opinion. These organizations managed at the very end of the legislative process of Schengen and Dublin to include the right of the UNHCR to analyze the articles concerning asylum but did not see at that time that it would lead to a politization of the UNHCR and especially to political nominations at its head. Although they denounced the risks of "compensatory measures", accused Europe of withdrawing into itself, of forgetting its duty to asylum seekers, they accepted the compensatory measures as "a necessary evil".

Their fight was a kind of rearguard action to introduce "safety clauses" of a judicial nature for countries where, in the name of effectiveness and speed, governments relied upon administrative procedures for dealing with asylum cases. From the beginning, it is necessary to note the delay of the Fortress Europe discourse formulation compared to the security discourse of sieve Europe. It is only at the time of the first public debates, around the beginning of the 1990s, that this discourse underlined its opposition towards the discourse on border securitization and immigration and to the theses on the necessary securitization of sieve Europe. The *Mouvement contre le Racisme, l'Antisemitisme et pour l'Amitie entre les Peuples* (anti-racist and peace movement) as well as the *Groupe d'Information et de Soutien aux Travailleurs Immigrés* (information and support group for the immigrant workers) argued that the logic of Schengen was anti-democratic. But they did not express this argument in 1985 or 1990. They waited until Schengen was put into practice in 1995. Nevertheless, they were among the few in France to understand the link between the control of foreigners at frontiers and the situation of immigrants already in the country, seeing a possible drift from border control to racial prejudice. The audience of these groups, however, is limited and they gave the impression that they were swimming against the tide, especially after Seville destroyed the hopes created at the Tampere meeting.[66]

Although perhaps isolated, these NGOs were not alone in adopting the discourse on fortress Europe. The European Parliament accepted aspects of it, in particular in its resolution of June 1987. But since then it has become less polemical, simply complaining about a "lack of democracy", and arguing primarily for reinforcing its own powers rather than for a change of policy. Governments of third countries (especially in the Maghreb and Central Europe) interpreted the Schengen and Maastricht tightening of police controls on immigrants and refugees as directed against them. They pressured the governments of the Twelve into contorted statements on emphasizing international co-operation with countries bordering the EU. But they were not successful, except perhaps in the case of Morocco. The migrants' countries of origin tried to introduce into the discussions with the EU about economic development a removal of the readmission agreements clause but they were blocked inside a kind of conditionality where if they want help from EU they needed to readmit their citizens, the third country nationals passing through their territory, and to support the efforts to eradicate drug transit and production.

At the rhetorical level, the European Council made statements about the risks of creating a fortress Europe. They were perhaps the most active in using this term. Some officials considered that the image of Europe abroad was being affected by anti-immigration measures and by the statements about an "invasion of immigrants". They insist that "this (Schengen) offends neighboring countries and the other nationalities living within the whole European Union and reinforces their belief that Europeans refuse to accept the fact that non-European residents are different" but very soon after, in 1995, they changed their language and accepted the idea that Schengen was an "*acquis*".

If one tries to summarize the reasons for the weakness of this discourse about Fortress Europe, it is due to the weak enunciative performances of their promoters, and also to historical hazards, which play a part in the game. The end of bipolarity has undermined the discourse about the stable environment of Europe, its unity, and its core values. The projects of free movement and citizenship were blocked by the "preliminary" questions of the European identity and of the borders of the Union. The promotion of free circulation of people and goods could no longer be considered one and the same freedom.

In countries other than France, humanitarian organizations faced the same difficulties. Statewatch published a disturbing report in England on the state of civil liberties in Europe and has for all these years been the center of resistance at the European level against the discourse of a sieve Europe endangered by migrants. They have criticized the lack of openness, of transparency of the Justice and Home Affairs ministries.[67] The debate concerning 'Fortress Europe' went further in the Scandinavian countries and included arguments to the effect that the opening of internal frontiers modified democratic practices by strengthening controls at external frontiers, by reinforcing controls over foreign populations already in the European Union, by increasing identity checks to locate illegal immigrants, and by toughening the conditions to obtain asylum.[68] Academics mobilized alongside the NGOs. Particularly strong criticisms of the securization of immigration questions were expressed in the Scandinavian countries.[69] Conferences took place in

Denmark, in Switzerland, in Belgium, in the Netherlands. Networks were constituted, including newsletters via the Internet. Electronic reviews and newspapers circulated. Those coming from Northern Europe and the Netherlands established an axis of resistance to the dominant discourses in Germany, France, and the United Kingdom. From 1995 on, one notes a slight transformation in power struggles. Little by little, secrecy surrounding the measures, having become the main target of criticism, was lifted. The civil servants of the various countries taking part in the meetings of the third pillar were all accused of being "eurocrats", even though at the same time, they often fought against the Members of the European Commission and considered themselves above all national civil servants. The Treaty of Amsterdam instigated new power relations by forcing the de-linking of immigration and asylum questions and questions of organized crime, even if the hopes of the NGOs concerning more transparency and democracy inside the third pillar were not met. The interference of NATO with European defense and with the third pillar complicated the situation and paved the way for new restrictions. Nevertheless the defeat of conservative governments in France and the United Kingdom partly changed the situation. Discourses in Tampere were more balanced than before, but in 2000 the lack of efficiency of the role of the different courts of justice and the decrease of the effective rights of third country nationals despaired the different NGOs even more. The aftermath of September 11 has reinforced the fears concerning the dismantlement of civil liberties, especially for foreigners, but not only for them. The Convention, which will give more power to the judiciary, is likely to limit the power of the professionals of (in)security and of the professionals of politics. The rule of law may go against some popular feelings and some policies but many judges share the "truth" constructed over the last twenty years and dare not challenge or defy their governments.[70] The resistance to the main discourses of the professionals of politics that Europe is endangered by migration is well developed in academic circles but often lacks widespread popular support.

As for the Sieve Europe narrative, various forms of argumentation structuring the discourse on Fortress Europe can be distinguished. The first one concerns an appraisal of difference and diversity as mutually enriching. It is based on a certain cosmopolitan ethic and an ideology of a world without borders between humans. Through the mass media, Daniel Cohn-Bendit, one of the green members of the European Parliament, became the main voice of this cosmopolitan conception. Paradoxically, it is hard to find such a conception in European NGOs, except in some Scandinavian countries, but it is as such that many American academics interpreted the Fortress Europe discourse. The second argument is grounded in a Grotian conception of life in society and rooted in the idea of multiculturalism. Borders exist between human beings, and even inside the States, between the basic communities: the boundaries between the latter are central, the former are not. So migratory flows must then be fixed according to a quota system that respects the equilibrium in the host countries. This discourse often emanates from humanitarian, cultural organizations or from immigrant organizations themselves. Its influence is significant in the Benelux countries and the United Kingdom, but rather marginal in France with *S.O.S racisme*. The third argument is based upon the defense of civil laws and freedoms. The measures taken to securitize immigration, insecuritize all the citizens, encourage racism, endanger the rule of States, and even evoke Fascism. Quickly, in the discourse of Fortress Europe, one accuses politicians (and sometimes also public servants in Brussels) of being responsible for racism and for transforming it into institutional racism by security laws, which criminalize immigration and transform asylum seekers into defrauders and economic refugees. The post-September 11 overreaction of politicians and their attempt to develop what could be considered as a permanent state of exception have reinforced this last argument and in the conclusion of this book this will be discussed in detail. But, even though critical theorists believe in some of the fortress Europe arguments, this discursive formation is built on *a mirror fear*, a fear of a revival of racism, of the re-birth of fascism. Even if they don't want to recognize it they are also driven by a discourse of fear and unease. They invert the argument while sharing some essential traits with their adversaries.

This fear of transformation of the liberal regimes into neo-fascist states often overestimates the danger to freedom, forgetting for example that, statistically, few of the rejected asylum seekers are in fact escorted back to the frontier; overburdened police officers often get the impression that it is them who are swimming against the tide. Tough policies recommended in the reports are not so often put into practice. They are still exceptional and do not develop into routines. Norms of fundamental rights are important and limit the possibility of changes against these rights.

This leads us to a central paradox, which is at the heart of the discussion. The groups that endorse the discourse on Fortress Europe trust and "believe" the governments and the professionals of politics evoking their capacity to control. So they are themselves prisoners of the myth that the politicians are in charge and that they efficiently manage the flows of people moving across frontiers. Instead of analyzing the efficiency of the practices they focus on the political discourses. They focused on the rationality of the governmental projects but not on the rationality of the control agencies. They discussed the state of exception strategy of some politicians but not the capacity for the professionals of management of fears and unease to (in)securitize the people. They confused hyper-politization and (in)securitization processes, as will be seen in the conclusion.

In that sense, the discourse on Fortress Europe is itself more a propaganda discourse than a description of the actual social practices. It is mainly a reaction to the discourse of Sieve Europe and its further development into a permanent state of emergency. So, the Fortress Europe discourse does perhaps describe a governmental ideology, or even a political strategy of certain political parties and intelligence services networks that are particularly cynical and ready to do anything in the name of national interest, but it does not truly describe generalized social practices.

Thus, even if it seems to be in opposition with almost all the elements of the Sieve Europe discourse, the Fortress Europe discourse shares the underlying presupposition of the former: if one has the political will, one can close the borders or at least control foreigners who want to enter a given territory. If one wants to change the norms of a liberal society one (if he is sovereign) can do it by suspending the normal law and creating an exceptional one. But these two assessments are wrong. Decisionism is an illusion. It is the illusion of the professionals of politics that they are in charge and manage the world and it is the illusion they want other people to share, but a critical discourse is critical not by opposing at the political level a conception of freedom of movement against the idea of controlling people's movement to avoid invasion, but by unmasking the managerial discourse of the professionals of politics and of security and their ideology of "will", of "mastering", of "ultimate decision".

The Myth of Mastering the Frontiers: Nobody in Control Despite the Will to be In Charge

The discourse of "sieve Europe", of "toughness" and the discourse of "fortress Europe", of anti-discrimination show, despite their opposition, a shared belief that governments can close the frontiers if they decide to. There is an additional assumption that the legal rules have a practical enforcement as soon as they are voted (and not before) and thus significantly change cross-border flows once they are passed. But one can legitimately discuss these two beliefs and ask some basic questions. For example does anyone, in the institutions, have a clear picture of cross-border flows of persons and of the methods of control? How is it possible to differentiate between the crossing of the same person many times and the crossing of many persons one time? How could we know if the same person goes back and forth or stays? Very often the statistics given by the authorities deal with crossings and speculate only about the real number of persons. But nevertheless the numbers construct an official truth, either about the increase of arrivals of migrants who want to settle inside the country in order to justify tough measures or to downplay migration by interpreting the same numbers as a rise in transborder activities and economic growth. Hence, statistics are not really helpful in that matter. The same is true for the impact of the different migration laws and their practical implications. Nobody knows exactly how they affect the crossings of persons and the millions of individual decisions. It is not clear how far tight controls of foreign populations advantage or block economic prosperity and free movement of goods and services. It is not evident that the will of the government to implement measures at the borders has a practical effect in preventing people from entering. It is mainly a matter of opinion, of beliefs and of interpretations of the different numbers concerning flows across borders, and a matter of the framing of the question of migration by the politicians of a specific country and their importance in the political competition.

    Demands from part of the population who feel unease are now well represented by some political parties and have voices in comparison to the lack of voices of the cosmopolitan claims. Although largely divided, it is said that the "public opinion" as "one" body wants the laws to be rigorously enforced even though these laws are sometimes based on erroneous assumptions about social practices. The will of power is there. Laws have to be enforced in any case, even the bad laws...There is a desire to make reality conform to political objectives, and to draw new official realities instead of changing policies. The political narratives are invested with "truth", even when they contradict everyday practices in the society. The political game has even integrated this gap and played with it. Hopes are expressed in each debate that new governments, unlike the old ones, will 'halt crime', 'declare war on drugs', 'eradicate terrorism', and 'control immigration'.

In respect to frontier controls, politicians are not ready to publicly accept that their governmental autonomy is reduced by economic interdependence (bolstered by discourses on deregulation and the benefits of international trade). As a matter of fact, the immigrant becomes a political opponent of all the local politicians and of the (in)security professionals who feel personally insulted that he or she has managed to cross the frontier, despite their interdiction and the passing of new tough laws. But at the same moment, the professionals of politics know very well that, even by coordinating their practices at the European level, by harmonizing their policies (through bilateral agreements of police co-operation and readmission agreements between the main countries of the Union, the Maghreb, Central and Eastern Europe, the multilateral agreements of Schengen, the Trevi action program, the complicated architecture of the Third Pillar of Maastricht, the treaty of Amsterdam, the recommendations of Tampere and Seville and the Convention that is to say more than twenty years of policies), they are, in fact, still unable to control the flow of people and the arrival of migrants in their country.

The decision to close the borders in a liberal regime has been tried in different periods but has always produced non-intended effects, which obliged those in power to open the borders again after a few days. Closing frontiers immediately generates queues of people and vehicles lasting for many hours and even days, a phenomenon which can be observed especially at the two land frontiers which are more controlled than the others: the German-Polish and the US-Mexican frontiers. The United States under Nixon attempted to close their frontier with Mexico with operation "Wetback" and, more recently, operation "Gatekeeper", continued as operation "Hold the line". The result in both cases was immediate economic damage, tensions between social groups and almost no effect on illegal immigration. The first operation was stopped after a few days, and the second was purely "symbolic" after a few days, and when implemented, succeeded only in diverting the traffic from Texas to New Mexico. The US debate on immigration, particularly in California, demonstrates that the building of a "technological wall" in Tijuana at the frontier with San Diego had a huge psychological impact but little practical effect. This example of reliance on technology using techniques derived from military experience – approaching the frontier like a front with strategic depth – is the product of a naive belief that machines compensate for the lack of staff. And the high technology system in California was jammed by the simplest counter-measures (chewing gum in machines, aluminum paper to baffle sensors). As Jean Paul Hanon shows technologies in Europe are perhaps less military in their origin, but a similar trend exists. All the same, even using the most sophisticated technologies, the systematic controls at European land frontiers remain ineffective.

Gerard Moreau, director of the International Migration Office in France in 1995, has emphasized the impossibility of conforming the practices to the parliamentary wishes to make border-crossing rules more restrictive. Tightening rules reduces the number of persons eligible to enter the territory; it does not block the crossings and the capacity to enter; hence, restrictive rules simply increase the number of illegal, expellable migrants. The annual number of crossings by land, air and sea at external frontiers, delimited by the agreements of Schengen, including France, Germany, the Benelux countries, Spain and Portugal (still excluding Austria and Italy), reached 1.7 billion crossings in 1998. 864 million people cross the German frontiers alone. Much of these crossings are local cross-border traffic, but clearly very strong economic and human links exist between the Schengen countries and their neighbors. Annual crossings of internal frontiers of the Schengen area number 1.2 billion. Movement in and out of the French territory totals 291 million each year – by air (with 600 airports), by sea (4 720 km of coasts) and by road (2 490 kilometers). 230 million crossings are counted at the land frontiers (762 roads between Dunkerque and Menton, Le Perthus and Hendaye), which are, with the exception of those with Switzerland, internal frontiers. To control these frontiers (by the operational staff of the Central Directorate for the repression of illegal immigration and employment (DICCILEC), the customs and the Gendarmerie), each official must control about 40 kilometers. Assuming that systematic controls are maintained and that the people entering the country do so through official checkpoints (which is not the case of people who want to enter illegally), it requires officials to check, including visa checks, all of the 230 million people crossing; yet, according to the best estimates, they check about 15 percent of the 130 million foreigners who need visas (about 20 million).

It is impossible to construct "the fortress", even with a strong political will, at least in liberal regimes. The dogma of sovereignty, which underpins our image of absolute control of the territory by the State, is associated with obsolete practices. The logistics, in terms of men and material, that such rhetoric supposes, will never be provided unless there is a change in the political regime itself. Even if the professionals of politics envisage to increase dramatically technology or personnel by a hundred times, this would not be sufficient.

The main European forums on immigration such as the ad hoc group on immigration set up by the Ministers of the Interior and of Justice in the eighties and after the different committees under Maastricht, and Amsterdam have investigated all the legal methods of stopping migrants and asylum seekers by a strict interpretation of the texts and by adding new techniques based on dissuasion, control and surveillance. But they know that the use of new technologies is hopeless in terms of strict efficiency. Nevertheless they are useful in order to obtain more financial means, more social power, more legitimacy as they can pretend to solve the problem in a scientific way. For this reason, the hyper-technologization will continue. It develops a brand new market of technologies of identification of different kinds and promotes opportunities of new carriers for the retired professionals of security coming from the military or the police services. And although the legitimacy of migration control is weak the same is not the case for organized crime or terrorism. So, the criminalization of certain groups (migrants, asylum seekers, diasporas... and eventually tourists?) will continue to justify the extension of the use of these technologies beyond the reach of terrorist or criminal activities. But this project of total information awareness is a technological dream, which will turn reality into a nightmare for both, the victims and the invigilators. The technologies will not work smoothly, they will be contradictory, arbitrary, and inefficient. As a matter of fact, all the officials we have met over the last ten years know that but dare not contradict their own interests by openly admitting it. General border controls (national or European) are simply quite impossible to achieve without changes in the economic and political system. The technological myth of electronic security is in practice hopeless. The new rationales are no more efficient than the traditional controls. The figures which follow illustrate this fact and aim above all at demonstrating that it is impossible to sort and filter border crossings according to objective and legal criteria, just as it is impossible to determine the motivations of those who cross borders on the basis of entrance modalities (tourism, transborder traffic, short stay for family visits, seeking employment or a better standard of living, exodus due to wars or famine, individual political persecution).

The ability to undertake systematic frontier controls belongs to the past, and probably to a mythical past. The politicization of police and security questions has not changed realities.[71] The recent turning of migration and asylum policies into matters of security has even exacerbated the gap between rhetoric and social practices. The blind alley of more and more controls has only produced negative effects. Frontiers will continue to separate societies with different levels of economic development but they will no longer act as filters helping to homogenize an 'inside' and an 'outside'. Work, social rights, citizenship, nationality and collective identities are no longer spheres, which coincide exactly with the physical boundaries of the State. But the uncertainty of European frontiers should not lead to a quest for a maximum security but for more reflection about possible options. A free society, it must be remembered, is one with open frontiers, open minds and plural identities.

Despite the security discourses, governments know that they have to deal with flows which seem to accelerate, enlarging the scope of the migrants largely beyond the immediate neighbors, and which also appeared to progressively change direction, consisting of flows from the poor countries of the South to the wealthy North and not only of people following a colonial expansionist movement or a flood of populations from neighboring countries. They are obliged to limit a large part of the virtual possibilities that the technological devices offer in order to control the frontiers. They cannot but play on a purely symbolic level and enforce the controls only when this symbolic level is too obviously challenged by the actual social practices. The bureaucratic struggles between the ministries of justice and home affairs and the ministries of industry and economy are the results of this contradiction.[72] Neither driven by freedom of movement, nor by a panopticon and maximum security logic, the practices of controls must take into account the permanent conflict between the symbolic will to master the move of the individuals and the norms of a liberal regime. We will see that it is "solved" by the constitution of a ban-opticon where freedom of movement for some coexists with the intensification of surveillance, control, and punishment for others.

Therefore, representing nomadism, mobility of people, like a transnational or trans-state problem framed in terms of migration, is in some way a narrow picture. It is the picture of the governments, not of the people. For them, migration is a story, which does not explain their lives, their choices, and their constraints. For the Western governments, on the contrary, nomadism of people is viewed as an attack on the sovereignty and integrity of the Nation; they only want to frame it in terms of migration. One consequence is that Western States are little concerned with changing the location of frontiers to their advantage by military means, but they are greatly concerned with the well-functioning of frontiers (meaning primarily policing and economic activities) and the purposes they serve. Unable to control most trans-frontier transactions, they are looking for a much more complex search to secure advantages and to increase power. Also, in cultural terms, frontiers have lost some of their sharp-edged quality. Participation in trans-frontier and sometimes-global cultures affect political identities and political institutions within States. The idea of more "inclusiveness", or "convergence and harmonization" towards different states sharing the same values is gaining weight within the European Union, but the same process of permeability of frontiers also creates anxiety in some parts of the societies and inside the political arena. The large majority of professionals of politics refuses the idea of a virtual global civil society legitimizing the right to move freely. They prefer continuing to frame the world through the system of interstates relations, and their right to control who is moving and where. More intimately, fear of migration is totally anchored in the fear of the professionals of politics, especially at the local, municipal levels, of losing one of the last remaining aspects of their power: the symbolic control of movement of people over the territorial boundaries. They hope to show that, at least, security remains their "thing", their task, that they are responsible for this domain. But they are caught in the paradoxes of the relationship between security (as a coercive practice and as the will to master through surveillance) and liberalism (as an economic practice necessitating more speed of movement and some freedom of movement, and as a libertarian value). They are prisoners of the changing relations between states and markets, and of the distribution of power between the elected politicians (or professionals of politics) and the people who take political decisions in regards to the economy such as bankers.[73] They do not know if they should see the frontier as a protection, a barrier that saves them from danger and from a new distribution of power, or as a closure, separating them from the global world and their own society. They do not know if they should develop frontiers as points of junctions, points of control, or if they should prefer displacing the frontiers in order to simplify the situation, thus hoping to resolve the contradiction and to enlarge their control.

Policing migration in the name of freedom: the European internal security discourse and practices In manipulating notions of frontiers and citizenship, civil servants of Schengen and of the EU, in charge of implementing free movement, and the Single Act, undoubtedly had the impression of treating a difficult, but certainly resolvable, technical and organizational question. They have in fact, without knowing, created a tool to transfer responsibility from the national politicians to European institutions in case of failure. But, they have not realized that they were dealing with such central matters of symbolic power, forms of legitimization, the consequences of which have only now become clearer. As they explained to us during interviews the difference between internal and external frontiers was seen as something simple and not as involving problems of sovereignty and identity. It is only ten years after that they have realized that they were apprentice sorcerers. Regarding the concept of frontier, they have called into question the relationship between authority, obedience and, to some extent, the very notion of state and of allocation of resources between citizens as well as the relation to otherness.

The Europeanization has played a major role here, increasing the politicians' fears as well as the anguish of parts of the population. Connected with institutional practices of racism by some security agencies,[74] the uncertainty about the boundaries of citizenship at the EU level, of the inside and the outside, reinforced security arguments and explains why a part of the "left" in France appeared to simply abandon its values and turn into a supporter of reinforcement of national controls and surveillance of the migrants already inside, while declaring that the controls needed to remain "humane". The de-localization of the control from the national border to another locus (the so-called external European border) was used to justify practices of control inside the country wherever migrants or minorities may live.[75] Since other countries, such as Germany and the Netherlands, were facing relatively similar situations, it was tempting to transfer the question of immigration to the European Union arena. But immigration policies and nationality entitlement cannot easily be standardized; they remain different because political interests, as well as the migrants' countries of origin are too diverse.[76] However, with the negotiation of bilateral agreements (commencing in the 1980s), the establishment of an ad hoc European immigration group (1986), the signing of the Schengen agreement (1985 and 1990), the Palma document (1989) and the Dublin Convention (1990), with the Third Pillar of the Maastricht Treaty (1992), and of Amsterdam (1997), and with Seville (2002), the countries of the European Union embarked on a course of transforming immigration from a national and political into a transnational and "technical" question, by presenting it as a matter of security technology.[77] This move was possible for different reasons but as explained in this book the main reason at the political level was the involuntary connection between discourses on freedom of movement and fears of immigrants. In the eighties, the reduction of frontiers as barriers (tariff/customs barriers) and the principle of free movement were directed to create a dynamic opening up of European societies. But, in the event, due to worldwide recession, all the rich countries tended to take a tough stance against migration of people, contrary to the Union's aspiration to encourage the free movement of people, initially for European nationals but with an inevitable widening to others, in the absence of practical and legitimate criteria for discrimination. If we closely examine the texts that were at the beginning of the discourses linking security and freedom of movement of people inside Europe, we can see that the White Paper of the European Commission on the Single Act had as its main theme the abolishment of barriers, creating by way of consequence anxieties among those whose jobs depend upon controls at frontiers (e.g. customs officers and border police). If the part of the White Paper on free movement was seen as "generous" (and in the spirit of the founding fathers of the Union), it also explained that protection against drugs and terrorism necessitated new forms of control and created at that time the idea to "compensate a security deficit".[78] Change in the global situation in the 1990s (end of cold war, first gulf war) has caused further problems for the straightforward idea of free internal movement with the controls pushed back to the external frontiers of the Union. Now, with the envisaged enlargement of the EU, it is uncertain which countries remain outside the Union and for how long.[79] The uncertainty about the borders of the EU plays a major role in the feeling of fear of the population but it also creates the opportunity for the rulers to manufacture unease and to use it as a domination device in a situation in which the control of some people is regarded as more important than the control of the territory at the borders.

The militarization of the border for a long period of time is incompatible with the liberal democratic regime. It is used only in limited areas, for public opinion reasons. Activating the frontier as a barrier signifies, in the end, putting in charge the ministries of interior and justice and creating tensions with liberalization of goods and especially services comprising the movement of persons. Doing that on a national level is a high-risk tactic as the neighboring countries might heavily complain. Only the US and the UK have tried this strategy. The US has imposed that the Nafta agreement excludes freedom of circulation. The UK has maintained its border controls and refused to join the Schengen area of internal free movement. Side effects were obvious in the case of the militarization of San Diego/Tijuana and El Paso/Ciudad Juarez urban agglomerations, or of Sangatte and Calais Dunkerque port zones, but their neighbors supported them. Nevertheless, it has caused the death of desperate people without solving any problems. On the contrary, it has created tensions between Mexico and the US, and between France and the UK. Germany, France, Belgium, the Netherlands and Luxembourg adopted another strategy dating back to the signature of the Schengen agreements more than fifteen years ago. These agreements, of 1985 and 1990, were based on the idea that removing the controls from what was called the internal frontiers would lead to increased freedom of movement and an acceleration of the economically important traffic on highways. But, in order to compensate for the internal liberalization, the controls needed to be stricter at the external frontiers. This situation was most favorable for those countries, such as France, that do not possess long external frontiers since the countries located at the periphery of the Schengen area bore the main burden of the costs of controls. It caused a real dynamic in favor of the extension of the internal area, with quite a large success; as a result, each country tried its best to hand over the responsibility of controls to its direct neighbor.

Now, except for the UK and Ireland, all other members of the EU have been accepted inside the Schengen area, plus Norway and Iceland to include all the members of the Nordic Union free movement area. Germany has already trained the polish border guards, not only at their common frontier but also at the Eastern border of Poland in order to push the control far from its own borders. Italy and Greece are promoting the enlargement of the free movement zone to the Southern

Balkans in order to avoid being in the "front-line". Only Spain has, from the very beginning, chosen a more military orientation. And the military navies of the three Southern countries are trained together to prevent a virtual large flow of "migrants" fleeing a civil war (Algeria scenario). Policing the "external" border of the EU is now a "hot potato" game in which nobody wants to bear the costs. Consequently, the key word has been "police cooperation". Everything is considered to be solved if the different police forces work better together. Some plead in favor of networking the national police services, others ask for the creation of a European police (project of a European Border Guard, existence of Europol and of OLAF). The notion of an "internal security" area common to all the European Union countries has been developed to justify this general tendency.

As explained in the present book, the activities of police forces, whether initiated by home affairs or justice departments, have been extended along two lines. First, the extension of police activities reaches *beyond national borders*, namely by the establishment of interconnections between the different countries. Second, new forms of control have considerably extended the sphere of police activity *beyond crime control*. The term "internal security" or "internal affairs" in use throughout Europe is an indicator of this double extension that is both, geographical (through increased European cooperation) and structural (in the light of the new tasks assigned to the different security agencies, which now clearly include migration control, even if it was completely denied at the beginning of Schengen when officials declared that its sole target was criminal activity).

After twenty years of discourses and more than ten years of practices, the idea that police forces have a legitimate task in regulating migration is rarely questioned. Only in the UK, the internal struggle between the industry ministry and a weak interior ministry permits the debate about the advantage of qualified migration to resurface and to evoke the rights of individuals to move. In the Schengen area, the debate (in Germany, the Netherlands and even France) was marginalized, and constantly subject to the idea of the national interest of the receiving country. The "normalization" of policing migration gives way to a new enlargement of the scope to the people to control and to reject. Western politicians consider that, now, the competition between East and West is over, and that accepting asylum seekers is much less a proof of morality than an economic burden for the regime. They still "accept" mobility of capital and mobility of rich people, of consumers in transit, of rich tourists, but they prefer refusing the same "freedom" of movement as soon as poor people, vagabonds, or people fleeing ecological, economic or political disasters are concerned. Migration of the poor, and of the people obliged to flee from their own country – that is asylum seekers – is then seen as the equivalent of an "invasion", based on the perception that these groups of people want to settle indefinitely in the prosperous economies in order to benefit from their welfare systems. Confusion between voluntary migrants and forced migration is created in some rhetoric through the notion of economic refugee. As a result, the level of protection that the refugees previously enjoyed decreases. According to that vision, every poor person coming from outside the society is potentially a threat. The image of the immigrant as a threat is reinforced by the constellation of links created with different kinds of fears of the majority group.[80] The immigrant thus becomes the core of an (in)security continuum where he is associated with the unemployed, the thief, the smuggler and the criminal – an image used and developed by political parties of the (far) right but also by major media programs.[81]

A professional culture of suspicion structuring an ethos that goes farther than any ideology is growing and explains why it is difficult to frame the debate along the lines of right versus left discourses and beliefs. Professionals of politics from the right to the left, as well as a lot of security professionals believe that individuals arriving at the borders are, by definition, "potential" liars. They are not to be trusted. Believing them signifies being naive and irresponsible. Of course, such discourses do not have the agreement and consent of all. They vary from the left to the right concerning the scope of suspicion and mistrust, but, for a majority of politicians and, in the name of "the defense of the society", the stance to be adopted must be tough.[82] Western politicians perfectly know the arguments in favor of more nomadism (enriching diversity at the cultural, economic and demographic levels). They know that they omit taking into account the pendular migrations, so important in agriculture for example, and that they refuse to understand the long-term strategy of the Diasporas as semi-settled migrants. But they also know that if, in the political competition, they opt for an open discourse while others play the card of a migrant invasion, they risk losing votes.

From all the interviews realized with politicians in France, the UK, Germany, Italy and the US, it seems that this tactical factor is considered central (even if counter examples may exist, in California for instance). So, migration is constructed politically. Or, to be more precise, markets and politicians construct (im)migration as a political and security problem.[83] And the politicians are neither demographers nor statisticians. They do not focus on the real number of people who are moving; they care about the social images of the groups, which are regarded as a problem.

They care also about another problem: their own role in our society as representatives of the state and the implications of immigration and nomadism in this structure. In that sense, the idea of "unity" of the people is central. Diversity is possible but not heterogeneity. Integration is a key word. The politicians analyze society as "one thing"; one "body". They frame the immigrant as a risk because of their conception of the state as a body or a container for the polity. It is an important point because it frames the question from the very beginning of the wording and has effects on the mindset of all the professionals of politics, as well as the "experts". The term migrant, when activated, and especially if it is an im-migrant, is seen as "something" destructive for the political body of the nation. The metaphor of the body politic which is embedded in the sovereignty myth, in the idea to successfully monitor the borders to re-assure integrity of what is "inside", in the practice of the "plans for protection of territory", in the surveillance technologies installed at the borders, creates an image of immigration associated with an outsider coming inside, as a danger for the homogeneity of the State, the society and the polity.

In that sense, the migrant is defined in opposition, inversion to the self-image of the dominant group. If foreigners fit the dominant image, they are not a problem, but even when nationals do not fit this image they become "dangerous" and are associated to the category of "immigrant". Even through strong differences between the US and Europe, and inside European countries, markets and politicians always distinguish between the high level profile migrants, who are welcome, and the "others", the "real" ones, that is the "poor" migrants, even in the case of naturally born citizens, who are often seen through the lenses of cultural colonialism.[84] Sayad has shown that immigration legislation is quite always the rationalization *a posteriori* of previous arbitrary administrative practices and not a discussion concerning the boundaries between citizenship, nationality and foreigners, or a rational-choice analysis of a migration regime (as mainstream IR theory continues to work). He has explained how we, as analysts, are prisoners of the state thinking concerning the framing of who is a migrant and who "we" are. The immigrant is not just a foreigner, but a certain kind of foreigner and sometimes not a foreigner at all. He could be considered a foreigner even if he is a national because he is associated with a social image of someone who is not like "us". He is an "outsider inside".[85] Immigrant is, in that sense, a shibboleth, a word, which encapsulates hints of danger.[86] Hence immigration is associated more with a poor economic status or racial belonging rather than with holding a foreign passport. The foreigners are, if they are rich, "impatriates", and refuse to be seen as immigrants. We can see that it is not the fact of crossing a border, of being an alien, that is at stake.[87] White Americans crossing European borders are less disturbing than Englishmen of Pakistani origin or French citizens of North African descent who just want to leave their own country. A poor national who looks like an Arab is more likely to be targeted as a migrant than a rich Australian or American as soon as questions of border control or even internal surveillance are concerned.

Conclusion: Frontiers Controls in (Il)Liberal Regimes: The Ban-opticon

Are liberal regimes (still) liberal? It depends on the meaning of liberal. Desmond King analyzing the transformation of welfare uses the notion of (il)liberal regime.[88] David Garland exploring crime and social order in the US and UK speaks of a "culture of control" inversing the paradigm of freedom as the principle and security as the exception.[89] Loïc Wacquant explains the link between the decrease of the welfare state and the raise of the control state by the construction of the migrant as a suitable enemy.[90] With September 11, some authors speak about a "fascisation" of the state in the name of security. But we are far from totalitarianism. The norms to justify the policies are still anchored in the idea of constitutionalism, of good life valorizing freedom in general and freedom of movement in particular. We are not going back to a "crustacean" type of nation state, we are evolving towards a global world, a "liquid modernity" where the major differentiation will consist of a small, globalized "elite", which will enjoy speed and freedom of movement, and a narrow group sorted out by the controls and trapped in the local with no chances to escape; the majority of mankind will belong to a third group, situated between the two extremes and establishing a balance between them.

This form of governmentality could be called, not a pan opticon, but a "ban opticon". The "panopticon" is too expensive in means, in missions, in social legitimacy. The surveillance of the borders cannot penalize the economy in liberal regimes. The traditional heavy security measures are obsolete as they are too visible both in terms of numbers of enforcement officers and armaments. Now, the State wants also to be unpretentious, unobtrusive. It delegates to the private sector the prerogatives of the use of violence with private military companies. It is ready to delegate to the great global firms transborder crossings and management of people working over different places. It does not exercise the function of control at the borders, but nevertheless intervenes and takes back its power where it seems necessary. The main mistake of the Bush administration is to have not understood this transformation and to have tried to come back to the crustacean form of State. In Europe, it has been taken into account. What is wanted by the professionals of politics and of (in)security is a proactive logic which anticipates the risks and the threats, locating the potential adversaries even before they have any consciousness of being a threat to others. The "targetting" is only on them. Those who are inside the "norm," by contrast, must not be controlled, this is the new imperative. The political program of liberalism at the world level is committed to freedom of movement.

That is why, instead of panopticon, the notion of Nancy about the Ban is used here. "The notion of Ban, he says, comes from the old Germanic terminology which indicates both exclusion from the community and the command and insignia of the sovereign." But, the Ban is more than a decision by the sovereign to suspend the law as Agamben has developed to analyse the state of exception. The Ban is linked with a general governmentality that here is called the management of unease which is developed through routines, through technologies, by the professionals of (in)security and not only by the professionals of politics in their conflicts with the Courts, the lawyers and the rules of law. The Ban is the way to exclude and to normalize, to play with the different possible futures and to try to monitor the future to control the present. So, it is a belief in technologies of "morphing", of "profiling", of computer data bases and their capacities to "anticipate" who will be "evil" and who is "normal", who is "allowed to benefit from freedom of movement" and who is excluded or controlled before they can use their freedom of movement.

So, in that (il)liberal program, some of the national and European police forces no longer want to be (if they ever were) the fire brigades of the crime, or the auxiliaries of justice acting after the committed crime. They refuse to act *a posteriori* and to play the traditional detective job. They believe that the rates of success are way too low and that they can't afford to take care of the small infractions, which supposedly are at the center of people's worry. Private companies are there to do that job. What the police have to do is to concentrate on the bigger virtual events of the future. They no longer want to be the assistants of either the penal system or the insurance companies. They no longer want to be the accountants of crime. Hence, they think that their role is to intervene upstream, in an active way, targeting specific groups that they have identified as dangerous and/or as victimized and uptime by running software which will help them to frame the future. In this logic of the Ban-opticon, the territorial borders of the state are then only one of the layers to operate for the technologies of surveillance and controls, the other ones are to control time and movement, speed and flux, present and future.

To give only one example of these technologies at the European level, one notices the mushrooming of data bases set up to risk-profile individuals. Concerning crime, besides Interpol's (not a new one), the Sirene System aims for a speedy traffic of judicial documents and information exchange. Since the treaty of Amsterdam and Tampere's meeting, the judicial system follows the example of other security agencies. It too operates at distance and networks. The Sirene system, the acceptance of criminal sanctions and procedures between States, the set up of liaison magistrates, the creation of Eurojust, and the neglect of the corpus juris create an imbalance between charge and suspicion, where both have access to the European Union resources, and a defense which stays at the national level and has no access to this information. But in the name of speed and efficiency, this fact is seen as a minor detail.

The Schengen Information System (SIS) regarding people is mostly a filing system designed to keep illegal immigrants from getting back into the EU. Managing crime is not its area of predilection. However, Schengen widens ceaselessly its sphere of power by imposing uniform visas, something which is becoming a norm not only inside the Union but beyond. In addition, derogatory controls of identity in the border zones (sometimes as far as 20 kilometers from the border) are becoming widespread in all countries, even in those where the concept of justifiable suspicion was paramount. Moreover, the police no longer fight the idea that Schengen is to create its own immigration police force (and that it is its priority) while only five years earlier most refused such a concept and only wanted SIS to deal with crime prevention and missing persons. This link between criminals' files and foreigners' files that SIS establishes strengthens the suspicions against foreigners and focuses the attention on small crimes and violations by making it a top police and customs priority.

But while these techniques accumulate and cross-reference data, they are not used for the elaboration of profiles. On the other hand, beyond Schengen, more sophisticated databases are being created and they are designed to focus on the analysis of risk-groups, not on their surveillance.

Eurodac will be a database that will store the fingerprint records of the refugees seeking asylum as well as the records of the reasons they gave for applying and of the reasons why they were denied entrance. This will help prevent multiple-entry applications but will also allow the authorities to spot stereotypical stories of asylum seekers. At the same time, FADO (false and authentic documents) is being created. It will be a secured network where information about false documents will be exchanged. The idea is to invert the principle and put the burden of proof of authenticity on the one handing out the document. Printrack International, an American company working in northern Europe, offers to beef up automated identifications of international travelers. The products they sell are the technology of cards with fingerprints, in harbors and airports, and that of retinal imprints. The purpose is to control identities in the most invisible way possible because, according to this company, individuals do not like being touched or slowed down when being controlled but if they don't realize that they are being controlled, then they don't protest. One can think in the future to extend this system beyond airports. The link between credit card and information on the identity is on the drawing board. It would be the same card that would contain the information, some of which only the police could have access to (that is, not even the cardholder). With Europol files, the profiling is more pinpointed. The idea is not to extend surveillance to all but on the contrary to refine it. On the other hand, people believed to be potential risks would be recorded. Interpol databases include only criminals actually wanted by the police. Europol files, on the other hand, include wanted criminals, suspects not yet subjected to judicial inquiry, informants, possible witnesses (that is people who could be called to testify because they happen to be neighbors or colleagues of a suspect), and victims or persons suspected to be so. So the idea here is to trace individual and social trajectories, to map out territories and borders between the populations at risk and the others, and to analyze and decide who is dangerous. We are at the heart of the proactive logic.

Nominative Europol files entered by the various national police and security institutions permit a concrete repressive action. In addition, there are analysis files kept by specific Europol staff who often entrust them to criminologists to establish the networks used by the populations under surveillance. An index file helps find correlation between index cards. These Europol files aim at anticipating the trajectories of networks, at tracing their path, at profiling each minority or Diaspora, and at defining those who need to be put under surveillance, to avoid a heavy and generalized surveillance.

These technologies allowing watching and punishing beyond borders via the collaboration between security agencies are mushrooming. As we indicated, these are signs that, at the European level, the police are increasingly networking and working at distance. It polarizes the policeman's profession. Two main types of police now exist within the national police force; the first one employs staff who are little or not at all qualified and whose job is to be visible and present locally. It is the auxiliary of the penal justice, of the mayor, of the chief commissioner or of the other police. It competes with private agencies. On the other hand, the second type employs few but highly qualified staff and is in touch with the other security agencies and social control institutions. This staff's two main characteristics are discretion and distance. Supposedly in osmosis with the high governmental spheres and the strategic private actors, these individuals have a mission to prevent crime by acting on these conditions in an active way, by anticipating where it will come from and who will perpetrate it. The idea being to draw "prospective" knowledge (from the evolutions) and become the center where reflection on the society's evolutions takes place. To create cells of information containing opened information, knowledge of the social sciences, and a technical and human, operational police information service is thus the ambition of all these professionals who consider themselves more professional and competent than the others. This dream of an epistemic community, common and consensual, haunts the life of these professionals who would pilot at distance – geographic and temporal via the anticipation – society's evolutions. They would be in a virtual place from where they could see everything, all the while being so discreet that no one could see them. We would only know about their executants – the police force, the judges, and the prison guards. Here, metaphorically, one is reminded of Jeremy Bentham's panopticon.

Thus this "system" is based on the faith in computer technology and statistical knowledge as well as on the studies of flux management and tracing analysis, from anticipated risks. It requires a different type of reasoning transversal to that of security institutions, and employs only the most professional staff, those who consider themselves the most competent. It establishes itself, then, by extolling collaboration as a permanent leitmotiv of efficiency to come. It establishes a relation between efficiency and speed of execution by trying ceaselessly to accelerate the processes of inquiry and judgment. In their phantasms, the policemen should know before the individual that he has the profile to commit a crime and should re-profile him or arrest him preventively. The judges should dispense justice on the spot, like a good company now knows how to manage zero stock.

So policing in the name of freedom is supposed to designate in advance who and what are the dangers. It supposes to "ban" some people, not to develop a class war or a panopticon with a global surveillance. It supposes to monitor the future. The argument of the imminence and danger of the next crime justifies in the eyes of the professionals of politics and (in)security a preemptive defense, because of the irreparable character of the action, it justifies the position of "not waiting until it is too late" as a website showing the twin towers and a nuclear mushroom cloud tries to suggest. It is the heart of the question about probability in the future and anticipation as fiction which is at stake. The belief of the imminent danger of the Apocalypse justifies at the same time "proactive" policing actions, "pre-emptive" military strikes, "administrative and exceptional justice, where anticipation of behaviour is considered a sufficient element to act. The decisions of those deciding are then based upon the "beliefs" they have in a rush and not upon wisely considered actions backed up by facts.

This anticipation or "astrological" dimension lies within the present tension regarding the fight against terrorism and its lawfulness as well as in the "immigration problem".

In such a situation, the major game for the politicians is to act along the lines of new technologies with the faith that they will solve the problem at the practical level, and to act along the lines of the old game of sovereignty and security motives versus freedom and economy at the symbolic level to focus on border control with the unspoken strategy to silence the de-localization of controls and the transnationalization of the bureaucracies of surveillance and controls. The political spectacle is not a shadow theater, with no effects, masking only the "real" practices. The language of symbolic politics is also crucial and could, at times, be "performative".

For example, speaking of symbolic controls at the frontiers is not to say that they are ineffective at all. They do have effects. If someone travels without the agreement of his own state, without a good set of papers, he can be at the mercy of the will of another state to accept him or to put him in jail or to send him back. The agreements between the Western democracies and more specifically the constitution of an area of freedom of movement inside the European Union have admittedly enlarged the zone of personal safety for the individuals regarding their right to travel, if they are national citizens of the member states. But, at the same moment, these agreements have put a cast of suspicion upon all the other persons living in the area. It has liberated from control a majority of travelers inside the area, but has paradoxically increased the level of controls for the people whose look differs from the norm, who are sorted out as dangerous.[91]

Patrick Weil has shown in his study that more and more controls are now carried out at the internal frontiers of the EU state compared to the period of the 1960s where they were said to be systematic.[92] It clearly contradicts the discourses about the "removal of the internal controls" inside the EU. But, as we will see, it is not a reason to advocate that the state is now more powerful than ever. The controls are more numerous but less significant than before, because they fail to reinforce the idea of equality by abandoning their systematicity, and they are not really effective. They increasingly function as signals sent to the other states concerning good police collaboration between governments, and do not represent a will to control the population willing to enter. So, the shared idea of a lack of control by the sovereign states because of the transformation of the size of the global activities, or because of Europeanization, is rather a myth, a conservative narrative coming from hyper nationalist discourses than an observation of the social practices. The same is true for the people who advocate that the raise of border controls is a sign of a new fascist state, and the raise of a fortress Europe. The number of people crossing the borders every day shows that we are far from the old technique of sealing the border with military forces.

As we have seen in detail the two narratives of a "sieve Europe" or of a "fortress Europe" are wrong. They prevent us from understanding the new technologies of controls, which are now more important than ever. These "exceptional" and "de-localized" controls permit to have a "low" cost of control (if compared to a systematic one) and the emergence of a general norm, which is the freedom to travel for individuals (the controls are the exceptions). It is this "displacement" which is important to study in details. It is a "configuration" where the controls are de-localized, dispersed, fragmented, transnational and done by networks of security professionals beyond the national frontiers. It is also only in this (il)liberal framework that a new kind of justification which is the "permanence of the exceptional", the "permanence of a quasi state of emergency" could develop. But, even if this rhetoric largely used after September 11 is proclaimed in the name of the core values of the state, sovereignty, identity, integrity of the people, the result is precisely to undermine the very notion of state and to accelerate the move towards a ban-opticon.

So, the State is perhaps not endangered at the level of the practices of control, synonymous with government, but nevertheless it is "conceptually" in danger if State is defined as the claim with some success of the monopoly of violence upon a population on a defined territory. Territoriality is at the edge of collapse because the frontalierization, the differentiation between inside and outside is not working anymore.[93] The professionals of politics, who represent the state in Western democracies, cannot implement what they pretend to do: control the movement of persons. And they are shocked by this fact. They know but cannot acknowledge it and try to live with the false pretences that they are in charge and that they could change the situation if they really want. But the professionals of (in)security in charge of the management of border controls are not ready to agree about an impossible political program concerning the sealing of borders, even after 11 September. They know that the immigrant, regarded as beneficial in a period of economic growth, has acquired in the eyes of the professionals of politics a negative image during economic recession, allegedly ruining the welfare state by fraudulent claims to Social Security and unemployment benefits.[94] But they know also that freedom of movement of people is an imperative and that the solutions for control are beyond the borders. Policing is done by profiling some specific groups before they could move, by following the traces of the people on the move by technologies of identification and mainly by a strategy of policing at a distance, through visa policies, and other forms of remote controls linked to data bases.

Notes

[1] I am grateful to Antonia Garcia-Castro, Philippe Bonditti, Emmanuel-Pierre Guittet and Christian Olsson from *Cultures and Conflits,* for their assistance in bringing this publication about.

[2] For a critique, see Elspeth Guild in this book and her forthcoming book on immigration law in Europe.

[3] Albert, Jacobson, Lapid, 2001 op. cit., Malcolm Anderson, *Frontiers: territory and state formation in the modern world,* Polity Press, 1996. Anderson and Bort, *Boundaries and identities: the eastern frontier of the EU,* University of Edinburgh, 1998. Groenedijk, Guild, Minderhoud, 2003, *In search of Europe's borders,* Kluwer Law International, 294 p.

[4] Day, A. J., *Border and territorial disputes,* London, Keesing's, 1987 and Prescott, J. R. V. (1987), *Political Frontiers and Boundaries,* London. Brown, Lester R., *World Without Borders,* New York, Vintage Books, 1973, Ganster, Paul, Sweedler, Alan, Scott, James and Eberwein, Wolf-Dieter, *Borders and Border Regions in Europe and North America,* San Diego/California, Institute for Regional Studies of the Californias, 1997. Foucher Michel, *Fronts et frontières: un tour du monde géopolitique,* Paris, Fayard, 1988.

[5] Campbell, David, *Writing security, united states foreign policy and the politics of identity,* University of Minnesota Press, Minneapolis, 1992; Sassen, Saskia, *Loosing Control?,* New York: Columbia University Press, 1996.

[6] Ceyhan Ayse, "Etats-Unis: frontière(s) contrôlée(s), identité(s) sécurisée(s)", *Cultures & Conflits,* 26/27.

[7] See Chapter 6. For Schengen see Boer, Monica den (ed.), *The Implementation of Schengen: First the Widening, Now the Deepening,* Maastricht: European Institute of Public Administration, 1997. Colvin Madeleine and Spencer Michael, "The Schengen Information System. A Human Rights Audit. A Justice Report", *Justice,* 2000.

[8] Elspeth Guild chapter.

[9] Albert, Mathias, Jacobson, David and Lapid, Yosef, *Identities, Borders and Orders, Borderlines,* University of Minnesotta Press, Minneapolis, 2001; Bourdieu, Pierre, *Raisons pratiques: sur la théorie de l'action,* Paris, Seuil, 1994; Bigo, Didier, "Security

and Immigration: Towards a Governmentality of Unease", *Alternatives/Culture & Conflits*, 2002.

[10] Outsider inside is the formula of Sayad Abdelmalek, "Immigration et pensée d'Etat" in *Actes de la recherche en sciences sociales*, September 1999, pp. 5, 15.

[11] Bigo, Didier, "Internal and external security(ies), the möbius ribbon", in Albert, Mathias, Jacobson, David and Lapid, Yosef, *Identities, borders and orders, Borderlines*, University of Minnesotta Press, Minneapolis, 2001.

[12] What is a political "problem"? See Edelman, Murray (1988), *Constructing of a Political Spectacle*, Chicago, University of Chicago Press.

[13] Giddens, Anthony, *The Nation State and violence, contemporary critique of historical materialism*, UCLA, Los Angeles, 1987.

[14] On these tautology see the seminal work of Sala-Molins, Louis, *La loi de quel droit?*, Paris, Flammarion, 1977, 171 p.

[15] Walker, R. B. J., *Inside-outside, international relations as political theory*, Cambridge University Press, Cambridge, 1993, XII-233 p. 23 cm, (Cambridge studies in international relations) 24.

[16] Tilly, Charles, *The Formation of National States in Western Europe*, Princeton, Princeton University Press, 1975.

[17] Noiriel, Gérard, *La tyrannie du national: le droit d'asile en Europe 1793-1993*, Paris; Calmann, Lévy, 1991. Noiriel, Gérard, *The French Melting-Pot: Immigration, Citizenship and National Identity*, Minneapolis, University of Minneapolis Press, 1996.

[18] Torpey, John, *The invention of the Passport Surveillance, Citizenship and the State*, Cambridge University Press, Cambridge, 2000.

[19] Hirst and Thompson, *Globalisation in question: the international economy and the possibility of governance*, Cambridge, Polity Press, 1996. Goldblatt, David, Held, David, McGrew, Anthony and Perraton, Jonathan, "Economic globalization and the Nation-State: Shifting Balances of Power", *Alternatives*, vol. 22, n° 3, Boulder/USA, Lynne Rienner, 1997.

[20] Hirschman, Albert, *Exit, Voice and Loyalty*, Cambridge, Mass., Harvard University Press, 1970.

[21] See Chapter 5. See US-Mexico borders, even with the rhetoric of war on drugs and now on war on terrorism.

[22] See the situation in Northern Ireland, the use of the art 2.2 of Schengen in the name of "drug tourism" in Netherlands, the vigipirate plan in France or now the war on terrorism. For details *Cultures & Conflits La participation des militaires à la sécurité intérieure*, vol. 1, 2003.

[23] Dandeker, Christopher, *Surveillance, Power and Modernity. Bureaucracy and Discipline from 1700 to the Present Days*, Cambridge: Polity Press, 1990. Lyon, David, *The Electronic Eye*, Polity Press, 1994; Marx, Gary, "La société de sécurité maximale", *Déviance et société*, vol. 2, 1988; Marx, Gary T., "The Declining Signification of Traditional Borders and the Appearance of New Borders in an Age of High Technology", Paper for the conference on Georg Simmel Between Modernity and Post modernity, Munich, Ludwig Maximilliams Universidad, 1994; Mathiessen, Thomas, "The viewer society: Michel Foucault's Panopticon Revisited", *Theoretical Criminology*, 1997, pp. 215-234.

[24] Hirschman, Albert, "*Deux siècles de rhétoriques réactionnaires*", Fayard, 1990.

[25] Koslowski, Rey, *Personal Security, State Sovereignty and the Deepening and Widening of European Cooperation in Justice and Home Affairs*, Conference Paper presented at the Conference "Dilemmas of Immigration Control in a Globalizing World" of the European Forum on International Migrations, MIG/59, Florence, European University

Institute, 1998; Jacobson, David, *Rights across borders: Immigration and the decline of citizenship*, Baltimore, John Hopkins University Press, 1996.

[26] Ganster, Paul, Sweedler, Alan, Scott, James and Eberwein, Wolf-Dieter, *Borders and Border Regions in Europe and North America*, San Diego, California, Institute for Regional Studies of the Californias, 1997.

[27] Kastoryano, Riva (Sous la Dir.), *Quelle identité pour l'Europe? Le multiculturalisme à l'épreuve*, Paris, PFNSP, 1998; Leveau Rémy, in Badie, B. and De Wenden, C. (eds), *Le défi migratoire, questions de relations internationales*, Presses de la FNSP, 1994.

[28] Rosenau, James N., *Turbulence in world politics, a theory of change and continuity*, Princeton University Press, Princeton, N.J., 1990, XVIII-480 p. Ruggie, John Gerard, 'Territoriality and Beyond: Problematizing Modernity in International Relations', *International Organization*, 1992, n° 472, pp. 139-74.

[29] Badie, Bertrand, and Smouts, Marie Claude, *Le retournement du monde sociologie de la scène internationale*, PFNSP, 1992, Paris.

[30] Strange, Susan, op. cit.

[31] Held, McGrew and Goldblatt, Perraton, op. cit.

[32] Gueheno, Jean Marie, *The end of the state?*, 1998.

[33] Badie, Bertrand, *La fin des territoires, Essai sur le désordre international et l'utilité sociale du respect*, Fayard, Paris, 1995.

[34] Hardt, Michael and Negri, Antonio, *Empire*, Harvard University Press, 2001.

[35] Foucault, Michel, *Surveiller et Punir. Naissance de la prison*, Paris, Gallimard, 1975; Ewald, François, *Histoire de l'État providence*, Paris, livre de poche, 1996; Bigo, Didier, *Polices en réseaux. Expérience européenne*, Paris, Presses de Sciences Po, 1996.

[36] Lequesne, Christian and Smith, Andy, "Union Européenne et science politique: où en est le débat théorique?", *Cultures & Conflits*, n° 28, Paris, Harmattan, 1997; Guiraudon, Virginie, Sociologie de l'Europe, n° 38-39, *Cultures & Conflits*, 1999.

[37] Rob Walker, "Europe is not where it is supposed to be", in Kelstrup, Morten, Williams, Michael C, *International relations theory and the politics of european integration, power, security and community*, London, Routledge, 2000, 306 p.

[38] Financescape, mediascape: Appadurai, Arjun (1990), 'Disjuncture and difference in the global cultural economy', *Theory, Culture and Society*, vol. 7, n° 2-3, pp. 295-310.

[39] John Crowley, "Locating Europe", in Groenedijk, Kees, op. cit.

[40] Concerning Sangatte, see the web sites of migreurope and statewatch.

[41] For developments on these subjects, see Didier Bigo, Elspeth Guild, "La mise à l'écart des étrangers: la logique du visa Schengen", *Cultures & Conflits*, n° 49-50, 2003.

[42] Mike King has first developed the notion of buffer zone which suppose three different concentric circles with different way to manage the border controls along the different circles. See King, Mike, *Conceptualising fortress europe: a consideration of the processes of inclusion and exclusion*, 17/04/94, Madrid ECPR.

[43] Paul Masson, *Résolution 263*, Paris, Sénat, 1999.

[44] Torpey, John, 2001, op. cit.

[45] Belgium, France, Germany, Luxembourg and the Netherlands. Italy joined almost immediately thereafter.

[46] I.e. persons who are not nationals of any Member State of the European Union.

[47] These provisions were superseded by the Convention determining the state responsible for examining applications for asylum lodged in one of the Member States of the European Communities (Dublin Convention) 14 June 1990 when it came into force in September 1997.

[48] D. Bigo, *Polices en Reseaux*, Presses de Sciences-Po, 1996.

[49] D. Papademetriou, *Coming Together or Pulling Apart? The European Union's Struggle with Immigration and Asylum*, Carnegie Endowment for Peace, 1996.

[50] C. Elsen, 'Schengen et la cooperation dans les domains de la justice et des affaires interiors. Besoins actuels et options futures', in M. den Boer, *The Implementation of Schengen: First the Widening, Now the Deepening*, EIPA, Maastricht, 1997.

[51] European Commission Staff Working Paper, *Visa Policy Consequent upon the Treaty of Amsterdam and the Integration of the Schengen Acquis into the European Union* SEC (19999) 1213; Brussels 16.07.99.

[52] See also, House of Lords, European Communities – 31st Report, Session 1997-98, Incorporating the Schengen *acquis* into the European Union, London 1998.

[53] Council Decision concerning the definition of the Schengen *acquis* for the purpose of determining, in conformity with the relevant provisions of the Treaty establishing the European Community and the Treaty on European Union, the legal base for each of the provisions or decisions which constitute the Schengen *acquis*, 8056/99 and 8054/99 Brussels, 12 May 1999.

[54] "The Council, acting in accordance with the procedure referred to in Article 67, shall, within a period of 5 years after the entry into force of the Treaty of Amsterdam, adopt: (1) measures with a view to ensuring, in compliance with Article 14, the absence of any controls on persons, be they citizens of the Union or nationals of third countries, when crossing internal borders."

[55] "The Council, acting in accordance with the procedure referred to in Article 67, shall, within a period of 5 years after the entry into force of the Treaty of Amsterdam, adopt: (2) measures on the crossing of the external borders of the Member States which shall establish: (a) standards and procedures to be followed by Member States in carrying out checks on persons at such borders; (b) rules on visas for intended stays of no more than 3 months, including: (i) the list of third countries whose nationals must be in possession of visas for crossing the external borders and those whose nationals are exempt from that requirement; (ii) the procedures and conditions which for issuing visas by Member States; paragraph (iii) a uniform format for visas; (iv) rules on a uniform visa."

[56] "The Council, acting in accordance with the procedure referred to in Article 67, shall, within a period of 5 years after the entry into force of the Treaty of Amsterdam, adopt: (3) measures setting out the conditions under which nationals of third countries shall have the freedom to travel within the territory of the Member States during a period of no more than 3 months."

[57] "The Council, acting in accordance with the procedure referred to in Article 67, shall, within a period of 5 years after the entry into force of the Treaty of Amsterdam, adopt: (3) measures on immigration policy within the following areas: (a) conditions on entry and residence, and standards on procedures with the issue by Member States of long term visas and residence permits, including those for the purpose of family reunion; (b) illegal immigration and illegal residence, including repatriation of legal residents."

[58] "This Title shall not affect the exercise of the responsibilities incumbent on the Member States with regard to the maintenance of law and order and the safeguarding of internal security."

[59] Van Outrive, L., G. Renault, J. Vanderborght, 'La collaboration policière en Europe', in *Déviances et sociétés*, vol. 20, n° 2, June 1996.

[60] It may be Samuel Huntington clash of civilisation 1994 opposing after many others the West and the Rest of the world, or Regis Debray tous azimut 1990 opposing Modernity to Islam. It may be also Robert Kagan drawing a line inside the west after September 11 between paradise and power, between the hobbesian world of the americans and the false

promise of the European Kantian paradise. For a critique, see Alker, Hayward R., "Pour qui sont ces civilisations?", *Cultures & Conflits*, n° 19-20, Autumn/Winter, 1995.

[61] Ceyhan, Ayse and Tsoukala, Anastassia, "The securitization of Migration in Western Countries", *Alternatives*, vol. 27, 2002.

[62] Bourdieu Pierre, *La distinction*, Ed. De Minuit, Paris, 1979.

[63] Lessana, Charlotte, Loi Debré, "La fabrique de l'immigré", *Cultures & Conflits*, n° 31-32, Paris, Harmattan, 1998, Autumn/Winter.

[64] Rea, Andrea (ed.), *Immigration et racisme en Europe*, Bruxelles, Complexe, 1998.

[65] See Chapter 7.

[66] Bigo, Guild (ed.), "De Tampere à Séville: bilan de la sécurité européenne", *Cultures & Conflits*, n° 45 and n° 46, Paris, L'Harmattan, 2002.

[67] Site statewatch.

[68] See the Newsletter *Fortress Europe*, edited by Nicolas Busch in Sweden.

[69] Mathiessen, Thomas, "The viewer society: Michel Foucault's Panopticon Revisited", *Theoretical Criminology*, 1997, pp. 215-234.

[70] For a more optimistic vision, see Elspeth Guild in this book.

[71] Nolutshungu am C., *Margins of insecurity, minorities and international security*, University of Rochester Press, 1996.

[72] See Elspeth Guild chapter.

[73] Strange, Susan, *The Retreat of the State. The Diffusion of Power in the World Economy*, Cambridge, Cambridge University Press, 1996.

[74] Rattansi, A. and S. Westwood, *Racism modernity identity on the western front*, Polity Press, 1994; Solomos, J. and L. Back, *Racism and society*, London, Macmillan, 1996.

[75] Bigo, 1996, op. cit.

[76] Guild, Elspeth, *Immigration Law in the European Community*, Kluwer Law International, The Hague, 2001.

[77] Bigo, 1996, op. cit.

[78] Bigo, Didier (ed.), *L'Europe de la sécurité intérieure Complexe Bruxelles 1992*, Busch Heiner, Grenzelose polizei, Munster, 1995; Lavenex, Sandra, "Asylum, Immigration and Central-Eastern Europe: Challenges to EU Enlargement", *European Foreign Affairs Review*, 1998, vol. 3, n° 2, pp. 275-294.

[79] Zielonka, Jan, *Europe unbound: enlarging and reshaping the boundaries of the European Union*, Routledge, 2002.

[80] See Chapter 5.

[81] Dal Lago, Alesandro, *Non Persone, l'esclusione dei migranti in una societa globale*, Interzone, Milano, Feltrinelli, 1999.

[82] The rhetoric of defending society is well explained by Foucault, Michel, *Il faut défendre la société*, Cours au collège de France, 1976, Seuil Gallimard, 1997.

[83] Waever, Ole, *Concepts of security*, Institute for political science, University of Copenhagen, 1997; Bigo, Didier, *Polices en réseaux: l'expérience européenne*, Paris, Presses de Sciences po, 1996, p. 358; Huysmans, J., "Migrants as a security problem: dangers of securitizing societal issues", in R. Miles and D. Thränhardt (eds), *Migration and European Integration. The Dynamics of Inclusion and Exclusion*, Pinter, London, 1995, pp. 53-72.

[84] Sayad, Abdelmalek, "Immigration et pensée d'Etat", in Actes de la recherche en sciences sociales, September 1999, pp. 5-15.

[85] Sayad, 1999, op. cit.

[86] Bourdieu, Pierre, *L'immigrant comme shebollet in Contre-feux 2*, Liber, Raison d'agir, 2000.

[87] Im-patriates, terminology constructed by inversing ex-patriates by some immigration lawyers of big companies to differentiate their clients from im-migrants.

[88] Desmond King in the name of liberalism, illiberal social policy in the USA and Britain in *Raisons Politiques*, n° 6, May 2002.

[89] David Garland, *The culture of control*, Oxford, Oxford University Press, 2002.

[90] Wacquant, L., "Des ennemis commodes", *Actes de la recherche en sciences sociales*, 1999, n° 129, pp. 63-67.

[91] Ban-opticon chapter. Michel Foucault, *Les anormaux. Cours au Collège de France 1975*, Seuil Gallimard, Paris, 1998.

[92] Patrick Weil in Cornelius, Wayne, Martin, Philip and Hollifield, James (eds), *Controlling Immigration*, Stanford, Stanford University Press, 1994.

[93] Walker, R. B. J., *Inside-outside, international relations as political theory*, Cambridge University Press, Cambridge, 1993, XII-233 p. 23 cm, (Cambridge studies in international relations) 24.

[94] See Chapter 7 by Ceyhan and Chapter 5 by Tsoukala.

References

Albert M., Jacobson, D. and Lapid, Y. (2001), *Identities, Borders and Orders*, Borderlines, University of Minnesota Press, Minneapolis.

Anderson, M. (1996), *Frontiers, State Formation in the Modern World*, Polity Press, London.

Anderson, M. and Bort, E. (1998), *Borders and Identities: the Eastern Frontier of the EU*, University of Edinburgh, Edinburgh.

Anderson, M., Den Boer, M., Cullen, P., Gilmore, W., Raab, C. and Walker, N. (1995), *Policing the European Union*, Clarendon Press, Oxford.

Andreas, P. (2000), *Border Games: Policing the US-Mexico Divide*, Cornell University Press, Ithaca.

Badie, B. (1995), *La fin des territoires: Essai sur le désordre international et l'utilité sociale du respect*, Fayard, Paris.

Badie, B. and Smouts, M.-C. (1995), *Le retournement du monde, sociologie de la scène internationale*, Dalloz, Paris.

Badie, B. and Wihtol de Wenden, C. (1994), *Le défi migratoire: Questions de relations internationales*, Presses de la FNSP, Paris.

Bauman, Z. (1998), *Globalization: The Human Consequences*, Polity Press, Cambridge.

Bauman, Z. (2000), *Liquid Modernity*, Polity Press, Cambridge.

Bayley, D. H. (1975), 'The Police and Political Development in Europe', in Tilly, C. (ed.), *The Formation of National States in Europe*, Princeton University Press, Princeton.

Bigo, D. (1992), *L'Europe des polices et de la sécurité intérieure*, Complexe, Bruxelles.

Bigo, D. (1996), *Polices en réseaux. L'expérience européenne*, Presses de Sciences Po, Paris.

Bigo, D. (1998), 'L'Europe de la sécurité intérieure: penser autrement la sécurité', in Le Gloannec, A. M. (ed.), *Entre Union et Nations: l'Etat en Europe*, Presse de Sciences Po, Paris.

Bigo, D. (2000), 'When Two Becomes One: Internal and External Securitizations in Europe', in Kelstrup, M. and Williams, M. C. (eds), *International Relations: Theory and the Politics of European Integration*, Routledge, London.

Bigo, D. (2002), 'Security and Immigration: Toward a Critique of the Governmentality of Unease', *Alternatives/Cultures & Conflits*, **27**, pp. 63-92.

Bigo, D. and Guild, E. (2002), 'De Tampere à Séville, vers une ultra gouvernementalisation de la domination transnationale', in *Cultures & Conflits*, **45**, pp. 5-18.

Boer, M. den (ed.) (1997), *The Implementation of Schengen: First the Widening, Now the Deepening*, European Institute of Public Administration, Maastricht.

Bourdieu, P. (1979), *La distinction, critique sociale du jugement*, Edition de Minuit, Paris.

Bourdieu, P. (1994), *Raisons pratiques: sur la théorie de l'action*, Seuil, Paris.

Bourdieu, P. (2000), 'L'immigrant comme shebollet', *Contre-feux 2. Pour un mouvement social européen*, Liber/Raison d'agir.

Brochet, C. (1995), '*J-2: les frontières tombent...pas les contrôles*', 24 mars 1995, *l'Argus de la presse*, Paris.

Busch, H. (1995), *Grenzenlose Polizei? Neue Grenzen und polizeiliche Zusammenarbeit in Europa*, Westfälisches dampfboot Verlag, Münster.

Buzan, B. (1991), *People States and Fear. An Agenda for International Security Studies in the Post-Cold War Era*, Lynne Rienner, Boulder/Col.

Ceyhan, A. (1997), 'Etats-Unis: frontière(s) contrôlée(s), identité(s) sécurisée(s)', *Cultures & Conflits*, **26/27**, pp. 203-254.

Ceyhan, A. (2001), 'La fin de l'en-dehors. Les nouvelles constructions discursives de l'ennemi intérieur en Californie', *Cultures & Conflits*, **43**, pp. 3-11.

Ceyhan, A. and Tsoukala, A. (2002), 'The securitization of Migration in Western Countries', *Alternatives/Cultures & Conflits*, **27**, pp. 21-33.

CIREFI (1994), *9 février 1994, Mesures pratiques de coopération entre services chargés des contrôles aux frontières*, Ronéoté, Bruxelles.

Colvin, M. and Spencer, M. (2000), 'The Schengen Information System. A Human Rights Audit. A Justice Report', www.justice.org.

Dandeker, C. (1990), *Surveillance, Power and Modernity. Bureaucracy and Discipline from 1700 to the Present Days*, Polity Press, Cambridge.

Day, A. J. (1987), *Border and territorial disputes*, Keesing's, London.

Edelman, M. (1987), *The Symbolic Uses of Politics*, University of Illinois Press, Urbana.

Edelman, M. (1988), *Constructing the Political Spectacle*, University of Chicago Press, Chicago.

Ewald, F. (1996), *Histoire de l'État providence*, Folio, Paris.

Foucault, M. (1975), *Surveiller et Punir. Naissance de la prison*, Gallimard, Paris.

Foucault, M. (1998), *Les anormaux. Cours au Collège de France 1975*, Gallimard/Seuil, Paris.

Foucher, M. (1988), *Fronts et frontières: un tour du monde géopolitique*, Paris, Fayard.

Ganster, P., Sweedler, A., Scott, J. and Eberwein, W.-D. (1997), *Borders and Border Regions in Europe and North America*, Institute for Regional Studies of the California, San Diego.

Garland, D. (2002), *The Culture of Control*, Oxford University Press, Oxford.

Giddens, A. (1987), *The Nation State and Violence, Contemporary Critique of Historical Materialism*, UCLA Press, Los Angeles.

Goldblatt, D., Held, D., McGrew, A. and Perraton, J. (1997), 'Economic globalization and the Nation-State: Shifting Balances of Power', *Alternatives,* **22** (3).

Groenedijk, K., Guild, E. and Minderhoud, P. (2003), *In Search of Europe's Borders*, Kluwer Law International, Nijmegen.

Hardt, M. and Negri, A. (2001), *Empire*, Harvard University Press, Cambridge.

Hirschman, A. (1970), *Exit, Voice and Loyalty*, Harvard University Press, Cambridge.

Hirschman, A. (1990), *Deux siècles de rhétoriques réactionnaires*, Fayard, Paris.

Hirst, P. and Thompson, G. (1996), *Globalisation in Question: The International Economy and the Possibility of Governance*, Polity Press, Cambridge.

Huntington, S. P. (1997), *Le choc des civilisations*, Odile Jacob, Paris.

Huysmans, J. (1995), 'Migrants as a Security Problem: Dangers of Securitizing Societal Issues', in Miles, R. and Thränhard, D. (eds), *Migration and European Integration. The Dynamics of Inclusion and Exclusion,* Pinter, London, pp. 53-72.

Jacobson, D. (1996), *Rights across Borders: Immigration and the Decline of Citizenship*, Johns Hopkins University Press, Baltimore.

Kastoryano, R. (1998), 'Quelle identité pour l'Europe? Le multiculturalisme à l'épreuve', FNSP, Paris.

Kelstrup, M. and Williams, M. C. (2000), *International Relations Theory and the Politics of European Integration, Power, Security and Community*, Routledge, London.

Koslowski, R. (1998), 'Personal Security, State Sovereignty and the Deepening and Widening of European Cooperation in Justice and Home Affairs', Conference Paper presented at the Conference, *Dilemmas of Immigration Control in a Globalizing World* of the European Forum on International Migrations, MIG/59, European University Institute, Florence.

Lavenex, S. (1998), 'Asylum, Immigration, and Central-Eastern Europe: Challenges to EU Enlargement', *European Foreign Affairs Review*, pp. 275-294.

Lessana, C. (1998), 'Loi Debré: la fabrique de l'immigré', *Cultures & Conflits*, **31/32**.

Lester, R. (1973), *World Without Borders*, Vintage Books, New York.

Leveau, R. (1994), 'Les jeunes issus de l'immigration maghrébine', in Badie, B. and De Wenden, C. (eds), *Le défi migratoire, questions de relations internationales*, Presses de la FNSP, Paris.

Lipshutz, R. (2000), *After Authority: War, Peace and Global Politics in the 21st Century*, State University Press, Albany.

Lyon, D. (1994), *The Electronic Eye*, Polity Press, Cambridge.

Marx, G. T (1988), 'La société de sécurité maximale', *Déviance et société*, **2**.

Marx, G. T. (1994), 'The Declining Signification of Traditional Borders and the Appearance of New Borders in an Age of High Technology', Paper for the conference on *Georg Simmel Between Modernity and Post modernity*, Ludwig Maximiliams-Universität. Munchen.

Mathias, A., Jacobson, D. and Lapid, Y. (2001), *Identities, Borders, and Orders*, University of Minnesota Press, Minneapolis.

Mathiesen, T. (1997), 'The viewer society: Michel Foucault's Panopticon Revisited', *Theoretical Criminology*, **1/2**, pp. 215-234.

Noiriel, G. (1993), *La tyrannie du national: le droit d'asile en Europe 1793-1993*, Calmann-Lévy, Paris.

Noiriel, G. (1996), *The French Melting-Pot: Immigration, Citizenship and National Identity*, University of Minneapolis Press, Minneapolis.

Noiriel, G. (2001), *Etat, nation et immigration. Vers une histoire du pouvoir*, Belin, Paris.

Nolutshungu, S. C. (ed.) (1996), *Margins of insecurity, minorities and international security*, University of Rochester Press, Rochester.

Prescott, J. R. V. (1987), *Political Frontiers and Boundaries*, Brown, London.

Rattansi, A. and Westwood, S. (1994), *Racism modernity identity on the western front*, Polity Press, Oxford.

Rea, A. (ed.) (1998), *Immigration et racisme en Europe*, Complexe, Bruxelles.

Rosenau, J. N. (1990), *Turbulence in World Politics. A Theory of Change and Continuity*, Princeton University Press, Princeton.

Ruggie, J. (1992), 'Territoriality and Beyond: Problematizing Modernity in International Relations', *International Organization*, **472**, pp. 139-174.

Ruggie, J. (1998), *Constructing the World Polity. Essays on International Institutionalization*, Routledge, London.

Sayad, A. (1999), 'Immigration et "pensée d'Etat"', *Actes de la recherche en sciences sociales*, **129**, pp. 5-14.

Schmitt, C. (1972), *La notion de politique et théorie du partisan*, Calmann-Lévy, Paris.

Sheptycki, J. W. E. (2002), *In Search of Transnational Policing: Towards a Sociology of Global Policing, Advances in Criminology*, Ashgate, Aldershot.

Sheptycki, J. W. E. (ed.) (2000), *Issues in Transnational Policing*, Routledge, London.

Solomos, J. and Back, L. (1996), *Racism and society*, Mac Millan, London.

Soysal, Y. (1994), *Limits of Citizenship. Migrants and Post national Membership in Europe*, University of Chicago Press, Chicago.

Strange, S. (1996), *Retreat of the State: The Diffusion of Power in the World Economy*, Cambridge University Press, Cambridge.

Tilly, C. (1975), *The formation of national states in Western Europe*, Princeton University Press, Princeton.

Torpey, J. (2001), *The Invention of the Passport*, Cambridge University Press, London.

Torpey, J. and Marrus, M. (1985), *The Unwanted: European Refugees in the 20th Century*, Oxford University Press, Oxford.

Van Outrive, L., Renault, G. and Vanderborght, J. (1996), 'La collaboration policière en Europe', *Déviances et sociétés*, **20**(2).

Wacquant, L. (1999), 'Des ennemis commodes', *Actes de la recherche en sciences sociales*, **129**, pp. 63-67.

Waever, O. (1997), *Concepts of Security*, Copenhagen Institute for Political Science, University of Copenhagen, Copenhagen.

Walker, R. B. J. (1993), *Inside-outside, international relations as political theory*, Cambridge University Press, Cambridge studies in international relations, Cambridge.

Wayne, C., Martin, P. and Hollifield, J. (eds) (1994), *Controlling Immigration*, Stanford University Press, Stanford.

Weil, P. (1991), *La France et ses étrangers*, Presses de la FNSP, Paris.

Wieviorka, M. (1998), 'Un nouveau paradigme de la violence?', *Cultures & Conflits*, **29/30**.

Zielonka, J. (2002), *Europe unbound: enlarging and reshaping the boundaries of the European Union*, Routledge, London.

Chapter 3

Who is Entitled to Work and Who is in Charge? Understanding the Legal Framework of European Labour Migration

Elspeth Guild[1]

Susan Strange sets out three premises as vital to understanding the modern world: first, the position of politics: the exercise of politics is not a monopoly of the state but equally exercised by non-state actors; secondly, power over outcomes is exercised impersonally by markets; and thirdly that authority in society and over economic transactions is legitimately exercised by agents other than states.[2] This chapter examines these three premises from the perspective of labour migration in Western Europe – a field which is perceived as a bastion of state authority. These three premises will be tested against the international legal framework of European labour migration to see whether the claim of states to a monopoly over this form of migration is justified, or whether Strange's observations about the limitations (often self imposed) of the state are applicable in this arena.

Over the past 50 years labour migration into and around Europe has been the subject of substantial legal and political debate. Labour migration involves at least three actors: first the state, which can be subdivided into the state of destination (the host state) and the state of origin (the home state). Western European states declare strong interests in the regulation of labour migration as regards promoting, preventing or controlling. Secondly, the employer has an interest in labour migration. This interest can manifest in a number of different ways, for instance the employer may rely on the host state to undertake recruitment for it, or it may recruit migrant labour directly either abroad or in the host state; alternatively it may move the production unit to suit the availability of labour (though the use of this option is often exaggerated). Thirdly the individual has an interest in labour migration both individually and as part of a network/family structure and strategy.[3]

This debate between and among the interests of these actors presupposes the successful expropriation by the state from individuals and private entities of the legitimate means of movement across international borders.[4] The regulation of labour migration between states requires the identification of foreigners whose access is controlled through state regulation. Nationals of a state are entitled, by international law norms, to enter to their state of origin. They do not then qualify for regulation as "labour migrants" within the legal definition of the term. The state's ability to identify persons outside its borders is determinant of the status of those persons on crossing the border. A classic example to illustrate the consequences of this state power of definition is the identification by West Germany of all nationals of the former East Germany as "own nationals" which meant their movement across the former border between the two states did not involve the states mechanisms of labour migration.[5] The Israeli law of return under which Jews are entitled to Israeli citizenship means the migration of Jews to Israel does not engage that state's rules on labour migration.

Strange's modern state is one characterised by a changing relationship of four factors of power: (1) position to offer security, (2) to offer or withhold credit, (3) to control access to knowledge, which includes the power to define the nature of knowledge and (4) control of production. In the field of labour migration, the fourth relationship, control of production, is implicit in the fact of control of labour movement. The definition of nationality or foreignness which is fundamental to the question of whether movement across borders is immigration or "return home" comes within the state's power to offer security – security of belonging which is offered to citizens and as differentiated from the more limited and precarious security of residence which may be provided to foreigners. However, the changing relationship of the state in all four areas defines its capacity to regulate labour migration once it has successfully dominated the right to do so. By the shift in control over the factors in relation to the individual and the company, the nature of the state changes over the periods outlined above.

Returning then to Strange, in the first part of this article, the period from 1949-1973 the first of Strange's axioms find a particularly strong expression: labour recruitment, while nominally controlled by the state, is in fact the result of politics exercised by non-state actors; secondly in the period 1973-1994 the second of Strange's premises can be tested – the interests of the market in labour migration irrespective of state interests in control are ultimately decisive of the accommodation of the market; thirdly, Strange's final principle that there is a legitimate exercise of authority over economic transactions including labour migration, by non-state actors, intersects with the new international legal framework commencing in 1994 where a regulatory system has been created within the WTO which is intended in its implementation to free some economic actors from close state supervision of labour migration. In Torpey's terminology, the state has licensed private actors to exercise some of its monopolistic powers.

As a tool to understanding the dynamic, the field will be looked at from the perspective of three key relationships:

1. The relationship between the individual and the state;
2. The relationship between the individual and the company;
3. The relationship between the state and the company.

As regards the state for the purpose of labour migration, what is meant is the bureaucratic state which has the capacity to confer nationality on its citizens and to recognise the nationality of aliens, thus to control their movement according to its purpose. This is the state which has monopolised the authority to restrict movement. The idea of a nation as the commonality of "place and people" provides the underpinning of the bureaucratic state's expropriation of the definition of belonging through nationality rights. It is that state which declares itself exclusively competent to determine insiders and outsiders which is then capable of extending certain labour migration rights only to some outsiders.

The individual in this study is always a natural person, national of a country to which the individual claims an identity of citizenship and to whom in turn the state grants the inclusion of nationality. The legal rules on acquisition and loss of nationality are particularly clearly defined in European states and increasingly the subject of national control.[6] With the exception of European states in formation such as in the Balkans, Baltics etc. statelessness is rare in European states. EU national rules on acquisition of citizenship are complex, discretionary and based on the individual's statement of commitment to the host state through long residence, mastery of the host state's language and often even renunciation of any foreign nationality. These rules are the building blocks by which the state exercises its control over movement. The elimination of statelessness, the joker in the monopoly over movement rights, was very much fuelled by European problems.[7] The legal relationship of the individual as a worker moving from his or her home state to a host state of employment is the aspect which will be investigated.

Companies also require definition.[8] The term "company" is used in preference to "corporation" (particularly as regards transnational corporation) because of its clear legal content. In practice "company" and "corporation" may be frequently interchangeable. In law they exist only by virtue of the varying national legislation which determines their incorporation and functioning.[9] Their economic strength or weakness may affect their ability to take advantage of one or more legal frameworks by changing their nationality. In the European Union context, at least, some rigidity on the change of nationality by companies has been inserted. They are held to be governed by the nationality of the state in which their central management and control and their central administration are positioned. The EU's legal regime does not give a company incorporated under the legislation of one Member State the right to transfer its central management and control to another.[10] Though this places no restraint on the more common form of change of "nationality" of companies: a take-over by a company based in another state. The much more rigorous control over the nationality of natural persons in comparison with legal persons demonstrates the importance of Torpey's premise that states' monopolisation of the right to authorise and regulate movement of persons has been intrinsic to the very construction of states (Torpey: 2000 p.6). The equivalent of a "corporate take over" of a natural person which results in a change of his or her nationality existed in 19th century European law where women on marriage to a national automatically acquired its nationality.[11] This form of "take over" beyond the control of the state (ie by virtue of the marriage choice of one of its nationals) became less and less acceptable with the emancipation of women.

Even in the EU legal framework, it is infinitely easier for economic activities to change their nationality by moving from the legal framework of a company of one nationality to one of another than for an individual. There is no fidelity test of long residence for companies, nor a language requirement. Restrictions in Member States which require a percentage of own national shareholders or levels of investment in the state are, in principle, contrary to Community free movement rules and permitted only where justified on grounds of overriding concerns of public interest. To this extent, companies are highly privileged in comparison with natural persons. However, before leaving this point, it must be pointed out that political and social constraints on the change of nationality of companies are an important reality. As Wyatt-Walker discusses, the take over of the British technology company ICL by the Japanese company Fujitsu in 1990 resulted in ICL's partial exclusion from the benefits of Community research and development projects. The approach of the Japanese parent to guarantee the independence of the UK subsidiary and to promise its floatation within a set period resulted in the "British" character of the company being politically and socially accepted. ICL was readmitted to the EU charmed circle of R&D companies in the field.[12] It is the relationship of the company as an employer of migrant labour both with the individual and the home and host state which is under consideration here.

Inter State Regulation 1949-1973: The ILO Framework

From the 1950s to the end of the 1960s the regulation of European labour migration was dominated by bilateral agreements between states. These agreements were primarily between Northern European host states, Germany, Belgium and the Netherlands being among the foremost users of the system, with countries with labour deemed surplus to their requirements: Spain, Portugal, Greece, Turkey and the Maghreb countries. The situation was characterised by collective state recruitment of labour complemented by state certification of labour until the discourse on labour migration was transformed by the rising unemployment rates in France and Germany.[13] This led to a political "stop" on state labour recruitment and sanction. This labour recruitment stop was accompanied by a change in the use of work permits. From these documents being the certification of the state's recruitment or acquiescence to private recruitment, they become the mechanism of the state's protection of the domestic market, and as such an expression of the right to work of own nationals.

The international framework of labour migration had been moribund during the inter-war period. However, the Convention for European Economic Co-operation concluded in April 1948 in connection with the Marshall Aid Programme contained at Article 8 a duty on member states to take the necessary measures for the progressive abolition of obstacles to the free movement of persons. This would be the spiritual forefather of the EC Treaty's provisions on movement of persons.[14] Close on the heels of that convention recognition was forthcoming at the international level by the International Labour Organisation of the changing climate as regards labour migration. ILO Convention 97 concerning migration for employment (1949)[15] which received substantial support from European Community Member States, set the stage providing a framework for both state and non state collective recruitment of labour. It was complemented by activity both within the Council of Europe regarding the treatment of migrant workers (though in the case of Council of Europe instruments such as the European Social Charter the rights of specific interest to migrant workers, such as security of residence and family reunification are reserved to nationals of contracting parties) and other instruments of the ILO. This activity, inter alia, gave legitimacy in the field of international law to the authority of the state's monopoly over the means of movement for work. An overview of the international regulation of labour migration follows:

International Treaties relating to Labour Migration: 1949-1999

Measure	UN/International Labour Organisation (ILO)	Council of Europe
Convention 97 on Migration for Employment	1949 parties[16] (EU): 8[17]	
European Convention on Establishment		1955 parties (EU): 12[18]
European Social Charter (original)		1961 parties (EU): all[19]
Convention 117 on Social Policy	1962 parties (EU): 3[20]	
Convention 143 concerning Migrant Workers	1975 parties (EU): 3[21]	
European Convention on the Legal Status of Migrant Workers		1977 parties (EU): 10[22]
UN Convention on the Protection of the Rights of All Migrant Workers; not yet in force; not ratified by any EU Member State	1990	

The rationale of 1949 is that labour migration is an inter-state activity which granted rights to host states (and by proxy to their companies and agents) by home states to carry out collective labour recruitment within the territory of the states of origin. The workers, who were the objects of the agreements, as necessary parts of the means of production, were made available by their state of nationality (ownership) to a host state normally for a limited period of time or at least with the understanding between the parties to the agreements that the workers would remain nationals of the state of origin and remain linked to that state. The role of the host state was to provide its domestic industry which, through nationalisation programmes, was increasingly an emanation of the state itself[23] with a solution to the national labour shortage by making available appropriately qualified migrant workers or by making available avenues whereby companies could take on migrant workers. The position of the individual was defined by reference to the interests of the state of origin which was, in effect, loaning or renting workers to the host state in return for the support which the workers were expected to send to their families in the state of origin. This policy objective found legal expression in ILO 97. As a measure adopted through the agency of the international workers' association, it enjoyed the legitimacy of classification as a measure to protect workers' rights. The contents, however, reveal a fairly complete accommodation of the interests of home and host states to the exclusion of some of the most pressing interests of workers themselves, in particular security of residence and family reunification.

ILO Convention 97: The Articles and Rights

Article Number	Content	State Oriented	Individual Oriented
1	Duty to provide information on national law and policy on immigration and emigration, conditions and general agreements on labour migration.	Directed at all members (ie states) of the ILO.	None.
2	Maintenance of adequate free service to provide migrants with accurate information.	Duty on states.	Benefit of information to migrant but no enforceable right.
3	Duty to prevent misleading propaganda relating to immigration and emigration.	Duty on states.	Benefit of information to migrant but no enforceable right.
4	Duty to facilitate departure, journey and reception of migrants.	Duty on states.	Benefit to migrant but no enforceable right.
5	Checking the health of migrants at departure and arrival.	Duty on states.	Benefit to state.

Continued ...

Article Number	Content	State Oriented	Individual Oriented
6	Non-discrimination duty: grounds: nationality, race, religion and sex; fields: remuneration (including family allowances), hours of work, overtime, holidays restrictions on home work, minimum age, apprenticeship and training, trade union membership, accommodation, social security, partial contribution rules for benefits and taxes.	Duty on state: the states "undertake to apply...".	Enforceable right for migrant. The non-discrimination obligation prevents migrant workers from undercutting domestic workers.
7	Co-operation between state employment services and guarantee of no charge for services to migrants.	Duty on state: ("undertakes... will...").	Enforceable right to migrant.
8	Migrants and their families (admitted permanently or after 5 years residence) will not be expelled on account of illness/injury contracted after entry.	Duty on state to refrain.	Enforceable right to migrant: the only right of security of residence.
9	Liberalisation of transfer of earnings and savings of migrants.	Duty on state.	Benefit to migrant in the context of the interest of the home state.
10	Provision for bilateral agreements between states.	No duty on states.	No immediate benefit to migrant.

As is apparent from the above, while the migrant worker gets the benefit of various undertakings by the states, few of these are enforceable. Those which are written in mandatory terms are characterised by the fact that they are designed to prevent migrant workers from undercutting domestic working conditions and provisions or to strengthen their tie to their home state. To this end the enforceable rights are those with which domestic trade unions were concerned to reduce the potential attractiveness of migrant workers over national workers.

Two of the most important concerns for the individual migrant are first whether he or she has a right to continued employment and residence and secondly whether he or she has a right to family reunification. Security of residence and work for the individual migrant is not provided for except where the worker becomes ill or disabled and thus the cost of his or her care is intended to rest with the host state where he or she was contributing to the economy. All other questions of a right of continued residence and protection from expulsion were left, in the European supra national context, to the European Convention and Court of Human Rights.[24]

Thus in respect of the relationship in law among the three actors: under ILO 97 the contracting states undertook to one another that they would behave in a particular way towards migrant workers (in other words the nationals of the other contracting parties by and large). The benefit was the securing of the same state undertakings from other countries – and here it must be remembered that most EU states were still net emigration countries up to and including the early years of the 1960s.[25] The rights granted were in the interests of the two states: to attract healthy workers ready to work in the host state and to maintain the links and encourage remittances by the migrant worker to the home state. The agency of the worker receives little or no consideration in the text of the convention itself. The concerns of the worker regarding his or her personal situation – security of work and residence and family reunification are excluded.

From the perspective of Strange's fundamental elements of the state – the host state is withholding security (in the form of security of residence) from migrant workers. This act is intrinsic to the state's expression of its right to control movement and residence. It would take a supra national human rights court (European Court of Human Rights) to break this monopoly of the state over security for aliens. The ECHR in the 1988 *Berrehab*[26] decision first held that the individual alien's right to family life guaranteed by Article 8 ECHR outweighed the state's monopoly over the grant or withholding of security of residence. This judgment has been followed by numerous more not only recognising the alien's right to security over the state's monopoly on grounds of family life but also on protection grounds.[27] While Strange's grant and withholding of credit finds little resonance in this Convention other than as regards the requirement of liberalisation of rules on transfers of savings, the monopoly over knowledge and its definition is critical. The Convention gives the state (both host and home) the right to define what information is made available to migrant workers on national law and policy. The state is required to exercise a degree of transparency but in so doing is entitled to define what knowledge is, and to control its availability.

Labour Migration: 1949-1973: A State or Private Activity?

In the literature over the 1980s, much emphasis was placed on the role of the state as the main actor in encouraging migrant workers to come to Europe.[28] This corresponded with political pressure for better treatment for migrant workers and their families after the 1973 stop on the grounds of the moral duty of European states in having "invited" workers to come. A second approach is also distinct in the literature of the period where the agency of the state is down played in relation to the agency of the individual – the decisions of migrant workers to migrate. In this version, the state is not responsible for the act of migration.[29] This emphasises the direct agency of the individual *vis-à-vis* the state particularly where the individual is a migrant. The perspective has become pervasive in the USA "A Polish worker in the United States during the 1970s reported 'The only way you got a job [was] through somebody at work who got you in. I mean this application, that's a joke. They just threw them away.'"[30] This approach of social scientists to move to a network construction of migration increasingly using the concept borrowed from economic sociology of "embeddedness" responds well to a changing position of the state's role in migration and labour. The state's ability to determine and control migration activities is much less tangible when the focus of research is networks where the individual and the company arc operating in Sassen's "socially conditioned activity space".[31] The framework within which research is carried out accepts that the room for manoeuvre of the state is limited to the field of control, borders and security. In this framework, labour migrants migrate as a result of embedded networks which include the complicity or partnership of companies against which the state's power of control is restricted to heavy handed border and expulsion measures focussed on adjusting the rules of legality/illegality. The two approaches exemplify Strange's shift on the positioning of politics – political scientists themselves are actors in the changing shape of politics.

How does the international legal framework of labour migration respond to the two different perspectives of labour migration: as a state activity or as a private activity? ILO 97 has two annexes each of which reflects a different approach to the state as actor in labour migration. The first annex is entitled: Recruitment, placing and conditions of labour of migrants for employment recruited otherwise than under government-sponsored arrangements for group transfer. The second is entitled: Recruitment, placing and conditions of labour of migrants for employment recruited under government-sponsored arrangements for group transfer. If the order of the two annexes is indicative of the importance in numbers of the two types of labour migration, then clearly the less state regulated form was of more pressing concern. Its definition by exclusion, in other words covering all activities except state recruitment, is also indicative of the relationship of state and private sector in 1949.

In the first annex recruitment is defined as "the engagement of a person in one territory on behalf of an employer in another territory, or the giving of an undertaking to a person in one territory to provide him with employment in another territory, together with the making of any arrangements in connection....including the seeking for and selection of emigrants..." What is missing from this definition is the situation referred to by the Polish worker: where the individual arrives in the host state and then looks for a job. Nonetheless, the underlying assumption of the convention is that there is a network relationship of some kind between the worker and the company which extends to the territory of the state of origin. The provisions relating to the annex are as follows:

ILO 97 Annex 1: Company Recruitment

Article	Content	Duty
3(1) and (2)	States which permit such recruitment shall restrict it to: public employment offices, public authorities authorised to operate with both host and home government approval; bodies permitted under international instruments; (to be granted free of charge – Article 4).	Duty on state to regulate activities of its agents.
3(3)	In accordance with national laws or bilateral agreements recruitment by prospective employers and their agents and by private agencies where in possession of prior authorisation and under supervision of the home state.	Duty on state to regulate private sector activity.
3(5)	Only the prospective host state can grant admission to its territory.	State reservation – control of the border.
5	Host and home states together must ensure that contracts between employers and migrant workers are provided to the worker either on departure or arrival which contain: conditions of work and remuneration; information about conditions of life; infractions are to be subject to sanction.	Duty on both host and home states for the benefit of migrant workers.
6	Clarification of the facilitation duty in Article 4 of the Convention. Reference to "family members authorised to join" workers but no undertaking about authorisation.	Duty on state but not enforceable.
8	Persons promoting clandestine or illegal immigration shall be subject to appropriate penalties.	Duty of home and host countries to benefit of host countries to maintain control of labour migration process.

The rights to migrant workers are most noticeable by their absence or laxity. The right to a contract is not placed necessarily on the host state but can be required of the home state. Nothing is mentioned about making contracts available in a language the migrant worker can understand. Nothing is included about the migrant's two main interests after finding employment: families and security. However, both host and home states are required to stamp out promoters of clandestine or illegal immigration, a theme which will return again and again to the stage, most recently included at the insistence of the EU Member States in the new African Caribbean and Pacific Agreement, a collective trade agreement with 71 countries in Africa, Asia and the Carribean.[32] This aspect of the state as controller of internal security is particularly relevant – it is important as a manifestation of a certain type of state – one with control over a certain territory for the purposes of defining an illegal activity. The assumption of the capacity of the home state to exercise this state role requires a detailed knowledge of the immigration rules of the host state. The definition of "clandestines" or "illegal immigrants" is a complex legal term of the host state imposed on the home state. Further, it is premised on the imbalance of power between the presumed parties: the anticipated practice is that the host state will define the elements of "clandestine" and "illegal immigrant" and require the home state to take action against agents promoting labour migration which the host state has classified as unlawful. In any event, the legitimacy of placing restrictions on the exit of a state's own nationals from the territory of nationality had been questioned. Such practices by Communist states during the Cold War period were highly criticised by Western States. The right, albeit qualified to leave one's state of origin was thus included in the International Covenant of Civil and Political Rights. The requirement of ILO 97 that states of origin enforce host states' rules against clandestines and illegal immigration presupposes that those home states will take measures to prevent their nationals, identified as potential clandestines in the host state, from leaving their state of origin. As regards Strange's premise regarding the power to define knowledge, this is a particularly stark example.

What the Annex does demonstrate is the licensing of the power to control movement, which it asserts, to companies and agents. The power to licence is shared by the two states – mutual recognition of their respective rights to control movement. The insistence of attaching clandestine and irregular migration is comprehensible through Torpey's theory of expropriation of the right to move. Any movement outside the control monopoly of the state must first be categorised as illegal and secondly combatted in the interests of the legitimacy of control for both host and home states. In Strange's modern world this is a definition of security by the state: insecurity is the result of failure to respect the state's monopoly. Knowledge is defined by the state which defines who is licensed, and controlled by the state and who is clandestine.

Turning then to ILO 97 regulation of state recruitment as contained in the second annex, what elements are found there? First the definition of recruitment varies from that applicable to the private sector. Here is included group transfer under a Government-sponsored arrangement, giving undertakings to migrant workers to provide jobs in the host state under a state-sponsored scheme.

ILO 97: Annex II – State Recruitment

Article	Content	Duty
3(1) (2) and 4	Restriction of recruitment etc. to public bodies (and bodies established under international instruments) of the host and home states by agreement; (and provision for information free of charge to the migrant).	Duty on host and home states to have a system.
3(3) and (4)	Subject to supervision by the home state recruitment may be carried out by prospective employers and their agents, private agencies, subject to prior authorisation and by regulation or agreement of home state.	Duty on the home state to regulate in conjunction with host state.
3(6)	Duty on host state to "ascertain whether there is not a sufficient number of persons already available capable of doing the work in question".	Duty on host state to protect domestic labour market.
3(7)	Reserve to state to control admission.	Reservation even in the case of state recruitment.
6	Duty on all states to supervise contracts: that the migrant gets a copy either on departure or arrival; the contract contains conditions of work and remuneration; information about conditions of life in host state; penalties for infractions.	Duty on both states.
7	As regards the facilitation requirement in Article 4 of the Convention, in respect of families, reference is made only to assistance for "members of the families authorised to accompany the worker"; also permission to transfer property.	No duty on state.
9	Where migrants fail, through no faulty of their own, to get a job the migrant is not to be responsible for the cost of the return trip.	Duty on host state for migrant's benefit.
10	Right to host state to change the employment of migrant workers without prejudice to national workers or arrange for resettlement elsewhere (subject to consent by the worker).	Wide right to host state to categorise migrants.
11	In respect of migrant workers who are refugees or displaced persons the host state shall find new jobs or resettlement in the event of job loss.	Duty on host state – this is an interesting intersection with the Geneva Convention on refugees and the Statelessness Convention.
12	Reporting on methods by host state for supervision of contractual obligations of employers to be subject of agreement.	No duty on any party.

Perhaps the most striking aspect of Annex II is how similar it is to Annex I – although formally it relates to state recruitment, the mechanisms envisaged are virtually the same as for private recruitment. An active role by companies and their agents is foreseen which is supported by the host state and the subject of approval by the home state.

What then, are the conclusions regarding the relationship of the individual worker, the state (host and home) and the company as regards the international legal regulation of labour migration during the period of heightened movement? Looking first at the relationship of the individual with the state: he or she is clearly the object of the labour recruitment activity but he or she is not provided an active role. The benefits which are set out for the worker are passive, regulated between the two states. He or she is "protected" in accordance with the interests of the host and home states. The proper interests of the individual to determine his or her employment and to live in security with his or her family are irrelevant to the agreement.

What is the relationship between the state and the company? Here it is evident that both the host and home states are relying on the agencies of companies either through their agents or as agencies in themselves, to carry out substantial parts of the recruitment and organisational aspects of the convention. The convention is clearly designed to fulfil the host states' commitment to provide labour to companies within their own states. The flexibility which host states are given to move workers, redefine their skills or even resettle them indicates the lack of agency which is expected of them in the face of the requirements of industry. The convention might well be characterised as a charter of the state (host) acting as a company or a company acting as a host state to carry out activities in recruitment. This is justified on the territory of home states not least because of the very substantial role of the state through nationalised industries as consumers of migrant manpower. Because there is no commitment to provide security, the worker is dependent on the company to retain his or her job or else risk expulsion. The mechanism of making admission (and residence) of the migrant worker completely dependent on working for a company means that the state gives to the company a huge coercive power over the worker. The complicity of the host state and the company is to exclude the agency of the individual worker. The implicit relationship between the host and home states is expressed through the worker – the lack of equivalence or balance between the two states expresses a different access to statehood between the two as developed by Strange – the concept of a state is by no means monolithic or universal. The interest of the home state is best served by the continuing employment of the migrant in the host state. The continued presence of family members in the home state increases the likelihood of substantial wage remittances by the migrant worker to his or her home state. Thus both residence insecurity of the migrant worker in the host state and the exclusion of family reunion in the host state are not necessarily contrary to the financial interests of the state of origin.

Finally, what is the relationship between the individual worker and the company? The company owes a duty to the worker to ensure that he or she has a contract before starting work and that the terms of that contract do not discriminate against the migrant worker as regards remuneration and working conditions. Beyond that the strength of the relationship between the host state and the company leaves a legal space which in practice is un-exercisable for the worker's relationship with the company. The state's monopoly over the definition and content of knowledge is expressed through the application of its national law on labour contracts. These national laws which determine the form and content of the labour/employer relationship are expressed as the only knowledge which must be imparted to the worker through the agency of the employer.

The constellation of relationships and rights strongly indicates the involvement of only certain state interests in the process. The emphasis of both the host and home states on the accommodation of the interests of companies in search of labour not available within the state indicates a strong involvement of labour ministries[33] in the settlement of the convention and the process of labour migration. The labour shortage was at the time seen as the responsibility of labour ministries, not industry ministries. The concerns of social affairs ministries regarding the consequences of migration on their areas of responsibility are limited to a health check on labour migrants before their departure, to ensure that they are not likely to be an immediate cost to health services. The right to non-discrimination in working conditions does include a reference to social security and other social affairs fields. However, the institutional interest of the non-discrimination provision is directed at protection of the national labour market, the side consequences of social responsibilities was not intended to become an issue because of the lack of security of residence of the migrant worker in the face of unemployment and lack of family reunification rights. Social costs come into existence when an individual has a right of residence not withstanding unemployment, and when he or she has family members in the host state. Unless a right to export benefits is included then the main advantage for the migrant worker will be health care. The exception is, of course, the host state's responsibility for disabled workers. Social issues of migrant workers would find regulation elsewhere (see in particular ILO 117 on Social Policy).

Just before moving on to the next period, it is worth noting that the interest of ministries with responsibility for employment are specifically accommodated in the convention. The non-discrimination provision in the main convention supplemented in both of the annexes: in annex 1 by the duty to prevent clandestine or illegal immigration and in annex 2 to permit labour migration only where there is insufficient national labour available. The duty to prevent discrimination in working conditions and remuneration is intended to prevent companies from enjoying a benefit by using migrant labour instead of domestic labour by applying a differential wage and benefit structure in respect of the latter. This is an interest of ministries responsible for labour: ensuring that companies' benefit in using migrant labour is limited to filling posts for which no national workers can be found either on account of the type of work (bottom of the labour market) or high skills (top of the labour market). The increasingly serious assumption by ministries responsible for labour of a duty to find work for national workers (the right of employment)[34] in the post war period would enter into competition with the interest of industry ministries in the field of labour migration only in the next period. The non-discrimination provision accompanied by an express exclusion of illegal workers and preference to national workers evidences this. The prevention of unauthorised labour migration ensures the control of the state over the process: unless the state sanctions labour migration the individual migrant will be clandestine and illegal. Such a classification renders the individual outside the protection of the company. The company can be divested of the benefit of the migrant worker, and in the logic of ministries responsible for employment, encouraged to find and train domestic labour. The framework of labour migration as a point of conflict between employment and industry ministries (or where both aspects are part of the same ministry, inter-ministry conflict) would become evident once the interests of the two ministries began to diverge after 1973. The solution was to privilege the agency of national workers and national companies by seeking to ensure as close as possible a convergence of their interests. This, in particular, required the protection of "middle" jobs – skilled and proportionately well paid, for national workers. The two ends of the labour market were open to migrant workers: the top end – which would gradually become the dominate concern of industry ministries[35] with the move out of heavy industry into high value services – and the bottom end which was the area of concern of the industry ministries in 1949 but which would increasingly become co-extensive with clandestine, illegal or highly precarious migrant work (such as work by asylum seekers etc.) liable to rapid changes in regulation and increasingly handed over to interior ministries as a security issue.[36]

The Interregnum: 1973-1994

In 1970-1990s there was a substantial change to the way in which labour migration was organised in Europe. As the states declared, in the mid 1970s, the end of collective labour recruitment, the private sector adjusted its role in the field arranging for themselves the recruitment of migrant labour.

Protecting the domestic labour pool The political commitment to guarantee a right to work for their nationals created a direct conflict with the interests of companies to recruit labour. Unemployment rose across Europe as states began to divest themselves of companies – nationalised industry. The concerns of the ministries with responsibility for employment, which had been paramount began to give way to those of industry. Industry ministries, increasingly shorn of their control function as regards nationalised industry developed a new role in relation to companies, initially the independent companies formed from privatisation. The closeness of personnel between industry ministries and privatised industries has been the subject of adverse comment. The new role of the industry ministries was to further the growth and success of companies. The influence of the large privatised industries cannot be underestimated. Also, the change of perspective implicit in European privatisation that private companies "do it better" leads inexorably to an increased importance of these ministries which would have consequences for labour migration. The differential between unemployment among own nationals and third country nationals indicates two things: first, in the earlier part of this period (taking the available figures from 1983-1995) the differential was less pronounced than at the end of the same period. The policies of reserving jobs for own nationals began to bite with time resulting in rising differentials of unemployment. However, the increasing security of residence of third country nationals also had the consequence of rendering the expulsion of unemployed aliens more complicated.

Unemployment Rates between Nationals and Foreigners: 1983-1995 (percent)[37]

Year	Germany: Nationals TCNs[38]		France: Nationals TCNs		Spain: Nationals TCNs		UK: Nationals TCNs	
1983	6.0	11.3	7.4	14.5	Figures not available		11.0	13.9
1986	6.1	12.0	9.6	18.6			11.3	15.3
1989	5.4	9.3	9.0	17.8	17.3	18.7	7.3	9.8
1992	6.1	9.2	9.7	18.8	17.7	13.8	9.6	14.0
1995	7.5	15.0	11.2	21.7	22.7	23.1	8.5	14.3

In the light of growing unemployment and the political consequences attendant on it, increasing emphasis was placed on employment ministries as responsible to individuals, specifically own nationals, to reduce unemployment. The responsibility of these ministries towards companies diminished. The role of the state in labour migration became increasingly one of dissuasion, through the creation of administrative obstacles to the certification of private sector recruitment of migrant labour. The general approach in the EU to combat unemployment was directed at increasing skills levels of workers to increase the chances of employment and improve the quality of employment. Taking France as an example, the percentage of young people who were studying at the age of 20 increases from 4 percent in 1967-68 to 70.3 percent in 1996/97.[39] At the level of the EU 15 by 1995 education levels of own nationals on average in comparison with third country nationals was as follows:

Educational Attainment: EU 15-1995 (percent)[40]

EU 15	Nationals	TCNs[41]
Low education level	37.3	52.1
Medium education level	42.6	33.7
High education level	20.1	14.2

The interests of employment authorities to increase skills levels of the national population and to ensure that jobs created in the middle ground of skilled work were available for them (as opposed to third country nationals) is evidenced by the figures on occupation of those in employment in the four EU states with substantial unemployment problems:

**Employment of Own Nationals and
Third Country Nationals in the EU: 1995 (percent)[42]**

Occupation	Germany Nationals	TCN	France Nationals	TCN	Spain Nationals	TCN	UK Nationals	TCN
Manager	6.1	3.3	7.9	7.4	8.3	8.4	14.9	16.8
Professional	12.0	5.1	10.6	5.7	10.0	12.8	14.7	19.6
Technician	19.7	8.1	17.4	5.0	7.3	7.0	8.3	6.9
Service worker	10.7	12.2	12.0	13.3	13.9	17.2	14.1	17.9
Craft worker	18.3	26.5	13.3	20.8	17.4	10.2	12.7	8.5
Elementary occupation	9.5	22.8	6.8	18.6	14.5	34.8	8.5	9.8

Of course these tables and the employment patterns which they reveal are strongly influenced by the social value accorded in each country (or indeed region) to different employment sectors. Nonetheless, there is a clear pattern of concentration of third country national workers at the top and bottom ends of the spectrum with less participation in the centre (with the exception of the UK where there has been a substantial advance of entry into the higher levels of employment – management level – third country nationals). Undoubtedly the changing role of the industry ministry in comparison with the employment ministry had consequences here. Their exclusion from the middle ground both by limitations on labour migration, for third country nationals already resident within the territory of EU states and differential access to or take up rate of educational opportunities over the period from 1973 to the mid 1990s has been effective.[43]

In some states like the UK, the state gradually withdrew from labour recruitment in general. The decline in power and efficiency of state recruitment systems went hand in hand with the rise of a new service industry of labour placement within many states. Responsibility for migrant labour certification remained primarily with employment ministries/authorities (often at the local level). The test applied became one of determining whether indeed there was a need for the admission of migrant workers to fill labour market gaps described by private enterprises. The rise in unemployment meant a change in culture within state agencies responsible for certifying labour migration – their duty to scrutinise the requests for certification of migrant labour – meant they were required to determine whether there existed a genuine market need for the skills. The industry ministry interest to the company to find workers became subservient to the employment authorities concern about national workers. Thus, the space for labour migration became increasingly squeezed to the top and bottom of the labour markets. This left little space for a migrant worker to rise within a line of work – either he or she was already at the top or he or she would be excluded the moment he or she aspired to improve his or her chances. The migrant's interest in a secure residence right independent of employment became paramount as only in this way would he or she be freed from control by the company and gain some control over his or her employment. A right of secure residence which provides free access to the labour market has developed in all EU Member States from approximately 1965 to the present with only one exception, Austria, where migrant workers remain subject to labour permit quotas.[44]

The standard against which the employment authorities labour certification function was carried out was the protection of domestic labour. The political priority was found in the continuing acceptance of state duty to ensure the availability of employment for all domestic workers. So long as the state accepted this duty the interest of companies to import migrant workers would be in principle illegitimate and only approved as a matter of exception. The resulting strategy of companies was to seek alliances elsewhere in ministries which were more receptive to their concerns – in particular in industry departments.

As Salt has described, the increasing activity of trans-national companies also meant a demand to move personnel with the company.[45] In particular senior managers went with company acquisitions abroad to ensure the bedding in of the new subsidiary or to set up new ventures for the parent company within the territory of other states. To accommodate this movement the category of "key personnel"[46] Salt developed the concept of the internal labour market of trans-national companies which operates much like an external labour market but limited to the space within one company and its subsidiaries.[47] This approach was embraced at least in the UK (to which government it was directed) and coincided or contributed to a change of the certification system of labour migration. However, it also coincided with a changing perspective of the UK employment authorities regarding their duty to reserve jobs for national workers – the increasing uncertainty about this duty also led to an increasing accommodation of the interests of the industry ministry within the certification procedure at least as regards trans-national companies.

One enduring aspect of the labour certification system, however, was its reserve for national companies (including national subsidiaries of companies based in other companies). Without a base in the state to which the migrant workers were to be sent, a company had little or no chance of obtaining the certification required.[48]

Creating conflicting interests The characteristics of the "certification" period were:

1. Friction between employment ministries and companies as regards the international movement of labour; the objective of these ministries to reduce domestic unemployment was not always reconcilable with the interests of companies to import migrant labour; in particular the

interest of trans-national companies to move staff internationally without substantial restrictions was not easily accommodated;

2.   The employment ministries' interest in the field was to limit as far as possible labour migration in order to "save" domestic jobs for nationals who were unemployed. The political sensitivity of labour migration meant that the state had every incentive to disguise labour migration as temporary in nature.

The fact of labour migration was formulated as high skills migration as opposed to low skills migration. The divide within the labour market became external and institutionalised; low skill labour migration became increasingly disguised as migration in other categories unrelated to economic grounds;[49] The exception to the high skill/low skill divide is found in Southern Europe where there was sufficient political will towards the mid to end 1990s to acknowledge the need for low skilled migration.[50]

The interest of the individual to have a secure status in the face of the employment authorities' interest to limit the long term basis of labour migration meant that a cut off of between 4 and 5 years for the acquisition of a residence right was achieved.[51]

The company's interest in keeping the employee for a long enough period to pay off the effort and cost of moving him or her had to find expression in a minimum period before an individual was entitled to change job.[52]

The relationship between the individual and the state was one whereby the individual had little agency; the application was driven by the company which had to be national in character; the individual only becomes entitled to rights after a period of residence and work on the territory; the minute that the individual is no longer protected by the employer the state will expel him or her; the state's control function as regards the labour market is particularly exercised as regards those persons who do not have corporate protection; this control function became increasingly the responsibility of the interior and justice ministries.

The relationship of the individual with the company: the individual remains dependent on employment in order to maintain a right of residence; without the continued good will of the employer, the individual will lose his or her right of residence.

The relationship of the company and the state: the state in the form of the employment authorities is opposed to labour migration which it will only permit under specific circumstances; the company will agree to the limitations so long as they do not hinder its operation completely and in return it gets a period of time when the employee is tied to the employer; to the extent that this arrangement is not satisfactory or becomes less and less satisfactory in particular to trans-national companies, they look to different allies within the state – specifically the industry ministries for assistance.

The field was restructured in particular to present the problem of the system as the failure to accommodate labour migration at the top end as this was the interest of trans-national companies in particular. The strength of these companies in the fields of finance and technology identified as desirable sectors by industry ministries, meant that there was a real will to find solutions: in Germany and the UK in particular from 2000 onwards there has been increasing recognition of this. The June 2000 statement of B, Roche (then British Minister responsible for employment) that the UK welcomed new skilled employment from outside the UK and the introduction of the so called Green Card Scheme in Germany designed to attract and facilitate high tech overseas workers to come to Germany are specific examples. These announcements are the result of longer strategies within the sector by trans-national companies and industry ministries.

In the high skills field, most Member States sought to accommodate under the guise of temporary labour migration the movement by companies of their existing personnel but limited this privileged treatment to their own companies.[53] The changing structure of employment began to affect the domination of the field of labour migration by the employment authorities. In particular the consequences of the restructuring of European economies changed the relationships of the three actors, not least changing the balance of interest within the state from employment ministries to industry ministries. The meteoric rise in importance of the services sector in comparison with manufacturing sectors began in earnest in the 1970s. For many types of services, where production and consumption are simultaneous, the movement of persons to provide the service in the place where it is being consumed is intrinsic, for example health services. As the services sector gained importance as a major component of international trade, so the interests of the services sector enterprises engaged in the trade began to conflict with immigration rules which impeded access to foreign markets. The high value added fields in services such as the financial sector, were an area of substantial competition among the industrialised world – the USA, Japan and South East Asia and the EU. Access to markets was critical to maintaining a competitive position.[54]

Services, GDP and Employment in OECD countries (percent)[55]

Sector	GPD: 1970	GDP: 1996	Employment: 1970	Employment: 1996
Finance and company services	16.1	21.4	6.2	10.6
Social services	8.8	13.0	10.5	18.0
Food and catering	19.6	14.7	18.8	19.8
Transport and communication	7.4	6.3	5.7	5.4
Public services	12.1	11.2	12.7	14.3
Total	64.1	66.7	54.0	68.2

The importance of the service sector as part of the European economy cannot be overemphasised as a factor in the changing legal framework of labour migration. The conundrum of the services sector is not only the involvement of persons as intrinsic to the activity itself in a way less apparent in respect of goods. However, the services sector, while rising dramatically between 1970 and 1996 as a proportion of the economy, is by no means exclusively high skilled. One of the criticisms of the services sector as regards job creation is its propensity to create low skill, insecure jobs – telephone sales, catering etc. Indeed, food and catering, traditionally associated with low skill jobs remained stubbornly throughout the period as the highest percentage of jobs (though its importance to GDP fell over the period).

Structuring access to private sector licensing of labour migration The most highly privileged part of the services sector was that in high skill and new technology fields. The interest was primarily to benefit the development of national industries even where that benefit involved alliances with foreign companies.[56] The leader in GDP terms are financial and other corporate services rising from 16.1 percent to 21.4 percent of GDP over the period 1970-1996. In respect of employment this sector is also important rising from 6.3 percent to 10.6 percent of jobs. This sector more easily fits itself into the overt regulatory scheme as a high skill sector where the justification of labour migration on the basis of a lack of national workers with the necessary skills can be played. Nonetheless, it must be remembered that the privileged position of companies seeking to import high skilled labour was always discriminatory – limited to companies based on the territory to the exclusion of those with no link to the territory and thus excluded except under particular restrictive immigration rules in the control of justice and interior ministries,[57] traditionally much less sensitive to company interests.

The theoretical argument of the internal labour market of trans-national companies provided a basis, at least in some EU states to permit the movement of higher skilled employees internationally without substantial obstacles. But what does this theoretical basis mean as regards the interests which the employment authorities were entrusted to protect: it is the acceptance that within a trans-national company there is little chance that national workers of medium to high skills will be disadvantaged by the operation of a labour market which is internal to a company. This acceptance indicates a different approach to trans-national companies than smaller enterprises. If the decision were one of the employment authorities alone then the importance of trans-national companies as important employers would need to be demonstrated to justify the differential treatment: in other words, it would have to be demonstrated that trans-national companies contribute highly to the reduction of domestic unemployment and thus deserve a more favoured position as regards the certification of migrant workers. If such a beneficial effect on the labour market is not apparent (as I will argue shortly) then other interests must be at stake. Here I will argue that the perceived benefit of trans-national companies to the industry ministries was the main reason for the privileged position which they enjoyed at the expense of the interests of the employment authorities.

The European Commission has invested substantial resources in the development of small and medium enterprises (SMEs).[58] The argument in favour of their preferential treatment is not least their contribution to employment throughout the Union. Taking France as indicative of most of the EU, the employment creation capacities of SMEs far exceeds that of larger enterprises:

Employment Creation: France 1975-1994 (percent)[59]

Size of enterprise	1977	1983	1989	1994
1-9 employees	18.4	22.3	24.1	26
10-49 employees	24.6	26.9	28.5	28.9
50-199 employees	22.2	21.8	22.7	22.6
200-499 employees	14.1	12.5	11.8	11.5
500 + employees	20.7	16.5	12.9	11
Total	100	100	100	100
Numbers: in millions	13,138	13,000	13,569	13,757

Clearly the importance of large companies as employers is decreasing. From the perspective of employment creation, the most important companies are the SMEs. The rationale then of employment creation for the simplification of labour migration rules for trans-national companies does not apply. Other factors are at work, which factors relate to the other capacities of trans-national companies and appeal to other national ministries than those charged with the protection of the domestic labour force. This then changes the relationship of companies with the state as regards labour migration. The rationale for a complex and exclusionary certification procedure for labour migration loses its legitimacy when it does not apply to some companies without the justification that those companies otherwise contribute to the employment of domestic workers more substantially than those excluded. The benefit of such companies to the EU must be searched for in other fields, the concern of other ministries. Thus the position of power in the relationship between companies and the state has moved sufficiently to justify a change in the approach to the certification of migrant labour. This development corresponds to Strange's second premise – the power over the outcome of labour certification is exercised impersonally by a market in which greater power is wielded by companies judged important on the basis of world wide turn over not contribution to any national employment market.

Failing to accommodate the bottom   In fact the more pressing problem was migration at the bottom end of the market. While there may be national unemployment levels which are unacceptably high, workers in the state may still not be willing to undertake some jobs. The pursuit of an aspirational employment policy – the focus on skills and training in order to achieve better employment and greater financial security – meant the devaluation of the social acceptability of jobs at the bottom end. The need to find workers whose hierarchy of values would not conflict with the acceptance of bottom end jobs and also who would not aspire with time to the middle employment market was the problem posed here. The bottom end jobs still need workers but they cannot be admitted in the guise of labour migration which has been highly circumscribed so other ways of filling the needs are found: for instance family members, asylum seekers are permitted to work for a while at least; domestic servants and agricultural workers, (highly limited categories), etc.[60] With the exception of family members, all the other categories are characterised by insecurity for the individual and the company as regards continuity of residence and hence ability to continue work.

The inclusion of even the low skills service sector in the framework of labour migration was only marginally politically possible. In spite of the problem of sectoral shortages, in particular in the agricultural, catering and cleaning sectors, the interests of the interior ministries in the exclusion of workers or ensuring the precariousness of their position took precedence over the interests of the individual and the company. Workers outside the protection of the employment ministries as informed by large companies (to the exclusion of smaller employers such as those in agriculture, catering and cleaning) meant that the demand side of this part of the labour market was left to its own devices by and large.

What then about the relationship of the state to the individual? The rationale of the protection of national workers began to disintegrate under the change in relationship of different ministries to trans-national companies, the logic behind the exclusion of migrant workers also lost its legitimacy. As this began to happen, the justice and interior ministry logic of control and exclusion moved in to fill the gap. The bottom end of the labour market needed to remain bottom end if it was to be kept from competing with the reserved middle labour market intended for own nationals. If the logic of including labour migration was no longer clearly defined by the employment authorities, at least the logic of exclusion of labour migration at the bottom end of the market could still fulfil its perceived function. The rationale of protection of the labour market together with protection of social security[61] created in the 1990s an increasingly shrill discourse in interior ministries about the need to exclude illegal workers from bottom end jobs. The political unwillingness to define into legality migrant workers at the bottom end combined with increasing measures against the employment of illegal workers both for the workers and their employers evidences a sharp increase in the use of the state's power over security to the detriment of individual migrants and employers.[62]

In Strange's terms, this period saw a segmentation of interests – larger corporate interests appear to benefit from an exercise of politics which is unrelated to their importance as employers but privileges them as high value "nationals" to a lighter control as regards their license to employ migrant workers than other companies, in other words, a higher level of security for them as regards their staffing choices than for other companies. The outcome benefits a part of the market, large multinational companies which enjoy "own national" status, in a manner which is fundamentally impersonal as regards the individual. The interests of smaller companies, despite their greater importance as employers, are accommodated to a lesser degree in particular where their interests are in low skilled labour (such as agriculture, catering, cleaning etc.). The state's monopoly of power over security for these companies is not licensed directly to the private sector.[63] Finally, the legitimate exercise of power to authorise labour migration, while resting with the state is increasingly licensed to some companies to the exclusion of others. The excluded sectors are of two kinds: foreign companies which are unwilling to set up a sufficient base in the European state to which it wishes to transfer or in which it wishes to employ labour migrants; companies based in the state which are insufficiently large (or otherwise privileged) to enjoy the looser licensing regime. These sectors thus have available a much lower level of security as regards the company's choices of deployment of labour, where that labour is foreign, than the privileged group. The change of the position of power both within ministries and within sectors of the economy led to the creation of a new framework for labour migration, the General Agreement on Trade in Services (GATS) part of the WTO. It is this next step in labour migration which will now be considered.

Corporate Regulation of Labour Migration: The WTO Framework? 1994-2000

The General Agreement on Tariffs and Trade (GATT) 1947 made no provision for trade in services and no provision on movement of workers. As the development of industrialised economies began to move more heavily into the services related industries not least through the 1970s, the USA and the European Community began to campaign for the inclusion of services in the new round of negotiations which led to the World Trade Organisation Agreement. They were successful notwithstanding substantial suspicion on the part of developing countries.[64] The result was the inclusion of the General Agreement on Trade in Services (GATS) as one of the integral parts of the WTO.

GATS includes both services which do not involve the movement of persons, such as television services, and those which do involve persons such as training services. The role of persons may be critical to service provision as there are many forms of service provision where the "product" is produced while being consumed. Stern and Hoekman identify three critical differences which may exist between goods and services all of which relate to the insertion of the individual in services: services cannot be stored but are consumed as produced, production and consumption take place simultaneously and services are intangible.[65]

The concept of an international market in services creates difficulties in particular as regards protection of consumers. Because of the difficulty of assessing and controlling the quality of services before their delivery, traditionally they have been fields of substantial national regulation. Anyone who has used legal services will be aware of the control problems which manifest in the field. The problem of consumer protection in the provision of cross border services has caused substantial headaches in Community law. It arises frequently in the area of the provision of professional services. Not least in recognition of the special regulatory problems which relate to professional services, the ECJ has permitted the maintenance of national rules of assessment and registration where they are non-discriminatory, suitable for securing the objective pursued, justified by an imperative requirement in the general interest and do not go beyond what is necessary for the purpose, in other words a substantial and unfortunately relative list of characteristics.[66]

Within the GATS framework, service provision can encompass three types of movement of persons: first where the consumer moves to the service provider. The second type of service provision in GATS is the equivalent of the right of establishment in Community law: the establishment of a commercial presence on the territory of another GATS member country. Thirdly, service provision includes the movement of persons from one country to another to carry out service provision which does not involve the establishment of a commercial presence. In Community law, the difference between service provision and establishment has only to do with the stability and permanence of the infrastructure of the provider. It is not defined in terms of the duration of the service provision. The Member States, however, in their annexes to GATS have without exception limited permission for persons to be present on the territory to carry out the final type of service provision, ie where there is no commercial presence, to three months.

The GATS system is based on a number of basic principles in respect of which either member countries are entitled to retain exceptions listed in the annexes or to which they may sign up in accordance with sectional annexes. The most important features include first, the principle of access to the market, ie, access to the territory. Here the basic principle is that member countries will provide to one another most favoured nation treatment (MFN – Article II GATS). For measures included in GATS, the best treatment which one member provides to another country must be extended to all GATS member countries. Exceptions and exemptions to the MFN treatment were permitted, but had to be tabled at the time of adoption and could not be added to subsequently. If one applies this principle to the three types of movement of persons within the GATS framework it means that access by persons seeking to use services, to provide services on a one off basis or to set up a commercial presence are entitled to the best conditions of entry into the territory of the EU available to any third country national. The exceptions and exemptions which are listed for the Member States are all based on their national laws. As Jackson describes this: "The obligations require each member to accord to services and service suppliers of any other members treatment no less favourable than that provided for under the terms, limitations and conditions agreed and specified in its schedule." This is a bottom-up approach, so that the GATS applies only to the tabled or bound sectors established in the schedules.[67] The Doha round of GATS negotiations was opened in 2001. The specific objective is to make progress in reducing or abolishing exception and exemptions which limit the scope of the agreement.

Once inside the territory, the GATS principle is that service imports are entitled to treatment "no less favourable than that [the country] accords to its own like services and service suppliers".[68] This equal treatment provision is expanded to ensure that it covers both direct and indirect discrimination: formally different treatment is permitted only so long as it does not modify the conditions of competition in favour of the services of service providers of the host country. Exceptions and limitations to this equal treatment provision are permitted and contained in the schedule of specific commitments. Again these are submitted for each state individually. The question arises, to what does this equal treatment provision attach when considering natural persons as service providers? Is it limited to the service or does it also cover the means by which the service is provided, the individual? This is critically important to the question of labour standards. If the natural person who is carrying out the service is excluded from the benefit of equal treatment with natural persons carrying out the same service but who are resident on the territory then the form of "social dumping" which was much discussed by the Member States in the context of the adoption of the Directive on Posted Workers[69] is relevant here. What is at issue in both contexts is the extent to which the competitive advantage of a company in bidding for a contract abroad can be based on the differential in wage related costs between the treatment of its own workers in one country and the minimum or sectoral standard in the country where the service provision is to be carried out. This issue is increasingly disputed in the field of movement of goods – in the context of the attempted opening of the Seattle round of WTO negotiations in November 1999, US President Clinton's insistence on fair trade which does not undermine labour standards in the destination country were aimed at this question. In the field of movement of persons, sensitivity is very high. The prospect of competition by foreign employees engaged under conditions substantially less generous than those in the destination country is unpalatable to many national authorities.

The GATS framework of labour migration is based on the principle that private enterprises are the determiners of labour migration – they select, recruit and move workers depending on the demands of the market as determined by themselves. The provisions of GATS are designed to ensure market access for service providers – in other words to restrict the power of states to impede access to their territory by foreign competitors in the services field through the use of restrictive labour migration laws. The GATS framework, while still weak in terms of enforceability promotes a very different approach to labour migration. The provisions are written in terms of the rights of companies based in one of the contracting parties. There is no mention of workers within the actual text of the GATS chapter. They arise only in declarations and annexes as the objects of continuing powers regarding admission, visas and expulsion. Thus individuals remain the object of the continuation of state control while companies are the beneficiaries of licence to exercise control: ie to require the movement of natural persons, their employees, from one state to another for service provision.[70] Companies are entitled to non-discrimination but there is no mention of individuals as entitled to non-discrimination, for example as regards wages or conditions of work in the host state. This is critical as it will be one of the major changes in the structure of labour migration. We have seen changes in the interaction of the state with migrant workers and employers – but all include a substantial degree of reserved discretion and involvement of the state. In GATS there is a movement away from this determining role to one where the company is entitled to enforce rights against the state regarding the movement of personnel.

One feature which is particularly important is the position of the company. The principle non-discrimination in market access for companies based in other contracting parties means that the interest of various ministries (including employment ministries) regarding creation and safeguarding of employment for own nationals, and secondly of industry ministries in reserving market share for "own" companies is no longer sustainable. Companies which do not enjoy the status of "belonging" to the state are entitled on the basis of the non-discrimination provision to access markets nonetheless and in order to do so to send their personnel to the state. The individual, at least on the face of the agreement only enjoys rights in so far as he or she is the appendage of the company, the company's interest is determinant for the individual.

What then does the development of this new framework mean for the relationship between the state, the company and the individual? Taking the first relationship between the state and the company – the state has "licensed" on a multilateral basis its monopoly on movement of migrant workers to companies. Under the GATS framework, it is for the company to determine where its employees are needed and to send them to that country for the purpose of service provision. Under the GATS annexes many limitations are placed on this right as regards sectors and purposes, but the principle is that these sectoral and other limitations will be removed as the system matures. The company is privileged to make decisions on labour migration which the states parties to the GATS are entitled to enforce through the dispute resolution mechanism.[71] In the GATS world, security remains within the power of the state: it must be accorded to companies from other states as regards their choices regarding deployment of personnel. It may be accorded to companies by their state of nationality to enforce the right of choice against another state through the WTO dispute resolution mechanism.

The relationship between the individual and the company is changed in that the individual, as a migrant worker, is increasingly dependent on the company for protection against the control capacities of the state. In the ILO framework, the protection of the individual migrant worker was, in theory at least, the responsibility of the state of nationality. In contrast with the ILO 97 framework GATS while an agreement among states, devolves power to companies. The individual is absent, the key player is the company whose rights are defined as against the exercise of sovereignty by a state. The ILO 97 framework is one of states agreeing the temporary use of workers defined as belonging to one state by another state which is intended not to acquire rights over them. It is about states and individuals with the company included almost as a mechanism of state policy. In GATS, the insecurity of the individual *vis-à-vis* the state (which will be discussed below) contrasts the power of the company to provide security to the individual. The company is placed between the state and the individual as the provider of security against the framework of state sponsored insecurity.

The individual appears in GATS only in declarations and annexes as the object of state powers on visas and other "heavy" control functions. As soon as the individual is outside the security framework of the company he or she is at risk of falling into the increasingly control oriented interior ministry mechanisms designed to define, identify and exclude irregular foreigners. In the ILO 97 system, it was the role of the employment ministries seeking to fulfil their role as providers of manpower to industry, to regulate the position of migrant workers. As these ministries moved out of employment recruitment directly, privatisation provided new approaches to the responsibilities of industry ministries muting the differences between state and company spheres, the relationship of the individual to the state changed direction. Industry ministries had an interest in promoting the company's power to protect its individuals and deploy them with little restriction. The interior ministries in their capacity of defining belonging to and exclusion from national identity, increasingly exercised the control function over foreigners.

At Odds with the Trends: The Community Framework?

The European Union has a very strong foundation as regards its immigration policy: movement of persons is part of economic integration. It is not by accident that the 1957 Treaty included as one of the four fundamental freedoms free movement of workers. The role of workers as the means of production was critical to the vision of European integration. Of the four freedoms: goods, persons, services and capital which found the basis of the Community, two, persons and services involve the right of movement to natural persons. The labour market function of the individual was the only basis for movement, but has provided an interesting counterbalance to the power of the company.

Over the period from 1957 to the 1980s, the EC Treaty provisions guaranteeing free movement of workers were recognised as having direct effect as the transitional periods came to an end. Together with the gradual enlargement of the Community southwards, the main migrant sending countries of Southern Europe were incorporated into the Community with the consequence of granting all those nationals a right of migration. The Community framework of labour migration is based on the principle that the individual has the right to choose to migrate or not for economic reasons. Instead of a mechanism driven by the state or private enterprises, the individual is left free to make the choice and respond to opportunities for economic activities anywhere within the combined territory where he or she may determine (rightly or wrongly) they exist. This is the underlying principle of free movement of workers, the self employed and service providers and recipients.

However, aspects of the other two frameworks can be found in the Community's approach to labour migration. The emphasis on equal treatment in working conditions, remuneration and social security is reminiscent of ILO 97. It is found in the EC Treaty and is incorporated into all the Community's third country agreements which include provisions on labour starting with the 1970 Protocol to the Turkey Agreement, the 1976 Maghreb Agreements (now replaced by the 1995/6 ones) and including the Europe Agreements with the Central and Eastern

European countries, Baltic states, Slovenia and the Cooperation and Partnership Agreements with the CIS states. Similarly, the GATS approach is to be found in the Community's interpretation of the right of an enterprise within the Community to send its third country national personnel anywhere in the Union to carry out service provision. Further the approach has been formally introduced into all of the post 1994 third country agreements of the Community which include provisions on services. A more sophisticated version of the GATS provision is included in the Europe and P&C Agreements, permitting enterprises to move their key personnel in order to carry out their service provision and establishment right.

In the Community, the fall of the Berlin Wall precipitated a rush to negotiate agreements with the restructuring countries of Central and Eastern Europe which began in 1990. The framework of extending agreements which included provisions permitting market access in the areas of both services provision and establishment has been widely used by the Community, and criticised in the WTO context. As regards persons, this included provisions of natural persons to establish themselves in business on the territory of the other contracting party, for legal persons to send their key personnel to the other contracting party either to establish the business there or to provide services. Yet at the same time, in the Europe Agreements there is also to be found provisions based on the particular Community approach to labour migration – the right to individuals as economic actors to make the decision of movement or not. In this case, the right of self employment for individuals contained in the Europe Agreements follows the Community pattern of leaving the decision in the hands of the individual whether Community national, or as in these cases third country national.[72] The integration, in this economic approach, of a high level of social security provided through a variety of differing national schemes with a co-ordination mechanism results in a specific European model.

The pre-eminence of an economic theory based on an integrated market where the factors of trade and industry are freed from national measures designed to privilege domestic industry from competition while at the same time protected from anti-competitive or monopolistic activity coincided with a period of unprecedented prosperity in Europe over the past 40 years. This model has, as an integral component, the protection of the individual both through the creation of free movement rights coupled with a strong social protection system. The development of what has been traditionally a complimentary external commercial policy designed to accommodate the European model has facilitated the Union's competition in an increasingly globalised marketplace.

The individual has been classified in law as the means of production, the provider or recipient of services, the holder of skills and valuable knowledge or the investor. This is then the basis for the right to move freely to apply his or her talents to the development of the internal market with a minimum of obstacles. The theoretical and legal foundation of the policy depends, inter alia, on the agency of the individual in determining what will be the most successful deployment of individual/personal capital in the Union. In this sense the Union from the beginning has taken an extreme free market approach to movement of persons: the individual and his or her enterprise are acknowledged as best placed to exploit market niches, develop trade and industry and bring about innovation and development. This understanding of commercial interest was transformed into a transparent right by the Court of Justice. This was central in protecting the effectiveness of the right in the face of Member State obstructionism. The relationship between State, individual and company was "deregulated" into an internal system where the Member State was no longer entitled to use labour certification as a means of controlling labour migration. The friction between ministries of employment and companies disappeared and the interests of the company and individuals regarding security of residence were irrelevant to the employment relationship. This is the European Community's clear and defined policy approach to primary immigration. It consists of creating clear and enforceable rights for individuals and enterprises to move for economic activities. Experience in the use of this approach has coincided with a period of economic growth and prosperity in Europe. One of the most serious complaints against the system of an individual right of free movement for economic purposes in Europe is the fact that it has not been possible to encourage sufficient numbers of persons to use their right so as to reduce the unemployment differentials among the Member States.[73] The abolition of administrative obstacles to free movement in the form of work and residence permits has also coincided with a continuous reduction in cross-border labour mobility in the EU.

Conclusions

Returning then to Strange's premises about the modern world, in the field of European labour migration it is evident that politics has not been a monopoly of the state but has been exercised throughout the post WWII period by non-state agents. The state has been divisible into different ministerial interests relating to various interests in industry, an understanding of which is critical to the regulation of labour migration. Secondly, the outcomes are the result of power exercised impersonally by markets in the demand of general labour, specialised labour and the maintenance of the value of the right to use migrant labour. Finally, the authority over economic transactions in the field of labour migration is increasingly exercised by non state actors. However, this authority is by way of "licensing" by the state. Where those transactions are not sanctions by those non-state agents, the state, in the form of interior ministries exercise their exclusionary powers in the interests of security to prevent the initiative to the individual to move and engage in economic activities without authorisation, first determined by the non-state actor and certified by a state actor. The development charted by this chapter is as follows:

1. Labour migration in the post war period is designed for the benefit of national companies. There is a high state role by employment ministries, in managing the process by facilitating the acquisition of foreign workers both overtly and covertly through simplified certification regimes;

2.   In the interregnum period, labour migration was discouraged by employment ministries resulting in conflict with companies through the deployment of increasingly impenetrable regulatory systems; this was accompanied by the segmentation of the labour market to top end labour migration – an interest of large companies which was taken up by industry ministries; middle level labour market reserved as far as possible by employment ministries for the domestic labour force; and bottom end migration left to regulation by interior and justice ministries on the basis of a very strong dissuasive and exclusionary principle; however, the whole system was still directed at national companies, even where trans-national companies had less and less of a "national" content;

3.   The GATS era where the protection of the domestic labour market and the protection of national companies are equally victims of the new framework of labour migration. The right is for companies to move personnel for service provision to any country; and the right of companies with no connection with a state to move personnel to the country for service provision.

The last phase of labour migration demonstrates most graphically Strange's premise that authority over economic transactions, even movement of labour, is increasingly exercised legitimately by agents other than states. The right to make choices about movement of labour is being transferred to the private sector on a transnational basis privileging not only national companies involved in cross border activities, but any company so long as it is based in a WTO signatory company to the increasing exclusion of employment ministries. However, the state has not disappeared from the scene. It remains the body which must give effect to the rights created by the GATS and holds the key for its national companies to gain access to the dispute resolution mechanism. Its role, diffused through different ministries, remains central as permissive and as the body responsible for commitments under international agreements such as the GATS.

The ministries left with a residual control over non-company sanctioned movement of labour are those of interior and justice which is exercised through the deployment of the concept of security. In the name of sovereignty and the duty of the state to provide security (not least of the identity of its residents), interior ministries exercise state functions[74] over movement of persons. In practice this control function is aimed at bottom end labour migration. The interests of interior ministries to provide security and of employment ministries to privilege national workers coincide only at the bottom end of the labour market where individuals seeking to move without the protection of companies do so in a framework of high insecurity. These renegades are outside the field of influence of the non-state agents' to exercise the labour migration function. Thus they constitute a threat to security because their movement is outside the new framework of authority. The value of the company's right to move employees is diminished if foreigners are entitled to move of their own accord to look for work. The loyalty of employees to the company which is exercising the control function is vulnerable if the employees can access rights through a direct relationship with the state.

The European exception to this framework is the valorisation of the individual as a factor of production to such an extent that he or she becomes the non-state actor entitled to exercise authority over the state by the choice of movement. This framework has a number of unexpected consequences. First, the demand by individuals to move for economic purposes is highly exaggerated when the discourse is compared to the reality in a system where the individual makes the choice. Secondly, by moving the authority to the non-state actor who is permitted to respond or not to the market, the refusal to respond to the market (ie the continuation of high variations in unemployment rates in different EU Member States) is more in evidence than the opposite. The state's power to exclude those persons defined as foreign is highly limited in the EU scenario – the expulsion or exclusion of nationals of other Member States is only permitted in circumscribed situations where there is an ongoing and future threat to public security by reason of the individual's presence on the territory which threat must satisfy a high threshold. The Strange premises are less easily demonstrated within a labour migration system which deprives the company of its participation in the state's certification structure and where the states control function on the grounds of security to expel and exclude individual foreigners is limited by supra national agreements.

By placing the individual at the centre of the equation with a right to move across borders in his or her capacity as an economic actor, European Community law changes the framework of Strange's factors of power: (1) the right to security of work and residence is provided from outside the state by EC law but it is the state which must carry out the Community's guarantee to the individual; (2) control over the offer of withholding credit is based on the state's right to define the individual's status as precarious. If the individual's residence is precarious, credit will be withheld; if it is secure, credit will be provided; here the state has also lost control over the definition of the individual's security of residence; (3) control of the access to knowledge – the supra national body's activities in disseminating information about the right to move and work limits the state's power to control access to knowledge; further the definition of the nature of knowledge – in this field perhaps the most important monopoly over the nature of knowledge is through the definition of who belongs and who does not – the creation of an identity, with the ability to define participation in it, becomes knowledge; (4) control over the means of production – in the Community model the state loses control over movement of migrant labour both as sending and receiving state. The means of production themselves, the workers, are entitled to make the choice of movement or not.

Returning then to the initial premises about the modern world, what conclusions can be drawn from Strange's approach as tested against the European Union and labour migration? Before looking at the three premises, an initial observation relates to the meaning of the state. This chapter has sought to emphasise the non-monolithic nature of the state. The European "state" is composed of different ministries with different interests and relations with one another. The approaches which these ministries take on labour migration have different consequences for the outcomes and the validity of Strange's premises. Considering then the premises, first, as regards the position of politics: throughout the period 1949 to the present the exercise of politics in labour migration is clearly not the monopoly of the state, or within the state, of one particular ministry. While the definition of identity was an exercise closely regulated by the state throughout the first period 1949-1973, the states' approach was divided between different ministries and other actors outside the state both in the form of international organisations (such as the EU) and companies created parameters and expressed interests which defined the politics of labour migration. Secondly, the impersonal exercise of power over outcomes by markets: the great testing period of this premise was the interregnum – 1973-1994 when the interests of the market in labour migration (ie continued access to labour migration) and the interests of (European) states diverged. However, this divergence was between the interests[75] of dominant ministries in the first period (employment/labour ministries) and those of ministries in search of new roles and forming new relations with the privatising sector (industry ministries) which led to outcomes in terms of maintaining systems for labour migration notwithstanding the dominant discourse of "closed" borders. On the third premise, the legitimate exercise of authority over economic transactions perhaps the most interesting observations arise in the field of labour migration: the role of the private sector in labour migration throughout the period from the legitimation of their role in ILO 97 to the licensing of their activities through GATS has remained constant. The exercise of authority over this kind of economic transaction has remained in substance shared between public and private. The exception to the forms and ways in which the premises operate is the European Union's approach to labour migration. Here the role of the state was diminished to a very low level, the right of choice of movement left to the individual and the private sector, but within a social model which permits to the individual a degree of choice over the decision to engage in labour migration or not.[76] The premises hold valid, but that validity depends on a very wide definition of their content so that events, developments and situations which are heterogeneous can be classified together. As soon as the role of the state is no longer monolithic but dissected as to the interests and activities of its ministries a different picture starts to emerge. When the non-state actors are companies, individuals or supra national entities the heterogeneity of their control over labour migration changes, though not necessarily in anticipated patterns.

Notes

[1]   Professor of European Immigration Law, University of Nijmegen, partner, Kingsley Napley: London.
[2]   S. Strange, *Retreat of the State: The Diffusion of Power in the World Economy*, Cambridge: Cambridge University Press, 1996, pp. 12-15.

3 For a review of recent work on the network analysis of migration see Michael Hanagan, "Labor History and the New Migration History: A Review Essay", in *International Labor and Working Class History*, n° 54, Fall 1998, pp. 57-79.

4 J. Torpey, *The Invention of The Passport Surveillance, Citizenship and the State*, OUP: Cambridge, 2000, p. 6.

5 J. Torpey, supra, pp. 146-147.

6 The move away from pure jui soli (whereby the sole fact of birth on the territory of the state cofers citizenship on an individual) in all EU Member States except Ireland is indicative of the increasing control of European states over nationality of individuals. By placing residence requirements on alien parents of children born on the territory before such children acquire nationality the State retains a greater degree of control over who acquires its nationality.

7 See J. Torpey and M. Marrus, *The Unwanted: European Refugees in the 20th Century*, OUP: NY, 1985.

8 For some interesting reflections on the legal personality of companies see F. van Hoof, 'International Human Rights Obligations of Companies and Domestic Courts: An Unlikely Combination' in M. Castermans-Holeman, F. van Hoof and J. Smith, *The Role of the National State in the 21st Century, Human Rights, International Organisations and Foreign Policy, Essays in Honour of Peter Baehr*, London/Boston/The Hague: Kluwer Law International, 1998, pp. 135-150.

9 C-81/87 Daily Mail [1988] ECR 5483; the law also regulates the potential for companies to work around it – see the "contournement de l'Etat", B. Badie, *Un monde sans souverainete, Les Etats entre ruse et responsabilite*, Fayard: Paris, 1999.

10 C-81/87 Daily Mail [1988] ECR 5483.

11 See for instance the British Naturalisation Act 1844 section 16 which provided "Any woman married, or who shall be married to a natural-born subject or person naturalised shall be deemed and taken to be herself naturalised, and have all the rights and privileges of a natural-born subject". See L. Fransman, *British Nationality Law*, Butterworths: London, 1998, p. 158.

12 A. Wyatt-Walker, "Globalisation, Corporate Identity and EU Technology Policy", in W. Coleman and G. Underhill, *Regulation and Global Economic Integration*, Routledge: London, 1998, pp. 141-157.

13 "In 1967, the unemployment in all the countries of the Community, with the exception of Italy, had increased fairly rapidly. In Germany and in the Netherlands especially the unemployment level amounted in the beginning of 1968 to well over double that of preceding years, with a peak of 527,000 unemployed in Germany in January 1968", H. ter Heide, "The Free movement of Workers in the Final Phase", in CMLRev 68/69, pp. 466-477.

14 K. Levin, "The Free Movement of Workers", in CLMRev 64/65, pp. 300-325.

15 120 UNTS 71.

16 Parties here means countries which have signed the relevant instrument. Signature/ratification courtesy: where an instrument has been ratified the date of ratification is included. If it has only been signed that date is then included. R. Plender, *Basic Documents on International Migration Law*, 2nd Ed. Martinus Nijhoff, The Hague, 1997.

17 Belgium, 1953; France, 1954; Germany, 1959; Italy, 1952; Netherlands, 1952; Portugal 1978; Spain, 1967; UK, 1951.

18 Austria, 1957; Belgium, 1962; Denmark, 1961; France, 1955; Germany, 1965; Greece, 1965; Ireland, 1966; Italy, 1963; Luxembourg, 1969; Netherlands, 1969; Sweden, 1971; UK, 1969.

[19] The European Social Charter only covers migrants tangentially. Its main concern is the securing of economic and social rights for persons on the territory. All the EU Member States are parties.

[20] Italy, 1966; Portugal, 1981; Spain, 1973.

[21] Italy, 1981; Portugal, 1978; Sweden, 1982.

[22] Belgium, 1978; France, 1983; Germany, 1977; Greece, 1977; Italy, 1995; Luxembourg, 1977; Netherlands, 1983; Portugal, 1979; Spain, 1980; Sweden, 1978.

[23] See M. van Creveld on this point, pp. 357-360.

[24] A right to continued residence was included in the Council of Europe's 1951 Convention on Establishment but the restriction on expulsion, the necessary corollary to make any right of residence indeed durable, was deprived of real teeth because it permitted expulsion on economic grounds.

[25] The UK ceased to be a net emigration country only in the early 1980s; in the Netherlands this took place earlier in the late 1960s.

[26] A 138 (1988).

[27] For a review of the cases see K. Groenendijk, E. Guild and R. Barzilay, *Security of Residence of Long Term Migrants: A Comparative study of law and practice in European countries*, Council of Europe: Strasbourg, 1998.

[28] In a very detailed analysis of the law and practice of migration from the 1950s-1970s published in 1984, S. Castles exemplifies this approach while recognising the element of individual initiative which accompanies state action: for the UK "The British government recruited 90,000 'European Voluntary Workers' (EVWs) from refugee camps and later Italy..." regarding New Commonwealth immigration "Some came as a result of direct recruitment by London Transport or the British Hotels and Restaurants Association, but the majority came in response to the labour demands of British industry" (pp. 41, 42); Belgium: "From 1945 to 1963 it took the form of organised recruitment in what was called the *contingentensysteem*. Workers were recruited through bilateral agreements with Southern European countries...After the *contingentsysteem* was abolished but foreign workers continued to come of their own accord." (p. 47); France: "In 1947 the French government set up the Office National d'Immigration (ONI) to organise recruitment of foreign workers...The impression of a highly organised system of recruitment is misleading. Prior to 1974 policies were pragmatic and unplanned, with various ministries often pursuing contradictory aims. The ONI's monopoly of recruitment of European workers became, more and more a fiction. The proportion of migrants coming as 'clandestines' (on tourist visas or without passports) increased from 26 percent in 1948 to 82 percent in 1968 [sources cited]" (p. 51); the Netherlands (after a consideration of other colonial related forms of labour migration): "The government made a series of bilateral recruitment agreements with Italy (1960), Spain (1961), Portugal (1963), Turkey (1964), Greece (1966), Morocco (1969), Yugoslavia (1970) and Tunisia (1970). The numbers of workers from the recruitment countries (excluding Italy) rose from a few hundred in 1960 to 46,000 in 1966." (p. 58); West Germany: "The state drew on the system set up to utilise foreign labour in the Nazi economy and on the subsequent experience of other Western European countries in devising a highly organised, official recruitment apparatus. The Federal Labour Office...set up recruitment offices in Mediterranean countries. Employers requiring foreign labour had to apply to the BfA and pay a fee. The BfA then selected suitable workers, testing their occupational skills, giving them medical check-ups and screening criminal and political records. The workers were brought in groups to West Germany, where employers had to provide accommodation – usually in wooden huts on the work site. The first bilateral recruitment agreement was made with Italy in 1955." (p. 71). S.

Castles with H. Booth and T. Wallace, *Here for Good, Western Europe's New Ethnic Minorities*, Pluto Press: London and Sydney, 1984. I have discussed this text in some depth as it is a particularly rich and detailed source of information about labour migration patterns in the 1950-1970s. The approach is also particularly rigorous acknowledging the informal sector's involvement in labour migration but stressing the states' responsibility. Similar approaches are to be found in the work of R. Cohen, M. Piore and others publishing in the 1980s on the subject.

[29] See for instance R. de Jongh, *FNV'ers aan het woord over buitenlandse werknemers, Uitgave 16 Centrum voor Onderzoek van Maatschappelijke Tegenstellingen*, Faculteit der Sociale Wteneschappen, Rijksuniversiteit te Leiden, 1984.

[30] Cited in Chris Tilley and Charles Tilley, *Work under Capitalism*, Boulder, CO, 1998, p. 191 and M. Hanagan, ibid.

[31] S. Sassen, "Immigration and Local Labor Markets", in *Economic Sociology of Immigration: Essays in Networks, Ethnicity, and Enterpreneurship*, A. Portes: New York, 1995, pp. 23-24.

[32] And incidentally, the source of the EU/US trade war regarding bananas – a produce which neither EU nor the USA produces in any particular quantities but which clientelist states of each depend upon.

[33] The titles of ministries are not always reliable indicators of the activities of those ministries; nonetheless, among the EU Member States there is a consistent division between ministries of labour which may include social affairs, industry ministries, ministries of interior or home affairs and ministries of justice (or exceptionally in the UK Lord Chancellor's Department). The interests of labour and industry in appearance at least belong to different departments in all Member States. This then suggests at least the possibility of divergent interests and constituencies.

[34] The history of the right to work stretches at least back to the French Revolution where the constitution included such a right. It became an important demand in the 1848 period throughout Europe. In Germany a system to give effect to the state duty to counsel and find employment for workers was in place before WWII. In France the objective of full employment found expression in the 1945 ordonance (4.10) and the creation of the national agency of employment in 1967. M-T. Join-Lambert et al., *Politiques sociales*, 2[e] ed Presses de Sciences Po et Dalloz: Paris, 1997, pp. 207-241.

[35] J. Salt, A. Singleton and J. Hogarth, *Europe's International Migrants: Data Sources, Patterns and Trends*, London: HMSO, 1994.

[36] K. Groenendijk and R. Hampsink, *Temporary Employment of Migrants in Europe*, Reeks, Recht and Samenleving: Nijmegen, 1995.

[37] Kiehl and H Werner, supra, Table 3.2.

[38] Third Country Nationals these figures include all non-nationals, including nationals of other Member States.

[39] D. Gambier and M. Vernieres, *L'emploi en France*, supra, p. 21.

[40] M. Kiehl and H. Werner, *The Labour Market Situation of EU and of Third Country Nationals in the European Union*, n° 32, Institut fur Arbeitsmarkt-und Berufsforschung: Nurnberg, 1998, Table 3.6.

[41] Third Country National: ie national of a country outside the EU.

[42] M. Kiehl and H. Werner, supra, Table 3.15.

[43] Source: M. Kiehl and H. Werner, supra, Table 3.6.

Education Levels 1995 (%)	Low	Average	High
Germany: own nationals	14.0	61.6	24.4
TCNs	46.1	41.8	12.1
France: own nationals	32.3	46.8	20.9
TCNs	64.4	22.8	12.8
Spain: own nationals	63.4	16.8	19.9
TCNs	48.7	18.2	33.0
UK: own nationals	43.2	34.3	22.6
TCNs	62.9	16.0	21.1

[44] K. Groenendijk, E. Guild and R. Barzilay, *The Legal Status of Third Country Nationals who are Long-Term Residents in a Member State of the European Union*, European Commission: Brussels, 2001.

[45] J. Salt and R. Kitching, "Labour Migration and the Work Permit System in the United Kingdom", *International Migration*, 28 (1990) 3: 267-294.

[46] A term which became incorporated into the EU legal framework of labour migration in 1991 with its inclusion in the EC Poland Agreement as a ground for an EU right of movement of workers at the instigation of the (Polish) company. It was included subsequently in all of the agreements with the Central and Eastern European countries, the Baltic states, Slovenia, Russia and the CIS states (though in respect of the CIS states there is no legal right as such to move key personnel – for this purpose Europe stops with Russia). It was also subsequently included in the GATS – part of the third period of labour migration to be discussed in this paper.

[47] J. Salt and R. Kitching, supra.

[48] P. Gulbenkian and T. Badoux (eds), *Immigration Law and Business in Europe*, Chichester: European Immigration Lawyers Group, 1993.

[49] The abuse of asylum in this category is particularly problematic. On the one hand, in numerous states asylum seekers are granted permission to work in periods of low unemployment, which permission is limited in practice if not in law to the low end of the market on account of the precarious nature of their residence, in periods of increased unemployment the right is removed. Increasingly they are accused of being illegitimate "economic" migrants on account of their position in the temporary labour market outside the sanctioned certification schemes.

[50] See special issue *European Journal of Migration and Law*, Spring 2002.

[51] This period is standard only for parts of Europe – excluding some of the new immigration states of Southern Europe – see G. Groenendijk, E. Guild and H. Dogan, supra.

[52] In Decision 1/80 adopted in 1980 under the EC Turkey Association Agreement and which reflected German work permit rules of the time, a requirement is that migrant workers stay with the original employer for three years before a work and residence permit would be issued for him or her to work for another employer; then a sectoral limitation for one year applied and finally the Turkish worker had free access to the labour market after four years; under the preceding measure, Decision 2/76 adopted in 1976, free access to the labour market was delayed until five years of employment either with the same employer or in the final year within the sector.

[53] K. Groenendijk and R. Hampsink, *Temporary Employment of Migrants in Europe*, Reeks, Rechts and Sameleving, n° 10, GNI, Nijmegen, 1995.

54 For an interesting analysis of the trans-national role of lawyers in this transformation see Y. Dezalay, 'Regionalism, Globalisation, and "professional society": between state, law and the market for professional services', in W. Coleman and G. Underhill, *Regionalism and Global Economic Integration*, Routledge: London, 1998, pp. 197-222.

55 Excluding Hungary, Mexico, the Czech Republic and Turkey. As represented in CEPII, *L'economie mondiale 2000*, La Découverte: Paris 1999, p. 84.

56 Wyatt-Wilson supra.

57 Gulbenkian et al. supra.

58 This approach was flagged in the European Commission's White Paper: Growth Competitiveness, Employment: the Challenges and Ways Forward into the 21st Century, Brussels/Luxembourg, 1993 and emphasised in the policies thereafter – see also V. Symes, *Unemployment*, supra, pp. 29 et seq.

59 D. Gambier and M. Vernieres, *L'emploi en France*, La Découverte, Paris, 1998, p. 13.

60 K. Groenendijk and R. Hamsink supra.

61 See vol. 2, issue 2, *European Journal of Migration and Law*, Spring 2000 on social security and migration in particular the contributions by Klaus Sieveking, Paul Minderhoud and Maija Sakslin.

62 A specific measure at European Union level indicates the political accord of the Member States on the exclusion of bottom end migrant workers and the tightening of state control over the definition of legality in order to exclude those categorised as illegal. These are the Resolution on limitations on admission of third country nationals to the Member States for employment (OJ 1996 C 274/3, adopted on 20 June 94) where the position of the Member States is stated to be "At present, however, no Member State is pursuing an active immigration policy. All States have, on the contrary, curtailed the possibility of permanent legal immigration for economic, social and thus political reasons." The year before the Member States had already adopted a Recommendation concerning checks on and expulsion of third country nationals residing or working without authorisation (1-2 June 1993) which recommend the establishment of systems of checks on suspect persons, including those given residence but not work permits, foreign spouses and others and the prompt expulsion of those held to be illegal (or in the case of foreign spouses to have failed to have lived with the sponsoring spouse sufficiently to give rise to a presumption of genuineness of the marriage). A later Resolution requires the introduction of sanctions against employers as well as workers.

63 Though see the work of Didier Bigo, Chapter 2 in this volume regarding the withdrawal of the state from the security sector.

64 W. Kennett, "The European Community and the General Agreement on Trade in Services", in N. Emiliou and D. O'Keeffe, *The European Union and World Trade Law After the GATT Uruguay Round*, John Wiley & Sons: Chichester, 1996, p. 136; N. Mukherjee, "Exporting Labour Services and Market Access Commitments under GATS in the World Trade Organisation", 1996, 30(5), Journal of World Trade, p. 21.

65 B. Stern and N. Hoekman, *Negotiations on Services*, 1987, 10 The World Economy, 1.

66 C-71/76 Theffry [1977] ECR 765; C-19/92 Kraus [1993] ECR 1663; C-106/91 Ramrath [1992] ECR I-3351; C-55/94 Gebhard [1995] ECR I-4165.

67 J. Jackson, *The World Trading System*, 2nd Ed, MIT Press: Cambridge, 1997, p. 309.

68 GATS Article XVII.

69 Posted Workers Directive 96/71.

70 In the GATS framework, service provision includes the concept which in European Community law is called establishment. That is to say where a company sets up a permanent presence in another country and sends personnel for this purpose, this is encompassed in the concept of service provision under GATS.

[71] This of course raises very important questions about the structure of GATS (and indeed the WTO) which gives rights to companies but standing before the dispute resolution mechanism only to states. The structure then requires a very close relationship between companies and ministries. The companies with the greatest interest in the benefits of the WTO are of course those which conduct substantial cross border business. The ministries most interested in the well-being of these companies are inevitably the industry ministries (not least in a Europe where privatisation has occurred over the past 20 years). The creation of substantial companies from what were previously parts of industry ministerial responsibility with individuals in senior positions both within ministries and these companies who both know one another and have worked together and thus knowledge of how to access public services is well understood in this part of the private sector.

[72] This has been confirmed by the Court of Justice in interpreting the right of self employment in these agreements – C-63/99 *Gloszczuk*, C-235/99 *Kondova*, C-257/99 *Barkoci and Malik* all of 27 September 2001, and C-268/99 *Jany* 20 November 2001.

[73] 1.7 percent of persons resident in EEA states (ie the EU 15 plus Iceland, Leichtenstein and Norway) are nationals of other EEA states (Eurostat Migration Statistics 1996, Luxembourg, 1997, p. 28).

[74] Or delegate state control functions to the private security sector.

[75] Protection of domestic jobs for the domestic labour market.

[76] In no Member State has access to social benefits been tied to the willingness or otherwise of the applicant to travel to another Member State to seek employment, though it is tied in most Member States to a willingness to take a job within the Member State itself.

References

Badie, B. (1999), *Un monde sans souverainete, Les Etats entre ruse et responsabilité*, Fayard: Paris.

Castles, S., Booth, H. and Wallace, T. (1984), *Here for Good, Western Europe's New Ethnic Minorities*, Pluto Press: London/Sydney.

CEPII (1999), *L'economie mondiale 2000*, La Découverte: Paris.

De Jongh, R. (1984), 'FNV'ers aan het woord over buitenlandse werknemers', *Centrum voor Onderzoek van Maatschappelijke Tegenstellingen Faculteit der Sociale Wteneschappen*, Rijksuniversiteit te Leiden.

Dezalay, Y. (1998), 'Regionalism, Globalisation, and "Professional Society": Between State, Law and the Market for Professional Services', in Coleman, W. and Underhill, G. (eds), *Regionalism and Global Economic Integration*, Routledge: London, pp. 197-222.

Fransman, L. (1998), *British Nationality Law*, Butterworths: London.

Gambier, D. and Vernieres, M. (1998), *L'emploi en France*, La Découverte: Paris.

Groenendijk, K., Guild, E. and Barzilay, R. (1998), *Security of Residence of Long Term Migrants: A Comparative Study of Law and Practice in European Countries*, Council of Europe: Strasbourg.

Groenendijk, K., Guild, E. and Barzilay, R. (2001), *The Legal Status of Third Country Nationals Who Are Long-Term Residents in a Member State of the European Union*, European Commission: Brussels.

Groenendijk, K. and Hampsink, R. (1995), 'Temporary Employment of Migrants in Europe', *Reeks, Recht and Samenleving*, GNI: Nijmegen.

Gulbenkian, P. and Badoux, T. (1993), *Immigration Law and Business in Europe*, European Immigration Lawyers Group: Chichester.

Hanagan, M. (1998), 'Labor History and the New Migration History: A Review Essay', *International Labor and Working Class History*, n° 54, Fall 1998, pp. 57-79.

Jackson, J. (1997), *The World Trading System*, MIT Press: Cambridge.

Join-Lambert, M.-T. et al. (1997), *Politiques sociales*, Presses de Sciences Po et Dalloz: Paris.

Kennett, W. (1996), 'The European Community and the General Agreement on Trade in Services', in Emiliou, N. and O'Keeffe, D. (eds), *The European Union and World Trade Law After the GATT Uruguay Round*, John Wiley & Sons: Chichester.

Kiehl, M. and Werner, H. (1998), 'The Labour Market Situation of EU and of Third Country Nationals in the European Union', *Institut fur Arbeitsmarkt-und Berufsforschung, Nurnberg*, n° 32, IAB Labour Market Research Topics: Nurnberg.

Levin, K., 'The Free Movement of Workers', *CLMRev*, n° 64/65, pp. 300-325.

Mukherjee, N. (1996), 'Exporting Labour Services and Market Access Commitments under GATS in the World Trade Organisation', *Journal of World Trade*, n° 30.5, p. 20-41.

Plender, R. (1997), *Basic Documents on International Migration Law*, Martinus Nijhoff: The Hague.

Salt, J. and Kitching, R. (1990), 'Labour Migration and the Work Permit System in the United Kingdom', *International Migration*, vol. 28, n° 3, September, pp. 267-294.

Salt, J., Singleton, A. and Hogarth, J. (1994), *Europe's International Migrants: Data Sources, Patterns and Trends*, HMSO: London.

Sassen, S. (1995), 'Immigration and Local Labor Markets', in Portes, A. (ed.), *Economic Sociology of Immigration: Essays in Networks, Ethnicity, and Enterpreneurship*, Russell Sage: New York, pp. 23-24.

Stern, B. and Hoekman, N. (1987), 'Negotiations on Services', *The World Economy*, n° 10.

Strange, S. (1996), *Retreat of the State: The Diffusion of Power in the World Economy*, Cambridge University Press: Cambridge.

Tilley, C. and Tilley, C. (1998), *Work under Capitalism*, Westview: Boulder, CO.

Torpey, J. (2000), *The Invention of The Passport Surveillance, Citizenship and the State*, OUP: Cambridge.

Torpey, J. and Marrus, M. (1985), *The Unwanted: European Refugees in the 20th Century*, OUP: NY.

van Hoof, F. (1998), 'International Human Rights Obligations of Companies and Domestic Courts: An Unlikely Combination', in Castermans-Holeman, M., van Hoof, F. and Smith, J. (eds) *The Role of the National State in the 21st Century, Human Rights, International Organisations and Foreign Policy, Essays in Honour of Peter Baehr*, Kluwer Law International: London/Boston/The Hague, pp. 135-150.

Wyatt-Walker, A. (1998), 'Globalisation, Corporate Identity and EU Technology Policy', in Coleman, W. and Underhill, G. (eds), *Regulation and Global Economic Integration*. Routledge: London, pp. 141-157.

Chapter 4

Where Does the State Actually Start? The Contemporary Governance of Work and Migration*

John Crowley

Introduction

What is the connection between "frontiers" and "immigration control"? At first glance, this is a rather silly question. After all, immigration, as entry into a country by a non-resident for the purpose of residence, obviously involves crossing frontiers or borders. Furthermore, a presumptively very tight connection is at the heart of current debate about immigration, which is regarded as a risk or pressure to be controlled by reducing the permeability of the border – or perhaps an opportunity to be mobilised by selectively modifying the permeability of the border. The "problem" of immigration, in other words, may seem to be illegal immigration, defined as the clandestine or otherwise fraudulent crossing of borders, and the solution more effective control, whether defined to restrict or selectively to promote movement of people. Conversely, progressive contributors to immigration debates are concerned to promote various interpretations of "free movement of people", which self-evidently involves, among other things, increased permeability of borders. The idea of a world "without borders" is widely considered attractive.[1]

At second glance, however, things are considerably more complicated. At least in the conventional territorial sense, borders do not *in fact* have a privileged position in either immigration politics or immigration policy, and furthermore that there are strong *theoretical* reasons not to expect them to. The purpose of this chapter is to look into both the facts of the matter and the underlying theoretical issues, describing in particular some of the mechanisms and sites of control that do not relate to the border at all. As shall be seen, welfare is of special interest in this respect. It is no coincidence that welfare issues are of considerable significance in contemporary migration debates: indeed, it is precisely as, among other things, *welfare states* that contemporary states are confronted with migration. Furthermore, the new forms of the penal or "carceral" state are themselves closely related both to welfare – of the retrenchment of which they may even very directly be the "dark side"[2] – and to the control of borders against migrants who are often *prima facie* suspect as "scroungers", traffickers or terrorists.

Yet, as shall be seen, the borders at stake are institutional as much as territorial. Access to welfare benefits is primarily related to *residence* – a legal connection between a person and a jurisdiction, which is in turn connected, but not reducible, to a territory. The existence in many countries, for the administrative and legal purposes of welfare adjudication, of a superficially contradictory notion of "illegal residence" undoubtedly complicates this picture: any attempt to conceive of radically deterritorialised jurisdiction comes up against barriers that are both practical and deeply embedded in the historically and institutionally structured *imaginaire* of statehood. Arguably, such barriers also point to a genuine and profound – albeit complex – *conceptual* connection between statehood and territoriality. Nonetheless, even illegal residence is demonstrably irreducible to a mere legal ratification of presence in physical space. On the contrary, the relevant criteria are explicitly and inherently *social*. The space occupied by the illegal resident claiming welfare benefits (in a broad sense, since access to public schooling is typically the most important practical issue) has rather more than three dimensions, of which the specifically non-physical ones tend to be the least significant. It is in this sense that immigration, and the borders that its control brings into play, reveal important and characteristic features of the contemporary state as such, and specifically underline the complexity, and in some respects the indeterminacy, of its territoriality.[3]

Immigration and Border Control

To question the connection between immigration and borders is not to deny that there is one. Indeed, immigration, as a sub-category of migration in general, has an inherent territorial dimension. Perhaps one might reserve the phrase "migration" for forms of movement in physical space that are set within a broader class of "mobility" which may not involve physical movement at all. With this in mind, the considerations in the following section underline the extent to which social space has dimensions irreducible to physical space, as revealed by such a straightforward notion as "social mobility" (e.g. between classes). Nonetheless, however convenient this kind of lexical clarification might seem, it is, in this case, profoundly misleading. For both legal and social purposes, immigration is *not* primarily a matter of territorial mobility – not, I might add, for subtle theoretical reasons, but as a fairly crude fact of ordinary usage. Both legal and statistical categories make a clear distinction between visitors and immigrants (who may be further subdivided into "temporary" and "permanent"). The criterion is change of *residence* – for a period of at least 12 months, for the purposes of the International Passenger Survey – which is not a strictly territorial notion. Of course, residence is a legal qualification of a certain kind of territorial status, but even permanent presence within the territory of a state cannot be equated with residence in it. The point is too familiar to be laboured, but it is worth noting that "illegal residents" are just one instance of a category that also includes, for example, such "legal non-residents" as diplomats and international civil servants. Furthermore, the law distinguishes for many purposes between kinds of residence, which derive from different kinds of connections between a legal person and a jurisdiction. It follows, again, that no jurisdiction can be exhaustively defined by territoriality. Conflicts of laws with respect to matters such as marriage and inheritance are thus typically resolved with reference to connections which, like "domicile" in English law, are in principle entirely independent from physical presence within a particular territory. To immigrate, in other words, is to attain a certain kind of status with respect both to a *society* and to a *jurisdiction*, which are related to a territory but not exhaustively defined by it.

It follows quite logically that the *politics* of immigration are not mainly about crossing territorial borders. No doubt xenophobia in the strict and literal sense has something to do with hostility to immigration; the "civilisational" bias summarised by the word "Islamophobia" typically expresses itself in suspicion of or even contempt towards Muslim societies – meaning, of course, societies predominantly composed of Muslims and *presumed* to be characterised primarily by Islam – as well as towards European Muslims. Nonetheless, the wide range of evidence about people's prejudices and the kinds of demands actually expressed in immigration politics suggests a rather more complicated picture.

Concern seems to focus on the *place* immigrants occupy within society rather than their mere *presence*. Of course, even to distinguish immigrants as a group and to relate them to "us" – whereas, for most other purposes, "we" do not constitute a reference group at all – is to take for granted a conception of national unity and homogeneity that is, in a minimal sense, xenophobic. Its character is indeed shown when it is formulated explicitly by politicians who affirm the constitutive mixture of, say, England or France to be "homogeneous", and any new form of mixture to be a solvent. But, typically, the more explicit the statement, the less plausible it seems, even to those who share the general sentiment.[4] It is because it is destabilised by being made explicit that common-sense xenophobia can be regarded as minimal. What is at stake in ordinary hostility to immigration is rather what immigrants are presumed to do: "to take the bread from our mouths", as well as "our" jobs and "our" daughters; to profit from a welfare system not designed for "them"; to behave as if it were "their" country; and furthermore to be supported in all of these deplorable activities by elites more sensitive to political correctness than to the needs of "their own" people, and who have in any case lost the capacity to control national borders. Undoubtedly, there is a circular relationship at work here, and historical and comparative evidence is not conclusive as to the relative significance of the various causal components. Nonetheless, it does seem true that highly marginalised migrant groups suffer *less* direct hostility (which is not to trivialise the necessary complicity of ordinary people in their marginalisation, or the "structural violence", in a fairly strict sense, that it involves), and conversely that racism tends to be positively correlated with structural integration and cultural assimilation, at least at a certain stage.[5] Without attempting here to offer a survey of the evidence, comparison of the timing of immigration politics in the UK and France provides some useful pointers. Partly for legal reasons (the peculiarities of post-1948 Commonwealth citizenship), partly because of the social geography of housing and employment, immigrants to the UK were structurally integrated at an earlier stage in the migratory process than in France; the UK also experienced significant political hostility to immigration from the second half of the 1950s. No doubt the existence in the UK of a strongly racialised official discourse was a facilitating factor, but it does not appear to have been decisive. Quite similar anti-immigrant sentiments and mobilisations appeared in France after migrants were structurally integrated by the shanty-town (*bidonvilles*) clearance programmes of the early 1970s and by the effects of nationality law on their French-born children.

Contemporary racism, in other words, operates most significantly among fellow citizens, and is superimposed on xenophobia only in specific contexts, often post-colonial, where migration patterns structured in dominance are themselves isomorphic with internal social processes. Islamophobia in countries such as the UK and France clearly exemplifies this configuration, since it implicitly relates the emergence of militant Islam in Europe with its political significance in, say, Pakistan or Algeria. This empirical connection is, of course, of enormous practical importance, but it should not be mistaken for a *conceptual* link.

It follows, most importantly for my purposes in this chapter, that shifting relations between "presence" and "place" as modes of social existence – to use words that are still very vague – are crucial for understanding changing patterns of migratory and post-migratory processes. Structural integration is not a timeless concept, but one that needs to be sensitive to the nature of the relevant social structures. It so happens that they have changed profoundly, notably in Western Europe, over the past two or three decades – in other words precisely the period of adaptation both to the long-term implications of post-war labour migration and to the new migratory patterns that have developed since labour migration was "ended". A number of major shifts are important in this respect, including chronic unemployment and the erosion of major public institutions such as the education system. The one I should like to focus on here, however, is the welfare system, which has been affected in the last 20 years or so, in most countries, by two superficially contradictory trends that have combined to raise its political profile. On the one hand, coverage has generally expanded, particularly in so-called "Bismarckian" systems within which the inherent limits of the employment-based "male breadwinner" model became apparent from the 1970s. As a result, a wide range of non-contributory income support benefits have emerged to respond to the needs of people excluded by standard contributory benefits. At more or less the same time however, and partly as a consequence of the same pressures, the legitimacy of the non-contributory and more redistributive aspects of most welfare systems has been challenged, financial constraints have become central to the dynamics of reform, and benefits have been made increasingly conditional. The two trends taken together produce a kind of "scissors" movement that places many immigrants in a vulnerable position: structurally included by institutional principles that are simultaneously normatively suspect. It follows that the kind of structural integration relevant for these purposes is *societal* and *institutional*. It is played out as much in welfare access procedures as in border control in the strict sense. As discussed in more detail in the final section, it can be meaningfully mapped only in a complex, multi-dimensional social space.

Unsurprisingly, in the context of these general political dynamics, immigration *policy* is not mainly about the control of territorial borders either. The

European Union offers a particularly interesting case in this respect, since aspects of the rhetoric of European integration explicitly refer to the "abolition of internal borders" as a desirable objective, and, for those countries that are signatories to the Schengen convention, abolition of passport controls at internal border crossings is regarded as a significant first step in that direction. Yet even a cursory study of the language and institutional processes shows that abolition of borders is misnomer.[6] While the Schengen system is closely linked to the development of new forms of freedom of movement – deliberately promoted as such and not restricted to EU nationals – it is also symmetrically concerned with new forms of immigration control.

The significance of these changes tends to be underestimated, presumably because free movement for "OECD nationals" (not a legal term but one that nonetheless conveniently summarises what is actually at stake) is not really politically controversial.[7] Yet they severely limit the relevance of the border as a control point for a potentially very large volume of movement, involving business travel and tourism as well as entry for settlement. Indeed the removal of visa requirements for settlement makes this distinction arbitrary as far as EU nationals are concerned. Borders are not just control points, of course, but also dividing lines between jurisdictions, and at this level too European trends are eroding their significance, albeit slowly and incompletely. Still, harmonisation of social, and to a lesser extent political, rights is more than just a set of technical changes. Furthermore, the reconfiguration of borders between European states cannot be interpreted simply as a displacement to the external border of the EU – although such may be the logic of Schengen in some respects. A degree of differential freedom of movement is extended by the absence of visa requirements for business and tourism to privileged third-country nationals – although the distinction between visitors and settlers is maintained in this case. And of course movement of people, although it is the primary focus of this chapter, is only one aspect of the border. From the point of view of the character of the contemporary state, movement of goods, services and capital is equally significant.

The reduced significance of the border is however not simply a consequence of freer movement of people. It is rather that differential freedom of movement creates new logics of control that for practical, institutional reasons are located elsewhere. The border in its conventional territorial configuration is thus eroded relatively – and not just absolutely – as a site of control. In so far as clandestine border crossing is of comparatively limited significance in the broader pattern of illegal migration, tighter controls on migration generally and the high political profile of illegal migration (at least in countries like France where until 1974 illegal migration was not an anomaly but a supposedly efficient system) inevitably shift the spotlight away from the border. Some of the alternative sites are external: consulates and airline check-in desks, in particular. Others are internal. In principle, the whole territory could be a site of control by spot identity checks, although in practice the process tends to be highly differentiated, focusing on a combination of target groups and target areas. Furthermore, identity checks are also to be conducted at sites not directly connected to immigration control (such as the gateways to welfare benefits), and indeed are often more systematic in such cases – although the effectiveness of controls is limited by restrictions on exchanges of information between state agencies governed by concerns about civil liberties. Furthermore, even to the extent that the border remains the juridical point of control, it increasingly becomes "control at" rather than "control of". In other words, precisely because restrictive immigration policies are associated with enhanced freedom of movement, the border is differentiated and selective. Thus in airports, which for logistical reasons tend to exhibit these tendencies in unusually pure form, passengers are increasingly "sorted" by destination, provenance and legal status (and to a lesser extent by class of travel or "frequent-flyer" status) for the purposes of control.

Some aspects of the processes that have just been sketched in very broad outline are peculiar to Europe – i.e. primarily to relations between EU member states and to a lesser extent to relations between the EU as such and the rest of the world. However, the contention of this chapter is that the reconfiguration of borders, and their subsumption in a broader field of border and boundary processes, has a wider significance. On the one hand, as noted earlier, it is misleading to regard the control of access to territory as being the most important aspect of concern about immigration, even in xenophobic discourse. On the other hand, features of the contemporary state that have little to do with territory lead to new forms of boundary control. For instance, the gateways that control access to social rights via the labour market or welfare mechanisms are by their very nature multiple, shifting and heterogeneous. Furthermore, while such mechanisms of control are often designed at least in part with restrictive immigration policies in mind – and to that extent are inseparable from border controls in the narrow sense – this is accidental: the logic of localised boundary control is in fact an essential feature of any administrative construction of rights. Even when not "about" immigration, therefore, they nonetheless impact powerfully on immigrants. Their effects, however, extend far beyond foreign legal or illegal residents to constitute a defining feature of contemporary governance and of perceptions of statehood and nationhood.

Dimensions of Statehood

To suggest that the theory of the state is less than adequately developed is, in light of the extensive literature devoted to the subject, rather odd. What is meant is that, outside specialist circles, statehood tends to be reduced to a kind of shorthand based on a rather uncritical summary of the classics (Max Weber in particular), which is either endorsed, or more frequently now rejected. The superficially straightforward question what to make of the contemporary features of the legal-political entities that go under the name of "states" – taking full account of the set of ideas that make the name supposedly meaningful – has been surprisingly neglected. If nothing fundamental had changed since the "sociogenesis" of the state – to borrow the vocabulary of Norbert Elias – this would not be very serious. But clearly the presumption must be precisely the opposite: that statehood has been profoundly transformed in the course of the 20th century. And if the presumption were to be rejected, this would require detailed conceptual and empirical analysis.

All this is, of course, trivial in the international relations context, where critique of
the Westphalian paradigm is commonplace. Surprisingly, there has been less
critical interest in the internal political sociology of the state. It is impossible
within the compass of this chapter to offer anything more than a very brief sketch
of the issues raised, but in light of the empirical points made earlier about
migration, welfare and territoriality, it is nonetheless useful to stress the limitations
of common sense, with particular reference to the supposedly canonical Weberian
definition.[8]

Simplifying very crudely, there are two standard approaches to the state, as a
historical, ideological and institutional construct, that are of relevance here. In one,
the state is characterised by political sovereignty, viz. the exclusive entitlement to
enact *laws*, understood as authoritative pronouncements obedience to which is
unconditional. The entitlement and its exclusivity are the key features. A tyranny
based on arbitrary rule does not thereby dissolve the sovereign state, so long as it
recognises no limits to its authority and is regarded, not necessarily universally, as
authoritative. To refer to this feature as *political* sovereignty is to add something to
the familiar purely legal perspective on sovereignty as authority that is general
(covering all matters), universal (applying to all within the jurisdiction) and
absolute (subject to no external authorisation). The authority that needs to be
understood here is legal in form, but political in origin. Those who claim
successfully to speak for the state, in other words, derive authority from the claim
because the state in turn represents something beyond its immediate institutional
manifestations: in a democracy, the people, to which it relates symbiotically; in
other regimes a range of supposed legitimising principles from the real movement
of history to race. The problem, notoriously, is that the political and legal
dimensions of the state are here juxtaposed rather than integrated. The relation
between them cannot be purely logical, but has an historical and sociological
character. The ability of persons or institutions successfully to claim a certain kind
of authority derives from their success in other areas: in imposing their power and
forging a language that makes such claims possible. It follows, first, that the
establishment of a point of origin for a supposedly sovereign order is itself a claim
that cannot be logically self-authorising. Secondly, history spills over into
sociology: because sovereignty has no logical origin, and because it presupposes
historically constituted patterns of belief and institutional behaviour, it has no
capacity *internally* to reproduce itself. As Foucault provocatively put it,
summarising this historicist line of argument against legalistic interpretations of
sovereignty, "politics is the continuation of war by other means".[9] In addition, even
in so far as legal-political sovereignty offers a valid description of certain
characteristic features of the orders we call states – given the prevalence and
historical stability of their constitutive beliefs – it cannot claim to be exhaustive.
Much that states do is unrelated to sovereignty, or derives from it only tangentially.
When states negotiate with powerful corporate interests, conduct public-health
campaigns using advertising techniques, and use various technical market-based
instruments to steer the economy, they are not acting as "sovereign" in any useful
sense of the word. Yet much of what contemporary states routinely do is, precisely,
either non-authoritative or non-legal, or both. This was the point of Foucault"s

notion of "governmentality", which he counterposed to legal statehood, and resurfaces under a different guise, but with similar analytical implications, in the currently fashionable notion of "governance".

The other standard approach to statehood is designed to respond to the conceptual and empirical limitations of the legal paradigm. Generally derived from Max Weber, the sociological analysis of the state characterises it by a political project: the monopoly of legitimate violence within a particular territory. An organised group that successfully executes the project is a state. The advantage is obvious. The project inherently has a history, and furthermore it is reversible. The definition also usefully accounts for important aspects of the real history of real states, which were established by the use of force against both external and internal competitors. Nonetheless, the Weberian definition remains disappointingly thin, axiomatically rather than analytically territorial, and more closely connected than might initially appear to the legal notion of sovereignty. The enactment of law ultimately determines the limits of legitimate violence, and conversely the monopoly of violence ultimately underwrites the unconditionality of obedience to law. The traditional notion of sovereignty, in other words, is logically implied by Weber's connection between legitimacy and the monopoly of violence. And indeed it is clear from his other writings, especially on bureaucracy, that Weber regarded the *legal* form as characteristic of the modern state. What is thin here is the historical perspective. At least in its Western European versions, the sociogenesis of the state undoubtedly reflects the liberation of monarchical or oligarchical power from feudalism on the one hand (the power of the "overmighty subject"), and from the limits imposed by religion or custom on the other. And in view of the military technology by which that liberation was accomplished, it is understandable that the modern state arose as a profoundly territorial institution. With regard to the contemporary state, however, such a picture of sociogenesis – essentially complete in the early 19th century in most of Europe – seems to leave out too much of vital importance. Gellner suggests plausibly that the monopoly of education is an essential feature of the modern state, and one could equally add taxation (crucially important in Elias's analysis of the medieval origins of the modern French and English states but often neglected) and welfare, as well as all the other functions – referred to earlier – that do not really fit within the sovereign-legal paradigm at all.

It follows that the undoubted *historical* connection between the monopolisation of violence and territorialisation has a far weaker *conceptual* basis than is generally admitted. As early as the 19th century, colonial expansion (which was an issue for most European states, although they were unevenly successful) seriously complicated the relation between sovereignty, territory, legitimacy and military capacity. Subsequently, changing military technology modified the significance of territory, partly as a direct consequence of aviation and guided missiles, partly and in many ways more importantly as a consequence of the transformation of military structures and mindsets that technology gradually induced. As in the 18th and early 19th centuries, the military in Europe and North America increasingly perform important internal-security functions, but the reason is not the absence of civilian law-enforcement, nor is the focus primarily territorial.[10] Terrorism merely exacerbates these features. Colonial expansion was in turn connected to capitalist development, which reshaped the state in its own right as mercantilism was superseded. Deleuze and Guattari no doubt overstate the case in making capitalism inherently deterritorialised, largely because they attribute to territoriality an unwarranted primeval or chthonic character, supposedly related to the "full organless body".[11] Nonetheless, the basic point, following Marx and Engels in the *Communist Manifesto*, that the "flows" of capitalism exceed any "encoding" remains entirely cogent.

The functions and processes of what the previous paragraphs might suggest calling the "welfare – colonial – education – tax – development – hygienist state" (the whole point of the enumeration being its rather haphazard nature) are thus set within the ostensible framework of the juridical sovereign state, but in fact profoundly transform its character. It is striking that this insight is common, from strictly opposite ends of the political spectrum, to Michael Oakeshott and Michel Foucault. The latter's familiar contrast between sovereignty and "governmentality" shares many descriptive features with the former's conception, largely ignored in social theory, of a characteristically modern "managerial state" (also called *"universitas"* and the "servile state").[12] In both cases, what is supposedly distinctive about this kind of political order is that it purports to mould its subjects by the terms of a collective project and implies a "pastoral" relation between ruler and ruled. Of course, Oakeshott's contrast is, unlike Foucault's, normative. The idea of a *res publica* ruled by *lex*, which derives from Oakeshott's reading of Hobbes (who, "precisely because he is an absolutist, is not an authoritarian"), serves as a standard by which the "servile" nature of the "managerial state" is to be assessed. Foucault, on the other hand, is unconcerned by any such assessment, and in so far as he implies a normative judgement is dismissive of juridical sovereignty as expressed in his, rather different, reading of Hobbes. Conversely, Foucault is preoccupied with the place of violence within political order, and therefore analytically respectful towards the historical and racial undercurrent he claims to have unearthed in the political theories of the classical age, whereas Oakeshott is largely unconcerned with the question. Nonetheless, however important, these distinctions should not obscure the fact that both theorists regard very similar features of the political orders of the late twentieth century as incompatible with juridical conceptions of statehood premised on territorial monopolies of violence.

In analytical terms, what is most importantly at stake is the relation of the state to the society of which it is, in legal terms, the regulator. Sovereignty in its pure form stands outside the polity and applies to it: the Hobbesian sovereign, we might remember, is not a party to the social contract. In the governmental or managerial state, on the other hand, the very idea of a "polity" is eroded: what appears in its place is a *society*, which is shaped by the state and in turn transforms it. The word "society" is *not*, it should be stressed, being used here as an equivalent of "human collectivity": rather as the name of a characteristically modern kind of human collectivity thought of in a characteristically modern kind of way – in a word, as the subject matter of "sociology". Hegel stood on the cusp of this epochal transformation. He believed that the state and civil society – as he borrowed and adapted the phrase from the 18th century thinkers of, in particular, the Scottish

Enlightenment – could be kept apart, despite their mutual and dialectical dependency, and therefore that what was most valuable in each could be simultaneously preserved. The conceptual price, however, as critics from Marx onwards have stressed, was a high one. The latent contradiction between civil society – conceived primarily in economic terms – and the state – conceived primarily in legal, bureaucratic and political terms – could be subsumed only within a neo-feudal *Stände* structure that seemed dialectically back-to-front. Seen from the aftermath of the revolutions of 1848 and the emergence of the "social question", the contradiction appeared insoluble except by the fusion of the state and civil society as, precisely, *society*.[13] The functions most characteristic of the contemporary state thus erode its *neatness* conceptually, institutionally and territorially. It starts at the point where its distinctive capacity – sovereignty, expressed in the utterance of self-authorising commands – begins to operate.[14] But *where* that point is remains an open question.

Territoriality and Social Space

Contemporary states enjoy, following the argument of the previous section, a symbiotic relation with *societies*, which profoundly shapes their character, to the point that the juridical trappings of sovereignty and territory are no longer adequate summaries of what they are essentially about. It is not strictly true that a state starts where its society starts. Societies, especially in so far as they are shaped by the economy, are not reducible to the states that structure and nurture them as self-conscious collectivities. Pending the hypothetical emergence of a global society endowed with the kind of institutional and imaginative basis that the Durkheimian tradition knows as "organic solidarity", the societies we are faced with, and within which the legal, political and ethical questions of immigration are raised, are "state societies", but not "of" or "owned by" the state. Nonetheless, the edges of societies – to use a deliberately vague word that encompasses the ideas of borders, boundaries, and frontiers – are also, in important respects, the edges of states.

An understanding of the nature of social space is therefore essential to clarification of the spatiality or territoriality of statehood. And, irrespective of any normative claim about the obsolescence of the nation-state, it is a *descriptive* feature of complex, highly institutionalised societies that their spatial organisation is institutional, technological, and symbolic, rather than territorial in the three-dimensional sense. Just as societies and states spill over their territorial borders, so conversely do they exhibit considerable topological complexity inside those borders. There is thus far more to be said about where the state "starts" than may appear at first sight. To make sense of it requires more detailed theoretical consideration of the nature of borders, boundaries, and frontiers.

Borders, boundaries, and frontiers are discontinuities in space.[15] On either side of them, things that might otherwise seem similar operate differently. Conversely, in their absence, things change continuously. Borders, boundaries, and frontiers exist in being *drawn*. No doubt some discontinuities are inscribed objectively in the nature of the phenomena they are used to describe – the distinction between an acid and a base, say, or between water in its liquid and solid phases. But even then it is significant that they *are* used to describe. It is not a feature of the phenomena themselves that they should be judged relevant to some actual or hypothetical observer. Furthermore, trivially, many discontinuities, especially in social space, are a consequence of a distinction rather than a reason for its existence. It follows that there are as many possible borders, boundaries, and frontiers as there are purposes calling for discontinuities. Some of these purposes are contingent and transitory, and there is therefore no reason to expect social patterns of discontinuity to be stable. Conversely, to the extent that they do in fact appear to be stable, such stability points to the need to understand the processes by which they are reproduced. And, of course, purposes may not be shared, so that discontinuities may need to be enforced in the face not just of random accidental violation, but also of deliberate trespass and fundamental transgression.

Other important consequences flow from consideration of what "space" means for present purposes. We tend to think of social borders, boundaries, and frontiers in terms of territory, both because we associate space with physical space and because many discontinuities observably are territorially inscribed. Movement from one area of physical space to another is, in such cases, constrained by walls and other barriers, or by impassable voids, or again by coercive technologies that are not themselves territorially ostentatious. Invisible lines that cannot be crossed, even for purely psychological reasons (in so far as these have a cultural and therefore collective character), are as significant in shaping social space as barbed wire and truncheons. In more abstract terms, the dimensions of social space correspond to structured sets of positions between which movement is both possible and susceptible of being impeded. There is, no doubt, nothing conceptually incoherent or practically absurd about the idea of state borders consti-tuting rigid, impermeable boundaries neatly dividing distinct and (at least in many important respects) uniform spaces on either side. Similarly, impermeable borders may rely on an empty buffer zone – one that socially, if not legally, is quite literally "no man's land". Both historical and contemporary examples of such borders are easy to find. Nonetheless, many regions, including Western Europe and North America, currently exhibit a tendency away from such impermeable borders. In Europe, in particular, the climate of European integration has encouraged (relative) demilitarisation and, more recently, its direct legal effects have removed or sharply circumscribed some of the purposes for which linear borders have traditionally been used (e.g. control of persons and goods). The idea, equally old and venerable, of border areas as zones of contact and exchange rather than as points of division has undoubted contemporary relevance.

This is not the whole story, however. Border *processes* as a whole have been reshaped rather than weakened. In Europe, economic integration has contributed to these changes, in particular by promoting increasingly differential controls on movement of persons and goods.[16] However, this shift is also made possible and encouraged by technological changes. Flows of persons or goods are physical: they can be mapped on to territory and involve expenditure of energy roughly proportionate to distance for any given mode of transport. In addition, they are naturally continuous in physical space: an object moving from A to B occupies, however briefly, each point on a path from A to B. Not all flows have this character. The movement of information, for instance, which obviously has growing contemporary significance, does not inherently require expenditure of energy proportionate to distance. Nor is it in any real sense continuous. While its physical carrier (e.g. electromagnetic waves) moves through physical space in the conventional sense, it conveys information only in the framework of a technologically determined sender-receiver system. The Internet is a well-known and important example of this, since its design is such that information transfer has no necessary connection to any particular physical pattern of signal transmission. Most financial flows involve information in this sense, and as a consequence territorial controls are of limited relevance to them. This does not mean, as is sometimes suggested, that they are impossible to control – rather that they demand non-territorial conceptions of jurisdiction and non-territorial intervention techniques. These are familiar, and not necessarily innovative in any way. Exchange controls, for instance, mainly involve procedures embedded in the routine operation of the banking system.

These features are not peculiar to information, but also characterise many current technologies for the transport of persons and goods. However, while the fact is very familiar, its significance is not always appreciated. Travelling by air, one occasionally passes almost precisely over some place where, other things being equal, one might wish to "drop in". But the image is a give-away. Although the place in question may be only a few thousand metres away, the effective social distance is infinite. The "drop" is impossible in practice, and life-threatening in principle. Hence the (trivial) fact that one of the most important external borders of France is embedded in the architecture of Charles-de-Gaulle airport. Nor is air travel inherently special in this respect. Gravity is undoubtedly part of the problem, but socially embedded technology is equally important. Thus, it is no less impossible, and for exactly the same reasons, to alight from a high-speed train at a unscheduled stop. As a consequence, the land border between France and the UK runs, in certain respects, through the middle of the Gare du Nord in Paris (although, unlike at the airport, it is not embedded in the architecture: it is materialised in a glass partition that stands out very visibly as a recent addition). And even more individual and flexible modes of transport, such as the motor car, share some of these features, as anyone who has missed a motorway exit will have noticed. Both the cultural and the technological features of modern travel tend to enhance its discontinuous character, as a kind of socially empty space between starting point and destination. Cultural conservatives, of course, will retort that such "travel", being entirely circumscribed by its "destination", hardly counts as travel at all.[17] What is important for present purposes, however, is simply that discontinuous flows require, if they are to be controlled at all, territorially indeterminate borders. Someone wishing to work out where one enters a contemporary state such as France cannot do so simply by looking at a map – not, at least, the familiar kind of two-dimensional map framed by physical geography that one finds in an atlas.

This analysis of the physical issues raised by migration needs to be complemented by a closer look at the social space to which migrants seek access. To be present in a territory is largely meaningless if one lacks the opportunity to work (legally or illegally), access to some kind of housing, enjoyment of the basic social entitlements that define "full membership" in the Marshallian sense, and so on. The situation of territorial presence and social absence is unusual in its pure form – which would, as Etienne Balibar suggests, be tantamount to a kind of apartheid[18] – but aspects of it, with respect to welfare in particular, are of massive significance for millions of foreign "quasi-residents" of the countries of Europe and North America. It is not simply a play on words to suggest that such "quasi-residence" places people in an ambiguous position with respect to society and the state, at once inside and outside. Of course, this position is often the result of the legal regulation of immigration and residence, and therefore an aspect of border control in the strictly territorial sense. But this is only a part of the story, and in some ways not the most interesting one. The processes that exclude people from certain structurally significant areas of state societies nominally shaped by citizenship are no less important, no less destructive, and no less normatively problematic, when they operate by reference to categories other than nationality or residence status.[19] If the idea of a symbiotic relation between state and society is taken seriously, then the borders we should be concerned with are those of inclusion, of membership, or of what it is useful to call – precisely because the term is so loaded and ambiguous – *belonging*.

Immigration, Welfare, and the Politics of Belonging

For present purposes, the "politics of belonging" is a generic expression to refer to the whole complex of processes by which multidimensional boundary maintenance differentially impacts immigrants and minorities, and thereby reveals the character of the "state society"/"societal state" itself.[20]

A helpful image in this respect is, I think, that of the queue for access to some place of entertainment such a nightclub, where the positional quality of admittance and the potentially arbitrary character of gatekeeping are crucially important. It is both a metaphor for, and an interesting example of, broader processes of discrimination. First of all, the bouncer has a social function that far exceeds his job. No doubt nightclub access is a positional good, but randomness is only one feature of the bouncer's filtering function, and probably not the most important. The probability of being turned away is invariably concentrated on a few specific social groups – the ones who are collectively regarded as "troublemakers", and each member of which is therefore held to be responsible for the behaviour of any individual. These groups exhibit, in detail, a wide variety of definitions. Where the clubowners' and bouncers' "local knowledge" is fine-grained enough, the blacklist may target specific housing estates, schools, gangs or even families. Nevertheless, in broad outline, the nightclub pariahs belong invariably, in each European country, to those groups habitually targeted by political xenophobia. They are in other words the children or grandchildren of immigrants who, for whatever reason, were generally regarded as unwelcome, and suspicion of whom extends to their descendants.

This kind of thing is important in two ways. Firstly, it is illustrative of the social dynamics of discrimination and, in particular, of its simultaneous symbolic and material impact and of its irreducibility to prejudice. Secondly, differential access to the club fits a pattern that can be observed in a wide variety of social processes. Membership of the nightclub is bogus: it is a fiction invented to make discrimination seem reasonable, and indeed lawful in many countries. Its social analogues are, of course, more tangible. To be a national of a country, for example, does confer certain benefits that genuinely distinguish nationals from non-nationals, such as immunity from deportation and full voting rights. Similarly, membership of the "social welfare club" – eligibility for certain benefits on account of nationality, age, residence, contributions, need or whatever – is really a condition of access to such benefits. But the conditions are necessary, not sufficient. In the terms of our parable, they are equivalent to permission to stand in the queue. They do not imply guaranteed access. On the contrary, as with the nightclub, there are a set of formal criteria that are public and can in principle be evaluated impartially, but there is also one supplementary informal criterion, which is in a sense public knowledge but cannot by its very nature be judged impartially, and which is at the discretion of the gatekeeper: whether one is a "troublemaker", whether one's face fits, in a word whether one *belongs*. In fact, *any* institutional procedure necessarily involves gatekeepers with at least some discretionary power.

Not to belong is to be constantly vulnerable to the accusation of *trespass* – even when in legalistic terms it is utterly groundless. Unlike formal membership (of which nationality is a convenient and important illustration), the processes of access exemplified by the nightclub queue, being inherently discretionary, cannot be reduced to something that neatly either exists or does not. Furthermore, the process is important in itself and not solely in its results, or more accurately it is inextricably tangled up with its results. The natural counterpoint of informal, fluid, vague, discretionary criteria for access is differential *suspicion*.[21] Some people's right to be in a place is challenged – they are trespassers until proved otherwise – whereas others are *prima facie* welcome. Such suspicion, even when it does not prevent access, may affect its meaning. In addition, if the level of humiliation is viewed as disproportionate to the benefits at stake, suspicion may in itself thin the queue, undermining ostensibly equal rights without the discrepancy really being apparent. The study of such informal criteria of belonging, and of the effects of their implementation, has a very wide application, which, as the nightclub example shows, is by no means limited to the state.

In more general terms, a queue is *always* a technique of flow management, but it is *equally*, inseparably, an opportunity for selective admittance, a border crossing, a point where the difference between "inside" and "outside" is ostentatiously established. Similarly, the bouncer's position shows that applying rules is *always* a process constrained by time and space, and never simply an algorithm itself reducible in principle to a rule. The point can obviously be generalised to any kind of selection process. The more exhaustively fair is the procedure for determining eligibility, the more understandably restless is the queue. "Understandably", because it is literally impossible to be fair to everyone: time is one of the resources being implicitly but very effectively allocated (assuming that positions in the queue are morally arbitrary: otherwise the issue of fairness is simply pushed back to an earlier selection procedure.) In other words, once selection has been established in principle and institutionally framed, it is very often impossible for it to be "fair" in any but the crudest sense. The general issue to which the nightclub parable points is therefore the concrete microsocial processes of resource allocation, in the broadest sense, leaving open their consistency with the various official discourses (including, but not limited to, those of the legal and administrative order) that frame them.

The desire to turn the spotlight on such processes is hardly original. In particular, it clearly overlaps to a considerable extent with established interest in various aspects of inequality or disadvantage as suffered specifically by migrant or minority groups, and in particular with the more indirect and institutional aspects of discrimination. There is, however, an important additional angle, i.e. that there is no reason to locate the production of normative frameworks regarding the demands of justice as they affect migrants and minorities exclusively in the field of discursive politics. Undoubtedly, these are relevant and important. But, often quite independently, selection procedures themselves thus become a kind of self-referential norm that is never made explicit, still less justified, but nonetheless determines both the social meaning of resources (anything from legal residence to unemployment benefit) and their factual distribution. Non-compliance with the "rules of the game" – which combine formal procedures with a wide range of background knowledge – once designated as such by gatekeepers whose *bona fides* may be unquestionable, leads to a lethal combination of shoddy service and technical ineligibility.

Of particular importance in this respect is welfare, which is in all West European societies a privileged site for the reconfiguration of membership, belonging and their relations through challenges to established procedures for defining entitlements. In this sense, it is a constitutive dimension of the state – which is, precisely, regarded as a *welfare state* – and to that extent access to it is access to the state. Precisely because "immigration" is not necessarily at the centre of debates about the current difficulties and necessary reform of the welfare state (although the "immigrant", especially if "illegal", does undoubtedly tend to be the paradigmatic "scrounger"), the connection has not always been made. Of course, xenophobic discourse in all countries seeks to blame migrants for funding deficits, but this has had little effect on policy. Perhaps the most important contemporary development, notably but not uniquely in the US and the UK, is the revival of distinctions between the "deserving" and "undeserving" poor that had virtually lapsed into obsolescence – an issue entirely separate from migration. The postnational paradigm in particular tends to focus on welfare rights as being unambiguously positive in terms of migrants' social membership, which takes for granted the procedures that give the abstract rights tangible content.

Yet a closer look at the way in which the welfare state actually works suggests that, as in the case of other administrative procedures for the allocation of resources and rights, processes of differential inclusion and exclusion are necessarily embedded in it for reasons that are not reducible to the possibly xenophobic prejudices inscribed in law or brought to their desk by the employees. The bureaucratic implementation of welfare necessarily involves distinctions based on criteria of eligibility implemented under pressure of time, as well as discretion in handling difficult cases. Almost regardless of their content, both these features will affect both practically and symbolically those claimants who are most vulnerable by marking them as targets for official suspicion – possibly making rights that are in principle entrenched effectively meaningless. There is indeed abundant research suggesting that welfare take-up is often lower than average among those who most need it, even when they are technically eligible. From this point of view, challenges to the welfare rights of immigrants or minority groups tend to reveal in amplified form what is going on generally.

For instance, all countries have rules restricting certain benefits to permanent residents, which is understandable (though not of course unexceptionable) both on abstract grounds of fairness and because abuses – so-called "benefit tourism" – do exist. What, however, do such rules actually mean? They mean two things which, combined, produce a much more complex picture. (1) All claimants are required to prove residence, in ways that may be arbitrary and difficult to comply with. There is therefore an unacknowledged "fast track" for those whose situations conform to bureaucratic preconceptions of *prima facie* eligibility. Whether such preconceptions reproduce socially normative stereotypes is almost irrelevant here: the technical dynamics are the same. (2) Some claimants, who are regarded *prima facie* as suspicious, for whatever rational or irrational reason, are told that their (officially sanctioned) proof is inadequate, and that they must provide more. The obvious problem that such rules create is that illegal residents, who may be made such by the operation of law rather than any fraud on their part, are excluded from benefits that, on grounds on fairness, should be theirs. Less obvious, but in some ways far more important precisely because it seems to lie beyond the confines of normative analysis, is that translating the rules into a bureaucratically streamlined algorithm (something that, for the reasons sketched earlier, can in fact never function as such) inevitably causes significant inequalities between claimants. More generally, the whole climate of financial crisis has highlighted fraud, which is recognised to be widespread even by those who are not sanctimonious about it. But the technical efficiency of a "clampdown" requires it to be targeted, and differential suspicion has major substantive consequences.

Furthermore, rules are inevitably norms – even if not intended to be. *De facto*, any welfare system defines, for instance, certain family relationships, gender roles, etc., as normal, and gives the definition teeth by making certain benefits conditional on compliance with it. The definition may be very flexible, but it cannot by its very nature be universally permissive – and in practice, of course, what it excludes tends to be culturally specific. The extent to which the welfare state is accidentally, but nonetheless coercively, assimilative is an important subject that has hitherto been inadequately researched. Indeed, even when rules are explicitly based on norms, the *implicit* norms that derive from their administrative implementation may be very different. For instance, the paradoxical effect of traditional forms of targeted welfare that, for any set of norms, they may promote "deviance" (in relation to those norms) is now recognised well beyond the confines of the utilitarian or moralistic variants of the New Right.

In T. H. Marshall's influential analysis, citizenship is equivalent to full and equal membership in society. Welfare rights are regarded as central in this respect, enriching the content and extending the scope of citizenship by mitigating the conflict in market welfare societies between equality of status and inequality of resources. This is true and important as far as it goes. However, Marshall's failure to distinguish clearly between the *reasons for* and the *effects of* the welfare state, as contributing to enhanced citizenship, can no longer be regarded as adequate – especially if, following the line of the previous paragraph, one entertains the possibility that actual procedures might make the reasons and the effects mutually opaque.[22] In addition, and for the purposes of this chapter more importantly, to be a member of a group and to enjoy the full benefits of membership is to be *recognised* as such, not simply, and perhaps not mainly, because recognition is a good in itself, but more fundamentally because its absence tends to erode technical entitlements and turn formal equality into a sham.

In certain contexts, the issue of recognition may be public and political, or even quasi-legal, and the boundaries that it draws symbolic speech-acts. This, however, is unusual. Boundaries are drawn in a complex, shifting social space structured by various kinds of "policing" operations that, as in the case of the welfare state, create distinctions and restrictions on mobility as much as they implement them. They simultaneously reflect views on what is right and proper – or rather derive from the dynamic interaction of such views, which are never consensual. Belonging is a property associated with these boundaries, which means that there are in principle as many forms and places of belonging as there are forms and places of social differentiation. In practice, of course, some boundaries matter more than others, and many overlap to a considerable extent. The nation-state is, in effect, a multipurpose overlap of effective and significant boundaries, in the two-fold sense that it offers a normative framework within which such overlap (of territory, political community, cultural community, ...) is desirable; and that the historical implementation of the framework has produced situations where, roughly speaking, such overlap exists.

This is why immigration looms so large in the politics of belonging – and *vice versa*; and also why the politics of immigration tend to correlate, as experience in all European countries suggests, with other boundary challenges, such as European integration or globalisation. Formally, anti-immigrant discourse tends to be characterised by a commitment to *neat* boundaries, and therefore also to a world that continues to make an established kind of sense. Conversely, immigration has the potential genuinely to erode or to blur such boundaries, especially when territorial welfare rights (and other forms of enhanced social control) raise the stakes of national belonging. This means that migration and postmigratory processes are among other things *epistemological* challenges – which is perhaps why they are so prone to evoke violent responses involving the symbolic redrawing of boundaries in physical space, or even on the human body.[23] A slightly different way of saying essentially the same thing is that the "dirty work" of boundary maintenance is necessarily performed *on* the boundary, and therefore usually in practice by those living on or near it (this is not necessarily a location in physical space), for whom the risk of ending up on the wrong side is agonizingly tangible – although the cognitive work may well be done elsewhere. This provides the link between the general considerations on belonging sketched here and the familiar political sociology of xenophobia and racism. However, boundaries are by no means exclusively of concern to xenophobes and racists. In fact, the xenophobic version of traditional "neat" boundaries has a curious parallel in anti-xenophobic attempts to draw alternative neat, albeit more partial, boundaries elsewhere (based on rights, or revitalised citizenship, or cosmopolitanism, or constitutional patriotism, or whatever). The analysis sketched here suggests that things are more irreducibly messy than either camp is prepared to accept.

Asking where the state actually starts is thus a roundabout but useful way of pointing to the limits of a juridical-territorial conception that we take too much for granted. It is correct as far as it goes to say that the state starts at the limits of its legal sovereignty, which are territorial as a first approximation. But if we take the analysis a step further such an answer is either tautological (is the state a defined *a priori* as a territory subject to sovereign jurisdiction) or false. If we consider the institutions in which the powers deriving from sovereignty are vested, scrutiny of what they actually do raises quite different questions. The state "starts" at a large number of points where access to the privileges it can grant – which may generically be called membership or belonging – is controlled, and most of these points are tangled up with social representations and processes that are not directly produced by the state and that impact on immigration without being directly connected to it. In contemporary governance, jurisdiction is just one aspect, not necessarily even the most important, of the state.

Notes

* An early version of this chapter was presented, under a slightly different title, at the 1998 Conference of the International Studies Association in Minneapolis.

1 The phrase is particularly resonant in French: *"sans frontières"*, which occurs particularly in the name of the humanitarian medical organisation *Médecins sans frontières*, and a range of parallel NGOs inspired by similar ideals. Unfortunately, it also conjures up – for readers of a certain generation – memories of the defunct multinational television game *Jeux sans frontières*, broadcast in the UK under the characteristically less idealistic title *It's a Knockout*.

2 See, in polemical vein, Loïc Wacquant, *Les prisons de la misère*, Paris: Éd. Raisons d'agir, 1999.

3 For a broader development of the themes sketched here, see Mathias Albert, David Jacobson and Yosef Lapid (eds), *Identities, Borders, Orders. Rethinking International Relations Theory*, Minneapolis: University of Minnesota Press, 2001.

4 Short, of course, of explicit racism, which remains significant in all European countries – especially, perhaps, in the UK. From a racist perspective, the historical mixture of populations can be portrayed with internal plausibility as not a mixture at all: because all the people involved were "white".

5 Whether a further stage of vanishing racism in a context of full integration and assimilation should be postulated is very much an open question: first because the evidence is limited and inconclusive, even in the United States; and secondly because the terms are themselves vulnerable to criticism. "Stages" of development imply a single point of migration into an otherwise closed system, whereas the real situation is a complex web of ongoing migratory relations that cannot be neatly cordoned off from

"internal" social dynamics. In addition, all developmental schemes are now justifiably regarded with suspicion because their analytical and normative components are notoriously difficult to disentangle. For some further consideration in the special case of political participation, see John Crowley, "The political participation of ethnic minorities", *International Political Science Review*, 22(1), 2001: pp. 99-121.

6   The following paragraphs borrow from John Crowley, "Differential free movement and the sociology of the 'internal border'", in Elspeth Guild and Carol Harlow (eds), *Implementing Amsterdam. Immigration and Asylum Rights in EC Law*, Oxford: Hart, 2001, pp. 13-33.

7   With some interesting exceptions, usually involving the acquisition of second homes. The emphasis on this issue is a striking illustration of the kinds of "presence" that are actually at stake here. While it may seem trivial, it is worth noting that Denmark successfully insisted on a Declaration appended to the Maastricht Treaty exempting it from general anti-discrimination provisions with respect to German-owned holiday homes, and that the same point has been prominent in negotiations over Polish accession.

8   A full treatment of these issues would require distinctions between national academic traditions that are not possible within the compass of this chapter. Specifically, the Weber-Elias paradigm of statehood is dominant in France in a way that is not exemplified in the English-language literature, within which, indeed, the notion of "the state" receives less attention. For some considerations on similar lines with respect to English-language political theory, see Chris Brown, "Borders and identity in international political theory", in Albert, Jacobson and Lapid, *Identities, Borders, Orders*, pp. 117-136.

9   Michel Foucault, *Il faut défendre la société. Cours au Collège de France. 1976*, Paris: Gallimard/Seuil, 1997.

10 Didier Bigo, "The Möbius ribbon of internal and external security(ies)", in Albert, Jacobson and Lapid, *Identities, Borders, Orders*, pp. 91-116.

11 Gilles Deleuze and Félix Guattari, *L'anti-Œdipe. Capitalisme et schizophrénie*, Paris: Éditions de Minuit, 1973, pp. 163-324.

12 Michael Oakeshott, "On the character of a modern European state", in *On Human Conduct*, Oxford: Oxford University Press, 1975, pp. 185-326.

13 The classic statement of this thesis is Jacques Donzelot, *L'invention du social. Essai sur le déclin des passions politiques*, Paris: Fayard, 1984.

14 The very narrow phrasing of this claim is deliberate. The state, understood in a slightly different sense as a quasi-agent that exists to the extent that identifiable actors successfully claim to speak for it and derive tangible resources from such success, may also exert *influence*, and such influence may extend far beyond its territorial borders. But nothing there is distinctive about either the state in general or the contemporary situation. What is important is rather the extent to which even sovereignty is demonstrably non-territorial in certain respects.

15 This section adapts material first published in John Crowley, "Locating Europe", in Elspeth Guild, Cees Gronedijk and Paul Miderhoud (eds), *In Search of Europe's Borders*, Dordrecht: Kluwer, 2002. For a complementary analysis from a geographical perspective, see David Newman, "Boundaries, borders, and barriers: changing geographic perspectives on territorial lines", in Albert, Jacobson and Lapid, *Identities, Borders, Orders*, pp. 137-151.

16 For more detailed discussion, see Crowley, "Differential free movement".

17 For a humorous development of these themes, see David Lodge's novel *Paradise News*.

18 Etienne Balibar, *Nous, citoyens d'Europe? Les frontières, l'État, le peuple*, Paris: La Découverte, 2001.

[19] For a similar approach to citizenship as a "bordering mechanism", see Martin Heisler, "Now and then, here and there", in Albert, Jacobson and Lapid, *Identities, Borders, Orders*, pp. 225-247.

[20] The following paragraphs draw heavily on John Crowley, "The politics of belonging: some theoretical considerations", in Adrian Favell and Andrew Geddes (eds), *The Politics of Belonging. Migrants and Minorities in Contemporary Europe*, Aldershot, Ashgate, 1999, pp. 15-41. Use of the word "belonging" as shorthand operates here in essentially the same way as the "IBO triangle" as deployed by the contributors to Albert, Jcaobson and Lapid, *Identities, Borders, Orders*.

[21] See further Crowley, "Differential free movement".

[22] I have discussed the limitations of Marshall's approach in more detail in "The national dimension of citizenship in T. H. Marshall", *Citizenship Studies*, 2(2), 1998, pp. 165-178.

[23] Arjun Appadurai, "Dead certainty: ethnic violence in the era of globalisation", *Public Culture*, 10 (1998): pp. 225-247.

References

Albert, M., Jacobson, D. and Lapid, Y. (2001), *Identities, Borders, Orders. Rethinking International Relations Theory*, University of Minnesota Press: Minneapolis.

Appadurai, A. (1998), 'Dead Certainty: Ethnic Violence in the Era of Globalisation', Public Culture, vol. 10, n° 2, Winter, pp. 225-247.

Balibar, E. (2001), *Nous, citoyens d'Europe? Les frontières, l'État, le peuple*, La Découverte: Paris.

Bigo, D. (2001), 'The Möbius Ribbon of Internal and External Security', in Albert, M., Jacobson, D. and Lapid, Y. (eds), *Identities, Borders, Orders*, University of Minnesota Press: Minneapolis, pp. 91-116.

Brown, C. (2001), 'Borders and Identity in International Political Theory', in Albert, M., Jacobson, D. and Lapid, Y. (eds), *Identities, Borders, Orders*, University of Minnesota Press: Minneapolis, pp. 117-136.

Crowley, J. (1998), 'The National Dimension of Citizenship', in T. H. Marshall (ed.), *Citizenship Studies*, pp. 165-178.

Crowley, J. (1999), 'The Politics of Belonging: Some Theoretical Considerations', in Favell, A. and Geddes, A. (eds), *The Politics of Belonging. Migrants and Minorities in Contemporary Europe*, Ashgate: Aldershot, pp. 15-41.

Crowley, J. (2001a), 'Differential Free Movement and the Sociology of the "Internal Border"', in Guild, E. and Harlow, C. (eds), *Implementing Amsterdam. Immigration and Asylum Rights in EC Law*, Hart: Oxford, pp. 13-33.

Crowley, J. (2001b), 'The Political Participation of Ethnic Minorities', *International Political Science Review*, vol. 22, n° 1, January, pp. 99-121.

Crowley, J. (2002), 'Locating Europe', in Guild, E., Gronedijk, C. and Miderhoud, P. (eds), *In Search of Europe's Borders*, Kluwer: Dordrecht.

Deleuze, G. and Guattari, F. (1973), *L'anti-Œdipe. Capitalisme et schizophrénie*, Éditions de Minuit: Paris.

Donzelot, J. (1984), *L'invention du social. Essai sur le déclin des passions politiques*, Fayard: Paris.

Foucault, M. (1997), 'Il faut défendre la société', *Cours au Collège de France*, 1976, Gallimard/Seuil: Paris.

Heisler, M. (2001), 'Now and then, here and there', in Albert, M., Jacobson, D. and Lapid, Y. (eds), *Identities, Borders, Orders*, University of Minnesota Press: Minneapolis, pp. 225-247.

Newman, D. (2001), 'Boundaries, borders, and barriers: changing geographic perspectives on territorial lines', in Albert, M., Jacobson, D. and Lapid, Y. (eds), *Identities, Borders, Orders*, University of Minnesota Press: Minneapolis, pp. 137-151.

Oakeshott, M. (1975), *On the Character of a Modern European State, On Human Conduct*, Oxford University Press: Oxford, pp. 185-326.

Wacquant, L. (1999), *Les prisons de la misère*, Raisons d'agir: Paris.

Chapter 5

Looking at Migrants as Enemies

Anastassia Tsoukala[1]

The last decades of the 20th century have been marked by many changes, such as the construction of the European Union, the creation of the Schengen space, the end of the Cold War, the globalisation process and the strengthening of transnational migratory movements, which unsettled the political and financial institutions as well as the ideologies and values of the European societies and led them to redefine themselves, as political entities, and to modify their external and internal policies accordingly. At the same time, these changes shook the very bases of the hitherto established conceptual and institutional order and accelerated the exclusion of certain social strata, thus contributing to the emergence of many anxieties and irrational fears within European populations. As, for obvious reasons, it is not possible here to fully analyse the impact of these changes, we shall limit ourselves to retaining only the fact that this impact has both real and symbolic aspects. Indeed, these changes not only provoked profound institutional reforms and revealed new financial and economic strategies, but also led to the weakening of national identities and to the calling into question of sovereignty. This weakening of the classic sovereign state, which can be observed in various fields, such as the creation of supranational bodies, the gradual establishment of a global economy, the abolition of national borders and the national currencies removal, has brought the borders issue into the heart of the European political debate and, consequently, the topic of the cross-border movement of persons, the liberalisation of which has been rapidly subject to restrictions, due to the fact that it has been considered potentially dangerous for EU internal security.

All European immigration policies have been developed according to these recent changes. They are thus presently characterised by the constant reinforcement of border controls, the hardening of the conditions of entry as well as of the deportation measures, the weakening of the legal status of asylum seekers and the establishment of immigration controls well before and after the border line, exerted, in the first case, by the introduction of new criteria as regards visa issuing, by the imposition of penalties on carriers transporting illegal migrants and by the reinforcement of co-operation with third countries, and, in the second case, by the extension of identity checks inside the territory of EU countries.

Although they are increasingly homogeneous, insofar as they are dominated by a securitarian reasoning, these immigration policies include several contradictions. The first of them becomes obvious when we note the divergence between the official statements on the security agencies' capacity to make borders "impermeable" and the number of illegal migrants present on the national territory of EU countries, which contradicts the official image of the efficiency of the border controls. Contrary to the generally accepted ideas, this situation results neither from the structural faults of the border controls nor from the incompetence of security agents involved in them. It results, above all, from the incoherence and the ambivalence of the very discourse on the need to adopt compensatory measures to the "security deficit" that would be provoked by the abolition of internal border controls within the EU. Resting mainly on myths and concealing many economic and political stakes, this discourse led to rather inefficient control measures, either because they were seeking to reconcile contradictory interests, or because they could not become efficient without jeopardising the democratic values specific to European host countries and, in a pragmatic way, without involving an exorbitant economic cost. Moreover, the efficiency of border controls in the fight against illegal immigration is all the more limited as, apart from the countries situated at the periphery of the EU, in most EU countries illegal immigration is no longer a problem of illegal entry but a problem of illegal prolongation of an initially legal residence.

Several contradictions are also observed in the economic and cultural arguments of this securitarian discourse. Indeed, as it is articulated around the threat that illegal immigration represents to the economy of the EU countries, it overlooks the fact that the arrival of this cheap and easily exploitable manpower allows or, at least, has allowed for many years the carrying out of some desirable short-term economic objectives, such as the decrease in production costs, the survival or even the growth of many enterprises and the rise in exports. This complex economic function of immigration has often been taken into consideration by the politicians, as is clearly shown by the fact that the repression of illegal migrants does not always go together with that of the principals, even if the latter are frequently at the source of illegal migrant trafficking. Besides, it should be reminded that the repression of the clandestine employment, in general, remains until now fairly weak in most EU countries and hardly corresponds to the genuine extent of the problem.

Moreover, the transformation of immigration into a threat to the EU societies has provoked confusions between legal and illegal migrants and/or between foreigners and nationals of ethnic or religious membership other than the one dominant in a given country, having thus created a climate of suspicion which aims indistinctly at all "foreigners". The impact of the social construction of this threatening figure of the migrant is so strong that it marginalises any argument pointing in the opposite direction. So, this securitarian discourse overlooks the contribution of migrants to the demographic rise in the host countries and the important role that legal migrants can play in regard to the survival of current welfare systems, threatened by the constant ageing of EU populations. It also omits to put forward the fact that EU societies themselves are nothing more than the result of multiple cross-breedings and that their civilisation is deeply marked, sometimes even determined by the contributions of migrants.

All these contradictions are simply revealing the multiplicity of issues underlying the elaboration and implementation of the present European immigration policies, which, in turn, reflect the multiplicity of the aspects of the migratory phenomenon. How can we explain, then, the predominance of a reducing, or even simplifying approach, flattening migration on the model of a multiform threat to EU internal security? Are there any mechanisms set up in order to allow the establishment and the diffusion of a migratory threat concept and to ensure its acceptance by the majority of the EU populations? In this case, we can no longer study the border controls issue and the role played in the matter by civil and military security agencies by dissociating them from the dominant discourse, which, owing to its declaratory aspect, has involved a genuine securitisation of immigration.[2]

In order to answer these questions, this chapter will first look at the process of the transformation of immigration into a "social problem", by analysing in particular the role played in the matter by politicians and security agencies. Then, this chapter will examine how migrants have been turned into "social enemies", by stressing the reasons and the criteria of this transformation. Lastly, the process of the social construction of the "migratory threat" will be examined by focusing on its formation and on the processes followed to this end.[3] The first two parts will try to cover all EU countries, while the last one will focus on two Southern European countries, Italy and Greece, where the migratory phenomenon appeared essentially in the 1990s, in order to observe the development of the processes from their very beginning.

The Problematisation of Immigration

The fact that European immigration policies are nowadays more and more influenced by a securitarian reasoning, presented as the most appropriate reaction to the seriousness of the migratory threat, should not be dissociated from the increasing politicisation of the immigration issue in Europe, which has placed it in the heart of the political debate throughout the 1990s. While complying with reasoning specific to the functioning of any political market, this politicisation reflects also the modification of the perception of the immigration in EU societies, since the late 1980s. Indeed, as these societies dropped their rather benevolent attitude towards migrants, which had prevailed all over the post-war period of growth, and radically changed their perception of them, migrants ended up being transformed into a serious threat to the internal security and well-being of the host societies.

Observed mainly at the symbolic level, this perception of migrants as bearers of multiple social threats rests on some categories of rhetoric arguments, which, formulated more and more openly by politicians, officials and the media, are articulated around three main principles: a) a socio-economic principle, according to which immigration is primarily associated with the rise in unemployment, the development of the parallel economy, the Welfare State crisis and the urban environment deterioration; b) a securitarian principle, according to which the rise in immigration is connected with many security problems, from petty to organised crime and from urban insecurity to fundamentalist terrorism; c) an identity principle, according to which migratory movements are threatening the demographic balance and the identity of the EU societies.[4] Immigration is thus set up as the source or, at least, an aggravating factor of the main contemporary social problems, justifying in this way the implementation of any measure presented as likely to handle what is currently regarded as a major social problem for the years to come.

If we admit, however, the principle that a social problem is not a verifiable entity but a construction serving ideological interests and that, consequently, its explanation should be integrated into a social construction process,[5] we notice that the immigration issue has been, above all, a major political issue. Indeed, the analysis of the political discourses held in Europe in the 1980s and 1990s shows clearly that racist and xenophobic discourses, as well as those related to the efficiency of border controls, played a very important role in electoral games, since it was around them that, by identification or by opposition, the electoral policies of the major political parties revolved.[6] Therefore, it seems plausible to affirm that the present politicisation of the immigration issue is reflecting primarily the adoption of political strategies mobilising the electorate on a racist and, consequently, on an ideologically opposed basis.

The politicians Such political strategies are in keeping with a fundamental element of the functioning of any political market, where the search of consensus constitutes one of the most effective means to achieve the top priority of politicians, i.e. the increase in their own power and in that of their party. In this respect, the choice of immigration as an electoral earning contribution ground can be judicious for several reasons. First, since immigration is one of the themes that occupy the political scene in a recurring or cyclic way, it does not necessarily require the adoption of innovating policies. Consequently, it can be the subject of pre-existent measures, which either have been already implemented towards migrants, or consist of a transposition of measures hitherto implemented in the fight against various criminal phenomena.

Furthermore, the immigration theme can easily occupy the front of the political scene, for more or less long periods, because of the breadth and the variety of the issues that are related to it, as well as of the impassioned debates that it can provoke within a given society. Such a focus on only one theme enables politicians to divert the attention of their electorate from the serious, complex and probably conflict-generating socio-political issues usually prevailing in their society and to obtain thus their temporary marginalisation, or even neutralisation.[7]

Lastly, as the electorate has always been concerned about immigration at a rather symbolic level, it can be widely satisfied by the adoption of symbolic measures, which are limited to simple declarations of intent, or lead to the adoption of measures hardly or not at all implemented, or give rise to genuinely implemented measures the efficiency of which remains however limited. Knowing that legislating is the supreme affirmation of the public action, politicians are entirely aware that "the promulgation of laws promising to solve or to reduce problems, even if everything indicates that they will not be successful, can be very efficient to quieting down dissatisfied people and to conferring legitimacy on the established authorities".[8] In this respect, it should be noticed that the possibility of satisfying the electorate through symbolic measures is all the more important as politicians are usually called on finding solutions to serious social problems, which involve hard conflicts of interests and, sometimes, disturbing and unpopular reforms. It should be stressed that, owing to its complexity, immigration is indeed on the point of becoming a subject likely to legitimate the established authorities since, generally speaking, the more the authorities get engaged into issues remote from everyday life, the less the public is able to grasp the motivations and the consequences of their decisions and, consequently, the more it tends to accept official interpretations as accurate.[9]

The security agencies However, the present problematisation of immigration and its subsequent securitisation cannot be ascribable only to the functioning of the political market because the politicians' actions overlap with those of public security agents, even if the latter follow a different reasoning, so that these two types of action end up being mutually reinforced.

The existence of a certain link between the transformation of a phenomenon into a "social problem" and the concern of some public security agents to preserve, or even to improve and to promote their functions, their careers and the budgets of their services has been often highlighted by many scholars.[10] Here, we should just specify that this need for constant reinforcement of the position of public security agencies, due essentially to power and influence struggles among the various agencies charged with the protection of internal security (national police forces, police forces having military status, customs, intelligence services, consulates, industries producing equipment for such institutions, etc.), does not result in the invention of entirely false problems. Observed primarily at the definition and hierarchical classification of the threats level, the influence of these agencies in the process of problematisation of a phenomenon appears through the proposed interpretations of it, which, profiting from the inherent ambiguity of most internal security issues, focus on the negative aspects of the phenomenon. Generally, this type of interpretation rests on two distinct processes, consisting respectively in the amplification of the "threatening effects" of a phenomenon and in the presentation of hypothetical threats as really imminent. As soon as these interpretations are stated, they acquire a particular force due precisely to the privileged position of those who have stated them, because, as these individuals are considered to be internal security experts, they "are invested of an established knowledge on threats and of a panoply of various technologies in order to cope with them".[11] Thus, although it has never been proved, the hypothesis that the free movement of persons within the EU would inevitably lead to a serious security deficit has been presented as an undeniable obviousness, thus causing the creation of the Schengen space, the functioning of which severely restricts the principle of the free movement of persons, established by the Single European Act. The credibility of the security agents' statements is so powerful that it is not really challenged even when their hypotheses/certainties are proved false. Thus, after the end of the Cold War, the prevision of the EU "invasion" by migrants coming from the Eastern European countries has been presented so firmly as accurate that it justified the reinforcement of border controls throughout the first half of the 1990s. The observation that, finally, this "invasion" never took place did not weaken the credibility of these discourses which, focused on the migratory threat concept, have simply modified its origin, by shifting it mainly towards the African and Middle Eastern countries, in order to justify the constant reinforcement of immigration controls.

Already observed in the handling of many criminal phenomena, from organised crime to urban violence, the influence exerted by the security agencies on the process of construction of the migratory threat is not at all unusual. What is new, in this case, is the fact that the implementation of internal security policies requires more and more often the assistance of the Army. It should be specified, however, that the increasing participation of the military forces in internal security missions, as from the 1990s, results from two different reasons. First, it is a more or less foreseeable consequence of the amplification process of the migratory threat and/or the threats related to various criminal phenomena (organised crime, terrorism, drug trafficking, urban violence, football hooliganism, etc.), which rendered the public responses to these phenomena more and more securitarian. But, this request for increased securitisation on the part of civil authorities could not have been satisfied if it had not corresponded with one of the new objectives of the Armed Forces which, after the end of the Cold War, were looking for new missions, likely to ensure the preservation of their budgets and of their manpower. In the absence of external cnemies, the Armed Forces started to convert themselves to internal security missions, in order to handle the new threats to the EU security, which were represented mainly by criminals involved in organised crime and by migrants.

The securitisation of immigration seems to be then "the effect of a field where no actor is the sole master of the game, but where the resources of each one in terms of know-how and technology are determining for the economy of the classification struggles as regards the way to hierarchise the threats",[12] and where the needs for reinforcing the politicians' and security agencies' respective powers converge in order to reduce the multiple dimensions of immigration to a single network of securitarian significance,[13] focused on the "new migratory threats".

The Transformation of Migrants into Social Enemies

The reasons Does this focusing on the migratory threat mean that we witness a new process of construction of social enemies? Even if it is not possible yet to answer this question, it seems more and more obvious that the public discourses held in most EU countries throughout the 1990s take up again the classic pattern of the social construction of internal enemies, already observed, for instance, during the persecutions of Jews in Europe, or during the "hunting for Communists" under McCarthy.

This transformation of migrants into social enemies seems, in the first place, to be closely linked to the rise of irrational anxieties and fears within European populations which, under the effect, on the one hand, of the construction of new supranational political entities, such as the EU, and, on the other hand, of the decline of ideologies and of the globalisation process, lost most of their previous certainties and reference points, while witnessing the rapid deterioration of their standard of living, or even the socio-economic exclusion of entire sections of their society. We notice indeed that the threats imputed to the migrants are related, above all, to the demographic stability, the cultural homogeneity, the internal security, the employment and the quality of the urban life of the EU citizens, reflecting thus the impact of the aforementioned changes on the EU societies. The link between the transformation of immigration into a "social problem" and socio-economic crises has been confirmed by many researches, conducted both in Europe and in the United States, which show that the anti-immigrant feelings emerge, according to the case, when the citizens of a country worry about the state of their national economy and think that immigration will be harmful to employment,[14] when they fear a future social decline,[15] or when they associate immigration with the themes of sovereignty, of integrity of borders, or of the transgression of the law.[16]

Therefore, it is not at all astonishing that migrants became the catalyst of all social conflicts and claims of the 1990s. Living in societies crossed by major identity crises, migrants constitute the ideal public enemy for all "identity" claims. Thus, according to nationalists, they sap the cohesion of the host societies, while, in the opinion of the supporters of regional or local patriotism, they alienate the ethnic purity of the native population. According to the supporters of urban values, they are criminals who threaten the everyday life security and deteriorate irrevocably the urban environment, while, in the opinion of the supporters of class values, they are "parasites" which jeopardise the working class conquests.[17] Lastly, according to the supporters of the Welfare State values, they are swindlers who abusively take advantage of the social security benefits usually destined to nationals.

Nevertheless, the spread of these perceptions would probably be less important if this reversal of the migrants' image did not coincide with a progressive modification of the very functionality of immigration in the EU economies since the end of the 20th century. In the current globalisation context of post-industrial societies, immigration corresponds less and less to the needs of the economic growth of the EU societies. As a matter of fact, this growth is nowadays characterised by a low demand in manpower and by a new deployment of the production process according to flexible criteria, manifested par excellence by the shifting of production to several Eastern European and third world countries. In this respect, immigration would be even harmful for EU economies, for it would be likely to reduce the availability of manpower in the emigration countries.[18]

These remarks should not, however, conceal the fact that the transformation of migrants into social enemies is not only a reaction to international or supranational events. This transformation seems to satisfy, at the same time, many needs which, situated at different social levels, are inherent to the functioning of any society.

At a collective level, the fact of turning migrants into social enemies enables the community to be defined and to recognise itself as such, by simple opposition to the figure of the foreigner. Therefore, the transformation of migrants into genuine scapegoats of our contemporary societies could also constitute a strategy for reaffirming the identity of the nation state, insofar as the exclusion of the foreigners involves the inclusion of the natives,[19] the perception of the migratory threat serving then as a factor of reinforcing the internal cohesion of the community.[20] Far from being static, this reinforcement can even involve the enlargement of the constitutive elements of a collective identity. Thus, putting forward an alleged *law and order* culture in Italy, practically non-existent before the 1990s, endows the national identity discourse with a new aspect, the transgression of the law by foreigners justifying therefore *ipso facto* their exclusion from the community.[21]

At the political market level, as we have already pointed out, the evocation of a threatening enemy allows politicians to obtain the desired consensus, by reaffirming their own engagements and by mobilising their electorate, which is presented then as the enemy's potential target.[22] But, at the same time, this evocation enables them to ease their own fears as regards the loss of sovereignty and, consequently, their loss of control over the political world, which have resulted from the aforementioned major political and economic changes. As these changes undermined the conceptual bases of the so-called Westphalian state, with regard to sovereignty, to national identity and to the keeping of law and order on a territorial basis, the political affiliation became increasingly vague, weakening thus the position of the politicians at the local and national levels.[23] Feeling threatened in the very quintessence of their function, politicians tend to legitimate again their role to their electorate and to instrumentalise to this end its fears and discomfort by designating a new "enemy".

This designation of a new enemy satisfies also, as we have already mentioned, several needs at the security agencies level. Being used in a context of power and influence struggles, it can reinforce the position of these agencies, by widening the field of their competencies, by facilitating the promotion of their know-how and of their technologies, and by allowing the preservation, or even the improvement of the budgets of their services, as well as the promotion of the careers of some agents. Far from being specific to public security agencies, these institutional competitions within the security field characterise also the private sector, not only because immigration controls are henceforth entrusted to private security agencies too (identity checks in semi-public places, control of persons and of luggage at the airports, etc.), but also, and above all, because the reinforcement of control technologies cannot be dissociated from the role played on the matter by private or semi-public industries producing this type of equipment for public security agencies.

Lastly, at the media level, the regular fuelling of the fear of foreigners that, as we will see further, sometimes reaches the paroxysm, fulfils two distinct functions. On the one hand, it can serve as a support to some political discourses, when these ones conform to the ideological position of the media. In this case, we witness the establishment of a dialectical relation between political and media discourses, which are thus mutually reinforced. On the other hand, the construction of the image of "the threatening migrant" by the media offers an unfailing source of strong sensations, for which a large part of the public remains still greedy. In this case, the presentation of the migrants by the media is primarily determined by commercial criteria rather than the ideological position of the media, and must comply only with the rules of the professional deontology.

The criteria Generally speaking, the transformation of a sub-population into a social enemy is carried out in two stages. Firstly, it is presumed that the members of this sub-population have one or more inherent features, which mark them as maligns, immoral, or perverted.[24] Secondly, these features are associated with current socio-economic or political problems and it is suggested that they are the source or, at least, an aggravating factor of these problems. Once this association is established, the presentation of the sub-population does not take account any more of the facts and, limiting itself to the reproduction of the already created stereotype, puts forward the image of the permanent threat to the well-being of the community.

Though, in theory, the choice of such a sub-population does not follow any rational criteria, its roots seem to be connected with the nature of the problems imputed to the "social enemies". If these problems are socio-economic, they will probably be associated with socially vulnerable or even marginal groups. Such was the case, for example, of Jewish or Roma communities in Europe. If, on the other hand, these problems are political, the "hostile" groups will be designated according to the ideological position rather than the social status of their members, as it is clearly shown by the persecutions inflicted to many dissidents to European communist regimes, or to American "communists" under McCarthy.

Therefore, the choice of immigration as a phenomenon implying multiple threats to EU societies is not at all extraordinary, since migrants, legal or not, are by far the most vulnerable members of a given community, both at the socio-economic and at the legal level. Even if legal migrants enjoy certain rights,[25] on the one hand they are usually employed in subordinate, precarious, and badly remunerated jobs, and, on the other hand, they can always be the subject of the non-renewal, or even of the withdrawal of their residence permit. Moreover, it should be stressed that this vulnerability goes beyond the first-generation migrants, as is clearly shown by the social integration problems met by the second or third-generation migrants in many Northern European countries.

This social vulnerability criterion usually goes together with a symbolic criterion. The success of the transformation of the migrants into "social enemies" is largely facilitated by the fact that migrants not only personify the "foreigner", the "other", which is so much feared for the cohesion of the community, but often bear on them the very marks of their alien status, such as the colour of their skin, or the external signs of their religious membership, even when they are the subject of a successful integration. Being guilty for having different life styles and socialisation modes, or for not perfectly speaking the language of the natives, migrants are regarded as inassimilable and are thus relegated to the rank of a "foreign body" to the host society, which, consequently, has no other choice than trying to get rid of them in order to ensure its own well-being.

The Social Construction of the Threat

The pattern The concept of the migratory threat has been elaborated in three distinct but interdependent stages, corresponding to official discourses, to scientific or pseudo-scientific analyses and to media discourses. These three mutually reinforcing and legitimating stages rest mainly on two broad themes, related respectively to demographic and internal security issues. The supporters of the migratory threat thesis evoke thus tirelessly the dangers that migrants represent for host societies, owing to their propensity to crime, and point out that these dangers will be increasingly important as the high birth rate in the emigration countries will undoubtedly cause the continuous rise of the migratory movements towards the developed countries. Yet, though this thesis is presented as accurate for resting on presumably scientifically irrefutable arguments, which justify the current immigration controls and plead for their constant reinforcement, it includes in fact many contradictions.

1. The demographic imbalance These contradictions can be observed, above all, in the discourse on the demographic imbalance in the emigration countries. Being formulated by several scholars and taken up again by both officials and the media, this discourse, which consists of demographic previsions, is elaborated at three levels. First, a standard prevision model is built, according to which the rise in the birth rate in the emigration countries will create an important demographic imbalance in relation to the population of the EU countries. It is then considered that this demographic imbalance will inevitably lead to important migratory movements towards the EU countries. Consequently, all EU societies have to take this data into consideration and to adopt in time policies allowing them to cope with these future dangers.[26]

But, as demography is not an exact science, it is at least imprudent to regard the conclusions of such studies as rigorously accurate. Standard previsions covering relatively long periods cannot include economic, social and demographic variables, such as the economic growth, the urbanisation, or women's emancipation, which are, by definition, random and may cause a fall in the birth rate in the emigration countries. Moreover, even if these previsions are proven right, the demographic imbalance will not inevitably lead to migratory movements towards the EU countries, because the transformations of the EU labour markets, which need less and less manpower, the economic growth of the emigration countries and the shifting of production to Eastern European and third world countries could reverse the current trends as regards immigration, by fixing the local manpower on the spot.[27]

2. The association of immigration with crime Many contradictions can be also observed in the thesis that associates more and more closely immigration with crime. This thesis, which is currently dominant in Europe, is in keeping with a broader securitarian discourse, which, creating a securitarian continuum among distinct phenomena, such as organised crime, terrorism, immigration, drug trafficking, money laundering, financial crime, petty crime and urban violence,[28] focuses on the threatening figure of the migrant, justifying thus the constant reinforcement of border controls and the adoption of restrictive immigration policies. One of the most obvious effects of the predominance of this thesis has been the progressive weakening of any distinction between migrants and asylum seekers, which, in its turn, reduced drastically the number of asylum seekers granted a refugee status. Being currently the subject of increasing suspicions, asylum seekers are divided in fact into "genuine" ones, who wish to avoid persecutions in their country of origin, and "false" ones, who wish to immigrate for economic reasons, the authorities considering in general that most asylum seekers are "false" ones.[29]

In spite of the fact that the existence of a particular link between immigration and organised crime has never been proven and that, on the contrary, many researchers come to the conclusion that migrants are hardly or not at all involved in organised crime activities,[30] official reports and publications of various security agencies (police forces, intelligence services, Armed Forces, etc.), as well as several judges "agree to regard immigration as a fact involving henceforth illegal migrants and drug trafficking, under the Mafia's control".[31] According to S. Palidda, this thesis reproduces in fact the pattern followed, from the beginning of the 1980s, by the American intelligence services with regard to the threats coming from the countries of the South, and in particular to the threat coming from Latin American drug traffickers.[32] It should be pointed out, in this respect, that the more the authorities harden their attitude towards migrants the more they stress the link between migrants and organised crime, by putting forward the discourse on the "human beings traffickers". The fight against this form of organised crime, which is presently placed under the mandate of the Europol Drugs Unit,[33] served even as a justification for the participation of Italy in the Kosovo war. Thus, the Italian Prime Minister D'Alema stated that the war in the Balkans was necessary in order to prevent Italy from being invaded by refugees and illegal migrants.[34]

Resting mainly on scientific or pseudo-scientific analyses, the thesis of "the criminal migrant", which relies primarily on statistical data and common senses, is frequently supported by politicians and police officers as well as by the media, creating thus a "security short-circuit" which renders immigration synonymous with insecurity.[35] Thus, in Northern European countries, some criminologists consider that the criminal involvement of migrants is facilitated by the fact that they possess a readily available infrastructure for the repatriation of criminal profits to their countries of origin, while their formal economic activities (restaurants, shops, etc.) enable them to carry out money laundering operations.[36] In Southern European countries, the public attention is drawn, on the one hand, to the criminal involvement of migrants and, on the other hand, to the development of foreign mafia networks operating on the national territory either in an autonomous way, or in co-operation with native criminals.

One of the major arguments of the supporters of the "criminal migrant" thesis is the overrepresentation of foreigners in European prisons throughout the 1990s. For instance, in Greece, in January 2000, foreigners amounted to 45.3 percent of the prison population; in Italy, in 1998, they amounted to 25.4 percent of the prison population, with an imprisonment rate nineteen times higher than that of the nationals;[37] in Germany, in September 1997, they amounted to 33.6 percent of the prison population, with an imprisonment rate five times higher than that of the nationals,[38] while in France, in 1995, they amounted to 29 percent of the prison population, with an imprisonment rate five to six times higher than that of the nationals.[39] It should be specified here that this high criminal involvement corresponds to very few types of offences, as most of the imprisoned foreigners are charged either with immigration offences, or with property or drug offences.[40]

Nevertheless, seeking to establish a link between immigration and crime by relying solely on police and/or prison statistics arises many methodological problems and induces inevitably to the error. First of all, any comparison of the criminal involvement of migrants with that of nationals is by definition problematic because not only are migrants usually young men, unmarried and poor – each one of these elements representing by itself a crime generating factor – but are also often discriminated against within the penal system of their country of residence.[41]

Then, we must always bear in mind that the police and prison statistics are only reflecting the police and judicial production during a given period and that this production can vary for many reasons. As far as police statistics are concerned, the usual methodological problems, related to data classification methods, go together with the fact that the police knowledge on crime varies according to several criteria. The police tend to know more about crimes that are under considerable social and political pressure, or about crimes that do not require much time and manpower to solve. Furthermore, the police pay much more attention to crimes which, when solved, have positive effects on their image. As this attitude is, for obvious reasons, closely associated with the prevailing political concerns in a given period, the current focusing on the repression of drug trafficking, which, inevitably, strikes in a disproportionate way some ethnic communities in the EU countries, reflects primarily the increasing attention paid to health and internal security issues at the local, national and European political levels.[42]

Moreover, the data on the criminal involvement of foreigners cannot be seen as exact for three other reasons. First, police statistics deal only with the officially recorded criminality. Foreigners tend thus to be over-represented for they are usually involved in highly visible criminal activities that, moreover, are the subject of an increasing repression. Second, presenting in an overall way the data on the criminal involvement of foreigners may produce spectacular figures but, at the same time, induces to the error, for many foreigners have been arrested only for immigration offences (illegal entry and/or residence, forgery, etc.) that do not represent any real threat to internal security. Lastly, as foreigners are usually involved in crimes characterised by a rather low solution rate, it is plausible to suppose that their crime involvement rate may be in fact much lower than that presented by the police data.

If we examine now prison statistics and compare the crime involvement rate of foreigners with their imprisonment rate, we see clearly that the latter is highly disproportionate. Actually, the over-representation of foreigners in prisons is due to several factors related to the functioning of the criminal justice systems of the EU countries. First, the courts impose rarely to migrants alternative sentences to detention, for migrants do not meet the usually required legal conditions for these sentences as, in most cases, they have neither a permanent address nor the external social support (family, permanent job, social network, etc.) which is usually taken into account as a factor facilitating social reintegration. The absence of these legal conditions can also explain the high rate of foreigners among pre-trial detainees.

Consequently, not only the crimes committed by most of the migrants involve, in theory, prison sentences, but migrants are placed in custody more often than nationals charged with equivalent crimes. The imprisonment rate of foreigners is furthermore increased in an artificial way owing to the detention of many migrants awaiting deportation. Lastly, the over-representation of foreigners in prisons cannot be dissociated from the quality of their defence during their trial, certain researches conducted in Italy, in the first half of the 1990s, having in fact revealed that lawyers had done a poor job defending foreigners during trials,[43] while, in the same period, Greek lawyers were denouncing the fact that foreigners were not always assisted by an interpreter during their trial.[44]

Often unknown or, quite simply, covered up, these factors are taken into consideration neither by politicians, nor by security agents, nor by the media, nor even by some scholars, who either content themselves with reproducing the securitarian thesis of "the criminal migrant" by mobilising to this end all available data, or seek to explain the "problem" by having recourse to culturalist theories. These theories, which impute the "propensity" of migrants to crime to their cultural features, have been developed mainly in Northern European countries and focused on the behaviour of the second-generation migrants. However, as long ago as 1938, T. Sellin explained that the high crime involvement rate of migrants was primarily due to their socio-economic position which, being determined by precarious and badly paid jobs, was resulting in "broken homes, inadequate education and leisure opportunities and an environment that could not develop in general".[45]

The process As we have mentioned before, the process of construction of the migratory threat rests essentially on political, police and media discourses. It should be reminded in this respect that, generally speaking, the perception of a social phenomenon by the members of a community is primarily determined by public, especially political discourses. Indeed, as M. Edelman affirms, our experiences are determined by the discourses made on the political events rather than by the events themselves, perceived in one way or another, so that the political language is the political reality.[46]

It is not possible, for obvious reasons, to fully analyse in this chapter the role played in the matter by the media. Therefore, we shall content ourselves with considering that, far from reflecting reality, the media structure "a" reality that ends up influencing, to various degrees, the public opinion. Of course, there is no direct causal link between crime fear and the way crime is presented by the media because, even if the media are the principal source of information, the public does not form its opinion solely by this way.[47] In fact, public opinion is formed and modified according to several cognitive, social and communicative processes and following various sources of influence, discursive or not.[48] Nevertheless, whatever may be the immediate effects of specific media messages on individuals, their influence, as regards information, on the structure and the contents of the social cognition of any social group is considerable and increases more if the public has no other sources of information;[49] its opinion tends then to be determined by the ideological pattern of the interpretations produced by the media.[50] Finally, we should point out that the development of this pattern is characterised by the fact that, when dealing with crime issues, the media do not seek to produce causal explanations, but rather tend to put forward a homogenising and standardising interpretation pattern.[51]

Before we analyse the principal discursive processes used for the social construction of the migratory threat in Italy and Greece in the 1990s, we should point out some semantic shifts common to all these discourses. First, the term "undocumented migrant" has been replaced in the 1990s by that of "illegal migrant", the meaning of which is not restricted any more to migrants entering the country illegally but covers also migrants stepping out from the state of legality while being already present on the national territory. Thus, it can designate nowadays any foreigner who has entered the country legally, as tourist for instance, but did not manage to obtain a residence permit, as well as the migrants who have been regularised but cannot meet the legal conditions required for the renewal of their residence permit.[52] Needless to say that this semantic shift is not at all neutral, for the term "illegal" conveys implicitly more threatening connotations than that of "undocumented".

Moreover, the spread of the notion of the migratory threat has been widely facilitated by the increasingly frequent use of aquatic terms to designate migratory movements ("migratory flows", "waves of migrants", "floods of migrants", "deluge of asylum seekers", etc.). While referring to the image of the perpetual motion of the sea, this association evokes the image of dams subject to the pressure of the water and being always likely to yield if this pressure becomes too strong. The metaphor is very clear: the waves of migrants will reach without delay the borders of the developed countries which, if they do not seek to protect themselves in time, will risk seeing them flood their territory and destroy everything on their way. These aquatic terms are so frequently used in political, media and even academic discourses that they quickly ended up being standardised and marginalizing the alternative term of "migratory movements". The acceptance of any recommended or adopted measure presented as likely to cope with these threatening waves has also been further facilitated by the use of some current words (such as "public", "official", "law", "general interest", "national interest", etc.) which, although they have no specific referent, contribute to legitimate governmental actions that, otherwise, might have provoked sceptical or even hostile reactions.[53]

1. Political and police discourses

a) Italy

Even though the problematisation of immigration acquired considerable dimensions only in the 1990s, the security agencies had already had a suspicious attitude towards migrants in the 1980s, a period when immigration was hardly existent in Italy. This suspicion is clearly expressed in the reports on the activity of these agencies, submitted regularly to the Parliament and the Senate, where the image of the "criminal" or "dangerous" migrant, related in particular to terrorism and organised crime, occupies a predominant place. In 1985, one of these reports affirms that there are many migrants present on the national territory and that some of them could take advantage of the conditions offered "by a particularly liberal system in order to carry out terrorist acts".[54] In 1988, another report affirms that the presence of many illegal migrants on the national territory does not only cause "public and social order problems, but also constitutes a potential threat, more and more serious, as a support of terrorism".[55] These fears having been proved unjustified, the rise in immigration in the 1990s quickly gave birth to other fears, now related to organised crime. In 1992, the link between illegal immigration and organised crime is put forward in another report, according to which "the criminal expansion of the citizens of an Asian country [probable reference to Iran] enables us to suppose that there is a network of logistic and operational co-operation related to illicit traffics".[56] In 1995, another report emphasises more the migratory threat, by including it into a widened insecurity context, created by both serious criminal phenomena and the political and economic development of the Western societies: "the need of the civil society for security grows constantly *vis-à-vis* the serious problems of organised crime, illegal immigration, Islamic fundamentalism, the decline of ideologies and the disorders of the financial markets".[57]

This perception of immigration was shared by the two principal extreme right-wing parties, the Northern League and the Italian Social Movement (MSI),[58] which articulated a major part of their electoral policy around the notion of the migratory threat. Wishing to put forward one of the central ideas of their political programs, i.e. Italy's cultural authenticity and ethnic purity, these extremist parties stirred the xenophobic feelings of the Italian society by emphasising the migratory cultural threat. A pamphlet, distributed in spring 1997 by a labour movement attached to the Northern League, affirms thus that "the ultimate objective of this invasion [of migrants] is not the conquest of a territory, but the alienation of a society, which, thanks to its efforts and sacrifices, and thanks to its millennial secular-liberal-Christian culture, was tending to relieve men from work, in order to transform it into a multiracial, materially and spiritually poor society, crossed by hatreds, tensions and conflicts specific to the Third World, increasingly close to Islamism and remote from Christianity", the ultimate aim of this strategy being "the similar transformation of the whole Europe".[59]

Although the rest of the political world did not take up these threats again, many politicians and officials adopted another extremist argument, the association of immigration with crime. From the mid-1990s, the political discourse stressed thus more and more often the fact that the migrants monopolised drug trafficking, that they were responsible for the rise in prostitution[60] and that, generally, their criminal involvement in Italy was much higher than that observed in other European countries – the association of immigration with crime being irrefutably proved by the over-representation of foreigners in the Italian prisons.

Increasingly dominant, this political discourse not only overlooked the factors explaining this over-representation,[61] but also rested on arguments that could not be objectively verified, since the number of illegal migrants present on the territory of a given country remains, by definition, unknown; so, on the one hand, any comparison with other European countries is impossible and, on the other hand, the establishment of a particular link between illegal immigration and crime is very questionable. Nevertheless, in a report submitted to the Senate in

September 1997, the minister of the Interior stated that, since 83 percent of the imprisoned foreigners were illegal migrants,[62] it was plausible to affirm that there was a close link between illegal immigration and crime.[63]

This statement, which constitutes the first official association of illegal immigration with crime, is not just the logical result of a process of construction of the migratory threat, set up as from the 1980s; it is also the official ratification of a mass hysteria campaign against the Albanian danger, which had reached its peak in 1997. Fuelled by the right-wing parties (in particular the Northern League), which exploited thus the urban anxieties and especially the new request for security expressed by a minority of the northern population, this campaign has been largely supported by the national press and ended by being legitimated by the government, which acted while taking for granted that the Italian society was hostile to migrants.[64] Indeed, the stereotyped image of the migrant and in particular of the criminal Albanian-migrant was so preponderant within the Italian society in the second half of the 1990s that, after some crimes imputed to migrants had been committed in August 1997, the whole country yielded to a genuine "moral panic", which led to a hostile and aggressive behaviour towards migrants and to a request for increased security. Acting under pressure, some delegates of the nationalist and national parties went as far as asking for the establishment of the death penalty for the "foreign murderers", some left-wing mayors proposed the introduction of a regional passport all along the Adriatic coast, and the government accelerated the adoption of the Turco-Napolitano draft on immigration, which introduced many new provisions related to deportation and to detention centres.[65]

It should be emphasised that, in the 1990s, legality became one of the central issues of Italian politics, giving rise to many law and order campaigns. But, this focusing on legality and, consequently, on the transgression of the law ended up causing the opposite effect, namely the rise of insecurity, because the more citizens were concerned about this issue, the more they became intolerant and the more they had the impression of living in a disordered society. Besides, as, apart from some Southern regions, organised crime does not cause a great deal of emotion among nationals, for they do not feel directly concerned by it, rhetoric on legality focused on petty crime, which is visible and directly concerns all citizens. The process followed to this end is carried out in three stages. Firstly, crime is assimilated to organised crime. Thus, the deputy chief commissioner of the national police has written that "organised crime and common crime are both faces of the same medal".[66] Then, any distinction between deviance and crime is completely wiped out and, finally, the criminal threat is personified in the figure of the migrant.[67]

The rise of the insecurity feeling and the transformation of its origin are clearly shown by the conclusions of a study conducted in 1998, in the region of Emilia-Romagna. According to them, the citizens' request for security no longer solely aims at denouncing a crime, but tends to become a request for security *vis-à-vis* the emergence of subjects regarded as incompatible with the desired urban civility and *vis-à-vis* the impoverishment and the deterioration of the urban environment of some social strata, who feel increasingly marginalised, or even socially excluded.[68] These fears are clearly revealed, for instance, by the fact that the complaints lodged to the police concern more and more often minor offences, never pointed out before, such as bicycle thefts, vandalism and various forms of incivilities.[69]

The supporters of the quality of urban life do not cease, therefore, to denounce that the population can live no longer because of the "presence on our territory of criminals, thieves, drug dealers, prostitutes, car window cleaners", confusing thus deviance with crime, minor offences with serious ones and offences with a victim with offences without one.[70] It should be pointed out that this confusion between deviance and crime is quite obvious in the eyes of the police officers, who note that migrants are primarily involved in petty crime and that it would be abusive to impute to them the recent rise in criminality in Italy.[71]

The impact of this confusion is all the more serious as a new political actor emerged in the 1990s: the citizens' committees. Acting in the name of the quality of urban life, these committees put pressure on the local and/or national authorities in order to obtain the reinforcement of the security measures in general and organise, now and then, punitive expeditions against migrants, held solely responsible for the rise in crime and for the deterioration of the urban environment. Occupying a sizeable part of the political scene, as delegates of the civil society, the citizens' committees seem hardly concerned with more serious forms of crime and overlook the fact that the committing of certain crimes imputed to migrants requires the participation of nationals, either as accomplices or as recipients of the act, or then they try to tackle the criminal-migrant issue in an overall way by associating all dealings of the migrants with organised crime. Thus, according to a report of a citizens' committee in Genoa: "[owing to] immigration, trafficking which was somehow organised became more diffuse [...], owing to immigration, all this is now under the Mafia's control".[72]

Furthermore, as the supporters of these theses seek to ensure the preponderance of their place on the political scene, they do not hesitate to denounce every association disputing the existence of the migratory threat and calling into question the association of immigration with crime. But, instead of trying to discredit the arguments advanced by the associations for the defence of migrants' rights, these denunciations take on an almost tautological aspect. Any action for the migrants is therefore regarded as an internal threat or, at least, as a "multiethnic illusion", which does not take account of the rise in crime and of the other dangers resulting from immigration.[73]

In spite of the fact that these anti-immigrant discourses are essentially similar to the ones observed in many other EU countries, the Italian case remains quite unusual for this mobilisation against migrants involved all political parties. This unanimity of the political world cannot be understood unless we take into consideration the fact that, as the anti-immigrant discourses were the object of a broad social consensus, the attitude to be adopted towards migrants became quickly a major electoral issue for all political actors, independently of the ideology of their respective parties. The reasoning underlying the positions of the left-wing parties, in particular, is clearly exposed in a press article which, in 1995, explained that the immigration problem stakes the very representativity of the left-wing parties with regard to their electorate, mainly composed of low social strata, which feel in the most negative and direct way the effects "of the undifferentiated flows of non-EU migrants and of the phenomena related to them, namely violence, illegality, insecurity".[74]

b) Greece

Despite the constant rise in immigration since the late 1980s and the amplification by the media of the crime involvement of migrants,[75] the notion of the migratory threat appeared in the political discourses only in the late 1990s.

Indeed, up to 1998, the conservative opposition,[76] worried though it was by the rise in crime, had avoided any overt criminalisation of the migrants[77] and had limited itself to proposing certain reforms with regard to the restructuring of the police force, the improvement of the police officers' training, the rise of their wages, the redefinition of their tasks and the reinforcement of the co-operation between the police and the Army as regards border controls. This moderate attitude was however gradually modified. In 1998, one of the Conservative Party leaders stated thus that the Greeks were living "in a mafia [...] and crime society",[78] while, in 1999, an executive of the party stated that "Greece is defenceless *vis-à-vis* the organised crime and the armed migrants".[79]

The same discursive shift can be observed in the discourse of the socialist government. While in February 1997 the Prime Minister stated that "in a period marked by economic crises and the rise in unemployment [...] the migrants are turned into scapegoats, to which one imputes the labour market crisis, the rise in crime and the marginalisation", in July 1999 he stated that "crime, which is connected with the wave of economic refugees towards the country, is a source of insecurity and is perceived by citizens as a threat to Greek society".[80]

This association of immigration with crime has been confirmed by all Ministers of Public Order throughout the second half of the 1990s. In July 1997, for example, the Minister of Public Order mentioned the possible existence of a co-operation between the Albanian, Greek and Italian Mafias[81] and, two weeks later, he stated that Greece witnessed "an outbreak of foreign crime; whereas, in 1996, migrants had committed 1 300 crimes, 550 of which had been committed by Albanians, in the first five months of 1997 they committed 2 300 crimes, 1 000 of which were committed by Albanians" and imputed this rise "to the easing of the border controls owing to the socio-political troubles in Albania".[82] Yet, if we compare these figures to those of the police statistics on 1996 and on the first half of 1997, we notice a considerable divergence showing that the Minister did not compare two statistically comparable volumes. It seems indeed that he quoted in an extremely selective way the 1996 figures, while those of the first five months of 1997 corresponded to the overall foreign criminality.

In 1998, this same Minister regularly denounced the xenophobic and racist reactions of the civil society as well as the sensational media coverage of criminality but, at the same time, he often pointed out the high involvement of foreigners in serious crimes while specifying that the emergence of organised crime in Greece was not worrying because its extent was very limited. This attitude became even more ambiguous in March 1998, when crime fear and xenophobia had reached their peak. The Minister stated then that, since Greeks were living in "a society marked by a high unemployment and illegal immigration rate", property offences were inevitable and recommended that "citizens should take some elementary self-protection measures" because "the time of insouciance, when people did not lock the door of their house and slept on their balcony, is quite completed".[83] Avoiding any comment on the causes of the phenomenon, he preferred imputing it to the fact that, as the regularisation was in process, all deportations had ceased since the beginning of the year, causing thus a temporary rise of the foreign criminality.

Though it has been regularly taken up by many officials as well as by police officers, the argument connecting the rise of the foreign crime to the suspension of the deportations is contradicted by the police statistics, which show that not only deportations never ceased in that period, but also that the number of migrants deported between January and April 1998 (35 586 persons) does not differ appreciably from that recorded during the same period in 1997. Nevertheless, the police kept on putting forward this argument for, on the one hand, it could thus explain its inefficiency in the fight against crime and, on the other hand, it could justify its requests for certain reforms which, expressed by both senior officers and the delegates of its trade unions, were widely covered by the media. Stressing the lack of manpower and the need for modernisation of the police equipment, senior police officers and trade union delegates called moreover for the adoption of a new law on the use of weapons in the exercise of their duties as well as for a more rational management of the police manpower.[84]

On 23 March 1998, following the death of two police officers in the exercise of their duties, the government announced the drawing-up of a draft on the use of weapons by police officers and, one month later, it announced the granting, over three years, of 100 billion drachmas[85] to the Ministry of Public Order, allowing thus the modernisation of the police equipment, the recruitment of 3 500 policemen and the reinforcement of border controls. Moreover, it announced the imminent vote by the Parliament of a draft on the creation of a Border Patrol, whose mission would be to fight crime and to ensure the security of the borders and of the Greek citizens.[86] Furthermore, the land and maritime border controls would be reinforced thanks to the establishment of a closer co-operation between the police and the Army. Lastly, the government announced the reinforcement of the municipal police competencies.

The adoption of these measures went together with the increasingly frequent confirmation of the association of immigration with crime. Thus, in July 1999, the Minister of Public Order stated that "although we should not consider that each illegal migrant is a potential criminal [...] it would be erroneous to minimise the existence of a serious imported criminality, related to arms and drug trafficking as well as to prostitution".[87] This association was also confirmed by a report of the national security forces, submitted to the Council of Ministers in August 1999, according to which illegal immigration is directly linked to common crime and to the emergence of certain forms of organised crime.[88] Besides, this point of view is shared by the majority of the Greek policemen who, according to the conclusions of an academic research, consider that illegal immigration and crime are closely linked.[89] It is, therefore, not astonishing that the media produce more and more often senior police officers' statements on the worrying extent of the criminal involvement of foreigners. In February 2000, the chief commissioner of the Salonika police stated thus that most of the crimes recorded in his district had been committed by foreigners and drew up a ranking criminals list, by nationality and by type of crime, according to which Albanians were involved primarily in hashish trafficking, prostitution, armed robberies and vehicle thefts; Bulgarians, in heroin trafficking, prostitution and vehicle thefts; Georgians, in the transport of stolen vehicles towards the former Soviet Union; Yugoslavians, in prostitution and Rumanians in burglaries.[90]

2. The media discourses   The reinforcement of immigration controls and the hardening of the immigration policies, which went together with the aforementioned political and police discourses, served also as a justificatory basis for the aggressions against migrants. Actually, these two reaction levels obey a dialectical logic, since the more authorities are severe towards migrants the more extremists consider that they act in accordance with the dominant opinion, the hardening of the immigration policies "legitimating" thus to some extent the anti-immigrant arguments. This interaction is even more reinforced if the fear of the threatening migrant is regularly fuelled by the media. Many German researchers considered thus that the aggressions against migrants that took place in the early 1990s at Hoyerswerda and Rostock could not be dissociated from the media coverage of the immigration issue during that period. In fact, the media had emphasised so much the migratory threat that the right-wing extremists had ended up believing that if they aggressed some migrants they would enjoy the sympathy of many of their fellow citizens.[91]

Of course, there is not any direct causal link between the media coverage of immigration and the numerous aggressions against migrants observed in Italy and in Greece during the 1990s, but that should not prompt us to forget that the media play a crucial role in the process of construction of the migratory threat, especially by objectifying the definitions advanced on the matter by the politicians and the security agents. Indeed, as a place of *agenda-setting* and of production of information, the media are ideally placed to establish and legitimate such definitions, by modifying accordingly their processes of presenting immigration. The more these processes are repetitive, stereotyped and regarded as evident, the more they confer objectivity on the alarmist definitions of reality by transforming them into a usual cognitive fund. Once these definitions are established, they are, in their turn, legitimated and confirmed by the existence of actors claiming to represent the local society, such as the citizens' committees in Italy.[92] Consequently, immigration becomes a national political issue, which cannot be ignored either by the political parties, supposed to represent the citizens, or by public authorities, supposed to ensure the citizens' protection.

The study of the Italian and Greek press discourses during the second half of the 1990s revealed that the process of construction of the migratory threat by the media has both quantitative and qualitative aspects. We observe thus a sharp increase in the number and the length of the press articles dealing with illegal immigration and, following an imperceptible semantic shift, dealing with immigration and asylum seekers in general. Far from taking a neutral approach, these articles focus on crimes committed by migrants. Inevitably, this selective approach ends up amplifying in an artificial way the criminal involvement of migrants, since the media start quoting all offences, even minor ones, committed by migrants, or even abusively impute to migrants several crimes committed by unknown authors.[93] This amplification of the criminal involvement of migrants relies also on the manipulation of the police statistics, as the media quote often the whole number of crimes committed by migrants during a given period, without specifying that most of them are just immigration offences. Moreover, even when they do present these statistics in a more analytic way, they fuel the image of "the criminal migrant" in two different ways. On the one hand, they focus on the crimes where migrants are over-represented; on the other hand, they do not specify that the number of crimes imputed to migrants does not correspond inevitably to as many authors, either because police statistics do not provide data on relapse (as it is the case in Italy[94]), or because, especially with regard to property offences, many crimes are often committed in a very short period of time by a few gangs, the members of which cross the border only for criminal purposes. Observed usually in Greece, this phenomenon, which has not been studied yet, facilitated on several occasions the confirmation of the link between illegal immigration and crime, for in fact the media confuse illegal migrants who cross the border for primarily economic purposes and may commit some offences with foreigners who cross the border for criminal purposes – the latter usually entering the country legally.

At the same time, the media increasingly pay attention to news on transnational migratory movements and asylum seekers and, often relying on demographic studies,[95] fuel the thesis of the "invasion" of the country by the migrants. This invasion, which is already visible, is supposed to be reinforced in the immediate future. The rise of the criminal involvement of foreigners acquires thus a quite different dimension, for this trend will be inevitably worsened in the years to come. The invasion theme is often the subject of sensational titles ("Italian coasts under attack";[96] "The invasion of the desperate";[97] "maximum alarm owing to the risk of a criminal invasion"[98]) which frequently go together with aquatic images ("migratory flows", "waves of migrants", "floods of migrants"). Once this threatening image of the foreign invasion is established, the image of the rise of crime which will result from it is no longer limited to illegal migrants, but also covers the asylum seekers: "Refugees, crime alarm" was quoting an Italian daily in 1997.[99] These confusions are all the easier as most nationals have often a completely erroneous image of the asylum seekers and/or the volume of the illegal immigration. As far as the volume of the illegal immigration is concerned, this ignorance is primarily due to the fact that the media production of police statistics on deported migrants induces to the error because, in most cases, these migrants return at once to the country which has deported them, so that the same person can be the subject of several deportations per year, or even per month.

The criminalisation of immigration involves, moreover, the implementation of further qualitative processes. First, the media put forward the foreign nationality of the alleged authors of crimes imputed to migrants. Nationality becomes thus an absolute constant of the definition of the migrants arrested for serious or even minor offences. According to the country, the emphasis is laid on the "Albanians", the "Rumanians", the "North Africans", the "Nigerians", etc. This anonymous presentation, which refers to ethnic groups rather than to individuals, reinforces the feeling of threat, while suggesting that immorality is an intrinsic feature of certain foreign cultures,[100] since criminal acts or behaviour are no longer imputed to individuals of such or such a nationality, but to the whole Albanian, Nigerian, Moroccan etc. culture, allowing thus the creation of stereotypes: Albanian-criminal, Nigerian-prostitute, Moroccan-thief, Rumanian-burglar, etc.

These stereotypes become all the more worrying in the eyes of the nationals as the criminal activities imputed to the migrants are frequently associated with criminal transnational networks, particularly Russian and Albanian. While regularly referring to the threat of the Russian mafia, the Greek and Italian press pays much more attention to the "Albanian mafia". The threat of the "Albanian Mafiosi" operating on the national territory, which was frequently mentioned throughout the 1990s, has been more emphasised after the Kosovo war. Thus, a Greek national daily quotes a secret report of the Greek intelligence services in order to put forward the fear that the country, hitherto "influenced by a small section of the Albanian mafia, based in Southern Albania", will be one of the privileged grounds of action of the powerful mafia networks based in Northern Albania which, following the evolution of the Kosovo war, started to move their activities towards the South.[101] If no concrete facts are available, the Greek press often fuels the image of the "Albanian Mafioso" in an abusive way, by using indistinctly the terms "mafia", "organised crime" and "gangs" even when it refers to simple thefts or burglaries imputed to Albanian migrants.[102] However, it should be pointed out that, while all property offences are usually imputed to "Albanian Mafiosi", the fields where, according to the Greek police, there is actually a certain link between migrants and organised crime[103] are seldom covered by the media. This silence does not simply result from the low visibility of these activities, but also from the fact that the committing of these crimes would be impossible without the participation of Greek criminals and/or the complicity of some Greek officials. Although the complicity of the latter is occasionally denounced by the media,[104] that of the Greek criminals is usually overlooked, or when it is mentioned, especially when related to drug or migrants trafficking, it is quoted in neutral terms.[105]

The image of the threatening "criminal migrant" is further reinforced thanks to two other processes. First, the media legitimate their discourse by calling for officials and police officers as well as for representatives of the civil society (such as the members of the Italian citizens' committees), while quoting, of course, the statements made on this subject by the politicians. Then, they associate the rise of the criminal involvement of foreigners with the general rise in crime, by having recourse on the one hand to police statistics and, on the other hand, to comments on the rapidity of the rise of crime at the national level and, should the occasion arise, at the European level. This presentation of the crimes imputed to foreigners goes together with the systematic use of sensational sentences ("nights of terror at the burglars' mercy"[106]), or of powerful images referring either to a general context of disorder and anomie ("Greece looks like Far West",[107] "Athens is comparable to

Chicago"[108]), or to a criminal context connected with emigration countries, where the Italian cities, for example, are described as "heroin souks" and "drugs casbah".[109]

Once the securitarian pattern of the threat is firmly established, the demonisation of the migrants relies also on the use of many figures of speech, which are either dehumanising or aim at stirring feelings of dislike and repulsion towards the migrants. The migrant is then called "anthropomorphic monster"[110] or "werewolf",[111] is presented as "sticky" and "muddy",[112] or is described as "a street slave".[113] These figures of speech not only emphasise the otherness, the alien status of the migrant, but also make conceivable, or even ordinary, the idea of the evacuation, of the elimination of the bodies to which they refer,[114] since their nature is proved to be deeply different from that of the nationals' bodies. Consequently, massive immigration controls and deportations are hardly criticised by the civil society and the aggressions against migrants become all the more probable.

This gap between nationals and migrants is all the more wide as it is underlain by the notion of the cultural otherness, which is regarded as particularly threatening to the identity of the native community. Thus, the Italian press often considers that the migrants cannot be integrated, because "the cultural gap" between them and the nationals is too wide and could threaten the authenticity of the Italian culture,[115] and puts forward the fear that the "character of the Italian cities" will be altered if migrants are established in central areas.[116] As a major part of the civil society takes this threat for real, it is hardly astonishing that, apart from certain exceptions, it did not react against the emergence of a new form of racism, expressed by the extreme right-wing parties, because there is actually a consensus regarding the values thus defended, the disagreement being limited only to the process used for this scope.[117] The separation between "us" and "them" is henceforth so rigid that the subjects "of exclusion of citizenship claims can hardly be put in the centre of an inclusion discourse",[118] likely to recognise any rights to them. This is also clearly shown in Greece where, following the first massive regularisation, a part of the national press has started to put forward the possession of a regularisation title by the foreign criminals ("the kidnapper was a green card holder", "we regularise even potential murderers"[119]).

This superposition of the cultural and securitarian threats leads, inevitably, to their mutual reinforcement, insofar as the more ethnic minorities are perceived as thick and inaccessible, because of "their languages, their incomprehensible value codes and their group loyalty", the more the image of ethnic criminals, members of a "secret society", is reinforced.[120]

This multiform migratory threat is presented as if it were so serious and imminent that the media turn themselves implicitly into defenders of the social values thus threatened. Either, then, they launch campaigns for the deportation of all illegal migrants, or they put pressure on the authorities for the reinforcement of immigration controls and the reestablishment of law and order. Of course, their position of "defenders of the society in danger"[121] does not lead them to suggest the committing of aggressions against migrants, or to justify such acts subsequently. But, this position often prevents them from denouncing the committing of such aggressions and from designating their genuine causes. Thus, the Italian press did not ever consider that the aggressions against migrants which took place in the 1990s and, sometimes, even led to the migrants' death, had xenophobic or racist causes. In most cases, these aggressions were minimised, or even ignored, or then they were regarded as "fatal" or as incidents without any particular meaning.[122] For example, the death of a Moroccan fallen in a river and prevented from regaining the river bank by certain natives throwing bottles, pieces of wood and other projectiles at him was "certainly not a fact ascribable to racism [...] but rather the tragic conclusion of a drunkards' fight".[123] Whereas the major national dailies paid a great deal of attention to the racist aggressions against migrants which have occurred in Germany or in other foreign countries, since the beginning of the 1990s, they never dealt with the rise of xenophobia in Italy, because it is not a legitimate public discourse object. When, then, some aggressions cannot be regarded as simple incidents, the media present them as the consequence of an "objectively" serious situation, connected with the presence of too many migrants on the national territory. They carry out a genuine inversion of roles, since they turn victims into wrongdoers and aggressors into victims, aggressions being simply the result of the incapacity of the authorities to handle the negative effects of the immigration. This attitude is clearly shown in the article of an Italian journalist who, commenting on the arrest and four days detention of a young Nigerian woman travelling on a bus without a ticket, wrote that the inhabitants of Genoa, far from being racist, were very patient and bore "the problem of the non-EU [migrants] and of the nomads, the unsuccessful solution to the immigration problem".[124]

3. The impact of the media discourses The media being only one of the factors fuelling the process of construction of the migratory threat, it is not possible to establish a direct causal link between their discourses and the development of the Italian and Greek immigration policies in the 1990s. This should not however minimise their indirect influence, insofar as not only they legitimate the definitions of the threat formulated by the politicians and the security agents, but also put pressure on the authorities, as platforms expressing the public opinion's needs and wishes.

From this point of view, the impact of the media discourses on the two immigration policies studied here seems to vary considerably from one country to the other. Of course, in both cases, the media construction of the migratory threat facilitated the implementation of restrictive immigration and asylum policies. But, we should note that these policies have been adopted only when the media discourses were in conformity with the government's will to harden its immigration policy. In this case, the media discourses are simply reinforcing the legitimacy of a political decision, the adoption of which is usually however determined by other factors, as it takes into consideration multiple issues, related to security, foreign policy, national economy, etc. Consequently, when, during a given period, the media discourses run up against the genuine wishes of the government, their impact on the national immigration policy is definitely weakened, or even abolished. Either, then, the government remains inert, or it acts against what is presented as the public opinion's wish, or it acts accordingly to this wish but limits the scope of its action at the symbolic level.

Thus, the strong rise in xenophobia and the various anti-immigrant campaigns launched by the media did not prevent the Italian and Greek governments from carrying out, in the 1990s, several massive regularisations. Moreover, the mobilisation of the public opinion by the media and the pressure thus put on the Italian government certainly compelled it to act but did not always ensure the effective implementation of the measures adopted under such a pressure. As a matter of fact, the Italian government has sometimes limited itself to adopting spectacular measures, very satisfactory in the eyes of the public opinion, without implementing them for as much. Such was the case in 1995 when, following a strong social mobilisation of many Northern towns against migrants, the government adopted a decree providing for the immediate deportation of all illegal migrants, of all migrants suspected of having committed a crime and of all migrants sentenced up to three years' imprisonment. This decree did calm down the public opinion, but it never entered into force.

Conclusions

This study of the social construction of the migratory threat in Italy and in Greece has revealed so many similarities between the processes followed to this end that it is possible to affirm that, in both cases, a wide implementation of the classic pattern of construction of social enemies is witnessed. Moreover, the demonstration of the multiplicity of the factors underlying the process of definition of the migratory threat can only call into question the current trend of the increasing reinforcement of immigration controls in Europe and, consequently, the role of the security agencies involved in them. It seems therefore obvious that the question raised by the weak legitimacy of the security system set up in order to cope with a threat thus defined cannot be tackled unless the impact of these internal security policies on the EU societies is taken into consideration.

It should be pointed out in this respect that the transformation of immigration into a multiform threat to the EU societies may satisfy several collective needs and certain logics specific to the political market and the security agencies functioning, but it is far from ensuring the well-being and the smooth functioning of the societies in question. First, the social cohesion of these countries risks to be sapped much more by the process of securitisation of the migrants than by the migrants themselves. Indeed, the implementation of this process in Northern European countries has caused numerous confusions between illegal, legal, and second-generation migrants as well as between foreigners and nationals whose ethnic or religious membership is other than that dominant in their country. These confusions not only create a climate of suspicion aiming indistinctly at all "foreigners", but are also likely to divide the social body into "nationals" and "foreigners", by reinforcing the adoption of discriminatory behaviour towards certain sections of the population,[125] by impeding the integration of some migrant populations and by contributing to the rise of racist aggressions. This weakening of the social cohesion of the Northern European countries becomes all the more worrying as their social foundations are also undermined by their "foreigners", insofar as the exclusion feeling and the discriminations undergone by some social strata, often composed of second-generation migrants and/or of nationals of colour, have without a doubt contributed to the triggering of many urban riots during the last decades. Although the effects of the process of securitisation of immigration are more visible in Northern European countries, the aforementioned threats concern also the Southern European countries. Of course, the confusions resulting from this process are, by definition, limited between legal and illegal migrants, but the general suspicion that henceforth lies heavy on all migrants impedes to a large extent their integration and, as we have noticed before, has already facilitated the committing of many racist aggressions.

These threats to the social cohesion of the EU countries go together with another threat, related to the very institutional and legal foundations of these societies. It is clear that this generalised suspicion towards "foreigners" has led to the establishment of a wide deviance control, accepted without much criticism by the civil societies in question as an integral part of the social protection mechanism against the migratory threat. The establishment and the legitimisation of such a control are all the more undermining the principles specific to European democracies as the identity checks *au faciès*, carried out as part of the fight against crime and illegal immigration, are addressed to both foreigners and nationals. The generalisation of this deviance control is even more threatening to the EU societies for its implementation calls into question the very protection of public order in these societies, insofar as its regular focusing on some "territorial targets",[126] which, in our opinion, cannot be dissociated from the triggering of many urban riots, is likely to be an important source of social disorder in the years to come.

There is no doubt that the construction of a "social enemy" fulfils numerous functions, related to collective community needs and to logics specific to the functioning of both the political market and the security agencies of a given country. There is no doubt that the construction of the figure of the "criminal migrant" facilitates, or even legitimates the implementation of restrictive immigration and asylum policies. But, the dangers resulting from these policies seem to be, by far, much more serious than the threats imputed to the migrants insofar as the implementation of this criminalisation process undermines the very foundations of the EU societies. Therefore, a paradoxical situation might be witnessed, where the process of securitisation of the immigration may end up jeopardising the very societies it is supposed to protect, becoming thus the subject of a genuine inversion of its initial purpose.

Notes

[1]   Associate Professor at the University Paris XI.
[2]   This securitisation has been only slightly counterbalanced by the improvement or even the recognition of some social rights to legal migrants and by the carrying out of massive regularisations in several EU countries.

[3] The analysis of the political, police and media discourses made on the matter rests on both primary and secondary sources.

[4] A. Ceyhan and A. Tsoukala, "Le contrôle de l'immigration: mythes et réalités", *Cultures & Conflits*, 26/27, 1997, p. 10.

[5] M. Edelman, *Pièces et règles du jeu politique*, Paris: Seuil, 1991, pp. 46-47.

[6] A. Ceyhan and A. Tsoukala, op. cit., p. 10.

[7] A. Dal Lago, *Non-Persone. L'esclusione dei migranti in una società globale*, 1999, pp. 115-116.

[8] M. Edelman, op. cit., p. 57.

[9] *Idem*, p. 58.

[10] D. Bigo, *Polices en réseaux*, 1996; M. Edelman, op. cit., p. 163.

[11] D. Bigo, "Sécurité et immigration: vers une gouvernementalité par l'inquiétude?", *Cultures & Conflits*, 1998, p. 28.

[12] *Idem*, p. 27.

[13] *Ibid*, p. 30.

[14] J. Citrin et al., "Public Opinion Toward Immigration Reform: The Role of Economic Motivations", *The Journal of Politics*, 1997, pp. 874-875; T. Espenshade and K. Hempstead, "Contemporary American Attitudes Toward US Immigration", *International Migration Review*, 1996, p. 539.

[15] T. Ohlemacher, "Public Opinion and Violence Against Foreigners in the Reunified Germany", *Zeitschrift für Soziologie*, 1994, p. 223.

[16] T. Espenshade and K. Hempstead, op. cit., p. 533.

[17] A. Dal Lago, op. cit., p. 11.

[18] S. Palidda, "La criminalisation des migrants", *Actes de la recherche en sciences sociales*, 1999, p. 43.

[19] J. Huysmans, "Migrants as a security problem: dangers of 'securitizing' societal issues" in R. Miles and D. Thränhardt, *Migration and European Integration. The Dynamics of Inclusion and Exclusion*, 1995, p. 59 f.

[20] M. den Boer, "Immigrants, Asylum Seekers and Criminalisation: The Interaction between Criminal Justice Policy and Criminology", 1996 (unpublished paper).

[21] A. Triandafyllidou, "Racists? Us? Are you joking? The discourse of social exclusion of immigrants in Greece and Italy", 1997 (unpublished paper).

[22] M. Edelman, op. cit., p. 129.

[23] D. Bigo, "Sécurité et...", op. cit., p. 33.

[24] M. Edelman, op. cit., p. 132.

[25] Of which illegal migrants are, by definition, deprived.

[26] A. Dal Lago, op. cit., pp. 160-161.

[27] *Idem*.

[28] See on this subject, D. Bigo, *Polices...*, op. cit., chap. V.

[29] M. den Boer, " Crime et immigration dans l'Union européenne", *Cultures & Conflits*, 1998, pp. 105-106; C. Butterwegge, "Mass media, Immigrants and Racism in Germany. A Contribution to an Ongoing Debate", *Communications*, 1996, pp. 207-208.

[30] M. Barbagli, *Immigrazione e criminalità in Italia*, 1998, p. 72.

[31] S. Palidda, op. cit., p. 45.

[32] *Idem*.

[33] M. den Boer, "Crime et immigration...", op. cit., p. 118.

[34] S. Palidda, op. cit., p. 45.

[35] *Idem*, p. 40.

[36] For a critical approach of this thesis, see M. den Boer, "Crime et immigration...", op. cit., p. 114.

[37] S. Palidda, op. cit., p. 41.

[38] *Idem.*

[39] P. Tournier, "La délinquance des étrangers en France – analyse des statistiques pénales", in S. Palidda, *Délit d'immigration*, 1997, p. 135, p. 145.

[40] H. J. Albrecht, "Minorities, Crime, and Criminal Justice in the Federal Republic of Germany", in Marshall, I. H., *Minorities, Migrants and Crime*, 1997, p. 101; L. Wacquant, "Des 'ennemis commodes'", *Actes de la recherche en sciences sociales*, 1999, p. 64; M. Barbagli, op. cit., pp. 50-52; S. Palidda, op. cit., p. 67.

[41] A. Tsoukala, "Le discours grec sur la criminalité des immigrés", *Hommes & Migrations*, 1999, op. cit., pp. 78-79.

[42] M. den Boer, "Crime et immigration...", op. cit., pp. 116-117.

[43] U. Gatti et al., "Minorities, Crime, and Criminal Justice in Italy", in Marshall, I. H., op. cit., p. 118.

[44] I. Courtovic, "To nomiko kathestos ton metanaston ergaton stin Ellada", in Marangopoulos Foundation for Human Rights, *The protection of the rights of migrant workers and their families*, 1994, p. 192.

[45] T. Sellin, *Conflits de culture et criminalité*, 1984, p. 98.

[46] M. Edelman, op. cit., p. 196.

[47] P. Schlesinger and H. Tumber, *Reporting Crime. The Media Politics of Criminal Justice*, 1994, p. 188.

[48] T. van Dijk, *Elite Discourse and Racism*, 1993, p. 242.

[49] The criminal involvement of migrants is one of these issues where the public is exclusively informed by the media.

[50] T. van Dijk, op. cit., pp. 242-243.

[51] P. Schlesinger and H. Tumber, op. cit., p. 204.

[52] A. Dal Lago, op. cit., p. 48.

[53] M. Edelman, op. cit., p. 186.

[54] Ministero degli interni, *Relazione al parlamento sull'attività delle forze di polizia e sullo stato dell' ordine e della sicurezza pubblica nel territorio nazionale*, Roma, 1985 (quoted by A. Dal Lago, op. cit., p. 122).

[55] Ministero degli interni, *Relazione al parlamento sull'attività delle forze di polizia e sullo stato dell' ordine e della sicurezza pubblica nel territorio nazionale*, Roma, 1988 (first semester), p. 25 (quoted by A. Dal Lago, op. cit., p. 122).

[56] Ministero degli interni, *Relazione al parlamento sull'attività delle forze di polizia e sullo stato dell' ordine e della sicurezza pubblica nel territorio nazionale*, Roma, 1992, p. 15 (quoted by A. Dal Lago, op. cit., p. 122).

[57] Ministero degli interni, *Relazione al parlamento sull'attività delle forze di polizia e sullo stato dell' ordine e della sicurezza pubblica nel territorio nazionale*, Roma, 1995, p. 5 (quoted by A. Dal Lago, op. cit., pp. 123).

[58] Now called National Alliance (NA).

[59] A. Dal Lago, op. cit., pp. 125-126.

[60] M. Barbagli, op. cit., pp. 48-49.

[61] See *supra.*

[62] According to the conclusions of a survey carried out in five major prisons of the country.

[63] M. Barbagli, op. cit., p. 108.

[64] A. Dal Lago, op. cit., pp. 25-26.

[65] *Idem*, pp. 27-28.

[66] G. di Gennaro, "Repressione democratica", *Micromega*, 1996, n° 5, p. 56 (quoted by A. Dal Lago, op. cit., p. 119).

[67] A. Dal Lago, op. cit., pp. 120.

[68] Perceived in an increasingly rigid way, the quality of the urban environment, morality and legality values are supported with great fervour because they are perceived as social inclusion criteria.

[69] S. Palidda, *Domanda di sicurezza e forze di polizia nei capoluoghi di provincia emilano-romagnoli*, 1998, pp. 11-12 (unpublished paper).

[70] A. Dal Lago, op. cit., pp. 81-82.

[71] *Idem*, p. 85.

[72] *Ibid*, p. 86.

[73] *Ibid*, p. 124.

[74] *Il Corriere della sera*, 18-9-1995 (quoted by A. Dal Lago, op. cit., p. 124).

[75] A. Tsoukala, "Le traitement médiatique de la criminalité étrangère en Europe", *Déviance et société*, 2002, 1, pp. 61-82.

[76] Nea Dimokratia.

[77] Although the Conservative Party did not disapprove formally of the statements of two of its delegates, who, during a parliamentary debate, stated respectively that they wished the creation of concentration camps for illegal migrants and the establishment of tax controls of migrants' income declarations, because "it is inadmissible that such controls are imposed to the criminals' hunters and not to the criminals themselves", *Kathimerini*, 21 May 1998.

[78] Statement of the former head of the Conservative Party, Mr Evert (*Elefteros Tipos*, 23 March 1998).

[79] *Kyriakatiki Eleftherotypia*, 30 May 1999.

[80] *I Kyriakatiki Avghi*, 18 July 1999.

[81] *Eleftherotypia*, 22 July 1997. In order to show clearly the abusive character of this statement, we point out that there has never been a Greek mafia in Greece.

[82] *Kyriakatiki Eleftherotypia*, 3 August 1997.

[83] *Eleftherotypia*, 23 March 1998.

[84] The legislation in force had been adopted in the 1940s.

[85] Approximately 330 million dollars. It is the largest sum ever granted to this Ministry.

[86] On the creation of this body, see: A. Tsoukala, "Le contrôle de l'immigration en Grèce dans les années qautre-vingt-dix", *Cultures & Conflits*, 1997, p. 61.

[87] *I Kathimerini*, 18 July 1999.

[88] *Kyriakatiki Eleftherotypia*, 1 August 1999.

[89] This opinion is shared by 65 percent of the policemen questioned (*Ependytis*, 18/19 December 1999).

[90] *Eleftherotypia*, 22 February 2000.

[91] C. Butterwegge, op. cit., p. 208; T. Ohlemacher, op. cit., p. 234.

[92] On this process, see A. Dal Lago, op. cit., pp. 73-74. The data for this paper come from all articles published on this issue by the following daily and Sunday newspapers: *Eleftherotypia, Eleftheros Typos* (1 January-30 April 1998), *Kiriakatiki Eleftherotypia* (1 January 1995-31 December 1999), *La Repubblica, La Stampa, Il Corriere della sera, L'Unità* (1 January-30 April 1997). They are occasionally completed by data coming from the personal press files of the author and from secondary sources.

[93] "The authors, probably Albanian, threw the corpse..." (*Eleftheros Typos*, 19-1-1998); "[the authors were] probably extra-Community migrants", quoted by M. Maneri, "Les médias dans le processus de construction sociale de la criminalité des immigrés. Le cas italien", in Palidda S., *Délit...*, op. cit., p. 55.

[94] S. Palidda, "La construction sociale...", op. cit., p. 235.

[95] On the ambivalences of these studies, see *supra*.

[96] *L'Unità*, 14 March, 1997.

[97] *La Repubblica*, 15 March, 1997.

[98] *Il Corriere della sera*, 18 March, 1997.

[99] *La Stampa*, 19 March, 1997.

[100] A. Triandafyllidou, "Nation and Immigration: a Study of the Italian Press Discourse", *Social Identities*, 1999, p. 78.

[101] *To Vima*, 18 July 1999.

[102] See, for instance: *Eleftherotypia*, 8 May 1997; *Eleftheros Typos*, 5 January 1998.

[103] Such as drug trafficking, prostitution and money laundering.

[104] See, for example, the articles on the role played by the officials of some Greek embassies in Eastern European countries as regards the fraudulent acquisition of the Greek nationality by many Russian criminals, or on the involvement of some Greek officials and police officers in the activities in Greece of an alleged "godfather of the Albanian mafia", published respectively in *Kiriakatiki Eleftherotypia* of 22 March 1998 and of 2 May 1999.

[105] See, for example: *Eleftherotypia*, 28 July 1994; *Kiriakatiki Eleftherotypia*, 17 September 1995.

[106] *Eleftheros Typos*, 9 March 1998.

[107] *Idem*, 25 February 1998.

[108] *Eleftherotypia*, 23 March 1998. See also: *I Kathimerini*, 4 April 1999.

[109] M. Maneri, op. cit., p. 56.

[110] *Eleftheros Typos*, 9 April 1998.

[111] A. Dal Lago, op. cit., p. 97.

[112] *Idem*.

[113] *La Gazzetta del Mezzogiorno*, 19 September 1994 (quoted by A. Dal Lago, op. cit., p. 72).

[114] A. Dal Lago, op. cit., p. 92.

[115] A. Triandafyllidou, "Nation and...", op. cit., p. 77.

[116] *Idem*, p. 79.

[117] A. Dal Lago, op. cit., pp. 102-103.

[118] M. Maneri, op. cit., p. 58.

[119] Titles published, respectively, on the front page of the national dailies, *I Vradini* and *Eleftheros Typos* of 17 July 1999 (quoted by L. Tsouknidas, *I Kiriakatiki Avghi*, 18-7-1999).

[120] M. den Boer, "Crime et immigration...", op. cit., p. 106.

[121] On the concept of the social defence *vis-à-vis* multiple internal threats, see: M. Foucault, *Il faut défendre la société. Cours au Collège de France 1976*, 1997.

[122] A. Dal Lago, op. cit., p. 29.

[123] *La Repubblica*, 20 July 1997 (quoted by A. Dal Lago, op. cit., p. 37).

[124] A. Dal Lago, op. cit., p. 78.

[125] This behaviour can be adopted by both ordinary citizens and officials, or even police officers.

[126] Namely disadvantaged districts.

References

Albrecht, H. J. (1997), 'Ethnic minorities and crime – the construction of foreigners' crime in the Federal Republic of Germany', in Palidda, S. (ed.), *Délit d'immigration, COST A2 Migrations*, Commission Européenne: Brussels, pp. 83-102.

Albrecht, H. J. (1997), 'Minorities, Crime, and Criminal Justice in the Federal Republic of Germany', in Marshall, I. H. (ed.), *Minorities, Migrants, and Crime*, Sage Publications: London, New Delhi.

Barbagli, M. (1998), *Immigrazione et criminalità in Italia*, Il Mulino: Bologna.

Bigo, D. (1996), *Polices en réseaux. L'expérience européenne*, Presses de Sciences Po: Paris.

Bigo, D. (1998), 'Sécurité et immigration: vers une gouvernementalité par l'inquiétude?', *Cultures & Conflits*, n° 31-32, pp. 13-38.

Bovenkerk, F. (1993), 'Crime and the Multi-Ethnic Society: A View from Europe', *Crime, Law and Social Change*, n° 3, pp. 271-280.

Butterwegge, C. (1996), 'Mass Media, Immigrants, and Racism in Germany. A Contribution to an Ongoing Debate', *Communications*, n° 2, pp. 203-220.

Ceyhan, Ayse and Tsoukala, A. (1997), 'Contrôle de l'immigration: mythes et réalités', *Cultures & Conflits*, n° 26-27, pp. 9-14.

Citrin, J. et al. (1997), 'Public Opinion Toward Immigration Reform: The Role of Economic Motivations', *The Journal of Politics*, n° 3, pp. 858-881.

Courtovic, I. (1994), 'To nomiko kathestos ton metanaston ergaton stin Ellada [The legal status of migrant workers in Greece]', *Marangopoulos Foundation for Human Rights,The Protection of the Rights of Migrant Workers and their Families*, Estia: Athens, pp. 182-193.

Dal Lago, A. (1997), 'The Impact of Migration on Receiving Societies. Some Ethnographic Remarks', in Palidda, S. (ed.), *Délit d'immigration, COST A2 Migrations*, Commission Européenne: Brussels.

Dal Lago, A. (1999), Non-Persone. L'esclusione dei migranti in una società globale, Feltrinelli: Milano.

den Boer, M. (1996), 'Immigrants, Asylum Seekers and Criminalisation: The Interaction between Criminal Justice Policy and Criminology', paper presented at the Round Table *Un nouveau champ de sécurité en Europe*, CERI/CNRS, Paris.

den Boer, M. (1998), 'Crime et immigration dans l'Union européenne', *Cultures & Conflits*, n° 31-32, pp. 101-123.

Edelman, M. (1991), *Pièces et règles du jeu politique*, Seuil: Paris.

Espenshade, T. and Hempstead, K. (1996), 'Contemporary American Attitudes Toward US Immigration', *International Migration Review*, n° 2, pp. 535-570.

Foucault, M. (1997), 'Il faut défendre la société', *Cours au Collège de France*, 1976, Gallimard/Seuil: Paris.

Gatti, U., Malfatti, D. and Verde, A. (1997), 'Minorities, Crime, and Criminal Justice in Italy', in Marshall, I. H. (ed.), *Minorities, Migrants and Crime*, Sage Publications: London, New Delhi, pp. 110-129.

Gregory, F. (1998), 'Policing Transition in Europe: The Role of EUROPOL and the Problem of Organised Crime', *Innovation*, n° 3, pp. 287-305.

Huysmans, J. (1995), 'Migrants as a Security Problem: Dangers of Securitizing Societal Issues', in Miles, R. and Thränhardt, D. (eds), *Migration and European Integration. The Dynamics of Inclusion and Exclusion*, Pinter: London, pp. 53-72.

ISPAC (1996), *Migration and Crime*, ISPAC: Milano.

Karydis, V. (1996), *I eglimatikotita ton metanaston stin Ellada [The crime involvement of migrants in Greece]*, Papazissis: Athens.

Maneri, M. (1997), 'Les médias dans le processus de construction sociale de la criminalité des immigrés. Le cas italien', in Palidda, S. (ed.), *Délit d'immigration, COST A2 Migrations*, Commission Européenne: Brussels, pp. 51-72.

Naylor, R. T. (1995), 'From Cold War to Crime War: The Search for a New "National Security"', *Transnational Organised Crime*, n° 4, pp. 37-56.

Ohlemacher, T. (1994), 'Public Opinion and Violence Against Foreigners in the Reunified Germany', *Zeitschrift für Soziologie*, n° 3, pp. 222-236.

Palidda, S. (1997), 'La construction sociale de la déviance et de la criminalité parmi les immigrés. Le cas italien', in Palidda, S. (ed.), *Délit d'immigration, COST A2 Migrations*, Commission Européenne: Brussels, pp. 231-266.

Palidda, S. (1998), Domanda di sicurezza e forze di polizia nei capoluoghi di provincia emilano-romagnoli, juillet (mimeo).

Palidda, S. (1999), 'La criminalisation des migrants', *Actes de la recherche en sciences sociales*, n° 129, pp. 39-49.

Sayad, A. (1999), 'Immigration et "pensée d'Etat"', *Actes de la recherche en sciences sociales*, n° 129, pp. 5-14.

Schlesinger, P. and Tumber, H. (1994), *Reporting Crime. The Media Politics of Criminal Justice*, Clarendon Press: Oxford.

Sellin, T. (1984), *Conflits de culture et criminalité*, Pedone: Paris.

Spinellis, C. et al. (1996), 'Recent Immigration and Protection of Migrants', Human Rights in Greece', *Chroniques*, September, pp. 119-154.

Tournier, P. (1997), 'La délinquance des étrangers en France – analyse des statistiques pénales', in Palidda, S. (ed.), *Délit d'immigration, COST A2 Migrations*, Commission Européenne, pp. 133-162.

Triandafyllidou, A. (1997), 'Racists? Us? Are you joking? The Discourse of Social Exclusion of Immigrants in Greece and Italy', *Non Military Aspects of Security in Southern Europe: Migration, Employment and Labour Market*, Institute of International Economic Relations and Regional Network on Southern European Societies: Santorini.

Triandafyllidou, A. (1999), 'Nation and Immigration: a Study of the Italian Press Discourse', *Social Identities*, n° 1, pp. 65-88.

Tsoukala, A. (1997), 'Le contrôle de l'immigration en Grèce dans les années quatre-vingt-dix', *Cultures & Conflits*, n° 26-27, pp. 51-72.

Tsoukala, A. (1999), 'Le discours grec sur la criminalité des immigrés', *Hommes & Migrations*, n° 1218, pp. 77-89.

Tsoukala, A. (1999), 'The perception of the "other" and the integration of immigrants in Greece', in Geddes, A. and Favell, A. (eds), *The Politics of Belonging: Migrants and Minorities in Contemporary Europe*, Ashgate: Aldershot, Brookfield, Singapore, Sydney, pp. 109-124.

Tsoukala, A. (2002), 'Le traitement médiatique de la criminalité étrangère en Europe', *Déviance et société*, vol. 26, n° 1, pp. 61-82.

van Dijk, T. (1993), *Elite Discourse and Racism*, Sage Publications, Newbury Park: London, New Delhi.

Wacquant, L. (1999), 'Des "ennemis commodes"', *Actes de la recherche en sciences sociales*, n° 129, pp. 63-67.

Chapter 6

The Control of the Enemy Within?
Police Intelligence in the
French Suburbs (*banlieues*) and its
Relevance for Globalization

Laurent Bonelli[1]

The processes of "globalization" remain deeply uneven in the populations they touch and in the ways in which they affect them. Whereas exchanges multiply, and, in the case of certain social groups, accelerate, others seem increasingly imprisoned in micro territories. But they are not an "outside" of the globalization. On the contrary, Arjun Appadurai has explained that the processes of globalization are always culturally located in these micro-territories and that it is this level which gives its real significance to the processes at work, not the discourses about globalization as a social distribution of good or bad.[2] So, what is the significance of the removing of the border controls and the so-called opening of citizenship to the other Europeans inside France? How far the removal of borders as a sign of globalization restructures or not the boundaries between an "us" and an "other"? Are the English or the German still the old enemies? Are the Russians under suspicion? No. Now the new enemies are considered by the police as already infiltrated, between us, part of us, but fortunately, marked by a certain kind of otherness which is based on religion and ethnicity as Anastassia Tsoukala explained in the previous chapter. They are different and even if they are inside the national territory, by chance it is said that it is possible to draw boundaries to discriminate them. They live in specific areas, they are among the "poor" and it is from "their location" that it is possible to control them and to anticipate what they are doing and for whom they really work. "Terrorism" has become the "word", the excuse for surveillance of the territories inhabited by some of the poor which are the most visible because they look as if they were the "outside" of the global world shared by the elites. Zygmunt Bauman has sketched the global picture of the creation of the folk devil of our age in his book, *Globalization: the human consequences*. He reminds us that "to exist locally in a globalized universe is a sign of social degradation and dispossession" and notices a general tendency to "criminalize cases which do not conform to the ideal standard",[3] and to discriminate those who are opposed to the dominant model (or those who do not participate in it). It is in this context that we need to analyze the police surveillance of the enemy within, when the within is less and less related to national or even European border controls.

In France this is particularly the case for the inhabitants of the *banlieues*,[4] excluded from the paradise of mobility, which characterizes a way of life (the elites' way of life) and the structures of power (economic and financial in particular). In the last years, an increasing number of political and media discourses about the dangerous nature of these zones and their populations has been observed. They refer to anomia and de-civilization processes, and insist that people move from deviant behaviors, linked to petty crime, to organized crime or Islamic terrorism. The urban jobless adolescent with foreign origins is frequently presented as the main threat to our society. As a consequence, we witness a rapid increase in the number of police forces deployed, new technologies of surveillance and the involvement of many social institutions in the social control of these populations. This chapter will reflect on the constitution and the effects of these discourses and knowledge that (re)builds internal borders and justifies measures of exception.

First of all, we have learned from the constructivist approach that the institutional answers are not a simple response to a given problem. On the contrary, institutions understand and frame a problem according to the answers which are usually offered. A social problem is not a fact in itself; it needs social work to receive the status of problem. Not all social transformations develop into a social problem. They are constructed by groups socially interested in producing a new category of perceptions of the social world in order to act on it. In short, in order to become a social problem, a phenomenon needs both objective transformations and a specific work of public enunciation and mobilization. This work should incessantly be called into question.[5]

Security agencies played an important role in this social construction of the reality and in the framing of the social problems. They are characterized by a form of specific authority that gives them a quasi monopoly on defining what is frightening, and on producing the pictures of the enemy. This authority is mainly based on the claim of knowing hidden and secret elements of the situation that other social agents are said not to be aware of.

Police Knowledge and Disaffiliation

The main set of knowledge relating to the *banlieues* and crime stem from police discourses. However, the police do not produce a singular and specific knowledge, but several kinds. Actually, if the police are an institution – a State institution in France – their tasks are carried out by several distinct structures. We can distinguish three of them: criminal police, intelligence services and urban police.

These three structures are very different from one another. They do not list the same hierarchy of threats, they do not assess situations the same way and, thus, they do not produce the same intelligence. It is an effect of the social trajectories of these different policemen. They seldom move from one service to another. Professional careers are developed mainly within the same service. This fact structures a distinct professional *ethos* linked to the institutional memory and social practices. Their stands tend also to be linked to the space they occupy in the field of security professionals.[6] Indeed, their intra-agency competitiveness and the incorporated history of each institution are the output of differentiated knowledge. The theoretical works of Graham T. Allison[7] demonstrate that institutional visions of problems are yoked to organizational routines that pre-date them and are reactivated by the fervour of new situations.

Different visions compete within the police force in struggles to define the hierarchy of threats and thus the importance of different services, both in terms of legitimacy and budgets.

The urban police were the first section to gather intelligence on these neighborhoods and on petty crime because, institutionally, it is their job to tackle this kind of crime. For a few years now, they have been facing two kinds of developments: the transformation of the social situation and of the deviant behaviors in the *banlieues*, and the increase in demands for regulating urban disorders coming from local politicians, schools, social workers and even citizens.

First of all, thanks to housing policies, the wealthiest inhabitants of these suburbs were able to buy houses and move out of the area. Meanwhile the economic crisis struck the unqualified workers mostly living in these neighborhoods. This double phenomenon of concentration/pauperization had very important effects on deviance issues. Violence among working class juveniles does not constitute a new phenomenon but its mode of expression appears to have changed. A deviant behavior (insults, physical violence, etc.) linked to a street culture was ended by the integration into the industrial world. This sort of behavior of virility, physical strength, anti-authoritarianism could be continued in the factory as part of the working class values. Throughout the years, professional integration had been linked to a passage to a more "classical" way of life.

Nowadays these groups can no longer integrate into a declining world; nor can they occupy the new under-qualified jobs they were supposed to get, because they do not have the required skills for jobs in the service sector.[8] As a consequence, they remain in the public space where they produce disorders. They are what Robert Castel calls *disaffiliated*: "they occupy a supernumerary position, in a "floating" situation in a kind of social no man's land, not integrated and without doubt unable to integrate, at least in the meaning of integration used by Durkheim as a belonging to a society forming a whole of interdependent elements (…) They are excluded from the productive exchange circuits, they have missed the modernization train and stand on the platform with very few luggage. Therefore, they can be objects of attention and arouse anxiety, because they pose a problem".[9]

The difficulties of different institutions (schools, public housing, public transportation) and local politicians to deal with this population produced a multilateral increase in demands for police solutions. Urban police benefiting from the real problems of local politicians to solve these issues have developed a discourse on the necessity for the police to "re-occupy" these areas. Thus they asked for more means (manpower, equipment) and more power on justice and politics. At the same time, this mobilization gave the urban police a key role, which had an effect on the other police services responsible for other forms of criminality.

From Urban Violence to Organized Crime and/or Terrorism

This effect was significant in the case of Criminal police services. In France, the Criminal Police (Police Judiciaire) are in charge of what is called "high policing", i.e. murders, bank robbery, and large-scale drug traffic. This police unit does not really deal with petty crime either. However, this police department decided to be interested in this "new form" of criminality because according to a high level policeman:

> "In strategic terms, the criminal police must not be away from the national apparatus designed to fight this type of criminality. It is a problem of credibility. Keeping away from urban violence means being marginalized, because the subject is at the center of political concerns" (Interview, Police Judiciaire Chief, May 1999).

The Criminal Police consequently justified their involvement by explaining why:

> "Criminals in the *banlieues*, some of whom are still under 18 years old, will take more and more importance and will constitute tomorrow's criminal tank of the Criminal Police. It is necessary right now to learn who they are, and what their behaviors are" (Interview, Police Judiciaire Chief, May 1999).

In order to do this, the Criminal Police obtained specific units: *the brigades de recherche d'enquêtes et de coordination* [BREC] and developed a discourse on this evolution towards more seriousness, which consolidated their own power in the institutional struggles inside the police.

However, the main transformations have affected the internal intelligence services. In France, the internal intelligence services are essentially the *Renseignements généraux* (RG).[10] They traditionally focus on political surveillance and subversion threats against the political order. It implies controlling politically organized groups (French or foreigners) that could contest this political order. They did not focus on petty crime at all. However, at the beginning of the 1990s, the usefulness of the RG was called into question and even their entire suppression was being envisaged. In this contest, the RG simply used the interest of politicians for urban disorder issues in order to re-deploy and prove their usefulness. They produced a new category of analysis: "urban violence".[11]

However, they imported their own methods of analysis and their framing of the social reality: Some practices linked to street cultures were reinterpreted according to their own framework, emphasizing the threats to the political and institutional order. The tools they created are interesting to examine: in their understanding, a murder is less important than the stoning of a police car or a graffiti saying "fuck the police", because murder is an individual act. Urban riots are the highest threat level of the scale, because they are collective.

The intelligence services became a very important force on *systematizing urban violence into a global threat.* They considered a number of relatively unrelated events to possess an organized and political character. Indeed, all intelligence service members have in common the fact that they attach a central role to political power relations. This means that their systems of representation and guiding principles are opposed to the world of the judiciary, for which the relationship with the law is primordial. These two activities, criminal and intelligence, are entirely separate, from their tutelage authorities (government/magistrate) to their targets (political/criminal) via their operational modes (prevention and pro-activity/repression). Their professional apprenticeship is effectively the constitution of *anti-subversive* mindsets, characterized by an interest in the political game, the practical ability to influence and control it, and an attachment to the legitimate order as well as its preservation.[12] It is the importation of the *logic of suspicion*, widespread in the police in general, into political activity and which explains in turn the recurrent visions of "plots" and "manipulation".

One of the clearest manifestations of this mindset is the degree of organization imputed by the intelligence services to their adversaries in case reports. They tend to see part of a global political strategy behind the slightest local initiative, and to consider groups or autonomous individuals as agents of an occult and structured organization.

From their point of view, acts as miscellaneous as car theft, smashing up a mail box, or a lack of politeness will ultimately lead the individual to organized crime or Islamic terrorism, and therefore to *a delinquent career*.[13] From this point of view, the riots are seen as politically manipulated by organized groups.

First of all, the intelligence services tended to believe that riots were manipulated by extreme left-wing groups, their traditional opponents. However, they realized that they were wrong...

Then, they thought that the riots were influenced by Islamic fundamentalists, another group they were monitoring. Urban violence was interpreted as being controlled by Islamic fundamentalists for the purpose of moving police forces away from the neighborhood, and the jobless urban youth were seen as recruits for terrorists. These analyses were nurtured by the involvement of some people, such as Khaled Kelkal, in terrorism. This young French national from Vaulx-en-Velin was involved in the attacks of 1995, and was tracked, then shot down by the gendarmes. While the DST, which has ever growing numbers of agents abroad and undertakes counterintelligence missions, described him as a member of foreign networks (the Algerian GIA) operating in France, the RG attempted to reconstruct the affair within the framework of the suburban housing estate where he was born, to demonstrate the risk of the radicalization of French youths of immigrant origin. As one contact emphasized:

> "Simultaneously, there is a geographical proximity and a proximity of origin between the groups at risk and young people living on poor estates. The manipulation of such groups is limited, but it exists. It concerns us on several levels: first, these groups are financed by trafficking, theft and the common crime committed by kids on estates. Then they pick up some of the anti-French Islamist discourse, which in the long term could enable autonomous terrorist groups to develop, although they don't exist at present. Finally, we are worried by the spreading of terrorist know-how. The training

that some kids have gone through, in Bosnia or elsewhere, the publications distributed, and so on, teach them how to make bombs and Molotov cocktails, so more and more youngsters have this know-how ..." (Interview, Direction centrale des renseignements généraux (DCRG) Police Chief, March 2000).

This "new threat" reaches one of the routines of counterintelligence: the surveillance of Muslim communities and especially locations of cult, leaders and religious associations. Indeed, the intelligence services of some countries of emigration have used religious infrastructures to control their own exiles for many years.

This form of surveillance increased therefore so long as the communities – notably those from former colonial empires – continued to grow. It is linked to the progressive settling of immigrant workers (partly because of the official end of working immigration in 1974).

But the intelligence services' interest in Muslim communities took a fairly sharp turn following international events linked to political Islamism. In France, the main staging posts in the development of specialist branches were the Iranian Revolution of 1979; the situation in the Middle East; and the attacks of the Fouad Ali Saleh network between 1985 and 1986. Then there was the Algerian situation post June 1991, which led to another wave of attacks in 1995. These events helped draw intelligence agents' attention on the activities of clandestine Muslim groups (especially armed Algerian Islamist Groups [GIA]), and work either to counter their violent activities on the domestic territory or to unsettle their logistical framework (propaganda, recruitment, financing circuits, etc.).

The intelligence services first investigated their functioning and locations. Using undercover working methods (tapping, shadowing, informers, etc.), they monitored mosques, sermons and cultural associations, anywhere they thought they may find "fundamentalists". As one contact indicated:

"Our work consists of operational work on people in *the* mosques. [...] We are criticised for seeing Islam as a security problem. I always say to myself that I'm not a Muslim. I've never studied Muslim culture. I know a bit about it, empirically learned from work. So I'm incapable of judging what a good Muslim is. [...] That Muslims practise their religion is normal and that's fine. On the other hand, I am capable of deciding whether people represent a threat to public order. It's my job. And as a terrorist act has to be commissioned by a *Fatwah*, delivered by someone qualified to do so, we are interested in people who have that power" (Interview, DCRG Police Chief, March 2000).

This is how they come to pay such close attention to Muslim institutions and groups, as well as their internal power dynamics and development. The challenge therefore is to identify who among the Muslim communities is likely to be enlisted to the ranks of radical groups. This task was approached by establishing "profiles" from standard "types", a *proactive* method whose aim, "from statistical correlations established on individual trajectories, is to produce data oriented towards repressive action, able to anticipate the probable behaviour of individuals with similar characteristics upstream of the commission of an infraction or crime".[14] Based on case studies of individuals involved in clandestine actions, the intelligence services draw up modal social trajectories and give priority vigilance to the activities of those who meet these specifications. Consequently, factors, for example, such as foreign origin (particularly from a Muslim country), visits to this association or that mosque (especially "fundamentalist" or "Salafist"), frequent travelling, an asymmetric career path and holidays abroad (in London, particularly) trigger the near-automatic attention of the intelligence agencies.

The suspicion is heightened even further for "converts". This national figure of the European called to Islam concentrates all the properties of "dangerousness" so far as they are defined by the intelligence services. As Yves Bertrand, former RG director (DCRG), indicated:

> "Dangerousness [...] is the clandestine. The clandestine is the networks. Remember that France was the first country hit by terrorist attacks in the mid-90s. Back then we discovered [...] the convert phenomenon [...] and its importance in the core of these networks. The converts played and continue to play the role played by the French in Algeria's National Liberation Front (FLN); the *porteurs de valise* [French nationals who aided armed Algerian independence groups] as we used to call them. In fact, they were much more important than simple *porteurs de valise*. I'm not making an ideological comparison, simply showing how it works."[15]

It is not so much the radical potential of the converts – due to the recent conversion and the raised ante that may accompany this – which worries the intelligence services, but rather their belonging to the national community and ability to melt into it. The image of *porteurs de valise* – aside from the fact that it demonstrates the persistence of social patterns born from colonial struggles – is interesting because it becomes the metaphor for the invisible enemy enjoying all the advantages bestowed by nationhood (free circulation, legal protection, administrative facility, etc.), and turning them against the interests of the State that granted them.

At the same time as they attempt to neutralize members of radical groups, the intelligence services are trying to dismantle the support networks that they suppose are established in areas comprising large immigrant populations arriving from mainly Muslim countries. This is why, for example, they monitor the friends and family of individuals suspected of taking part in radical actions. As DST director Pierre de Bousquet de Florian explains:

> "We also work a lot on their surrounding. Some activists, without ever having lived in France or with few links here, may still have attachments: a cousin or friend, a sister and brother in law. Without having organised networks, they can still benefit from fairly voluntary complicity and friendly or family solidarity susceptible to culminate in logistical aid."[16]

Here we find the classical figures of a counter-subversion methodology that mechanically deduces attitude systems from social, affective or cultural proximity, and consequently establishes grounds for surveillance.[17]

We should be especially prudent here. Social disqualification, which is the condition of a number of youngsters from working class areas in large French cities, can lead young people to reconstruct and "fabricate" their identities – especially religious ones – aimed at restoring some sort of *dignity*.[18] However their apparent radicalism (notably in their discourse) has nothing to do with that of clandestine groups. In the same way as the surveillance of individuals who have joined violent action insists on the singularity of the trajectories and life stories rather than on a systematic "career",[19] profiling, and the interpretations it authorizes, is contemptuous of the differential modalities and groundings of religious commitment and incorporate this heterogeneity into a single "threatening" category. It throws suspicion upon a large part of the Muslim community, by linking all cultural and religious elements, facts and activities with terrorist potential.

These interpretative schemes create confusion between the radicalism of groups such as al-Qaeda, the image of a conquering, homogeneous and warrior-like religion, threatening to the West, that has been constructed in certain strategist think tanks,[20] and the rise in power (although it remains relative) of the claims made in connection to practicing Muslim worship and the renewal of religious organizations within western countries.[21] This transposition simultaneously accredits the theses of the dangerousness of Islam and casts doubt upon the loyalty of immigrant communities, consigned to function as "terrorist breeding pools", authorizing hasty generalizations. Thus, police chief Richard Bousquet, for example, insists that: "the human breeding pool that can deliver our disaffected city and suburban areas to radical Islam is still swarming with "re-Islamicized" Arab kids and converts mixing with criminality and ready to join the terrorist adventure on the order of a brain in the international Jihad".[22] This generalized suspicion of foreigners bears echoes of the *fifth column*[23] and the *enemy within*, and largely outstrips the framework of terrorism, becoming a threat to national cohesion itself.

The fight against the "terrorist threat" does not restrict intelligence service surveillance. The RG also pay considerable and particular attention to proselyte Muslim groups, such as, for example, *Jama'a at-Tabligh*. Through telephone tapping, the services are aware that some militants have received injunctions calling on them to preach in working class urban areas, on the socio-economic exclusion of the teenagers there. Their observations confirm this. They also remark the role that religious groups or leaders can play in appeasing tensions in urban areas, and the moderating influence that they can have on "deviant" behaviour among the younger members of the community. Being unable, however, to measure the direct impact of this discourse on teenagers and young adults in these urban districts, they fall back on the vague notion of "communitarism", a kind of Arab-centrism that exalts a "Muslim" identity, deemed a threat to the Republic. The indistinctness of this category permits the reactivation of the image of Republican integration, linked to the historic model of the development of the State and characterized by centralization and the elimination of regional and cultural differences. It also offers scope to bring anyone who seems to contest this standard model back into line. Through the prism of the anti-subversive mindsets of intelligence service agents, communitarism begins to look like something of a coherent whole, endowed with central organizations and advancing in disguise, something whose *political* purpose must have daylight shed upon it. Under questioning by members of the French parliament on the "Islamic" headscarf, Yves Bertrand (ex-DCRG) explained:

> "I believe *they are testing our ability to respond* and are seeking other areas. [...] I think that orders are given and, beyond the school, the market place, taken in its broadest sense, is now the target, aiming at certain categories of personnel. Obviously, they are not going to turn to executives. Presently, they are approaching more modest categories. I'm thinking, for example, of manual workers, [...] and young supermarket cashiers" (Debré, 2003).[24]

Whether a violent threat for society or a danger for the Republic, fundamentalist Islam appears therefore to the eye of the intelligence services as *a priori* problematic. For them, it combines a trans-national dimension (consistent with foreign manipulation), strong communities established in western States but occupying low positions in the social hierarchy, and an ideology hostile to the prevalent social and political order. This Islam presents itself as something of a global subversion project susceptible to replace communism, fatally wounded by post-Fordist capitalist restructuring and the collapse of the USSR. It assumes its place within the discourse of power and normalization as described by Michel Foucault, in which society is "threatened by a number of heterogeneous elements which are not deemed essential to it and do not share the social body, the living body of society, in two parts, which are in some ways accidental. This will be the notion of infiltrated foreigners, the theme of deviant sub-products of this society".[25] From here flows the discourse of the irreducible "otherness" of Muslims, the focalization on converts and hardening of the police response.

New Structures and their Effects

All this information contributes to create an image of these zones as dangerous and, consequently, to justify the establishment of specialized structures. These structures are very different from the normal ones and constitute real *exceptional* structures.

Thus, the police forces set up multiple units of intervention: *brigades anti-criminalité* [BAC], *unités mobiles de sécurité* [UMS], *compagnies départementales d'intervention* [CDI], *forces de maintien de l'ordre fidélisées* [CRS or *gendarmes mobiles*]; criminal units: BREC; or intelligence units with the "urban violence" sections of the *Renseignements généraux*. The recent reform of neighborhood police forces also affects these priority zones.

The justice system has also developed specific structures (local criminality treatment groups [GLTD], prosecutors' correspondents or delegates, houses of right and justice [*MJD*]) as well as specific procedures (*traitement en temps réel de la délinquance* [*TTR*], immediate appearance courts, etc.). Finally, other institutions have built their own practices such as National Education in the violence zones, with the standardized information protocols sent to the prosecutor and the police.

The inflation of these structures in the poor neighborhoods and the choice to repress minor criminality as a matter of priority has had three major effects.

First of all, one witnesses in the zones defined as "sensitive", hostility in the relationship between the police forces and the people who live there. Some do not hesitate to denounce the "military attitude" of the specialized units, which intervene in these districts. This military attitude becomes obvious not only in the methods used (stop and frisk...) but also in the police agents' behaviors. They extend to other institutions, for example in the public transportation security services.

The vocabulary changes into a more warlike register. Jean-Pierre Havrin, police force adviser for the former home office minister J-P. Chevènement stated as follows:

> "In the urban ghettos, there are citizens and there are hooligans. Often, we mix up the young people and the hooligans. And the hooligans should be well targeted. And I believe that with a neighborhood police force like the one we've put into place, there will no longer be mistakes. One carries out surgical operations, surgical strikes. The hooligans are identified. One separates the hooligans from the remainders."[26]

Some police chiefs, like Richard Bousquet, representative of the main police chiefs trade union (*SCHFPN*), speak about the "zones of security that surround the stairwells, of effective functioning army logistics, of drug infantrymen, etc.".[27] The logics of action are complementary to the warlike register. Justifying the use of the Security Mobile Units (UMS), the Préfet of a Parisian suburb explained:

> "They are a major tool used to dam urban violence in the suburbs. As soon as there is a brawl between gangs or a crew [of police force] in difficulty, I have thirty well-built guys who can be on the spot in 10 to 15 minutes. That calms them... Patrolling the block is nothing if the cavalry does not support it. The neighborhood policeman does not stop anybody if he's not backed up. It is out of question that I give up my cavalry" (Interview, January 1999).

The central police chief described an ordinary day in the urban ghetto as:

> "It is like in Kosovo, over there. We are on a pacification mission. The heights must be held, like soldiers hold the peaks... We need more updated material. We don't use the *flash-ball* [specific gun shooting rubber balls], which was the best 5 years ago. Now the police have shock grenades that send a strong puff of wind and they use riot guns. The bullets are made of rubber but for the police officer, what must be done is the same: to point at somebody with a riot gun. Before, these collective weapons did not leave the police station, and were used only for very specific and targeted missions. Now the orders are to hold the place at all costs, even under manpower. And it must be held, but..." (Interview, Urban Police chief, April 1999).

The most immediate result of these logics is the massive increase in outrage and rebellion in these areas, which provides statistical evidence of the intolerant relationship between police officers and young people. Moreover, one witnesses a massive spread of illegitimate police violence.

This strengthening is also very obvious in the penal field. Minor crimes, which previously did not attract police and judicial attention, are now the subject of criminal charges. The sanctions for minor criminality offences were strongly weighed down. The severity of the immediate appearance courts compared to the ordinary jurisdictions is particularly characteristic. The *traitement en temps réel* [TTR[28]], for its part, has radically transformed the exercise of justice for minors. Instead of being subject to civil court procedures, children are now directly engaged in the criminal courts. In the same way, actions that did not directly engage the justice system before are penalized today, in particular by means of criminal mediation.

Then, one sees the initial stages of police and judicial enquiries in fields of activities to which they did not previously extend. This rationale comes to constitute the prism through which social questions are viewed in these districts. The structural prevention disappears with the advancement of the delinquent prevention. Socio-cultural concerns and/or public health are examined only as long as they contribute to the maintenance of social order. The only question now is what is likely to produce criminal behaviours.

Furthermore, the police seek to enroll the efforts of social services on behalf of their mission, in situations which exceed their *savoir faire*. This mobilization of services and administrations, formerly separated from the field of security, is accompanied by a transformation of their power and strengthens the reach of control of these institutions. As Richard V. Ericson and Kevin D. Haggerty explain: "there is no limit to police participation in the construction and management of social problems. [The police are] shaping the knowledge requirements of other institutions in order to assist these institutions in the risk management of the specific part of the population for whom they are responsible".[29] And from this point of view, the equation: *young people with social, economic or professional difficulties* equals *criminal* appears to become obvious. Thus, the neighborhoods *in danger* are transformed into *dangerous neighborhoods*.

In contrast to the United States, France has not yet chosen to massively increase the number of agents involved in repression (i.e. police, magistrates and penitentiary personnel), this focus implies that entire sections of criminality being disregarded, in order to privilege the fight against its most benign, "visible" forms in the public sphere. Thus, the Ministry of Justice itself recognizes that the *fast track procedures* – which represent more than 90 percent of the activity of certain courts – "privilege and overemphasize the treatment of small and average criminality, to the detriment of the economic or financial criminality".[30] Described as long and enduring by the Minister of Justice, these procedures lead to a dissipation of the activity of the magistrates, who must abandon more complex affairs. In the same way, the number of police investigators assigned to the economic and financial sectors remains ridiculously low whereas France is one of the countries with the highest ratio of security forces/population in Europe. The weak enforcement of laws concerning fraud at work, commercial or environmental crimes is in stark contrast considering the importance of these areas.

Political Management of Crime: Towards a New Governmentality?

The increasing management by the police of the consequences of *disaffiliation* is also the consequence of structural political changes.

Petty crime and deviant behaviors have not always been political issues. They were more or less considered in terms of social and/or moral pathology. However, they became central in the generic heading of *insecurity* at the end of the Seventies, when, for the first time, a separation between *crime* and *the fear of crime* occurred. This rupture was fundamental, because it was at the origin of the political management of crime and topics left before to the security professionals. The invention of the fear of crime as *public opinion on security*,[31] allowed politicians, particularly local ones, to become involved. Public statements on the subject multiplied throughout the 1980s and 1990s; politicians would specialize in security and consequently build their careers on it.

According to an expertise on the matter, the political experts contribute to the increasingly technical approach that will erase little by little the political cleavages that opposed a right wing guarantee of security against a left wing follower of freedom in the Seventies. Agreeing on the nature of the problem, the diagnosis and the solutions needed, they tend to produce a consensus concerning the priority to fight specified forms of criminality.

This agreement on the problem is also a consequence of the spread of the Front National (extreme right party) ideas, and of the disappearance of alternative knowledge concerning poor districts, from the political field (decline of the working class representatives: French Communist Party and neighborhood organizations) or from other institutions, as social prevention services which are struck by the structural transformations of the *banlieues*.

The almost unshared domination of the police expertise on urban disorders in the political world and in the media is enforced by a particular category of social agents: the "independent experts".

They appeared in the mid-1990s and acted as go-betweens between the police officers and the politicians or the media. Basing their expertise on their proximity to the police officers, they shaped the dominant views and discourses according to their expertise. Claiming an academic identity, they reinterpreted police analyses in the light of theories of the rational choice. Importing economic theses into the analysis of crime, they transformed the delinquent into a *homo oeconomicus*, into a rational being who chooses criminality according to a cost/benefit calculation. Linked to the conservative *doxa* of "individual responsibility" for their acts, these schemes presuppose that adolescents in the poor neighborhoods make an easy choice that is rational and consistent in a system of delinquent values when compared to conventional values within which work remains the central aspect. This interpretation voluntarily disguises the social causes of apparent disorders in these zones of relegation. They convey the idea of social danger in these neighborhoods (here we observe a return to the end of the

19th century ideology defining the working class as dangerous). They also provide the framework for a moral and condescending discourse about the degeneration of working class families. Severity would thus be justified on the grounds of irreversible criminality.

These schemes were all the more effective as various governments were unable to stop or to reverse the processes of urban and social segregation. In the poorest zones of the country, unemployment increased and the activity rate collapsed. As a consequence, a subsistence economy developed oscillating between legal and illegal.

At a moment when the space for maneuvering for the government was reduced, due to economic regulations, we observe a return of punishment – both in discourses and practice. As Michel Foucault argued, the capacity to punish, to mark the bodies, is related to the affirmation of power.[32] It is important to notice today in France, but also in the United Kingdom, in the United States, in Belgium, as well as in other countries, that a return of punishment is taking place, at a time when the sovereignty of these States is challenged in economic and financial matters. In short, punishment could be interpreted as the last fortress of the sovereignty of politics.[33]

We observe a new form of *governmentality* which changes the political management of fears. The development of the State was linked (particularly in the post war Welfare states) to the building of institutions in order to reduce the social fears and the uncertainty of citizens: unemployment, retirement, etc. Today, "governments are unable to promise anything more than "work flexibility", i.e. to further increase uncertainty and its painful and invalidating consequences".[34] It is therefore not very surprising that the real problems involved in uncertainty are reduced to the fear of crime, which becomes a *new technology of power*.

These technologies lead to inequality of treatment depending on the social profile of law enforcers. They confuse law and order with the pacification of the poor neighborhoods, and contribute to the linking of crime to the poor, and therefore its criminalization. The districts of relegation in France, the ghettos in the United States, are seen as the perfect grounds for criminality. A criminality limited to street criminality.

However, it remains to be seen whether these choices, which (re)build and enforce social borders, constitute in time the best way to ensure the "security" of the State and society, to support the cohesion of its citizens and to strengthen the legitimacy of its democratic institutions.

Notes

[1] Lecturer in politics at the University of Paris X—Nanterre and member of the Centre d'études sur les Conflits. Co-editor with Gilles Sainati (2001) of *La machine à punir. Pratiques et discours sécuritaires*, L'Esprit Frappeur: Paris, 320 pages.

[2] Appadurai, A. (1996), *Modernity at large: cultural dimensions of globalization*, Public worlds; v. 1. Minneapolis, Minn.: University of Minnesota Press.

[3] Bauman, Z. (1999), *Le coût humain de la mondialisation*, Hachette, Paris, pp. 9 and 12, French translation of (1998), *Globalization: the human consequences*, Columbia University Press, NY.

[4] The "banlieues" are French poor neighborhoods located in the periphery of large cities. They are characterized by a high level of public housing and important rates of unemployment, youth and migrants.

[5] See for example, Bourdieu, P.; Chamboredon, J. C. and Passeron, J. C. (1983), *Le métier de sociologue*, Mouton, Paris, 359 pages, and Edelman, M. (1991), *Pièces et règles du jeu politique*, Seuil, Paris, 253 pages.

[6] On this topic, see Didier Bigo (2004), "The Globalisation of (In)security and the Ban-Opticon", *Traces: a Multilingual Series of Cultural Theory*, n° 4, University of Hong Kong Press.

[7] Allison, G. T. (1999), *Essence of Decision, Explaining the Cuban Missiles Crisis*, 2ᵉ Ed. Longman.

[8] See Bourgois, P. (1995), *In Search of Respect. Selling Crack in El Barrio*, Cambridge University Press, particularly chapter 4, "Goin' Legit: Disrespect and Resistance at Work", pp. 114-174.

[9] Castel, R. (1999), *Les métamorphoses de la question sociale. Une chronique du salariat*, Gallimard, Paris, pp. 665-666.

[10] There is another one, la Direction de la Sûreté du Territoire (DST), but more specialized on counterintelligence.

[11] See Bonelli, L. (March 2001), "Les Renseignements généraux et les violences urbaines", *Actes de la Recherche en Sciences Sociales*, n° 136-137, pp. 95-103.

[12] Bonelli, L. (2004), "Formation, conservation et reconversion de dispositions anti-subversives. L'exemple des renseignement généraux", in Sylvie Tissot (ed.), *Reconversions militantes*, Limoges, Presses universitaires de Limoges.

[13] These visions, generally wrong – as shown in judicial data – find an academic support (or justification) in criminological concepts like "incivilities" developed by American authors like J. Q. Wilson and G. Kelling in their well known theory: "*Broken Windows*". For them, these small disorders are the starting point of a delinquent *continuum*, which starting from insignificant acts will lead to much more serious actions, if they are not stopped in time: "*the proliferation of incivilities is only the sign that there is a generalized rise of criminality. The first deviant acts, however tiny they seem, if they spread, brand a district, act as a magnet for other deviances, are the sign of the end of social peace. The spiral of the decline starts, violence settles in and with it, all the forms of criminality: petty crime, theft, robbery, drug dealing, etc.*" See Wilson, J. Q and Kelling, G. (March 1982), "Broken Windows: The Police and Neighborhood Safety", *The Atlantic Monthly*, and in France, Roché, S. (2001), *La délinquance des jeunes*, Seuil, Paris, 303 pages.

[14] Bigo, D. (December 1997), "La recherche proactive et la gestion du risque", *Déviance et Société*, vol. 21, n° 4, pp. 423-429.

[15] Hearing of Mr. Yves Bertrand, director general of the RG, 9 July 2003, report by Mr. Jean-Louis Debré, *sur la question du port des signes religieux à l'école*, n° 1275, Assemblée nationale, December 2003.

[16] *Libération*, 6 December 2002.

[17] Rogin, M. (December 1997), "La répression politique aux Etats-Unis", *Actes de la recherche en sciences socials*, n° 120, pp. 32-44.

[18] See Césari, J. (1998), *Musulmans et républicains. Les jeunes, l'islam et la France*, Bruxelles, Complexe, and Sayad, A. (1999), *La double absence. Des illusions de l'émigré aux souffrances de l'immigré*, Seuil, Paris, 344 pages.

[19] Beaud, S. and Masclet, O. (2002), "Un passage à l'acte improbable? Notes de recherche sur la trajectoire sociale de Zacarias Moussaoui", *French Politics, Culture and Society*, vol. 20, n° 2; Khosrokhavar, F. (2003), *Les nouveaux martyrs d'Allah*, Paris, Flammarion, pp. 271f. In another register, see Leveau, R. (1989), "Réflexions sur le non-passage au terrorisme dans l'immigration maghrébine en France", *Etudes polémologiques*, n° 49, 1/1989, pp. 141-156.

[20] See notably Huntington, S. (1996), *The Clash of Civilizations and Remaking of World Order*, New York, Simon and Schuster. For a radical critique of the conditions of drafting and reception of this thesis, see the special edition of *Cultures & Conflits*, "Troubler et inquiéter. Les discours du désordre international", n° 19/20, Autumn/Winter 1995.

[21] Césari, J., *Musulmans et républicains...*, op. cit.

[22] Bousquet, R. (1998), *Insécurité: les quartiers de tous les dangers*, L'Harmattan, Paris, p. 151.

[23] For example, the military review *Le Casoar* (n° 142, July 1996, p. 24) describes the situation in deprived areas with a high concentration of populations with foreign origin as follows: *"the links preserved by these migrants with their countries of origin can render them susceptible to calls from it when differences arise with our country. The famous fifth-columns, evoked during many previous conflicts, would then already in place".*

[24] Hearing of Mr. Yves Bertrand, director general of the RG, 9 July 2003, report by Mr. Jean-Louis Debré, *sur la question du port des signes religieux à l'école*, op. cit.

[25] Foucault, M. (1997), *Il faut défendre la société. Cours au collège de France 1976*, Gallimard-Seuil, Paris, p. 70.

[26] "Vous avez demandé la police?", *la Marche du Siècle* – France 3 – 19 January 2000.

[27] See Bousquet, R., *Insécurité: les nouveaux risques*, op. cit., pp. 121-122.

[28] Accelerated court procedures in respect of charges relating to minor offences.

[29] Ericson, R. V. and Haggerty, K. D. (1997), *Policing the Risk Society*, University of Toronto Press, pp. 73 and 75.

[30] *Rapport au Garde des Sceaux sur la politique pénale menée en 1999*, Direction des Affaires Criminelles et des Grâces, April 2000, p. 27.

[31] See Bourdieu, P. (1984), "L'opinion publique n'existe pas", in *Questions de sociologie*, Minuit, Paris, pp. 222-235.

[32] Foucault, M. (1975), *Surveiller et punir*, Gallimard, 360 pages.

[33] See Garland, D. (1998), "Les contradictions de la 'société punitive': le cas britannique", *Actes de la Recherche en Sciences Sociales*, n° 124, pp. 53f, and Garland, D. (2001), *The Culture of Control: Crime and Social Order in Contemporary Society*, University of Chicago Press. See also Christie, N. (2003), *L'industrie de la punition. Prison et politique pénale en Occident*, Autrement, Paris.

[34] Bauman, Z., *Le coût humain de la mondialisation*, op. cit., p. 177.

References

Allison, Graham T. (1999), *Essence of Decision, Explaining the Cuban Missiles Crisis*, 2e Ed. Longman: London.

Appadurai, Arjun. (1996), *Modernity at large: cultural dimensions of globalization, Public worlds*, vol. 1, Minn.: University of Minnesota Press, Minneapolis.

Bauman, Z. (1999), *Le coût humain de la mondialisation*, Hachette: Paris.

Beaud, S. and Masclet, O. (2002), "Un passage à l'acte improbable? Notes de recherche sur la trajectoire sociale de Zacarias Moussaoui", *French Politics, Culture and Society*, vol. 20, n° 2.

Bigo, D. (2004), "The Globalisation of (In)security and the Ban-Opticon", *Traces: a Multilingual Series of Cultural Theory*, n° 4, University of Hong Kong Press.

Bigo, D. (1997), "La recherche proactive et la gestion du risque", *Déviance et Société*, vol. 21, n° 4, pp. 423-429.

Bonelli, L. (2004), "Formation, conservation et reconversion de dispositions anti-subversives. L'exemple des renseignement généraux", in Sylvie Tissot (ed.), *Reconversions militantes*, Presses universitaires de Limoges: Limoges.

Bonelli, L. (2001), "Les Renseignements généraux et les violences urbaines", *Actes de la Recherche en Sciences Sociales*, n° 136-137, pp. 95-103.

Bourdieu, P. (1984), "L'opinion publique n'existe pas", *Questions de sociologie*, Minuit: Paris, pp. 222-235.

Bourdieu, P., Chamboredon, J. C. and Passeron, J. C. (1983), Le métier de sociologue, Mouton: Paris.

Bourgois, P. (1995), *In Search of Respect. Selling Crack in El Barrio*, Cambridge University Press: Cambridge.

Bousquet, R. (1998), *Insécurité: les nouveaux risques*, L'Harmattan: Paris.

Castel, R. (1999), *Les métamorphoses de la question sociale. Une chronique du salariat*, Gallimard: Paris.

Césari, J. (1998), *Musulmans et républicains. Les jeunes, l'islam et la France*, Complexe: Bruxelles.

Christie, N. (2003), *L'industrie de la punition. Prison et politique pénale en Occident*, Autrement: Paris.

Direction des Affaires Criminelles et des Grâces (2000), *Rapport au Garde des Sceaux sur la politique pénale menée en 1999*, pp. 27.

Edelman, M. (1991), *Pièces et règles du jeu politique*, Seuil: Paris.

Ericson, R. V. and Haggerty, K. D. (1997), *Policing the Risk Society*, University of Toronto Press: Toronto.

Foucault, M. (1997), *Il faut défendre la société. Cours au collège de France 1976*, Gallimard-Seuil: Paris.

Foucault, M. (1975), *Surveiller et punir*, Gallimard: Paris.

Garland, D. (2001), *The Culture of Control: Crime and Social Order in Contemporary Society*, University of Chicago Press: Chicago.

Garland, D. (1998), "Les contradictions de la 'société punitive': le cas britannique", *Actes de la Recherche en Sciences Sociales*, n° 124.

Khosrokhavar, F. (2003), *Les nouveaux martyrs d'Allah*, Flammarion: Paris.

Leveau, R. (1989), "Réflexions sur le non-passage au terrorisme dans l'immigration maghrébine en France", *Etudes polémologiques*, n° 49, 1, pp. 141-156.

Rogin, M. (1997), "La répression politique aux Etats-Unis", *Actes de la recherche en sciences socials*, n° 120, pp 32-44.

Roché, S. (2001), *La délinquance des jeunes*, Seuil: Paris.

Sayad, A. (1999), *La double absence. Des illusions de l'émigré aux souffrances de l'immigré*, Seuil: Paris.

Wilson, J. Q. and Kelling, G. (1982), Broken Windows: The Police and Neighborhood Safety, *The Atlantic Monthly*, March 1982, Atlantic Monthly Group: Boston.

Chapter 7

Policing by Dossier:
Identification and Surveillance
in an Era of Uncertainty and Fear

Ayse Ceyhan[1]

Introduction

The post-Cold War decades have been characterized by a dramatic emphasis on identity and identification means and technologies. Knowing with certitude who is who and assigning a recognizable identity to an individual, group or entity has become an important task for state authorities and law enforcement agencies. More recently this preoccupation has been reinforced by September 11 and the war against terrorism, leading even countries that were traditionally unconcerned by centralized identification means to think about their creation. In effect, like the American and British discussions about the adoption of a national identity card or the Japanese constitution of a computerized ID system (Yuki Net), more and more governments seek to adopt new technologies of identification in order to securitize identities and identification means and monitor the movements of people inside a given state as well as across borders. Many assign an ID number in a nationwide computerized system to their citizens. This trend, however, engenders severe criticisms. Critics worry about loss of privacy and fear government officials will misuse information for improper ends such as harassing those who are deemed "risky people", a category whose definition is quite blurry and that can encompass different people or groups. Governments affirm that the underlying idea is to modernize the cumbersome bureaucracy by making it easy to obtain personal information through nationwide databases. But they also acknowledge that the process intends to pursue not only efficiency and modernization but also public order, security and anti-terrorism objectives allowing them to gather information about people in an effort to keep better track of them and to monitor their movements inside and outside the national territory. This chapter will analyze this appetite for identification and identity in the context of a post-bipolar, post-Westphalian and globalized world. It will examine how it is intrinsically related to the transformations of security preoccupations and to the perceptions of the enemy in the new context as well as to the fear of the unknown and uncertainty. This will be illustrated by a historical look at French and American approaches on identity and identification means and an analysis of the contemporary technologies utilized to securitize them. This chapter will conclude by stressing the shift to a new form of surveillance generated by these transformations.

The Context

According to the Weberian foundation, this process, in its national framework, has its roots in the long term processes of bureaucratization of the modern state. Bureaucratization is understood here as the establishment of a durable state administration based on a centralized control of the means of violence within a delimited territory in the enforcement of its order (Weber 1947). On the one hand the state bureaucracy claims the monopoly over the legitimate use of violence and establishes a supervisory control of subject populations (whether this control takes the form of the Foucauldian Panopticon model or of an invisible and extraterritorial control as in the Baumanian "liquid modernity"), on the other hand the state's claim to enforcement of order requires the privilege of a monopoly over the legitimate crossing of borders by persons. This in turn leads to the claim to hold a monopoly over identification and means of identification of individuals under the state control by issuing documents such as the passport or the ID card (Torpey 2001). But today the Weberian model, which relies essentially on territoriality, is dramatically challenged by the processes of globalization and transnationalization and the creation of regional entities such as the European Union (EU), where borders are suppressed inside the Schengen area.[2] In the new framework characterized by moving borders, access to the territory, and free movement people are more and more monitored by a network of national and transnational security agencies, bureaucracies, mobile control units (Bigo 1996), and private companies such as the airline carriers (Lahav 1998). Their tasks include checks on persons and transport of goods not at traditional checkpoints but almost anywhere, issuance of visas, constitution of centralized databases and patrolling the external borders of the Union.

In order to better understand the sense of the focus on identity and identification means one needs to remember the context of the dramatic transformation of the concept of security at the end of bipolarity (Buzan 1991). Security is no longer framed by the clear-cut distinction of the inside and the outside but by the interpenetration of the domestic and the external security realms (Bigo 1996, 2000) and its scope has been deepened and enlarged to new sectors such as the political, the environmental and the societal (identitarian) (Buzan 1991, Waever 1997). In this framework the "enemy" is no longer the Communist as it was during the Cold War. With the collapse of the Berlin Wall, all security agencies, including the traditional external security agencies are looking inside the borders in search of an "enemy within" (Ceyhan, Peries 2001). This transformation has led to the creation of a domestic security concern in which the new figure of the enemy is not represented by a unique image and has multiple faces: supposedly it might be the migrant, the citizen with foreign ancestors, the dual-national, the commuter, the poor, the people living in poor suburbs, the foreign student, the anti-globalization protester etc.

It is noteworthy to remember that in the aftermath of September 11, the focus on the internal enemy has been dramatically intensified in the US. The Homeland

Security policy has made border controls and domestic security the cornerstone of the fight against terrorism. With the concentration in one agency (the Homeland Security Department) of all border control and security agencies, the US administration foresees the establishment of a greater control mechanism over who enters or leaves the territory and over the "risky people" inside the country. Supposedly, these people are often legal migrants from non-Western countries, essentially from the Middle East and Central Asia. They are regarded as posing a threat and endangering national security by creating a demand for false identity documents and business for smuggling networks that could also assist terrorists. This fear has led to the reinforcement of surveillance and identification technologies that would permit the government to gather information about and supervise subject populations.

Identity in Question

What is identity for security agencies and bureaucracies? Ultimately, it relies on bureaucratically constructed biographies. In this sense it is established through the collection of a certain number of data providing basic information on who the individual is (name, gender, nationality, birth place and physical description). For this purpose, states created ID cards and passports. But today it seems that identity is more than this basic information. It is not only a state's certification of national belonging or citizenship but rather, it looks like a knowledge on the past and present behaviors, acts, aims of a person, his/her projects, morality, relations and networks. Identity thus becomes more than the simple registration of nominal and individual identifiers.

In fact, knowing with certitude who is who is difficult even if documents certify it. Even though bureaucratically speaking this can be established through official documents issued by state authorities, it is not easy to fix and locate an identity for ever. In effect, identity is complex, never pre-given, unified nor singular and is multiply constructed across different, often antagonistic discourses, practices, positions, and strategies (Hall 1996). Identity has multiple meanings regarding the processes by which it is constructed, the social fields in which it is utilized, and the social position of individuals who use it as means of control and surveillance. In this perspective, identity can be the processes that produce subjectivity and construct us as subjects through specific strategies of enunciation and modalities of power (Foucault, 1969, 1975, Althusser 1993, Hall 1996). It can arise through a narrative presentation of the self (Hall 1996). It can produce and require recognition (Taylor 1992). It can be based on excluding somebody and establishing a violent hierarchy between differences (Derrida 1994). It can be assigned by one individual to another and may certify national belonging (Noiriel 2001). In consequence, the ways by which identities are created and proclaimed are multiple and different.

In this chapter, identity is used as a constructed representation of the self with relation to "significant others" produced in particular historical and institutional contexts and fields with specific discursive formations and practices emerging within the interplay of special modalities of power (G. H. Mead 1963,

Foucault 1975, Hall, 1996). Since identity is created in the interaction between self and society, it is formed and modified in a continuous dialogue with the social, cultural, and political environment. In the context of the transformation of this environment with globalization and de-territorialization, identity is becoming composed not of a single, but of several, sometimes contradictory or unresolved components as a result of structural and institutional change. As Stuart Hall assesses "the very process of identification, through which we project ourselves into our cultural identities, has become more open-ended, variable and problematic"[3] and "since identity shifts according to how the subject is addressed or represented, identification is not automatic".[4] In this respect, it becomes more and more difficult to cling on to identities assigned to individuals by bureaucratic process and the means that certify them. But with the rise of ever more varied technologies of identification, people are increasingly subjected to imputed identities of which they are not even aware. The question raised here is: how do individuals as subjects identify or not identify with the biographies to which they are summed, how do they perform, resist or negotiate the roles and positions they are assigned with? To what kind of control and surveillance do these processes lead?

To Be or to Do?

When comparing France and the US in regards to the question of the identity of a person or a group, Michel de Certeau asserts (1981, p.14) that contrary to Europe where identity can be addressed as what a person or a group *is*, in the US, it is only what they *do*. In France, like in most European countries, identity relies on bureaucratically constructed biographies that take into consideration the place of birth, the family, the social status etc. In that sense, identity is a sign of bureaucratic and social existence. In the US it relies on internal and external migrations, social and geographic mobility, exchange and production. In other words, the "European dogmatic focus on identity is contrasted by the American unconcern *vis-à-vis* place, origin and document" (de Certeau 1981, p. 14). This means that in the US, one does not need an established document in order to exist socially. Michel de Certeau highlights that contrary to France, there is no identity card[5] in the US. Americans replace it by the driver's license and the credit cards which detain "the capacity to cross the space and the participation to the game of contracts".[6]

But since the mid-eighties, we have been witnessing the reversal of this difference between the two approaches of identity. Today, it seems that "to be" is increasingly mixed with "to do" in both countries. I will argue that this transformation is dramatically linked to the problematization of migration and the focus on borders in the post-bipolar and post-Westphalian world. In effect, in the US, the unexpected change started in the nineties in California that surprisingly became the forerunning state in the problematization of immigration and in the convergence with the focus on identity and the securitarian rhetoric produced in France. Hence it is in California, once described as "the place of internal and external migrations where life consists of crossing the border constantly",[7] that the debate on identity and identification means started in 1994 with the adoption of the Proposition 187 that singles out the migrants as the cause of the social and economic problems of California and prohibits undocumented migrants from receiving any public welfare service and denies schooling to their children (Ceyhan 1997). One of the issues raised by this law was the question of the establishment of identity through official documents. Stressing the need for more secure identity documents, it introduced the question of bogus documents presumably utilized by illegal aliens and the criminal stealing of identity documents (especially the Social Security number) and transformed it into a public concern. Vehement debates generated around this question had even led to the proposal of the creation of an identity card *à la française* and involved the securitization of identity and employment eligibility documents.

Among the surprising consequences of the Proposition 187, there was the quasi-consensus of all parties, even of those who battled against it, such as the Democrats, on its provision fighting against fraudulent documents. Hence, two years after the adoption of this state law, its fraudulent document section was largely transposed into federal law (Illegal Immigration Reform and Immigrant Responsibility Act and Immigration and Nationality Act of 1996). State and Federal lists of documents acceptable for proving identity, employment and welfare eligibility for migrants were established, accompanied by an alarming discourse on the proliferation of false documents especially used by illegal migrants. Basically, these documents were the driver's license, the Social Security number (SSN), the green card, and the passport with visa. But with the rapid and epidemic growth of identity thefts by almost all means like the misuse, over-use and easy access to Social Security numbers, in 1998 the Congress passed a law to criminalize them and the administration decided on the adoption of high-tech identification means such as biometrics (fingerprint readings, facial and voice recognition systems, hand geometry etc.). These technologies became the cornerstone of the post-September 11 security measures established with the Enhanced Border Security and visa Entry Reform Act of 2001.

In France also, the focus on identity documents and the fight against sham documents have been reinforced with the transformation of migration into a security problem. Started in the end of the seventies, the suspicion concerning undocumented workers as potential usurpers of identity allowing them to cross borders, obtain monetary or welfare benefits, and avoid detection by law enforcement agencies had led to the establishment of unconditional proofs of identity. Politicians and law enforcement agencies assumed that the lack of a very high standard of documentary proof of identity was leading to a security risk. Finally, national ID cards and passports for citizens, passports with visas of entry and stay for third country nationals, and resident cards for migrants were recognized as documents accepted for establishing identity. Furthermore, with the adoption of a tightened immigration legislation called Pasqua Laws in 1993 reinforcing border controls and toughening the entry and the stay of migrants, the question of the identity checks was posed. After long debates, French authorities established identity checks not only at the borders but also inside the territory and decided to secure identity documents against fraud. As for justification, they put forward security and public order concerns as well as compensatory security measures *vis-à-vis* Schengen agreements that suppressed internal borders and allowed the free movements of EU nationals inside the Union (except the UK and Ireland).

How to analyze such a passionate focus on identity and identity documents in both countries? What kind of evidence is there on the connection between identity documents and security?

Paradox of Globalization: A Neurotic Focus on Borders in a "Borderless World"

One of the core features of globalization is the weakening of traditional borders whether physical, temporal, or cultural. In some ways with this process it becomes more difficult to draw clear-cut lines separating individuals and groups from each other and from their environments as it was in the past.

With the development of globalization, the shifting of borders and the enhanced multiplication of transnational flows, the interesting element here is the appearance of subjects with multiple identities and not dependent on unique and clearly identifiable physical spaces (Beck 1999, Bauman 2000). These subjects might be individuals whose identities are not structured with reference to an exclusive territorial state like in the Westphalian model and the Weberian formula. These people might have multiple senses of belonging and might behave in multiple environments. Thus they might have various allegiances related either to smaller, fragmented local units or to extraterritorial boundaries. Like the increasing number of persons with dual-national identities, they might commute between multiple places and deploy a variety of different cultural references.

The phenomenon analyzed as de-territorialization (Badie 1996) or "unbundling of territoriality"(Ruggie 1998), e.g. the loss of the exclusivity of state related territorial boundaries and the de-linking of territory and identity, poses serious problems to the traditional Westphalian conceptions of state, border and identity. Basically, the Westphalian order is characterized by a constitutive link between state, territory, identity, and security. According to this, borders delimit territory, separate sovereign states. They are mythomoteurs of identity and they distinguish between the domestic and the international (Anderson 1996, pp. 2-5, Foucher 1991). But today, clear-cut borders do not separate states, and identity is no longer exclusively defined by them. Borders are challenged in their function as mythomoteur of identity. The multiplication of dual nationalities, tangled identities, transnational spaces and new benchmarks etc. threatens many of the well established social and cultural assumptions and definitions providing certainty for the lives and acts of States. Facing this challenge, a fear of epistemological and security related uncertainty preoccupies political actors and security agencies. Since the eighties, it seems that the unknown concerns not only the future but also the present (Lipschutz 2000) and this perception transforms the conceptions of risk (Beck 1992) and techniques of risk-profiling and risk-testing.

The loss of the traditional role of territoriality and the growing feeling of uncertainty dramatically affect the legitimization of the state, which is notably linked to the control of its well-defined territory, clear-cut borders, and to its monopoly over the legitimate means of movement. The state understood as nation-state considers itself to be in position to identify and to control people crossing its borders, distinguishing among its own citizens and those of the other states, and filtering out the "undesirable people" at its gates. This is why we have been witnessing the discursive sticking of French, European, and American politicians, bureaucrats and law enforcement agencies to the territorial Westphalian state and asserting its monopoly over the control of borders even though borders are shifting and moving inside the EU. In effect, when it comes to the questions of migration, terrorism, and security, almost all refer to borders and to border controls in their discourses, even though their security preoccupations shift to the internal issues and the reality of borders is changing (Ceyhan 1997). Thus there is a significant focus on the stiffening of border controls and the multiplication of identity checks even if in reality, because of international humanitarian regime constraints (Soysal 1994) and the loss of their effective capacity of controlling territory and people, more and more states are losing control of their national borders (Bigo 1996).

This focus on borders attributes a paradoxical character to globalization. On the one hand, discourses of globalization magnify the free movement of goods, services, and persons and advocate the suppression of borders. In some regional inclusive units such as the European Union, internal border checks for EU nationals are relaxed (albeit some limitations). On the other hand, securitarian discourses stem the tide by urging the establishment of more and tougher border controls and by reassessing the role of the state to distinguish between its citizens and foreigners, between desirable and undesirable persons. According to these discourses, states must continue to regulate the free movement of persons and to assert its monopoly over the legitimate means of movement. This implies the continuation of the practices associated with verifying the identity of persons and with the identification documents as being a major preoccupation of states even as they open up their borders for free movements of goods and of certain categories of persons (Torpey 2000). This complex situation leads to the adoption of more and more sophisticated devices and technologies of border control and surveillance as we can witness at the Mexican-American border (Ceyhan 1997b, Andreas 2000). These technologies encompass satellites, night and day visual surveillance, sensors, voice identifiers, vehicle immobilization and scanning tools, databases to detect illegal migrants, fingerprint system (biometrics) etc. This hi-tech protection of borders leads to the securitization of identities via controls at the borders (in the US and at the external borders of the Schengen Area) and inside the territory. To justify this, in the European Union one evokes the European construction and the loss of security that the free movement of persons inside Europe may result in as well as the presumable "invasion" by migrants, whereas in the US, the argument brought forward is the steady creeping hispanization of the society and the fight against drugs coming from Latin America (especially from Colombia and Mexico). After September 11, the US administration included to this justification process the fight against terrorism and the alleged relationship between immigration and terrorism.

The Problematization of Migration

In fact, this discourse is underpinned by the assumption that the migration flows from the countries of the South constitute a real danger to the state and to its well being as a political and cultural entity. Even though France and the US have different histories, immigration traditions, and integration policies, one can notice a rhetorical similarity between them *vis-à-vis* immigration and the place of migrants in the society since the eighties. In contemporary French and American politics, migrants are more and more cast as an object of fear and as a threat than suitable candidates for *E Pluribus Unum* solutions. In both cases a new figure of the migrant as an adversary has been introduced by a securitarian discourse in which questions related to border crossing, illegal migration, asylum, terrorism, crime, incivilities, urban violence, and drug trafficking are linked to each other and constitute a *continuum of threats* (Bigo 1996).

But addressing migration as a problem is not new. In the US, it started a long time ago, in 1790 with the first regulation on naturalization (Naturalization Act), and in France after the French Revolution. Foreigners in general and migrants in particular were suspected of importing "strange" qualities into a community to which they did not belong originally. Almost all anti-immigration discourses put emphasis on the strangeness of migrants, portraying them as being different, strange and non-assimilated to the society. As Simmel stated (1964), the concept of strangeness was an undecided condition between the inside and the outside and led to the question of the belonging of foreigners to the group from which they cannot stem. In present days, this question continues to structure discourses against immigration to Western countries.

Since the end of the sixties, the transformation of migration into a political problem has been realized along different thematic axes and approaches such as socio-economic, humanitarian, public order, welfare, identitarian, and securitarian approaches (Huysmans 1997, Ceyhan and Tsoukala 2002). Each of them involves different actors and institutions and implies specific forms of regulation of social interaction and exchange. In the eighties, the approach of migration has been considerably transformed. Rather than being correlated to the labor market, migration questions have been interrelated with the crisis of the welfare state (migrants considered as free riders of welfare and as tax burdens) and with the questions of identity and culture. More and more cast with different, "strange" cultural characteristics they have been transformed into cultural others that infiltrate the country and disturb its harmony. In consequence, state control functions do not only rely on borders but also on the access to social rights via welfare mechanisms. This leads to the shifting of controls and the constitution of bifocal controls processed both at the border and inside the territory (Ceyhan 1997). In other words, we may assume that we are witnessing the de-linking of security from its exclusive affiliation with the territorial state and corresponding redefinition of security in terms of collective identities and welfare benefits.

Since the nineties, the main feature of the problematization of migration has become the amalgamation of different issues under the designation of an enemy supposed to represent them. This is obtained by establishing a virtual coupling of different questions that are not necessarily linked to each other. As Murray Edelman (1988, pp. 11, 21, 129) asserts, the amalgamation leads to the equivocal construction of problems. It creates a political spectacle that focuses on an enemy, which is more likely to be a blurry concept. Enemy is purposely not well defined. The situation of vagueness permits what is not granted by a clear definition: the arbitrary and the uncertainty of the language. Language with its multiple and sometimes contradictory meanings is at the source of many controversies that remain unresolved. The non-resolution of controversies is, for Edelman, what characterizes problems as political. Language may reproduce the situation of vagueness or may lead to a process of nomination, which is accompanied by the attribution of cultural and moral attributes. Furthermore, the amalgamation permits the constitution of new coalitions of actors and this may sometimes occur between strange bedfellows such as the cooperation between police and social security agencies. It also permits the negation or the denial of more serious and real social issues, it creates political benefits, structures public opinions and influences the policy agenda.

The problematization and the securitization of migration are accompanied by a neurotic focus on identity documents and are underpinned by the assumption that there is a continued attempt on the part of persons involved in illegal border crossing, criminal activity, terrorism, and economic hardship to counterfeit or to alter genuine documents by a variety of methods. Security agencies and politicians believe that fraudulent documents permit their users to create new identities allowing them to travel internationally, gain entry, obtain monetary and welfare benefits and avoid detection by law enforcement agencies. For them, the uncertainty created by the challenge to the Westphalian state is triggered by the insecurity resulting from the chaos of borders and the emergence of the multiplicity of individuals or groups that act on the international and domestic realms. The question they ask is how to cope with this situation and how to identify people and deter the undesirable ones?

Identification Means and Controlling the Free Movement of People: Passports and Visas

As John Torpey (2001) highlights, states always sought to monopolize the legitimate means of circulation inside their territory and at their borders. They also sought to establish the identity of people living in and moving inside and around their territory. For this purpose, they have developed technologies of identification that would prove with certitude who is who. These technologies create, gather, process, and disseminate all identifiers capable of identifying individuals (Castells 1997).

The history of identification means starts long before the constitution of the Westphalian state. In France for instance, throughout the pre-modern period, identification was a matter of collective regard at the village level where the priest was the only person in charge of keeping registers. But this need of identification and control became more visible when states intended to regulate the movements of people inside their territory and across the borders (Noiriel 1991, 2001). The first measures to control identity over a larger territory were undertaken under the Absolute Monarchy with the 1667 Royal Order forbidding changes in names during one's lifetime. Also, this preoccupation led to the creation of a documentary proof of identity under the form of either the passport (internal and external) which is essential to travel and to cross borders or the national ID card.

Today, the main functions of passports rely on international recognition of the states. They symbolize the sovereignty of states and their mutual recognition by other states on the international scene. Thus they permit their holders to be recognized as a member of a national state. Their practical utility is to regulate the movements of people across the borders.

Normally, passports should permit their holders to leave a country, to enter another one, and to stay there for a certain time. But these days, not all passports suffice to realize this function. Especially those which are issued by the countries of the South do not permit their holders to travel and to stay abroad automatically, as do passports issued by the Western countries. Actually, with the transformation of migration originated from the countries of the South into a securitarian problem and with the focus of Western countries on the control of their borders, single passports do not permit the free circulation of people coming from what are called "countries of risk". Seemingly, border control agencies do not regard them as providing sufficient information on the identity of their holders. Here arises the crucial question to define: what is identity for law enforcement agencies? If it is, as indicated before, collecting a certain number of data providing basic information on who the holder is (name, nationality, birth place and physical description), passports must suffice since they contain them. But if identity is more than this information, if it is knowledge on the trajectories, the past and present behaviors and acts, on the aims, projects, and morality, on the relatives, relations, networks etc., for border control agents, passports do not suffice to provide proper information on these.

Why are Western governments not satisfied with the single passport? There are several reasons and rationales for that. Firstly, they refuse to be satisfied by the information issued by the authorities of the countries that they deem "risky". They suspect them of being false or partial. Secondly, they would like to carry out themselves, via their consulates and liaison officers, the identification of foreigners in their home country and the control of their documents before the departure (remote control). Thirdly, they intend to anticipate who is likely to become a security risk if allowed to enter an EU country. These preoccupations led to the establishment of visas to identify, to control, and to supervise people who are motivated to travel. Are they real tourists, or do they in fact plan to immigrate or to apply for asylum? Do they have relatives established in France or in the US? Are they criminals? Do they have relatives that have committed crimes in Western countries? Do they have terrorist ties etc.? Guided by this preoccupation, Western governments have been creating an increasing number of sophisticated identification schemes and control devices such as computerized databases, smart cards, magnetic strips, DNA tests, biometrics, facial recognition techniques, palm recognition systems, iris scans etc. in order to make a background check and to search the criminal or the terrorist past and networks of visa applicants. For instance since 1999, German consular authorities in Turkey require DNA tests from Turkish visa applicants who have their relatives in Germany for a criminal background check.

What is a visa? Basically it is a proactive identification and surveillance technique established by a foreign authority on an individual in his country of origin. It authorizes or forbids someone to enter a country. The EU defines the term "visa" as an "authorization given by or a decision taken by a member state which is required for entry into its territory with a view to: an intended stay in that member state or in several member states of no more than three months in all, transit through the territory or airport transit zone of that member state or several member states".[8] The visa regime is part of the community *acquis* and the candidate countries to join the Union are expected to adopt it when they will become full members.

In their fear of fraud and false visas more and more authorities focus on security features. For that, they create technical specifications which lay down universally recognizable security features that are clearly visible to the naked eye. But they also create supplementary secret technical specifications such as laser prints which aim at preventing counterfeiting and falsification of the visa (laser visa).

The main features of the EU visa regime are threefold. First, it establishes a common visa processing system the aim of which is to avoid that an applicant whose visa application is refused by one EU country applies to another one and gets authorization to enter the Union. It establishes common consular instructions and criteria to be applied in the same manner by all Schengen countries. Secondly, it establishes a common "negative" list of countries whose nationals must be in possession of a visa when crossing external frontiers of the Union. In this respect the first list was adopted in 1993. Concerning the visa requirements for nationals of Third Countries, the first regulation, which was adopted by the EU Council in 1995, was subsequently annulled by the Court of Justice in 1997 because the Parliament had not been consulted prior to its adoption. Another regulation came to be adopted in 1999 with the same title. This new regulation set out a list of 101 "risky countries" whose nationals must be in possession of a visa when crossing the external borders of the member states and traveling inside the Schengen area. These countries are likely to constitute a security risk for Western countries. Under the Treaty of Nice of 2000 which decided that visa, asylum, and immigration policy are to be decided mainly by the co-decision procedure (the shift to the rule of qualified majority), article 62 reiterated the above definition of a visa. A new regulation[9] re-established a common list of countries whose nationals require a visa to enter the EU for short stays (Black list) and a common list of those excluded from this requirement (White list). The Black list contains 131 countries and 3 territories, the White list 43 countries and 2 territories. Also, it removed Romania and Bulgaria from the "negative list" but it continued to include Turkey with which it has already established a customs union.[10] Concerning the constitution lists of "risky countries" it would be relevant to remember that the paternity of establishing lists does not belong to the EU. The US has been establishing lists of risky people or countries since her first legislation on naturalization and immigration in 1790. More recently, she created the Visa Waiver Program in 1986.

This program established by Congressional act as a pilot program was transformed into a permanent program in 2000. As for February 2002, 28 countries are exempted from visa to get into the US. Consequently the US defines risky countries as "countries not listed in the Visa waiver Program". But this explanation is far from being sufficient. It does not reveal the real purpose of visa which is in fact to avoid the entry of people supposed to pose a threat to the welfare and the labor of the US. The purpose is then clearly to avoid the economic and fiscal burden of migrants coming from poor countries. To this concern authorities added the fight against organized crime, drug trafficking and terrorism. After September 11, the US administration clearly listed five Muslim nations as sponsors of terrorism: Libya, Syria, Sudan, Iran, Iraq. But at the same time authorities established a second list that they decline to make public. This second list called "visitors who raise national security concerns" encompasses 26 countries which are mainly Islamic nations. The applicants from these countries are required to give fingerprints at the ports of entry to be checked against criminal and terrorist databases and to stay in touch with the authorities during their stay in the US.

The third feature of the EU visa regime is the creation of the Schengen Information System (SIS) which is a network database containing information on people who are deemed security risks. Basically, its aim is to identify and exclude these people from the Schengen territory. Technically, it brings together national lists of people to be excluded into a single network which can be accessed online by visa officers and border police. The question that arises here is about this category of "risky people". Again, as stressed above, this category is blurry and depends on contexts, the social construction of agents and countries. This is why it may encompass various people. Originally SIS referred to transnational crime and illegal migration as risky categories. But this list has been enlarged by SIS II which was adopted in 2001 to "visa overstayers", "resident permit overstayers", "violent troublemakers" like hooligans, anti-globalization protesters, *"flagrento delicto* border crossers" etc. Also, SIS II has established databases of issued visa and people involved in terrorists activities (whose access is restricted to Europol). By the same token it raised the question of who is allowed access to it. Even though it is still under discussion, the idea is to create different levels of access and to permit the online access of various agents such as Europol, Eurojust, public prosecutors, magistrates, asylum, and immigration authorities, border police, security and intelligence services.

This system raises many controversies about its real purpose, the data protection, the nature of information sought on individuals, its secrecy and its lack of accountability to elected bodies. But the main concern is about its target population which is composed of "Third Country" nationals; i.e. people originated from non-Western countries who are considered a "security threat" to the EU and who receive the closest scrutiny and surveillance (Preuss-Laussignotte 2000).

This technology of control and surveillance of foreign people in their own countries, before they leave (remote control) and via transnational databases (SIS) is very relevant to address the transformation of borders and border controls in the post-Westphalian world. Today, borders and border controls do not necessarily converge with national territory, but they are moving. With the establishment of visas, border controls are not exclusively processed at national borders but definitely in the country of origin of migrants, by European and American consular services, law enforcement agencies, liaison officers, secret services, and also by private security companies that operate at the airports to check the documents and visa of travelers before they board the plane. This process that challenges the traditional Weberian framework of territorial borders can be characterized as the extension of borders from physical edges of the national territory to consulates, airport check-in desks, aircraft doors, immigration controls, customs, and to a zone of 30 km inside from the physical border in the US, 20 km in the EU where immigration police and border patrol can check the documents of people.

The Exclusivity of the National Identity Card in France

If passports and visas serve to control the movement of persons, a various number of other documents have been created to prove the social and administrative existence of individuals. In France the principal document for this purpose is the national identity card.

The move towards the establishment of national identification occurred in 1792 after the Revolution. People had to carry an internal passport to go from one place to another. To this, the National Assembly added another document by adopting the decree on civil status (*Etat civil*). The objective of the decree was to assign a civil identity to citizens as opposed to Church-managed identity of that time. Hence with the civil status, identification was thought to contribute to generate a sense of national belonging by implementing a civil ritual that would replace the religious one. It was also seen as a way to unify the French nation which was characterized at that time by strong regional and linguistic diversity. This led to a massive Frenchification of names in regions where local languages were dominantly used. And finally, it was characterized by a strict procedural uniformity which was due to the bureaucracy's methodology based on standardization of identification patterns and centralization of information about individuals. But application of the decree encountered resistance during the first decades of its enactment. The main one came from the Catholic clergy who was reluctant to hand over its registers and accept civilian competition. This was also triggered by the citizen's preference for religious identification rituals of the new-born babies instead of civil identification. However, decades after, once the bureaucratic machinery was set in motion in the Weberian sense, centralized administration demonstrated an unbeatable efficiency to assign identity as well as to verify and control it.

As Gérard Noiriel asserts (2001, p. 255), France considers the identity card the material proof of legal and social existence of an individual. Its main characteristic is its collection and conservation of information in files. In fact, since 1851 France had been constituting databases and centralized information. It is interesting to bear in mind that the national identity card takes its roots in the aim of French authorities in the nineteenth century to control and to get rid of non-desirable foreigners and marginal people. Over the century, a police document originally designated to control stigmatized people, had been generalized to the whole French society under the Vichy regime and had become a symbol of national integration.

The establishment of identity on paper and into files was due to a police officer, Mr. Alphonse Bertillon (Noiriel 2001, p. 326). In 1880, Bertillon designed a method of identification combining the photograph, the anthropometrical measures and the portrait of targeted people, who were mostly prisoners. This information, which was handwritten, was conserved in files and put into a central database. This method was soon after applied to non-desirable foreigners that French authorities wanted to control, to put under surveillance, and even to expel. In that respect, the decree of October 2, 1888 obliged foreigners to declare their identities, and in 1914 all foreigners were required to possess an identity card issued by French authorities. Later, this obligation was extended to prostitutes, erratic people, felons and to mad people as well. But the generalization of this technique to the French population was realized under the Vichy regime. With its regime of exception in 1940, Vichy obliged every French citizen under the age of 16 to obtain a card containing a photograph and a finger print. It might be said that the Vichy regime realized the bureaucratic plan of centralization imagined under the Third Republic: to generalize a technology that would keep the marks of everybody on paper files. It also established the distinction of population through racial belonging, by adding a special mark to identify Jewish population.

After WW II, the Fourth Republic suppressed the obligation to possess an identity card with the decree of 1955. But since then, in practice, it has become an unconditional proof of identity. In that respect, France constitutes an interesting example of the difference between law and police practice. Actually the law does not require French citizens to possess and carry a national identity card. The only document that is obliged by law to be possessed are civil status documents (birth, marriage, etc.) (*Syndicat de la magistrature* 2002). But even though it is not required by law to possess an ID card, the non-presentation of such a document during a check may put the citizen in a difficult position. In effect, police or gendarmes can retain citizens for a verification of identity at the commissariat or gendarmerie. The authorized detention time is 4 hours. This practice stirs criticism from Civil Rights organizations which constantly remind that it goes against article 5 of the European Convention of Human Rights that forbids all types of arrests except when there is clear evidence to suspect someone of committing a crime.

In the eighties, with the finger pointing towards undocumented migrants as being the cause of the economic and social problems, and with the suspicion of their usage of false documents, a debate was generated around the securitization of identity documents. France started to create the computerized identity card in 1987, the US generalized it in the early nineties.

French law distinguishes between citizens and foreigners and puts the latter under a discriminatory regime. With reference to the decree of November 2, 1945, foreigners are submitted to a special regime and are obliged to posses and to present the documents which allowed them to enter the country, to stay, to work, and to travel (*Syndicat de la Magistrature* 2002). I have started the analysis of the identity card by stressing that it was first issued to control foreign people in France. But with its generalization to all French citizens, law enforcement agencies needed to create a separate document to identify, to file, and to centralize the foreigners living in France. This need became more urgent after the May 1968 events directed by the student movement leader Daniel Cohn-Bendit, who was a German national born in France. Since then, French administration had worked on the creation of a document that would allow foreigners to stay and work in France. Hence the establishment of the *carte de séjour* which became in 1983 the *resident card*. But since the eighties, the securitarization of immigration has rendered the attribution of the resident card more and more difficult. In consequence, a great number of persons live in France without possessing this document. It would not be out of interest to remember here that for many years this document did not allow people to travel around but just to live and to work in France. The question whether its holders could travel inside the European Union as freely as do the EU member state nationals led to multiple debates within the Third Pillar discussions of the Maastricht Treaty of 1992. At first, the majority of EU member states was reluctant to integrate this question within the Community level and preferred to regulate it nationally. But with the assignment of questions related to migration and to asylum to the First pillar in the Amsterdam Treaty (1997), the free circulation of resident card holders inside the Schengen area came to be discussed and to be accepted at least by five of the full members that signed this agreement (France, Belgium, Luxembourg, Germany, Netherlands). It should be reminded that the resident card issued by one of the member states of the European Union does not allow its bearers to live and to work in another member state. It only allows the circulation of its holders.

American Unconcern Vis-à-vis a Single Document Challenged

In the US, as highlighted before, there is no federal identity card and contrary to the wishes of some politicians and law enforcement agents there is an apparent unconcern *vis-à-vis* a single federal document. But this does not mean that there are no verifications and checks and no other means of identification. As Michel de Certeau pointed out, in the US, identification schemes are mostly created through the social spaces such as work and welfare (the Social Security number), banking (credit checks), vehicles (driver's license), or for administrative reasons. These latter mostly concern migrants and are established to control their entry and stay, verify their eligibility for work and welfare, and monitor their movements. Consequently, with the enforcement of the Immigration Reform and Control Act of 1986 (IRCA), the INS[11] divided the documents accepted to establish identity and employment eligibility into three groups: 1) those that establish both identity and eligibility, 2) those that establish identity, and 3) those that establish eligibility for employment and welfare benefits.

After September 11, the US administration pushed both the public and the private sectors to seek the documentary proof of identity of individuals. For instance in its effort to cut the flow of money to terrorists, the Bush administration announced proposals requiring Wall Street firms to verify the identity of new customers. If the rules are finalized, firms would have to develop plans to seek documentary evidence of customer's identities, collect government issued data such as Social Security numbers and in some cases, run credit checks. According to this project every US customer would be required to submit a Social Security number or a taxpayer identification number, while non-citizens would have to submit an alien-identification number or similar official identification from a foreign government including a photograph, fingerprint, or other proof of identity.[12]

Documents acceptable for establishing both identity and employment eligibility are: Social Security number (SSN) for all citizens and for foreigners; alien registration receipt card or permanent resident card, an unexpired foreign passport that contains a temporary I-551 stamp, an unexpired employment authorization document that contains a photograph. Documents acceptable for establishing identity only are: state issued driver's license or identification card containing a photograph, passport, school identification card, voter registration card, US military card, permanent resident card for aliens and Native American tribal document. And finally documents acceptable for the sole purpose of employment authorization and welfare benefits are: Social Security number, certificate of birth or certificate of birth abroad issued by the Department of State, identification card for use of resident citizen in the US, and an unexpired employment authorization issued by the INS.

This division into groups means that identification occurs differently in different spaces and purposes. The distinction between the purpose of identity, welfare, and employment leads to the circulation of numerous cards issued by different public and private agencies such as the INS, the department of State, the Social Security Agency, the Attorney General, the City Hall, Public and Private Schools etc. Each card has its own symbolic meaning and may enable the holder to obtain different benefits in respect of their social position and immigration status.

One of the highly sought after documents is the Social Security number (SSN) which is basically a government-issued data. Originally it was created in 1935 as a means of administrating the Social Security System. In 1961, the Civil Service Commission started to utilize the SSN to identify all federal employees. A year later, the Internal Revenue Service required taxpayers' SSN to appear on all completed tax returns. The computer revolution enabled the widespread use of SSN for many purposes. It may enable its holder to obtain various benefits such as welfare and credit and in the meantime it can be used to establish employment eligibility. In addition, the possession of a Social Security card gives credibility to the bearer. According to the federal law, this number is not intended to serve as a national identification means. But in practice, because of the centralizing function of its number, it has become a *de facto* national identifier. It contains all the background information on its bearer and is used in every field of public and private lives of citizens and foreigners as an identifier. It contains their credit and health histories, their welfare situation, and can be checked by all private and public agencies. With its quick check facilities, it constitutes a guarantee of the social status of its bearers.

In 1996, with its immigration and welfare reform bills, the Congress ordered the Social Security Administration to develop a prototype of a counterfeit-resistant, tamper-proof Social Security card that provides individuals with "reliable proof of citizenship or legal resident alien" status. In doing so, the Congress implicitly recognized it as an identifier. Thus the state justifies its appetite for secure identification and information as a counterpart to welfare services it provides for citizens. Hence the fabrication of technologies to identify who is eligible for this service and who is not.

But in the day-to-day life of the Americans the most widely accepted identity document is undoubtedly the driver's license. It is issued by states and can be obtained with the support of a birth certificate. The problem is that each state has its own driver's license and the conditions of its obtaining vary from one state to another. In the nineties, with the production of securitarian discourses in California, the driver's license was criticized for being easily obtainable and allowing undocumented migrants to acquire unauthorized benefits. One of the consequences of the anti-immigration atmosphere generated by Proposition 187 was to impose on migrants the possession of a permanent resident card for its acquisition. If this practice was enforced in California during the nineties, the Federal Court stated against its securitarian feature and asked for the suppression of the possession of a permanent resident card as a condition for the acquirement of a driver's license. This change has been utilized differently by political opponents in their struggle for power in California letting the former governor Gray Davis to authorize the issuance of driver's licenses to illegal workers and leading the new governor Arnold Schwartzenegger to suppress it.

The Constitution of a "Dossier Society" As Bauman (2000, pp. 2, 3) asserts, the new global environment is characterized by a move towards a "software-based modernity" where there is an increasing appetite for information in public and private spheres. With this change, information has become a raw material which can be processed, altered, multiplied, sold or exchanged through many technological means (Castells 1997). The interesting element here is that the focal object of information is the individual. In effect, information on almost every person, about his/her private, professional and public life is obtained and stocked in different computerized databases (Marx 1994).

The main feature of the new means of identification is the mixture of high security features such as biometrics with databases constituted by a variety of files containing (un)officially selected information on an individual's life: employment, immigration status, health, financial situation, criminal history, driving history, insurance, education, itinerary, family etc. Consequently, it can be asserted that the enhanced development of identification and surveillance technologies leads to the creation of what Laudon calls a "dossier society" (Laudon 1986) assigning a recognizable identity to individuals and attributing an "official life" to them with which they must live in accordance. The "dossier society" is thus constituted through the use of computer records, data storage, matching, merging, and linking various information to support decision-making coordination, control analysis and the visualization in a territory, place or organization. It integrates distinct files originally serving unique programs and policies (such as the fight against criminality) into more or less permanent and centralized databases. This new device impacts dramatically individual's life and identity, and the ways of controlling it.

In this perspective it can be affirmed that with the enhanced means of classification and data processing, the ways of defining the self have greatly expanded: As Gary Marx noted forcefully "We become not only the sum of our own biographies but a part of broader social types believed to have the potential to behave in certain ways. Individuals are defined according to being in or out, above or below some cutoff point, according to a differentiating standard" (Marx 1997, p. 490). In fact, the "dossier society" created by law enforcement agencies and private actors such as banks or corporations works to the detriment of the individual to the extent that others gain access to, or create data about, him/her and distribute this for controlling and surveillance objectives.

But the "official life" created by "the dossier society" invents new identities that do not necessarily correspond to the reality of individuals. They must live accordingly and behave defined by the new representations. How are these identities created? What are the value choices made by the key actors? Concerning migrants for instance, do they reflect the social images that the law enforcement agencies produce on migrants and on presumed fraudulent document users? Who is authorized to use this information? We have seen that in the US, private actors such as employers and banks have the right to consult it. In France, there is an increasing tendency to integrate different files (social security, taxes, crime, immigration status, bank, education, and health) into a centralized and permanent database. One of the surprising elements of this trend is the adhesion of almost all political actors to it. For instance in France, the bill allowing the interconnection of administrative databases was proposed in 2000 by the Communist Party that, theoretically, should have opposed such an initiative. How and in what legislative ground the information contained in different programs could be shared by a multiplicity of actors (law enforcement agencies, administration, school administration, employers, banks etc.)? To what extent is the privacy of individuals still guaranteed? Who will control, audit, and oversee these systems?

It should be remembered here that the increasing creation of databases in Europe has been fostered by the adoption of Schengen agreements. The necessity of information transmission between its members, the goal of rapid search of targeted people and the constitution of networks provoked the necessity to constitute more and more sophisticated databases such as the Schengen Information System (SIS) and Europol. As indicated before, SIS is a computerized information system on persons, stolen vehicles, and objects for the use of border control authorities, customs, and national police. It relies on increased policing behind borders and extensive cross-border police cooperation between Schengen members.

Considering the computerized character of the "dossier society", can we assert that it alters the face to face relations? Laudon affirms that with this system decisions made about people rely less and less on personal face to face contact, on what they say or even what they do. Instead, decisions are based on information that is held in national systems and interpreted by bureaucrats in distant locations. Decisions made about them are based on comprehensive "data image" drawn from diverse files (Laudon 1986). But I would affirm that when it comes to identity checks, decisions made about individuals rely on the mixture of information systems, bureaucratic obligations (obligations to make a certain number of arrests or expels) and face to face relations, the behavior of actors, the environment and the social construction of target groups. In regard to this latter point it is important to analyze why some groups are targeted and why others are not. According to Edelman, social construction of target groups refers to the cultural characteristics of popular images of persons or groups whose well-being and behavior are affected by policy (1988). These characteristics are normative and evaluative portraying groups in positive or negative terms through symbolic language, metaphor, and stories (Schneider and Ingram 1993). This construction is oriented by the new preoccupations of security that appeared in Western countries. With the partial de-linking of security from its exclusive affiliation with the territorial state and corresponding redefinition of security in terms of collective societal identities, there is an increasing focus on cultural characteristics of targeted groups.

The new security environment leads to the creation of techniques of risk-profiling and risk testing which allow for different degrees of intensity of checks depending on the risk criteria fulfilled by certain categories of persons and locations such as suburbs, border areas, immigrant neighborhoods etc. One of the questions that arises here is about the technique of profiling that is more and more used by police and law enforcement agencies. To what extent is the foreign appearance a determinant factor to stop, to check and to interrogate someone? Even though it is not legally recognized in many countries *profiling* seems to be commonly used. The French police practice this technique on people with dark skin and located in "risky" environments and suspected to be out of law.

In effect in the US, even though the Supreme Court with the US vs. Brigani Ponce decision declared that an immigration officer cannot rely on Hispanic appearance as the only factor, that it requires the INS officer to have clear facts that justify a reasonable suspicion,[13] in practice there are common ethnic and culturally biased features used by law enforcement agencies. These features are: unfamiliarity with English, manner of dress and behavior, geographic location and type of neighborhood, presence of an old model car, nervousness and attempt to avoid questioning (Gittel and Gittel 1988). These features were confirmed by a federal appeal court who affirmed that Border Patrol agents can now consider ethnicity as a basis for traffic stops.[14]

September 11 made the prevention of future attacks security and defense priorities of the US. Accordingly, increasing control of the borders and the foreigners living in the US and supervising the "risky people" became the keystone of the Homeland Security policy. In that respect, Congress and the administration have implemented dozens of measures among which the most important is the Border Security bill approved by Congress in May 2002.[15] The bill admits that it is possible to distinguish terrorists from immigrants and provides for a layered screening system that uses technology and linked databases to identify those with criminal and terrorist ties before they enter the US. This led to the proliferation of lists of suspected and known terrorists and databases which became a key part of intelligence gathering and analysis. But this policy operating with increased reliance on suspicion raises critical questions about who the enemy is. How can one determine who is a suspected terrorist? Who should be targeted for investigation? Who should be watched? What are the criteria to be used to identify a terrorist? Admitting that it is impossible to implement all security measures and to track everybody, the administration chose a discretionary approach:[16] applying the law only to some people who will correspond to the profile of a terrorist. The Justice Department created this profile after the characteristics of the 19 hijackers of September 11: young males from Muslim countries where the terrorist network is active. Profiling efforts are thus undertaken with the targeting of males aged between 16 and 45 from 26 Muslim countries who are singled out during checks and face supplementary background checks at the borders. Their visa applications and border crossings are registered in an effort to keep better track of them (NSEES).[17]

Under changes ordered by the Attorney General in the enforcement of Homeland security policy, the FBI is authorized to use commercial databases in order to constitute profiles in its efforts to prevent acts of terrorism in the US. Now even if they do not have a specific suspect or legal basis for suspicion, FBI agents could generate lists of potential suspects based on a profile using such criteria as race, religion, travel, bank accounts, and even grocery-store purchases. Such profiles can be highly specific, but they can also generate misleading and bogus information and lead to misuse. It is important to remember that much of that personal data comes from supermarket loyalty-club programs and credit-card purchases. This practice goes against privacy requirements and the guarantee that commercial data collectors would not turn this data over to law enforcement.

These examples seem suitable to express a fundamental change in the nature of identification and surveillance. This change occurs in a de-territorialized world characterized by fluidity, mobility, multiplicity and slipperiness where power is moving with the speed of globalization and transnationalization. Regarding this context I would assume with Bauman that the new surveillance conveys the advent of the post-Panopticon era which alters the relationships between the two sides of the surveillance relation: the observers and the observed or the surveillants and the surveilled or the routinizers and the routinized. Actually, Panopticon happened in an era of mutual engagement between these two and was territorially rooted (Foucault 1975). As Bauman argues, "in the Panopticon model, routinizers were not truly fully free to move. In effect in the Panopticon model the surveillants were assumed to be 'there nearby in the controlling tower' ".[18] But nowadays more and more surveillance seems to be realized extraterritorially through a network of transnational supervisors, mobile border police forces, and databases and does not occur with neither surveillants nor surveilled fixedness to a single place.

However, if new surveillance is becoming extraterritorial, it is not loosing the disciplinary power of its predecessor (the Panopticon). In effect, it aims to control and to regulate the behavior of individuals by assessing what is useful and what is harmful to the society. In order to concretize this form of political technology, the population has to be known in its present and probable future behaviors. As Foucault assessed (1975), discipline was exerted through a continuous, uninterrupted process of supervision of the activities of people and was both the product and the means of accumulating knowledge about individual behavior. This explains the focus on the individual. As we have seen, nowadays any individual in any place of the world can become subject of surveillance and control. Like Foucault asserted, people are not managed "en masse" but individually and in detail in regard to specific bodily movement, gesture and behavior. Indeed surveillance and identification processes and technologies are mainly about the individual's trajectory, itinerary, movements, affiliations, networks, projects and even soul. In the field of identification a growing corpus of technologies and scientific discourses focuses on body parts with DNA tests, iris scans, palm analyses, voice recognition systems etc. These techniques serve to secure the knowledge about individual's behavior in the form of scientific evidence.

It is also interesting to remember that obedience to this disciplinary power means obedience to standards and norms. Today this tends to be achieved through enticement and seduction rather than by coercion and appears in the disguise of exercise of free will (Mathiesen 1997). But even though individuals know overtly by law or by advertisement or just figure out that they are subject to identification and surveillance, the "dossier society" continues to keep its secrecy. In effect individuals are far from seeing and identifying the surveillants who might be located thousands of kilometers away from them. Neither are they aware of all information contained in numerous databases that manage their private, public and transnational lives.

Notes

[1] Dr Ayse Ceyhan is a political scientist. She teaches at the Institut d'Etudes Politiques (IEP) of Paris and is a researcher at the Center for Conflict Studies.

[2] Composed of 13 out of the 15 EU member states with the exception of the UK and Ireland. It was created by the Schengen agreement signed in 1985 between France, the Federal Republic of Germany and the Benelux countries. It provided for the objective of a gradual abolition of internal border controls and the creation of external borders. In 1990 the same countries signed the Convention implementing the Schengen agreement which contained detailed provisions for the removal of checks on persons at the internal borders and their replacement by controls on entry at the external borders of Schengen countries. To compensate for the loss of internal border controls the Convention also includes measures to enhance cooperation between immigration police and judicial authorities.

[3] Stuart Hall, *Questions of Cultural Identity*, London: Sage (1996), p. 277.

[4] Ibid., p. 280.

[5] In the sense of a federal issued identity card. Otherwise, there are state issued identification cards.

[6] Ibid., p. 11.

[7] Ibid.

[8] EU Official Journal L 234, 03.10.1995; EU Official Journal L 72, 18.03.1999.

[9] EU Official Journal L 81/1 2001.

[10] The EU signed in 1963 the Ankara agreement with Turkey. Accordingly Turkey should have become a full member after having realized a customs union with the EU. Turkey fulfilled the conditions for the customs union which foresees the free movement of industrial goods between the EU and Turkey, the establishment of a common customs

tariff towards Third countries and the adoption of community *acquis* on the matter. The EU and Turkey signed the Customs Union agreement in 1995 which entered into force in 1996. But despite this, the EU seems still reluctant to accept Turkey on the list of its future full members.

[11] Immigration and Naturalization Service.

[12] "Bush Will Let Financial Firms Tap Social-Security Information", *The Wall Street Journal*, July 16, 2002.

[13] US vs. Brigani-Ponce, 422 US 873 (1975).

[14] Ruling of May 14, 1999.

[15] Enhanced Border security and Visa Entry Reform Act (Public Law no 107-103, formerly HR 3525).

[16] Tamar Jacoby, "Immigration Reform and National Security", *The New York Times*, September 16, 2002.

[17] National Security Entry Exit System.

[18] Zygmund Bauman, *Liquid Modernity*, Cambridge Polity Press, 2000, p. 4.

References

Althusser, L. (1993), *Ecrits sur la psychanalyse: Freud*, Lacan, Stock: Paris.

Anderson, M. (1996), *Frontiers, State Formation in the Modern World*, Polity Press: London.

Andreas, P. (2000), *Border Games. Policing the US-Mexico Divide*, Cornell University Press: Ithaca.

Badie, B. (1996), *La fin des territoires*, Fayard: Paris.

Bauman, Z. (2000), *Liquid Modernity*, Polity Press: Cambridge.

Beck, U. (1992), *Risk Society, Towards a New Modernity*, Sage: London.

Beck, U. (1999), *What is Globalization?*, Polity Press: Cambridge.

Berger, P. and Luckmann, T. (1967), *The Social Construction of Reality. A Treatise in the Sociology of Knowledge*, Allen Lane: New York.

Bigo, D. (1996), *Polices en réseaux. Expérience européenne*, Presses de Sciences Po: Paris.

Bigo, D. (2000), 'When Two Becomes One: Internal and External Securitizations in Europe', in Kelstrup, M. and Williams, M. C. (eds), *International Relations Theory and the Politics of European Integration*, Routledge: London.

Buzan, B. (1991), *People States and Fear. An Agenda for International Security Studies in the Post-Cold War Era*, Lynne Rienner: Boulder, Col.

Castells, M. (1996), *The Information Age*, 3 volumes. Vol. 1 (1996): *The Rise of the Network Society*, vol. 2 (1997): *The Power of Identity*, vol. 3 (1998): *End of Millenium*, Blackwell: Oxford.

Ceyhan, A. (1997), *Migrants as a Threat: A Comparative Analysis of Securitarian Rhetoric in France and in the US*, ISA Conference, Toronto.

Ceyhan, A. (1997b), 'Etats-Unis: frontière(s) contrôlée(s), identité(s) sécurisée(s)', *Cultures & Conflits*, n° 26-27, pp. 203-254.

Ceyhan, A. (2001), 'La fin de l'en-dehors. Les nouvelles constructions discursives de l'ennemi intérieur en Californie', *Cultures & Conflits*, n° 43, pp. 3-11.

Ceyhan, A. and Peries, G. (2001), 'L'ennemi intérieur: une construction politique et discursive', *Cultures & Conflits*, n° 26-27, pp. 61-90.

Ceyhan, A. and Tsoukala, A. (2002), 'The Securitization of Migration in Western Countries', *Alternatives*, n° 27, pp. 21-33.

Dandeker, C. (1990), *Surveillance, Power and Modernity. Bureaucracy and Discipline from 1700 to the Present Days*, Polity Press: Cambridge.

De Certeau, M. (1981), 'Californie, un théâtre de passants', *Autrement*, n° 31, pp. 10-22.

Derrida, J. (1994), *Politiques de l'amitié*, Galilée: Paris.

Edelman, M. (1987), *The Symbolic Uses of Politics*, University of Illinois Press: Urbana, Ill.

Edelman, M. (1988), *Constructing of a Political Spectacle*, University of Chicago Press: Chicago.

Edelman, M. (1991), *Pièces et règles du jeu politique*, Seuil: Paris.

Foucault, M. (1969), *L'archéologie du savoir*, NRF Gallimard: Paris.

Foucault, M. (1975), *Surveiller et Punir. Naissance de la prison*, Gallimard: Paris.

Foucault, M. (1989), *Sécurité, territoire et population. Résume des cours*, Julliard: Paris.

Foucher, M. (1991), *Fronts et frontières. Un tour du monde géopolitique*, Fayard: Paris.

Gordon, C. and Gordon, G. (1988), *Immigration Law and procedure. Practice and Strategies*, Matthew Bender: New York.

Hall, S. (1996), *Questions of Cultural Identity*, Sage: London.

Huysmans, J. (1997), 'European Identity and Migration Policies: Socio-economic and Security Questions in a Process of Europeanization', in Cederman, L.-E. (ed.), *Constructing Europe's Identity Issues and Tradeoffs. The Central European University*, Political Science Working Papers, n° 9, Budapest.

Lahav, G. (1998), 'Immigration and the State: the Devolution and Privatization of Immigration Control in the EU', *Journal of Ethnic and Migration Studies*, vol. 24, n° 4 (October), pp. 675-694.

Laudon, K. (1986), *The Dossier Society. Value Choices in the Design of National Information System*, Columbia University Press: New York.

Lipschutz, R. (2000), *After Authority, War, Peace and Global Politics in the 21st Century*, State University Press: Albany.

Marx, G. T. (1994), *The Declining Signification of Traditional Borders and the Appearance of New Borders in an Age of High Technology*, Conference on Georg Simmel: Between Modernity and Post modernity, Ludwig-Maximilians-Universität Munich.

Mathiesen, T. (1997), 'The viewer society: Michel Foucault's Panopticon Revisited', Theoretical Criminology, n° 1-2, pp. 215-234.

Mead, G. H. (1963), *L'esprit, le soi et la societe*, PUF: Paris.

Noiriel, G. (1991), *La tyrannie du national: le droit d'asile en Europe 1793-1993*, Calmann-Levy: Paris.

Noiriel, G. (1996), *The French Melting-Pot: Immigration, Citizenship and National Identity*, University of Minneapolis Press: Minneapolis.

Noiriel, G. (2001), *Etat, nation et immigration. Vers une histoire du pouvoir*, Belin: Paris.

Preuss-Laussignotte, S. (2000), *Les fichiers des étrangers au cœur des nouvelles politiques de sécurité*, Unpublished PhD Thesis, University of Paris X-Nanterre.

Rosenau, J. N. (1990), *Turbulence in World Politics. A Theory of Change and Continuity*, Princeton University Press: Princeton, N.J.

Ruggie, J. (1998), *Constructing the World Polity. Essays on International Institutionalization*, Routledge: London.

Schneider, A. and Ingram, H. (1993), 'Social Construction of Target Populations for Politics and Policy', American Political Science Review, vol. 67, n° 2 (June), pp. 334-347.

Simmel, G. (1964), 'The Stranger', in Wolf, K. H. (ed.), *The Sociology of Simmel*, The Free Press: New York.

Soysal, Y. (1994), *Limits of Citizenship. Migrants and Post-national Membership in Europe*, University of Chicago Press: Chicago, Ill.

Syndicat de la Magistrature (2002), *Vos papiers. Que faire face à la police?*, Esprit Frappeur: Paris.

Taylor, C. (1992), *Multiculturalism and "The Politics of Recognition"*, Princeton University Press: Princeton, NJ.

Torpey, J. (2001), *The Invention of the Passport*, Cambridge University Press: London.

Waever, O. (1997), *Concepts of Security*, Copenhagen Institute for Political Science, University of Copenhagen: Copenhagen.

Weber, M. (1947), *The Theory of Social and Economic Organization*, Parsons, T. (ed.), Free Press: Glencose.

Chapter 8

Policing at a Distance:
Schengen Visa Policies

Didier Bigo and Elspeth Guild

Moving Frontiers Controls Afar from the European Union Borders

As we have seen, identity, borders, and orders are intimately related.[1] Sovereign narratives of the national professionals of politics desperately try to continue linking them to the state border, despite the transformations that occurred due to new transport technologies and the desire of people to move. The idea to "seal" the borders is obsolete and nightmarish, especially if politicians try to implement it by adding arbitrariness to inefficiency. The detention of foreigners at – or even on their way to – the borders of the EU is a large-scale phenomenon. September 11, 2001 has created such a fear of a globalization of violence that the impetus to set up a homeland security department has been overwhelming within the community of professionals of politics, particularly since the US government tried to impose its "solution" on the other Western countries. Nevertheless, the professionals of security are doubtful about these "solutions" and "narratives" as they know that they are inefficient and that their inefficiency will be denounced by other politicians in the future. Hence, they largely prefer to begin the control of frontiers abroad, at the point of departure of the people on the move, but as discretely as possible, for they know how much this globalization or transnationalization of control is potentially destabilising for the rhetoric of the sovereignty of nation-states. The strategy of the European Union expressed by the Schengen visa policies began in the eighties with the development of a dual role. The states continued to issue and verify passports and travel documents at their borders but added another dimension to their previous responsibilities. This new aspect consisted of the creation of intergovernmental agreements concerning visas and the establishment of common data bases, exchange of good practices, common manuals, and, finally, what was called a common visa between the Schengen member states. This last chapter will examine how the technologies of control are now far from the borders and could therefore be defined more precisely as remote control tools. Consequently, the differentiation between the internal and the external created by the process of "bordering-debordering" is increasingly intersubjective. The frontier controls are less material and objective. They are activated through different devices responding to only one certain type of person and differentiating between those who belong and those who do not belong.

What is the idea behind policing people wishing to migrate from a distance? It is here that the examination of insiders and outsiders begins. The idea does not relate exclusively to the practices of national police or border guards. Rather, it is used to describe the mechanisms whereby the controls, which used to be carried out by national officials at national borders, are now carried out by foreign officials at the external frontier of the European Union and by private sector actors in the security field on behalf of carriers and to whom is passed the obligation of checking valid travel documents for the purpose of entering that part of the European Union.[2]

Against this reasoning which is focused on the official physical border, the concept of a border is breaking away from the territory in a sense that it is no longer the physical boundary, the limit or the envelope. It has been argued elsewhere the importance of this transformation of meaning of the border to the individual.[3] This argument enables one to understand how the individual "activates" various controls by movement and thereby meets the virtual border long before physically crossing the border of sovereignty. Depending on whether the individual has the nationality of a Member State of the Union, a third country, a country subject to a visa obligation, he or she will not meet any border, will meet it only once or twice on the territory of the arrival country, or will meet it within his or her home state at the consulate and at the airline counter. The frontier has thus an increasingly different meaning which relates more and more to the act of leaving one's country of nationality than getting into another. The frontier is activated in terms of surveillance and differs from individual to individual because it aims less to protect sovereignty than to define identities, discriminating between the "desirables" and the "undesirables". Some foreigners are no longer aware of the borders because they are perceived as others of ourselves – citizens coming from the other countries of the Union or even from European Economic Area or the United States. On the other hand, for some other foreigners – nationals of countries outside the Community, belonging to the Community's visa black list, without substantial financial resources, the border is activated repeatedly, with a much higher likelihood of access being denied or at least subject to many more administrative obstacles.

Rather than talking about "remote control", the phrase "policing at a distance" is used in order to describe a logic that is still being constructed. It is worth noting at this early point that this terminology is already being borrowed and redeployed in a military logic that is also under construction. The stake of the notion "policing at a distance" is in that sense the control by specific procedures and technologies of the movement of people before the individuals enter a given territory.

From this perspective, this chapter on remote policing differs from Zolberg, who uses the concept of remote policing to focus on the assignment of police officers or private actors with police functions outside their national territory,[4] and is closer to the research of Noiriel who, without using the term remote policing, describes remote identification procedures.[5] These procedures are extremely important in the process of construction of a national territory. Changing control and supervision technologies also brings about transition from face to face control based on local and historic relationships, to the checking of documents based on national and class profiles. The current Communitarization process and its relation to identification, supervision and control technologies is central to these changes. Is there still a continuity with the practices of the nation state? Is there a breach with the de-territorialization of the national space of controls and its re-territorialization within the European Union, via the computer technologies of networking control and surveillance (for instance in the form of the Schengen Information System, Eurodac etc.), and this in an era of control globalization (EU-FBI, Echelon etc.). The issue then becomes one about the relationship between the authorities managing these computer data-bases, the identification of people and the identification and meaning of documents. This chapter will be divided into two parts. The first one will focus on the EU's Schengen visa policy as the main example of current frontier control technologies as well as on their efficiency and legitimacy. The technologies of control are nowadays used abroad to police the people. This policing, however, is not carried out by official policemen. Instead, the consulates and embassies, actually tools of foreign affairs, are now mainly engaged in policing the borders and "internal security" issues. They are considered "a first line of defense against the virtual invaders". The common consular instructions are clear and quite cynical as they explain what is often masked in the rhetoric of the ministries of foreign affairs and cooperation with Third World countries. Hence, it is important to look at them in detail. The second part will deal with the question of how transnational networks of professionals of (in)security of the European Union frontiers may transform the present control and surveillance situation. We will also analyze the nature of their relationship with American professionals of politics and their policy. It is not possible, however, to draw conclusions concerning the transformations of the management of frontiers controls on a global scale. Nevertheless, this specific example provides lines of thought along which one can analyze the post-September 11 policies of control and surveillance differently and show that the danger for civil liberties are less and less located at the actual state borders. Instead, they are far from where the civil rights activists are watching. They are less visible and restructure the world into two spheres: one composed of people allowed to travel and a second one, of people who are banned from it without any possibility to protest since they have no appeal against the decisions and are miles away from the border because they cannot even board a plane or leave their own country.

The Schengen Visa: Who Controls the Legitimate Means of Movement?

The issue of visas is central.[6] The European Community has been responsible for the designation of a list of countries whose nationals must always be in possession of visas to pass into the territory of the Union since 1993. However, until the entry into force of the Amsterdam Treaty and the activation of the Schengen *acquis* into the control of borders of the Union, the visa national designation power was incomplete. Now it is exclusively for the European Community to determine the world in four categories: (1) Member States whose nationals have a right to enter and reside on the territory of one another which right can only be circumscribed in very limited circumstances; (2) countries with an especially privileged relationship with the Union whose nationals enjoy equivalent rights – the European Economic Area; (3) favoured countries which appear on the "white list" of the Community visa regulation, which means their nationals do not require visas to enter the territory of the Union; (4) countries whose nationals are by definition as such suspect – those on the regulation's "black list" who must always have a visa obtained abroad before arriving at the borders of the Union.[7]

It is the management of control by different entities of national police forces at the borders which is at stake. The primary control has moved to the consular authorities in those countries whose nationals are subject to a mandatory visa obligation. It is the visa process, more than the passport, which allows a selective sorting of those who will or will not be allowed to move "freely".[8] The visa obligation denotes a suspicion towards a country or a nationality as a whole. The granting of the visa is an exception to the exclusion. It is a re-establishment of confidence in an individual notwithstanding that his or her country of nationality is one which as a whole has been designated suspect.

The list of countries subject to a visa obligation is, if one applies the logic to its extreme, a generalized form of the so-called "rogue states". It denotes suspicion, mistrust and fear about the nationals of that state. In particular it manifests as a suspicion towards unstable countries, countries at war and poor countries.[9] In this area one of the first political objectives of countries subject to the visa obligation is to be withdrawn from this list, especially if they are in the list of candidate countries for Union membership. They understand that their chance to accede to the Union is governed by a withdrawal of suspicion and the acceptance of the their citizens as not constituting a prima facie threat to the Union.

The Bulgarian example here is interesting. When the Visa Regulation was adopted much discussion took place about the continued inclusion of Bulgaria and Romania on the list while all the other accession states in Central and Eastern Europe were excluded from the visa requirement. The two countries were included on the list but the Commission was instructed to draw up a report on the adequacy of border practices in each of them for presentation to the Council. At the European Council meeting in December 2000 the political decision was taken to remove Bulgaria from the black list. It was inserted on the White list. Romania was also withdrawn from the black list according to the wording of the Regulation but visas were still required of all Romanians seeking to enter the Union territory pending a second report by the Commission on the adequacy of Romanian border practices and a decision to remove in practice Romanians from the visa requirement. The Commission proposed such removal in October 2001. However, it appears that the fact of withdrawing Bulgaria from the list of countries subject to visa is less an efficiency measure (harmonization of the list of countries subject to a visa or the so-called problems of illegal migration crossing its own territory in direction of the Union), than evidence of acceptance by the Union of symbolic engagements that the Bulgarian authorities would take against corruption, in favour of a global legislation and recognition of the accendancy of the Union's economic influence in comparison with that of the United States. Between the official discourse regarding the Schengen *acquis* (now integrated into the Union's *acquis*[10] which under the terms of the Amsterdam Treaty the candidate countries have to implement) and their capacities to implement these measures, there is a substantial gap.[11] They are asked "to make gestures of good will" as regards legislation and in exchange the designation of "suspect" will partly be erased and some facilities will be financed.[12] In political terms, it is not therefore certain that the question of visas is connected to security and migration requirements.

Visas are mainly demanded by the authorities of Member States which do not want fast enlargement to second wave candidates, and plead for a "pause". Conversely, they are countered by those who support politically faster enlargement of the Union which leaves none out, on account of the risks which that frustration would create. Those who believe in security arguments are mainly in the ministries of Justice and Interior. The Foreign Affairs and Labour ministries favour enlargement. Simultaneously, though, free movement of persons from applicant countries is increasingly called into question, even for first wave countries, and even countries in favour of rapid enlargement. Indeed, the Greek and Austrian examples are used to illustrate that the principle of entry into the Schengen Agreements was not followed by immediate effects and that they had to prove – in front of a committee composed of the participating Member States – the effectiveness of their capacities to control their frontiers in order to participate in the border control free area. Thanks to this precedent, German-Polish frontier controls would not be lifted with the date of accession nor indeed necessarily after Poland establishes strengthened controls at its Eastern border.[13] The German government has argued for a 7-year transitional period though a Bundes Kriminal Amt official pleaded for ten years starting from the effective entry of the applicant countries in the Union.[14] If this reasoning, accepted in the EU's Justice and Home Affairs Council, though countered by both the European Commission and Parliament, is followed, there would be a further de-linking of the area of freedom, security and justice as regards movement which would be ensured only between some countries – the older and the richer ones – and the police collaboration area which would exist among all the Member States having accepted the Schengen *acquis*. This de-linking is well understood by the United Kingdom which plays with it in order to maintain controls at its borders but also to participate in remote control as well. For Bulgaria consequently, as for Hungary or Poland, the issue of abolition of border controls and full free movement within the Union is still far away. The issue of white and black visa lists, of imposition or not of visas seems then to say less about safety and migration imperatives, than about the social construction of more or less shared fears concerning the Other and about the way Europeans seek to construct an image of themselves, a common identity.

It is in this categorization of identities and not simply of security that the Schengen visa and the strategies of remote control must be analyzed. Describing remote control means then to understand the relation between the legal principles implemented and the supervision and control instruments deployed. The objective of the system is to make sure that individuals who are not wanted by any one of the participating States are not permitted to enter the territory. Thus the rules concentrate on who has to be excluded and provide very little information on who can be admitted. Due to the underlying principle of the system, namely a crossed recognition of national decisions rather than harmonization, the choice of legal mechanism for implementation has unexpected implications. The lifting of control at borders between States means for example that a positive decision on an individual's admission is probably respected by default – thus the Parties have to make fewer controls of identity at borders but their mistrust regarding the other administration can cause them to strengthen controls inside the country, in some sensitive areas or in places populated by a minority of third country nationals.[15] The cross recognition of negative decisions requires even more specific measures. When the internal security concept (the first reason for a refusal of admission to the EU territory) is not harmonized, the refusal of admission to the individual by another State is based exclusively on the invocation of security by another Member State. The effective decision of exclusion is divorced from an examination of the reasons why the individual is a threat. For example, in the Netherlands, the legal mechanism to carry this out is to be found in Article 109 (4) and (5) of the Aliens Law 1999 which locates the Netherlands border for the movement of persons at the extremities of every Member States and integrates the internal security of every Member State to Dutch internal security.

Despite the heterogeneity of local implementation, the legal logic of the EU visa is summarized by three principles.

First principle: no third country national can have access the Union territory (with or without a short term visa) if he or she constitutes a risk to the security of any Member State. States must therefore be able to identify the individuals who constitute a threat to their own security and to the security of the other Member States. This is done via the consultation of the databases of national police forces, international databases like Interpol and via the link between national databases of the other Union States created by the operation of the Schengen Information System (SIS) and the Sirene (the national database linked to the SIS). Within the SIS are to be found the names of those individuals who already having been in the territory of the Union for one reason or another are designated as "undesirable". That is translated into a registration on the list of those who must not be admitted to the EU territory. This list is based on national appreciations of risk which are not exclusive but left open ended (Article 96 Schengen Implementing Agreement 1990). The definition of these people as undesirable is based on what they have done or represented when they were within the territory of the Union. It is here that the question of divergent perceptions of what constitutes a risk and of what is security becomes central. What is perceived as a risk to security in one State is not inevitably identical to that in another. This difference in risk appreciation as it refers to the activities of the individual the last time he or she was in the Union only becomes visible when national courts start calling into question the legitimacy of the system. As regards the SIS and this ground for exclusion from the EU territory, the relationship between individual and risk is made on the basis of an individual already known and already having been on the Union's territory. This leads to the next principle of the EU border.

Second principle: there is an assumption of admissibility (not as strong legally speaking as a presumption) regarding an individual in possession of a short-term visa delivered by one of the other participating States. Consequently the visa is recognized as valid in order to enter the common territory (though there are explicit exceptions which can justify the refusal, ie security which falls within the competence of the police at the borders, these are rarely exercised). This supposes that there is a system of co-ordination so that each State accepts the visa issued by the other's authorities and does not repeat the control. That also supposes reciprocal confidence marked by a belief in the effectiveness of controls carried out by the administrations of other Member States. Theoretically, the "uniform" EU visa is designed to avoid the nuisance of multiple controls for people and is a pledge of reciprocal confidence. The practice is somewhat different. Until December 1998 there were three lists – the white list of countries whose nationals never had to get a visa to enter the EU; a black list of countries whose nationals always had to get visas to enter and a grey list of countries whom some EU states required visas and others did not. Thus the variable geometry of threat and risk was accommodated within a "mutual recognition" system. Of course the practical consequences were absurd. For example, a Colombian national could enter Spain without a visa and travel to any other Member State once within the border free territory even though technically he or she would have required a visa to enter that other state. The accommodation of differing perceptions of threat by Member States was more important than the actual exclusion of persons designated as prima facie threats. The existence of the grey list, evidence of the symbolic nature of the EU construction of risk, was finally abolished in 1998.

The variable geometry is still very much in existence in the interpretation of the criteria for a visa. These are not interpreted in the same way by the consular agents of the Member States. Can a system like the one under consideration, limited to co-ordination of national systems, be integrated into the logic of EU integration? In what respect can we speak about a common visa policy and a uniform visa? The intention of the Common Consular Instructions[16] on the issue of visas is to identify those groups of people who are more likely than others to have among them individuals who constitute a risk to a Member State. This group is then subject to an additional level of control regarding their potential access to the territory of the Union. The problem is how to identify these risk groups, then to separate the *bona fide* from the others. The first tool is by reference to the country of origin: nationals of a country on the visa black list are, by definition, a risk. The second instrument is the Common Consular Instructions on visas which categorize individual nationals of black list countries according to a risk intensity scale (which includes "migratory" threat). For these people, specific controls including a face to face interview and document screening is systematic. It is up to the individual to prove that he or she does not constitute a risk and that he or she can be regarded as bona fide. This means that for these people the real border of the EU has moved to within their own country and is no longer, or no longer exclusively, at the border of the state they want to enter. It is at the consulate level that their entry is examined and not when they pass the physical border of the state. It is here that the remote control concept is meaningful. The border is activated before entry into the territory.

This change is due to an inversion of the logic of control, partly linked to the end of bipolarity. The justification system reverses the relation between the individual and the state as regards who or what is dangerous. It is no longer the relation between the EU and other states that determines the treatment of their nationals. This involves rather the evaluation of individuals and their suspected behaviour which determines the characterization of the state. Thus, the diplomatic logic which affiliates individuals to a dangerous political regime is partly erased by a transformation of the state into a dangerous one if its population or a minority of it is regarded as a risk by the Union. The ideology of the regime counts less than the migratory risk which a part of its population might constitute. Relations are no longer on a state to state basis, but on an individuals or minorities to groups of states basis, and this transnationalization has substantial consequences for consular practices.

Applying general rules to individuals is no longer adequate, rather it is a matter of identifying, and selecting, from risk profiles built on previous individual statistics, what group of people is likely to constitute a risk, and then to apply it to individuals who might fulfil some of the criteria. This morphing technique or pro-active policing is sometime used in relation to crime control and is now applied to those seeking visas. A police logic is introduced into consulates. Thus Interior and Justice ministry personnel become important aids to consular staff either on the spot in the form of security attachés, or via training aimed at transforming consular staff duties, or via links with the various national central authorities. This vertical and national co-operation is completed by horizontal co-operation between EU States at the local level via formalization of consular co-operation which facilitates regular meetings of *visa officers* of EU States (Ireland and United Kingdom included) in capitals and large cities worldwide, and even sometimes of transversal co-operation where the local authority depends, in a certain case, on central authorities of other EU countries, in relation to the attribution of a threat criterion to a specific minority as regards a specific State (annex 5B).[17]

This construction of suspicion at the level of individuals leads to the introduction of private actors at key moments in the process. For instance travel agencies begin to play a role in the management of visa requests, airlines are caught in a web of legislation requiring the certification of documents held by people, and finally private security companies provide wide ranging controls on persons and documents in airports. This enables Member States temporarily to avoid the contradictions between a State to State diplomatic logic, and a logic of remote policing which focuses on the so-called undesirable or dangerous individuals.

Third principle: once within the common territory, the individual is allowed (but that can also be liable to exceptions for security reasons) to travel in the whole territory for a three-month period without any additional control at the internal borders of the participating States. This principle of internal freedom of movement is supposed to compensate for inconveniences caused in the previous phases. But, in practice, identity checking is applied to those who do not have the appearance of "European" or welcome foreigners. The criterion of poverty is, together with skin colour, one of the most powerful control triggers. Suspicion attaches to the image of the migrant which the profiling technique has created and then applies also to citizens of the State who share that image. We will not develop here the discussion regarding technologies for identity controls within the borders and at internal borders. The momentum of remote or upstream policing is meaningful only when related to the momentum of a downstream or inner policing.

It would only be with a common visa policy and uniform implementation by the consular authorities that we could find consistency and some kind of unification of the territory. The European Union as a single territory would have then the technical means to exercise from afar, via a uniform visa, a claim to a monopoly over the legitimate entry mechanisms for foreigners coming from high risk countries. The Union would not encroach directly on the official attributes of sovereignty via the issuing of passports and the physical border control, but would supplement them.[18] As the Commission indicates, the establishment of the nationality at the border is crucial for the management of cross-border flows.

The border, for the nationals being on the list of countries with a visa obligation, is located at their starting point, in third countries. The first border for these people is at the consulate of a Member State in their own country. It is far from the physical border of a State. The crucial decision for them will be taken in this consulate, within the framework the consular co-operation of the Fifteen, and in their own country.[19] The request must be made in one's own country for controls to take place. This virtual relocation of the border, placed before the trip – and not after – is central in the strategy of the Union and of the Commission. It aims "to dry up flows from the source" according to one official interviewed during this study.

It does not apply therefore to every country but only to the so-called high risk countries –which are described only by reference to the three general criteria – see *supra*.[20] It is a two step process: the first is the decision to put these countries on the visa list, which defines them *prima facie* as risk factors for the Union's security. Then simply, the individual decision on each request can reconsider the exclusion. The first step, (the drawing up of the countries list), now falls within the competence of the Commission which seeks to harmonize States positions among themselves in eliminating the additional lists some States had created. However, the Commission considers that granting or refusing visas on an individual basis is the exclusive competence of the Member States.[21] Paradoxically, this reverses its role *vis-à-vis* the threat since it stresses the danger of individuals more than government policies of third countries.

The Commission, in the preamble to the proposal for a Regulation establishing the list of third countries whose nationals are subject to a visa obligation in order to cross the external borders, and the list of those nationals who are exempted of this obligation, explains its position in these terms:

"The Amsterdam Treaty constitutes a remarkable step forward for the European integration into the field of the visas policy in relation to the Maastricht Treaty. The latter by introducing Article 100 C into the EC treaty, put into Community law only two aspects of the visas policy (on the one hand the determination of third countries whose nationals have to be provided with a visa at the time of the external borders crossing of the Member States and, on the other hand the introduction of a standard visa model). However, the Amsterdam treaty put into Community law all the other aspects of the visas policy by incorporating them into the new title IV of the EC treaty "Visas, asylum, immigration and other policies connected with free movement of persons" which aims at the creation of an area of freedom, security and justice. At the same time, a protocol annexed to the Amsterdam treaty incorporated the Schengen *acquis* into the Union, which includes the whole *acquis* in visa matters to which Schengen states had reached".

Thus there are two sources for the current law: the previous Community law and the secondary legislation stemming from Schengen Agreements.

1. Pre 1999 Community Law

On the basis of (former) Article 100 C, the Council adopted Regulation 2317/95[22] which, after it was annulled by a judgement of the Court of Justice (10 June 1997), was replaced by Regulation 574/99[23] determining then third countries whose nationals must have a visa at the time of the crossing of the external borders of the Member States.

Regulation 574/99, like previous regulation 2317/95, only includes the common list of the third countries whose nationals are subject to the visa obligation. For the third countries not appearing on the common list, Member States remained free to choose whether to impose a visa obligation or not. Practice varied among Member States most often connected with the colonial traditions and the cultural and linguistic links.

2. Schengen Law

Under the Schengen Agreements from 1985 onwards, some Member States developed closer co-operation in the field of visas. This co-operation was given Community legitimacy in regulations 2317/95 and 574/99 which specified that they did not oppose more thorough harmonization among the Member States, the scope of which went beyond the common list.

The Schengen states[24] coordinated their visa policy more thoroughly that regulations 2317/95 and 574/99 required. The harmonization was done gradually and by the time of Schengen integration into the European Union, included:

1.   a list of 32 third countries which were not found on the list of regulation 574/99 and whose nationals were subject to the visa obligation in all the Schengen states;
2.   a list of 44 third countries whose nationals were exempt from visa requirements by all the Schengen states (there was no equivalent under regulation 574/99).

For only one third country, Colombia, Schengen states had not reached a harmonized position. This situation was eventually resolved by including Colombia on the list of the countries whose nationals are subject to visa. Spain, in spite of its strong links with Colombia, justified this new restriction to the Colombian authorities on the basis that they could not derogate from the Community decision which was taken according to qualified majority vote in the Council.

The Schengen *acquis* has been adopted into Community law following the entry into force of the Amsterdam Treaty and the borders sections are now an integral part of the Community legislation. Among the measures mentioned in Article 62(2)(b) EC under the heading "the rules on visas for intended stays of no more than three months" is "the list of third countries whose nationals must be in possession of visas when crossing the external border, and those whose nationals are exempted of that requirement". The regulation fulfils Article 62(2)(b) and includes two exhaustive lists of third countries.[25]

The new regulation aims to harmonize the visa rules applicable to third country nationals. Member States no longer have a choice over which countries to impose visa requirements or not. Although the new regulation is formally the consequence of the Amsterdam treaty, it is the direct descendant of (former) Article 100 C. When the Commission submitted its first visa regulation proposal in December 1993 it interpreted the provision such that the Council determined the third countries whose nationals would not be subject to visa requirements.

The standardization of the list of countries does not prevent the maintenance of a limited number of derogation and exception insofar as necessary to leave the Member States the possibility to derogate or make an exception for some categories of people, in particular for reasons of international or customary law – (for example sailors or holders of a green card in the United States are exempted of a transit visa).

In accordance with the rules of division of powers an explanation must be given in each proposal by the Commission of how it complies with the requirements of subsidiarity. The answer here is as follows: Article 62(2)(b)(i) confers an exclusive competence on the Community to decide the list of the third countries whose nationals are subject to the visa requirement and those whose nationals are exempt.

The choice of recourse to a regulation rather than a directive is explained by various reasons: the lists do not leave room for manoeuvre to the Member States "to transpose" the lists. Moreover, a transposition delay of one or the other Member State would involve practical difficulties, some of which could call into question the operation of the arrangement of the visas resulting from the Schengen *acquis*' integration into the Union. The new regulation was adopted on 15 March 2001 by the Council[26] and entered into force on 10 April 2001.

As the Commission indicated, the regulation does not cover all the questions, but is specific. It does not: (a) apply to instruments which do not engage Article 62(2) like the long-term visa or the airport transit visa; (b) lay down the procedures and conditions of issuing visas; (c) determine the conditions of intra-Community movement of the visa holders or of the exempted individuals because this will be fixed by an instrument based on Article 62(3); (d) include provisions on the crossing of external borders (for example: non admission at the border or exceptional admission on a humanitarian basis; issuing of visas at the border). The regulation does not affect the possibility that exceptional measures can be taken in

individual cases. Article 64(2)EC provides for limits to the duration and the
conditions for such measures and establishes the procedure to be applied.

In order to explain why countries are on the list the Commission states in the
explanatory memorandum:

> "To determine whether nationals of a third country are subject to the visa requirement
> or exempted from it, regard should be had to a set of criteria that can be grouped
> under three main headings:
>
> • illegal immigration: the visas rules constitute an essential instrument for
>   controlling migratory flows. Here, reference can be made to a number of
>   relevant sources of statistical information and indicators to assess the risk of
>   illegal migratory flows (such as information and/or statistics on illegal residence,
>   cases of refusal of admission to the territory, expulsion measures, and
>   clandestine immigration and labour networks), to assess the reliability of travel
>   documents issued by the relevant third country and to consider the impact of
>   readmission agreements with those countries;
> • public policy: conclusions reached in the police cooperation context among
>   others may highlight specific salient features of certain types of crime.
>   Depending on the seriousness, regularity and territorial extent of the relevant
>   forms of crime, imposing the visa requirement could be a possible response
>   worth considering. Threats to public order may in some cases be so serious as
>   even to jeopardize domestic security in one or more Member States. If the visa
>   requirement was imposed in a show of solidarity by the other Member States,
>   this could again be an appropriate response;
> • international relations: the option for or against imposing the visa requirement in
>   respect of a given third country can be a means of underlining the type of
>   relations which the Union is intending to establish or maintain with it. But the
>   Union's relations with a single country in isolation are rarely at stake here. Most
>   commonly it is the relationship with a group of countries, and the option in
>   favour of a given visa regime also has implications in terms of regional
>   coherence. The choice of visa regime can also reflect the specific position of a
>   Member State in relation to a third country, to which the other Member States
>   adhere in a spirit of solidarity. The reciprocity criterion, applied by States
>   individually and separately in the traditional form of relations under public
>   international law, now has to be used by reason of the constraints of the Union's
>   external relations with third countries. Given the extreme diversity of situations
>   in third countries and their relations with the European Union and the Member
>   States, the criteria set out here cannot be applied automatically, by means of
>   coefficients fixed in advance. They must be seen as decision-making instruments
>   to be used flexibly and pragmatically, being weighted variably on a case-by-case
>   basis."[27]

The appreciation of what is public policy can vary appreciably from one
Member State to another. In the case of Donatella Calfa (C-386/96 of 19 January
1999), the Court of Justice was confronted with this difficulty. The case involved
an Italian national convicted of a soft drugs offence, possession for personal use, in
Greece and sentenced to three-month's imprisonment and expulsion including a
ban on return (ever) to Greece. Was expulsion and a prohibition on re-entry

compatible with the principle of freedom of movement of persons and European citizenship? The Court first of all pointed out that Member States can take expulsion measures with regard to a Community national on grounds of public policy. The Bouchereau[28] judgement had established the principle that expulsion could only be justified on grounds of public policy where the perturbation of the social order which any infringement of the law involves constitutes a genuine and sufficiently serious threat to the requirements of public policy affecting one of the fundamental interests of the society. Because the Greek provision carried an automatic ban on re-entry, it was contrary to Community law. However the crucial point for these purposes is that the appreciation by Greece of soft drugs as a ground for expulsion was not challenged by the Court even though possession for personal use is tolerated in the Netherlands and recently was legalised in Portugal, and de facto in Germany. The Court recognizes therefore a certain "margin of appreciation" of the states to determine what belongs to public policy which does not help clarify the concept.

As regards the ground of international relations, the European Union adopts two positions regarding people to be excluded. First, each Member State must exhibit solidarity with the other Member States and respect the presence on the black list of a country whose nationals do not necessarily present a problem for it. Secondly, the assessment of countries is not taken independently of other countries located in the same regional area: for instance Algeria will not be considered independently of its geographical situation, but in relation to all the Maghreb countries. The Union imposes its vision of regionalism on other parts of the world.

Is the admission to the EU of an individual dependent on the appraisal of his or her country as a threat? If he or she is a national of a high risk country, according to the Commission's criteria, he or she is subject to a visa requirement, whatever his or her personal qualities. Does the assessment of a country on the visa list sanction its government policies – ie international relations criteria – or illegal social practices – public policy and migration criteria? The dichotomy between the diplomatic character of interstate relations and the illegal character of the activities of the individual put forward by the Commission masks a vision in terms of "transversal threats to internal safety" coming from some communities of third countries. The implicit criterion which connects the three explicit criteria is the suspicion of transnational population flows which would affect the internal security of the Union. The construction of suspicion certainly slices through the attitudes of governments towards one another, through their "rogue states" lists or their perceived narcotic-trafficking countries but also converges on low GDP states or states in conflict where their people might have reasons to flee. In addition to the attitudes of governments, what concerns the Commission is that these population flows can be considered dangerous because they generate terrorism, religious radicalism, criminality, because they could contain candidates for migration (something the European Union does not want) or because the political situation is such that they might flee their country and seek asylum.

Here is the construction of a continuum of insecurities that are linked together and which include, beyond governmental actors, social practices of some groups from these countries. The charge of potential illegal individual migration cannot properly mask a reasoning which plays on "flows" and not on individuals and an argument which assimilates criminality, illegality, regular/irregular migration and asylum. Within the list there is a hierarchy of the most suspect countries. The classification on alphabetical grounds may hide another gradation of threats. If so, who produces it and is it implemented uniformly? Is it possible to exchange fears regarding risks by Communitarising them or does each State establish its priorities finally, little interested in the management of the others, fears? This will now be considered in more detail to see whether it is the threat of the individual – criminality – which is at stake, or geopolitics – ideology – or if it is a fear of destabilising identities – massive flows coming – migrants or refugees – legal or irregular. The first hypothesis is that threats are built by national considerations and that the SIS is the reflection of them. Each country has its own management and its own fears. States exchange or share these fears with the other Member States. They are seldom concerned, at least at the border, with fears of the other Member States about individuals who are not registered in the SIS. Nevertheless some categories of fear are being integrated into Community law more quickly than others – for example those cross-border fears of Gypsies which very quickly develops into a suspicion about Romanians in general. It is probably at this level that there is a link between SIS and Europol in so far as the analysis teams of Europol aim to build the categories which are then applied by States for their Schengen data on the undesirables, and are also deployed by consular agents.

Of the three criteria used by the Commission, only the criterion of foreign policies would call into question the Commission's claim to responsibility for the entry mechanisms of individuals coming from high risk countries. The Commission also uses a different argument focusing more on individuals taken as population flows. But, who is finally responsible for refusing visas to people? The consular authorities of the Member State where the application is made or the authorities who establish the criteria? Can the Commission avoid criticism when it establishes the criteria which will be applied? To answer these questions at least in part, the extent to which the conditions for granting and refusing visas are harmonized will now be considered. It is therefore necessary to differentiate states from their nationals. Nationals of one or other state may be considered a threat or dangerous. This threat or danger, embodied by individuals, reflects back on the state, which will be black listed.

The key to the system of EU border control is not in the systematic checking of documents at borders, but in the methods of profiling and of identifying threats coming from foreign countries. The first step to identifying these threats and risks is profiling according to nationality with the imposition of obligatory visas on nationals of high risk countries. The second step is to identify individuals who do not constitute a threat among individuals of a high risk nationality and to make sure that only these people will get visas. This is the task of national Ministries for Foreign Affairs and diplomatic and consular authorities on the spot.[29]

Standardization is presented as existing because of the fact that whichever EU consulate the candidate approaches the same type of visa allowing travel throughout the European territory will be issued (if at all). This is the standard account. But the details of the instructions are more complicated and call into question the singularity of the Schengen visa, as well as whether such a visa is actually valid throughout the whole European territory.

On the legal level, the uniform Schengen visa is not a single visa for two reasons. It is a visa delivered by one of the EU States and which permits entry into the others, but which can still be made subject to checks at internal borders. In addition, there are nine types of Schengen visa which have different legal consequences.

As the consular instruction points out "visa shall mean an authorization given or a decision taken by a Member State which is required for entry into its territory with a view to an intended stay in that Member State of no more than three months in all; or transit through the territory of that Member State or several Member States, except for transit through international zones of airports and transfers between airports in a Member State..."[30] Indeed, because the visa system is a network of national systems (i.e. between Member States), the refusal of entry at the border of a person provided with a Schengen visa depends on exceptional situations. In practice, if the visa is granted by the state to which the official belongs, the entry refusal at borders is quite possible because the threat is defined by the state itself, and that opposes *de facto* the police force only to its consular authorities. Apart from the exceptional case, there is no dispute because the police force has discretionary authority.

On the other hand, although refusal of entry to an individual with an EU visa issued by another state is still possible at internal borders, this refusal is much more delicate because it is tantamount to a criticism of lack of vigilance against the state which delivered the visa, or an accusation that the state of first arrival has not carried out a proper check. This means that a national police official is passing judgement on consular authorities of another Member State or its authorities at the external borders. Internal diplomatic relations of the EU States are engaged. How can a visa issued by a German consulate not be honoured by the Dutch police? The border police in some countries though (notably France and Germany) check people issued EU visas by "doubtful" consulates – for instance Greek consulates in the Middle East and in Africa.[31]

In some interviews officials stressed the risk of visa shopping where applicants choose the "easiest" consulate and obtain a visa giving access to the whole EU territory. But this hardly takes account of the constraints on applications. The individual can seek a visa only at the consulate of the Member State where he or she will remain longest and has therefore to prove that there are reasons to approach this consulate. In addition, it is almost impossible for an individual to seek a visa other than in his or her country of origin. Finally, any attempt to make an application in more than one consulate is regarded as the proof of fraud and justifies refusal. Thus the rules of application are strictly limited on grounds of nationality – that of the State. The integration of the Union is not apparent here.

It is to avoid tensions among Member States that co-operation among consular officials is so strongly recommended by the Commission. If all take part in a decision, differences of appraisal which can be problematic at the border will be limited. The EU visa is a national *de facto* visa which gives facilities to enter the

territory of the other States but which does not ensure the entry into a single
territory where freedom of movement is guaranteed.

In addition, "uniform" in fact includes various types of visas. According to
the Common Consular Instructions there are nine types of Schengen visa grouped
in five categories and to which three other types of national visas related to the
common visa must be added.[32]

The five categories are as follows: airport transit visas, visas permitting a
foreigner travelling from one third state to another to cross the EU territory, short
stay visas, multiple entry visas, and collective visas.

As the consular instruction describes, visas are defined as follows:

1. a travel visa valid for one or more entries provided that neither the
    length of a continuous visit nor the total length of successive visits
    exceeds three months in any half-year, from the date of first entry;
2. a visa valid for one year entitling a three month visit during any half
    year and several entries;
3. a visa valid for more than one year but for a maximum of five years
    entitling a three month visit during any half year and several entries;
4. airport transit visas which entitle an alien to pass through the
    international transit area of airports;
5. transit visas which entitle aliens who are travelling from one third state
    to another to pass through the territories of the parties;
6. transit visas issued to a group of aliens provided that they enter and
    leave the territory as a group;
7. group visas limited to a maximum of 30 days stay on the territory for
    groups of between 5 and 50 persons travelling on a group passport
    provided they enter and leave the territory as a group.

Concerning the long-term visas, the Commission stressed that a visa for a
stay longer than three months is a visa delivered by each State in accordance with
its own legislation. However, it will also act as a uniform transit visa enabling its
holder to enter the territory for the duration of transit, not exceeding five days,
unless the holder does not satisfy the conditions of entry or is registered in the SIS.
Concerning the two other types of visas: visa with a limited territorial validity and
visa delivered at the border, the instructions regarding treatment at the border are
confidential. The uniform visa is not a single visa. It includes various types of
visas, corresponding to different modes of travel or stay. The application of the
rules is liable to variation depending on the State's view of what is more
problematic. In addition, the uniform visa is not automatically necessary – there are
rules on issue of visas at the border as well.

Among the most impressive of variations used to be the price. For several
years the price varied according to the national consulates. Now with the
introduction of the Euro the fee has finally been harmonized. Nevertheless, the
money charged for the uniform visa issuing varies according to the type of visa as
shown by the following table:[33]

A. Airport transit	EUROS 10
B. Transit (one, two or several entries)	EUROS 10
C1. Very short sojourn (30 days)	EUROS 30 + 5 EUROS from the 2nd entry in the event of multiple entries
C2. Short duration (90 max days)	EUROS 50
C3. Multiple entries with a validity term of a year	EUROS 50
C4. Multiple entries, max 5-year validity	EUROS 50 + 30 EUROS per additional year
D. National visa for a long stay	Fixed amount by the Member States, these visas can be free
- limited territorial validity	Amount at least equal to 50% of the amount fixed for the category A visas, B or C
- delivered at the border	Double amount of the corresponding category of visa. These visas can be free
E. Collective, categories A & B (of 5-50 people)	10 EURO + 1 EURO per person
F. Collectives, category C1 (30 days) 1 or 2 entries (of 5-50 people)	EUROS 30 + 1 EURO per person
G. Collective, category C1 (30 days) more than two entries (of 5-50 people)	EUROS 30 + 3 EURO per person

These prices were set, after a debate between those who wanted them to be high enough so as to have a dissuasive effect against unwanted migration and those who wanted to facilitate freedom of movement. The latter prevailed. But to this fee must be added the cost of the passport and especially the cost of translating and legalising documents required to accompany the application. For example we were told that sometimes bank statements over a two year period and issued by the bank were required. Applicants also have to prove that they have at least 40 Euros per day for the duration of their stay and a return ticket. Some consulates require sight of the money before the departure while others are satisfied with a signed statement.

Indeed, the rules about which state has responsibility to consider a visa application are admirably complicated. The issue of a Schengen visa depends on the internal rules at national consulates and on local practices. Because there are several possible interpretations of the rules, in practice, there are many variations. The result is that consulates of some states accept very easily the responsibility for considering an application while others do not. Greek consulates are often singled out as the most "generous" ones, and the French as the most "strict". We were not able yet to obtain statistics on applications for Schengen visa and the results by national consulates in a given country.

It is very difficult to obtain significant data on the comparison of consular practices, even where one is looking at only one third country. We were provided with contradictory information. Some imply that comparative statistics exist but are confidential; others that they do not exist and are not a priority in view of the other activities which consulates have to carry out.

Some NGOs advised that in cases where the responsible State refuses to accept an application, claiming that another state is responsible, and that second consulate does not want to look at the visa request either, the applicant finds him or herself in orbit around the consulates with no remedy and no way to force one of the consulates to consider that application. These cases seem rare. Most of the time the request is informed. But what are the practical considerations for granting or for refusing to issue a visa?

We have already examined the inversion of burden of the proof for individuals from black list countries. It is up to the individual to prove that he or she will not be a risk if allowed into the Union. Depending on the person's nationality he or she will have to explain why he or she is an exception in comparison with fellow nationals who are, by definition, threats or risks to the European Union. The individual must submit documents proving that he or she is neither a criminal, nor a potential migrant seeking to settle irregularly on the territory of the Union. The role of the interview(s) at the consulate here can be decisive, if the individual gets a chance to be interviewed.

There is a heterogeneity at work within in the legal system itself. This reflects the fact that weaving a network of national laws does not lead to harmonization or even convergence. Differences are simply arranged in such a way as to be recognized as legitimate. States describe their practices with the wording of the Community rules. Implementation depends on the way States see their interests as well as risks and threats which would affect them or would affect their society. This is demonstrated in the practices of physical frontier controls, into the supply of data to the SIS and even into the management of visas.

The Commission seeks to distinguish two levels (1) the management of visas applicants and (2) the lists of the countries subject to visa requirements. The Commission has succeeded in brokering agreement among the Member States to reduce the differences concerning the list, but management of applications by the consular authorities is far from being an expression of a uniform, coherent and global policy. The consular officer's right to assess is strengthened via co-operation among consulates and even hinders coherence at the national level. What happens to visa applications at the French consulates in Jeddah and Accra comes to have less in common with what happens to visa applications at the French and German consulates in Jeddah or Accra. While some States, for example Germany, set up risk profiling via ready-made templates provided to their consular officers, others reject this approach. But the consular network in place in each capital takes over, first informally, by telephone between consulates in one place in connection with individual applications, but increasingly formalized. The cooperation is structured around lists of individuals who are considered bona fide and those who are not. In a few cases, it was suggested that these exchanges also take place via emails. This network certainly has a legal basis with the consular instructions and the Council recommendations aiming to develop cooperation though these lists are not specifically sanctioned. There is no explanation of the criteria used to decide whether an applicant is considered bona fide or not, nor are there any data protection rules which could provide a remedy to a person refused a visa because he or she has been included on one of these informal lists. A visa refusal may lead to a minimum of many years of exclusion from the territory of the Union. The practice of stamping passports of applicants to indicate that they have made an application (which has not been successful) means that there is an easy first control to exclude those who try a second time for a visa. The lists ensure that the possibility of getting a new passport will not help. The legitimacy of giving the authority to officials to choose on a case-by-case basis who is a "migratory risk" and who is not must be questioned. The perception of migration as a risk is, itself, debatable. When one considers that (a) visa refusals are not necessarily reasoned (or justified) (b) interviews are not compulsory, (c) documents required vary according to the consulate approached and according to the country, (d) the fees themselves vary according to the type of visa, and (e) some consulates advise applicants to withdraw their applications rather than risk a refusal (which means the individual has no remedies against refusal and the consular officials do not have to give reasons for a refusal as there has been no refusal), the term uniform visa, as an instrument of a common policy is particularly empty.

Nevertheless, the Commission, and some governments, are convinced that the management of transnational flows of persons has to be carried out in countries of origin – the high risk countries – and via the Ministries for Foreign Affairs, through a logic of remote policing. Control at physical frontier via the border guards is considered archaic. The remote management provides a role for the Commission in its claim to manage *de facto* requests of entry, throughout the whole European territory, of high risk foreigners. And this claim gives the Commission a key role in respect of the monopoly on the legitimate means of movement of persons without engaging in a head-on attack on the monopoly of Member States to control the legitimate means of movement via the passports and identity documents.

Conclusion: The Relations between Actors, New Developments in Technology and Individual Rights

Relations between States and Individuals

The theory of sovereignty has long served as the basis on which governing powers could establish a watertight boundary between internal and external rules, between an ordered society and international anarchy. On one hand respect for law and concern for society, on the other war and diplomacy. On one hand, within the Weberian state, rationality prevailed, with an optimal range of choice for the individual, and the promise of democracy; on the other, in the world between states, destruction threatened, nations vied for power, with conflict the expected issue. There was a clearly defined "Us" and a clearly defined "Them", clearly defined fellow-countrymen and clearly defined foreigners. The theorists of realism tended to overestimate these differences, and by considering them as immutable, mistook otherness for enmity.

Liberal theorists have, on the contrary, relativized this notion of the frontier as a cut-off point, and have emphasized the part played by transits across frontiers, seen as a positive form of interconnectedness. Economists as well, adopting a liberal approach, have questioned the claim made by states that they, and they alone, have the right to control the movements of people between nations and authorize their exits and entries. The concept of the frontier has become deterritorialized; it is no longer the boundary, the limit, the edge, the checkpoint separating within from without. Europeanization together with globalization have modified the procedures that had made a state's territorial frontier to become an institution. Such procedures have disconnected the frontier as a line from the frontier as a zone and from the frontier as the site of official control. There is now a dialectic between freedom of movement and protection of the frontier, a dialectic that cannot be reduced to the classical liberal paradox of the "back door", the door that remains open within the context of a closed frontier, to allow for negotiation between private enterprise's need for a workforce and the mistrust of foreigners born of security imperatives.

It is more accurate to say that this dialectic has established a new set of operational norms that govern who can move and who can't, a dialectic that takes the form of a "dromocracy", in which the powerful are those who hold sway over rates of movement, who determine the rate of movement of others, and disqualify those who stay put.[34] In this new state of affairs, it is increasingly considered illicit not to be on the move, not to get things going, at least as far as well-off consumers are concerned. On the other hand, the injunction to move, with the idea of accelerating the rate of flow, creates in and of itself backwaters and storage zones where those who have not the means to move, or who cannot do so without outside help, are increasingly numerous: asylum seekers, people who are too poor to leave the neighbourhoods where they have been parked ...[35] When they are within, they are usually banished out of sight, away from public areas and towards the storage facilities provided for them. When they are without, they are intercepted upstream or, if they succeed in getting through somehow, the "flow" is directed toward "hoop net" or transit camps like Sangatte where they wait to be repatriated. On both sides, both within and without, whenever those who are poor and disaffiliated want to join in as tourists or consumers – but with the limited means at their disposal – they become suspect. Yet it is impossible to admit as much; so other justifications are put forth.

The novelty as regards the European Union will no doubt prove to have been the decision to make of this contemporary phenomenon of movement, of rapid movement, a "right" that when transgressed can lead to sanctions against states at the hands of European courts of law. Even if, in terms of everyday practice, there was no real need to wait on Europeanization for people to move about fairly freely, the Union established it as a fundamental liberty for all, unlike for example

NAFTA in North America. The dialectic between liberty and security has been modified in the European area (in Schengen as well as in the United Kingdom and Ireland) by the adoption of measures designed to ensure free movement for all, including even foreigners living within European borders (although a frontier does still exist between the Schengen territory and the British-Irish territory). These measures, had they been drawn up in a unified code, could have had a significant impact for freedom, but rather than push them to this conclusion, the tendency has been to cut back on them by adoption of rulings that are contrary to this spirit, rulings which were designed to exercise closer control, to refine and prioritize rather than do away with controls. The Schengen Informations System network is situated at the heart of this contradictory pull of forces, attempting on one hand to adopt a common policy in regard to outside nations, while at the same time maintaining the attributes of sovereignty through the issuing of passports and visas to individuals. Conflicts have arisen, but these conflicts are not between nations but transnational conflicts between governmental departments. Ministers of Justice and of the Interior have tried to impose security "imperatives" as the essential, while Foreign Affairs and Finance Ministers, as well as judges of the bench, have opted for the primacy of global diplomacy and respect for rights in order to minimize the security issue. The past fifteen years of Schengen negotiations bear witness to this evolution and to the chaotic interplay between those who press for more detailed information on foreigners so as better to keep watch over them, and those that consider it more important to establish freedom of population movement as the accepted norm. Government leaders have often sided with Ministers of the Interior and rehabilitated policies of control that are even stricter than in the past since, now that the communist adversary no longer exists, freedom of movement cannot serve as a marker of the difference between dictatorship and democracy. This turn of events has greatly weakened the rights of asylum seekers who, instead of having the right to be protected, in the sense of sheltered (tegere in Latin), are to be protected – but in the military sense of the term, that is to say to be guarded and confined (praesidere).[36] The fact that government leaders did act in this manner was due as well to their own fears and their own misgivings about the future. They have had to deal in political terms with the climate of anxiety stemming from the years 1992-93, set off by the belief of an imminent massive influx of immigrants from the east (Russia) and the south (Algeria); the handling of their fellow citizens' constant sense of insecurity has become a routine political issue, whereas in the past such questions had only cropped up episodically. The situation was destined to last and to undermine the renewed confidence in the future of liberal democracy; despite recent vacillations the security issue serves as a political litmus test and provokes shifts in party allegiance that are particularly advantageous for the right.

It is in this context that the policies governing the issuing of visas and the developing of policing at a distance by the professionals of (in)security management should be analyzed. The individual no longer has any intrinsic value, he/she is apprehended as part of a collective entity, as a disrupting flow, often dehumanised by the use of terms such as mass, crowd or flux. Procedures for issuing passports or visas reflect this approach. Visas are not granted through a process of "weighing" individual characteristics, but on the basis of membership in a predefined group.

Relations between States and the European Commission and between the
European Commission and Individuals

The existence of a Schengen visa has further complicated the relations between the state and the individual. The state no longer exercises even de jure monopoly rights over the movement of individuals. By adopting the principle of free movement of peoples the European Union impaired the exercise of the state's monopoly. Nations have been obliged to negotiate with each other in order to set up a collectively implemented control system to be applied to their own citizens and to all foreigners living within European borders. The separate territorial status accorded to the United Kingdom and Ireland made it impossible for there to be a simple one-to-one correlation between European territory and the areas to which the reciprocal governmental agreements concerning free movement applied. The succession of stopgap measures adopted by the "Schengen laboratory", then by the "Schengen *acquis*", as well as the laborious edification of pillars in Maastricht, which were to be redefined in Amsterdam, certainly did nothing to clarify the situation. The Commission attempted to handle the crisis by the adoption of a common set of rules for granting visas to passport holders. The policy recognized the right of free movement between friendly nations (with no need for visas) in return for security checks on those entering from without the Union and the adoption of measures designed to keep unwelcome foreigners out. Within the Commission itself, depending on whether one civil servant belonged to title IV of the first pillar or to the third pillar, he/she takes a different view about free movement or the reinforcement of coercive measures. The last ones, as they applied also for poor tourists has heightened tensions, re-enacting the ideological conflicts within parties and within governments. Fine-sounding discourses about mutual confidence and harmonization of policies have masked the increasingly embittered struggle to preserve room for manoeuvre within the new framework. The resort to exceptional measures and the lack of confidence in contractual partners have prevented harmonization; and whenever a semblance of harmonization has been achieved, it has been on the basis of a common agreement to reinforce repressive methods that are hardly democratic. The solution that consists of using visa-issuing policies as a means of avoiding the complaints of NGOs stationed around international waiting zones and frontier areas has been stepped up. The strategy of adopting security measures that no longer operate on site but by remote control has strengthened suspicion as regards foreigners, adding a racial taint, for the distinction between the two types of countries, visa and non-visa, bears a striking resemblance to the European stereotypes of racial inferiority that informed the colonial imagination. Poverty has emerged as a criterion that curtails freedom of movement; the immigration menace justifies preventing those without resources from travelling or placing them under far stricter surveillance, especially when compared to the wealthy. States have on occasion shown little interest in the political regimes of neighbouring nations, but have indicated concern for certain minorities within those nations or concern for individuals who, whether by choice or constraint, have become displaced persons in their own countries.

It is in this way that the relationship between the State, the Commission and individuals has been modified, as certain individuals are now promoted as undeclared enemies of the state, replacing or alongside former regimes considered as hostile. The Europeanization of control procedures governing the issuing of visas has shed light on the discrepancies between who we are, what are our values and who we suspect of not adhering to those values. Control techniques have been changed; a closely guarded security perimeter has been given up in exchange for an upstream protection system that cuts off the flow of those considered as dangerous before they reach the border. Reliance on categories that class individuals according to the degree of risk they represent has allowed states to abandon the process of judging candidates individually, a process considered as too lengthy, and to abandon as well use of nationality as a single criterion, considered as too all-inclusive. Criteria situated in-between that of judging each individual case and that of relying on national identity have been tested, criteria such as minority status, ethnicity, coming from areas known as dangerous etc.; in so doing the terminology of sociologists and criminologists comes into play, along with their methods. Remote control in terms of space has gone hand in hand with remote control in terms of time whereby an individual's risk factor is supposed to determine how he/she will behave.[37] Yet these methods of justifying the decisions taken are still in their early stages; the arbitrary character of the principles evoked is still all too evident. Individuals find many ways in which to resist, by seeking support from within institutions that are there to defend their rights, or by finding means to get past the barriers. The result is a spiralling effect in that control procedures are then designed to operate independently of the individual's participation, to treat him as an object, to reduce him to nothing but a body and no longer a person capable of dialoguing with the various administrations and even outwitting them. Hyper-technologization is then seen as the solution that will grant the state, or the state together with the Commission, the last word as regards the movement of "persons".

Technologization as the Ultrasolution

September 11th provided the opportunity for renewed efforts to technologize the process of identification by enlisting biometric methods that, it was hoped, would operate independently of an individual's capacity to act or to speak.[38] The frontier and the defence of the frontier were once again considered as sacred causes, the United States in the lead. The concept of an electronic shield that would ward off terrorist attacks was the successor to the anti-nuclear missile shield. But in short order, the Homeland Security Department let it be known that it considered that the security of American citizens could only be assured by measures taken well outside its frontiers, and not simply at border crossings.[39] To be sure, the national Security Entry and Exit Registration System was tightened up by requiring more probing interviews with nationals from countries figuring on a list that was literally identical to that of Annex 5b of Schengen; but the major thrust consisted of rethinking passport and visa procedures and opting for increased technologization in this domain.[40] The Homeland Security Department even tried to challenge the monopoly over foreign relations exercised by the State Department and Department of Defence, in particular regarding relations with British allies. Support for Homeland Security Department policies and for reform of the Immigration and Naturalization Service came largely from a number of private enterprises that had already done research on the collection of biometric data but had not found a market for their products.

A sizable number of firms took advantage of the September 11th opening. To take one example, ZN Vision Technology boasted, in a letter dated October 18th 2001, of its automatic facial recognition system that, according to its promoters, could verify the identity of a document holder by comparing his facial features with those of the photo figuring on the document.[41] These companies insisted they were capable of disclosing the true identity of a person, with no need to consult the documents that he presented. According to them, the solution was to invest in an expanded technological program in which the governments of the developed countries would create biometrical data banks connected by an electronic network or via individual identity cards. Governments could then act jointly, without affording the individual in question any opportunity to intervene actively in the system and "adjust" it to his own advantage. In their promotional literature these companies try to get across the concept of a biometric control system that would operate without the individual being aware of it; in facial recognition systems as well as iris recognition systems, once the basic data have been recorded, the individual simply passes through a security gate without stopping and with no human contact whatsoever.[42]

The annual Milipol trade fair that is held alternately in Qatar and in Paris launched a global campaign of invitations extended to companies specialized in all branches of the security and security services industries supplying police forces worldwide. Over the past four years, the number of companies offering these skills has risen dramatically. Many of them had worked previously on Ronald Reagan's Strategic Defense Initiative program, but had shifted – in the absence of a Soviet threat – to programs aimed at the individualized surveillance of persons crossing national borders and at the development of biometric methods and precision electronics.

These commercial proposals for curbing terrorism and illegal immigration, as well as detecting false documents, through the application of biometric techniques have been adopted in extenso by a number of political figures and by certain Ministers of the Interior in the European Union, acting in unison with the Homeland Department. There has been much talk of biometric data concerning the DNA and concerning fingerprints, data that was to be stored on electronic chip cards, but it appears that these systems have been momentarily abandoned as too costly, and attention has turned to techniques for which the initial collection of data requires little cooperation on the part of the person concerned (iris recognition or facial recognition). The more cumbersome systems (fingerprinting and DNA) would then be reserved for people consigned to camps or imprisoned, people that are expected to stay put for long enough to effect these controls, whereas the other techniques, that are relatively unobjectionable, would be used to keep track of global population flows. People in camps and detention centres were to be subject to electronic fingerprinting once the Eurodac system became fully operative.[43] The official inauguration of the system took place on January 15th 2003, but in fact processing by fingerprinting had begun one year earlier for asylum seekers and illegal immigrants held in detention centres. The millions of people passing through airports and air terminals, or even travelling on motorway networks or to cities such as London (now that the Congestion Charge system is operative), could be monitored by video surveillance; facial and iris parameters would be fed into recognition software that in a matter of seconds would launch an interception warning on detecting a suspect profile. But the technical problems involved in perfecting the recognition capacities of these programs means that, while waiting for them to be reliable, a somewhat simpler technique is being tested, one which relies at least in part on paper documents and on the willingness of the holder of these documents to present them for inspection – while at the same time obtaining precise body measurements and providing information without the individual's participation. In the near future an electronic photograph will be required on all passports and visas; this photo will then be fed into software capable of registering facial structure, and the resulting reading will be compared by the same software to a camera image of the individual presenting the document. In theory at least, the software can even tell brothers apart and thus guarantee with absolute certitude that the photo is that of the document holder. The Americans intend to require from now on that all countries issuing passports adopt the same technical norms, providing data that can be scanned electronically and electronic photographs, and they threaten to suppress the visa "waiver programs" for any country that refuses to comply.[44] Leaving aside the science fiction aspect of biometric technology that is fast becoming a reality, and that the media make much of, applied research is for the most part concentrated on these latter types of programs, which means that it is by tightening passport and visa procedures (in particular visa procedures for the Union) that, it is hoped, "solutions" will be found.[45] The prospect of high-tech visas will no doubt make it more difficult to produce counterfeits and will tie together pre- and post-control procedures, but this identification/recognition system operating at the European and the transatlantic level – a digitalized version on a planetary scale of the anthropometric methods devised by nineteenth-century criminal police – in no way solves the problem of what persons or groups of persons are to be so controlled.[46] Technology cannot provide answers to political dilemmas.[47]

Individual Rights and Individual Resistance

A close examination of the procedures for obtaining a visa, and of the way in which the control policies are applied, reveals how far we actually are from the harmonization that is on the official declarations. To be sure, there are a great many people travelling within the Union and the Schengen area. First of all, those who don't need a visa. Then those who manage to obtain one. But for the latter the process is a succession of frustrations. These mini-tragedies of daily life reveal Europeans' contempt for other people, and threaten to destroy the international climate. To obtain a visa after having been unfairly treated as a suspect engenders a sense of injustice, even if one ends up by obtaining the visa in time. Focusing on the potential danger the individual represents, rather than on the nature of his country's political regime, has turned visa-issuing into a complex affair. It has revived the old idea of the "undesirable" or "unwelcolme", revived it without the least sense of shame and in forgetting what it connoted under the Austro-Hungarian Empire. The term has entered the everyday language of Schengen administrators and only a handful of British are still shocked by it. A consensus has emerged in regard to this category of undesirables and has created a folkdevil phenomenon, but not a homogeneous one. Those that are "undesirable" in one country are not necessarily "undesirable" in another, so a stock exchange market whereby European fears are exchanged via technical surveillance systems linked to more or less obscure pressure groups, doesn't really provide a real answer to the problem.

It is certainly legitimate to bar criminals from entering a country, but considerably less legitimate when it is a question of migration flow, and not at all legitimate when a person is just on the move for tourism and refused a first entry because he/she belongs to a suspect immigration group. There is no justification for keeping people with little means at their disposal from joining up with their families that are in Europe or even simply visiting them.

The techniques used to "discourage" poor people, or those belonging to certain ethnic groups, from obtaining visas run counter to the concept of an open Europe, in particular when applied to those coming from nations that count on joining the Union or being numbered among its "friends".

The right of free movement, the right to travel and visit other countries, should take priority and security concerns be the exception. Yet, in certain European countries – but not all – priorities are reversed, and the "dangers" and "risks" of infiltration from the outside are exaggerated as they become caught up in political conflicts and when security becomes a high-stake political issue. A sense of unease and social anxiety have created a climate that is largely hostile to foreigners coming from the third world whose colour sets them off. It is essential not to foster this climate, but to combat it by refusing to accept the stereotypes fabricated by the merchants of fear who then make their living off them.

Political leaders as well as government officials should use their influence to counter such fears instead of simply acceding to them as if they were the voice of public opinion. Words must be found that will convince people of advantages of openness, of Europe's capacity to integrate and of the benefits that accrue from a widespread policy of freedom of movement. The recent expansion of the European Union has dissipated fears of the invasion of rich countries by their poorer neighbours. As has been pointed out on several occasions, the entry of Greece into the Union was not followed by hordes of poor Greeks pouring into Germany and France.

We cannot continue to base our policies on categories as ambiguous as that of "undesirable". It is not the right to protect against certain criminals that is to be denied, but the right to extend internal security precautions beyond the realm of criminality, which can hardly be done in an atmosphere of international cooperation and is of questionable legitimacy.

Likewise, the system of "policing at a distance" by which people submit to processing far from the countries in which they can appeal if their rights are endangered, creates an impression of cynicism – if that is the purpose – or is simply inept. It is unacceptable that identity control systems be transnational, while the right of appeal is strictly limited in territorial terms. Neither judges nor concerned citizens will stand for it.

In conclusion, the freedom of movement that the rhetoric of the European Union links with a better and safer life for citizens and foreigners living inside the EU has not been implemented in a way which has enhanced freedom for the people. It has destabilized the boundaries of national justice and of fundamental rights of citizens and foreigners, opening opportunities for more controls to occur "in the name" of freedom. Securitization has been undertaken through discourses of fear management, but also through a technologization of policing, and has been the result of both political games, media games and security professionals' games. The interplay of these segmented games, where each of them has its own rationale, has created a new form of governmentality at the transnational level that we may call Ban-opticon. Nobody really wanted what happened and we are far from a naïve vision of class war of the dominants, or from a plot theory by the police. The intentions are often meaningless, but the social effects are meaningful. It is in the name of protection, in the name of more freedom and with the belief to achieve this goal that the different actors have been motivated. All were not cynics. They were for a large part true believers of the norms of freedom of movement. But the results of their actions – what we have called the fields' effects of the development of a way to police at a distance and by dossier – correlated with the identity crisis of some professionals of politics in their belief to represent society, as well as the social transformation affecting the travel and movement of the people around the world. This has created new forms of discriminations and inequalities both at the local and the transnational levels.

The frontier is less and less the place for the effective controls. The different national governments have known it for a long time, even if they also know too well that it is better for them to continue with the old myth of territoriality embedded inside a certain kind of sovereignty of the national Western state. The deterritorialization of surveillance, the creation of profiling trying not only to monitor the stock of people inside and the movement of those crossing the borders, but the destination of these people and the anticipation of how and why they move. This has created a specific futurology where "experts" try to predict who will be dangerous with the highest technology but with the same results and beliefs as the priests of ancient Rome. The social behavior of the people is under this form of policing at a distance less important than the expectations by the police, the intelligence services, the politicians or the journalists of what they will do in the future. They are put under surveillance not for what they have done but for what it is "predicted" they will do. In that sense we have moved from a "territorial state" concerned with space and localization, to a "population state" concerned with time and traces of the past for the monitoring of the future. And perhaps only Foucault and Philip K. Dick have been clever enough to interpret this transformation the world is currently witnessing. The European Union is at the crossroads between territorial and population surveillance with fierce combats between the professionals of (in)security to impose their view of what is effective and what is dangerous. Here, the role of the rule of law is central. First, by drawing the lines of who are the excluded, but also by "grouping" who are the "normal people", who are the "Europeans", who are the "real" tourists, the "real" consumers. It is a way to avoid the displacement in time, which is enacted by the idea of a permament state of emergency. It is a way to defend the present against the invading future. But it is also a "fix", which needs to be seriously discussed and linked with the democratic process of who draws the lines of the rule of law. What is the role of the excluded, of the "abnormals", of the "banlieues" within this game of definition of the norms? Resistances emerge from each locus of control, but hope to reappropriate its own future is limited. The global surveillance goes hand in hand with a "dream" world of fear, which may have a dangerous tendency to self-fulfilling prophecy. The evanescence of the enemy creates a feeling that he is everywhere, and even "inside" us. Each bit of freedom is a bit of risk and each risk is a potential danger. The "normalization" is then even more important than the process of exclusion of some categories along the lines of scapegoating and folk devil habits. The relation to freedom or (un)freedomization for the majority is redrawn by the ban of the excluded and by the definition of who the (ab)normals are. The fact that freedom of movement is now more important than the right to live in a specific place has destabilized the previous notions of migrants, asylum seekers, refugees and foreigners. Freedom of movement has become an "imperative", a "desire", which is everything except a choice.

If this book has succeeded in showing that we need to ask ourselves what kind of freedom we want, what kind of (un)freedomization we are ready to accept in the name of our own protection against our own fears, why we have to challenge the assertion of the professionals of (in)security and of the professionals of politics concerning our fears and our unease, perhaps it has contributed to open a different path, an oblical light which disturbs the Ban opticon and its normalization. And in this accumulation of dark clouds coming from the fear of an Armageddon unlocked by a group of "terrorists", against whom all the governments need to collaborate to protect us, it is even more urgent. We cannot live with fear of the worst case scenario, with the sense that the Apocalypse is for tomorrow. We cannot accept that some groups of professionals manage our fears along the lines of their own interests and their beliefs that they act to save us, to protect us. We have to stand up and define what we consider as a danger, an opportunity, and a freedom instead of accepting the globalization of individual surveillance, the computerization of the traces of our movements through biometrics, and the monopoly of the professionals of (in)security concerning the framing of our fears, our freedoms, our desires.

Notes

[1]   Albert, Lapid and Jacobson, *Identities, Borders and Orders*, University of Minesota Press, Minneapolis, 2000.

2   While the central element of the EU border policy is found in the development of the Schengen Agreements from 1985 onwards, this is now incorporated into the EC Treaty and applies to all Member States except those which have opted out under the specific provisions of their protocols to the EC and EU Treaties – Denmark, Ireland and the UK. However, the policy of remote control of migration is equally applied by these states. Indeed they participate in the EU borders law for these purposes – Denmark as a party to the Schengen Agreements (1985 and 1990); the UK by opting into the common measures on the export of the borders – common consular cooperation, carrier sanctions and similar measures. Hanon, Jean-Paul, *Les coopérations policières aux frontières Schengen germano-tchèque et germano-polonaise, Les cahiers de la sécurité intérieure*, (41), Paris, IHESI, 2000, Cruz Antonio; *Carrier Sanctions in four community states;* Nederlands Juristenblad; 1991 and Cruz, Antonio, 1993: Schengen, ad hoc Immigration Group and other intergovernmental Bodies, Brussels: Briefing Paper no. 12 of the Churches Committee for Migrants in Europe, Guiraudon Virginie "Policy change behind gilded doors", PhD Harvard, 1997.

3   E. Guild, *Moving the Borders of Europe*, inaugural lecture: 30 May 2001, University of Nijmegen.

4   A. Zolberg, "Bounded States in a Global Market: The Uses of International Labor Migrations", in Pierre Bourdieu and James S. Coleman (eds), *Social Theory for a Changing Society* (Boulder: Westview/Russell Sage, 1991).

5   G. Noiriel, *Etat, nation et immigration vers une histoire du pouvoir* (Belin: Paris: 2001).

6   This discussion of visas is limited to visa which permit individuals to pass the border for a short stay of up to three months. The issue of long stay visas is only in the process of incorporation into Community law.

7   The EC visa regulation OJ 2001 L 81/1. There are 131 countries and three territories on the black list. The white list contains 43 (plus two territories).

8   Here, however, is one of the limits of the excellent approach made by John Torpey regarding the European territory and its underestimation of visas role: Torpey, John, *The Invention of the Passport, Surveillance, Citizenship and the State* (London, Cambridge University Press, 2000, 211).

9   Bauman, Z., *Globalisation: the Human Consequences* (Columbia University Press: New York: 1998).

10 European Commission Staff Working Paper, *Visa Policy Consequent upon the Treaty of Amsterdam and the Integration of the Schengen Acquis into the European Union* SEC (1999) 1213; Brussels 16.07.99.

11 See Amato, Giuliano and Batt, Judy, *Final Report of the reflection Group on "The long-term Implications"* (Badia European University, 1999).

12 See Savona, Ernesto U., *Dynamics of Migration and Crime in Europe: New Patterns of an old Nexus*, Courmayeur, Conférence de l'ISPAC,1996, octobre.

13 Here we have contradictory information. The political statements regarding Eastern frontier controls take into account the Eastern enlargement and preparation for the abolition of controls at the EU borders with the accession states. But officials speak about need for maintenance and indeed strengthening of controls at the existing Eastern borders of the Union – i.e. at the borders with the accession states.

14 Conference: July 9 and 10 2001, Centre for European Policy Studies, Brussels.

15 But see the presentation of K. Groenendijk on the maintenance of the controls of the people at the internal borders after the entry into force of the Implementing agreement Schengen in 1990: Article 62 EC and Borders of the EU: Conference on 11/12 May 2001, ILPA, Meijers Committee, London.

16 OJ 2000 L 238/332.

[17] Council recommendation concerning local consular cooperation as regards visas (third pillar) encourages "local cooperation on the visas, comprising an exchange of information on the criteria of issuing of the visas and an exchange of information on the risks for national safety and law and order or on the risks of illegal immigration" (Article 1 OJ 1996 C 80/1).

[18] This discussion could perhaps build on the work of Noiriel and Torpey regarding documents and in particular the passport to look further at the meaning of visas. See J. Torpey, *Cultures & Conflits*, 31.32 1998.

[19] While not express in the Common Consular Instructions, in fact consulates refuse to entertain visa applications from persons who are not either nationals or permanent residents in the state where the application is made.

[20] When the list of criteria is reduced to the shorthand of common parlance, what becomes embarrassingly apparent is that it in fact is no more than a way of describing poor countries and those in conflicts which produce refugees without actually using the words.

[21] Interview with senior Commission official carried out in June 2000.

[22] OJ 1995 L 234/1.

[23] OJ 1999 L 72/2.

[24] These were at first five of the original six Member States (Italy was late to join) but by the time of the Amsterdam Treaty all Member States were members with the exception of Ireland and the UK.

[25] These two lists are attached to the regulation.

[26] Regulation 539/2001 adopted on 15 March 2001 establishing the list of the third countries whose nationals are subject to mandatory visas when crossing the external borders OJ 2001 L81/1.

[27] Document 500PC0027: Commission Proposal – COM (2000) 027 final.

[28] 30/77 [1977] ECR 1999.

[29] For convenience we use the term consular official or officer.

[30] Part I paragraph 2.1 of the common consular instructions.

[31] Interviews with officials and individuals in June 2000.

[32] See further table of fees.

[33] OJ 2000 L 238/332.

[34] On the concept of "dromocracy", see Paul Virilio, *Vitesse et politique* (Paris, Editions galilée, 1977).

[35] See Zygmunt Bauman and Gérard Noiriel. Noiriel, in an historical survey of the subject from the French Revolution on, concludes, in what is a paradox in appearance only, that individuals have never been as subject to confinement as after the proclamation of the principle of free movement of peoples.

[36] I am indebted to Emmanuel-Pierre Guittet for these remarks concerning the semantics of protection. On the concept of protection see Didier Bigo (*et al.*), *La fonction de protection, op. cit.*

[37] On this issue, and on the parallel with Philip K. Dick's "Minority Report", see Didier Bigo, "La recherche proactive et la gestion du risque", *Déviance et société*, 1997, vol. 21, 4, pp. 423-429. See also "globalisation of (in)security", *Traces, op. cit.*

[38] In this respect similar to the reaction after Orsini's attempted assassination of Napoleon III, with the subsequent development of identification techniques. See, here again, Gérard Noiriel's work on the subject.

[39] See the studies by Philippe Bonditti, *L'antiterrorisme aux Etats-Unis. Dela menace soviétique aux Rogue States. La construction de l'ennemi terroriste depuis 1980*, DEA thesis, IEP, Paris, September 2001, and *Les organisations de lutte antiterroriste aux Etat-Unis*, DAS report, 2002.

[40] For the Annex 5 B see Didier Bigo and Elspeth Guild, "La mise à l'écart des étrangers: le visa Schengen", *Cultures & Conflits*, Paris, L'Harmattan, 2003, 192 pages. See "The Enhanced Border Security and Visa Reform Act 2002" (EBSVRA) and the so-called Lincoln technique that includes digitalised biometric data on the visa ("C. Powell's Testimony before the Select Committee on Homeland Security, 11/07/2002").

[41] See the annex to the second volume of the document produced by the ZN Vision company: "Reconnaissance faciale automatique pour la sécurité du transport aérien".

[42] A number of promotional pamphlets claim, with a certain cynicism, that it is not the fact of the control procedure itself that bothers people, but the awareness that their identity is being controlled.

[43] Eurodac went so far as to produce a promotional CD-Rom justifying these techniques on the basis that they fostered free movement and protected the rights of genuine asylum seekers. As regards justifying the unjustifiable, see Martin Heisler's theoretical study, ISA Chicago 2002, soon to published.

[44] On the controversy set off by the Commission's acceptance of the United States demand that all those travelling to the US have in their possession, before their arrival, the documents required for an identity check – and on the plans for passport-issuing procedures that would deny other states the right to set their own rules (and thus exercise the right of sovereignty over "their own" people) – see Mark Salter, *Rights of Passage: The Passport in International Relations* (Boulder, Lynne Reinner, 2003). See also studies by the ELISE group (http://www.eliseconsortium.org) and by Statewatch (http://www.statewatch.org).

[45] For a critical assessment of these measures see Steve Wright, "An Appraisal of Technologies of Political Control", Omega Foundation, European Parliament, Scientific and Technological Options Assessment, 06/01/1998 (which provided the groundwork for the criticisms contained in the report on Echelon and the UE-FBI plan).

[46] The VIS (Visa Information System) that is now being set up would appear to be a step in this direction.

[47] This concept of a transatlantic process of identifying people, that would take precedence over national procedures, should be seen in the light of research done by historians and political scientists working on questions of surveillance. See in this regard the colloquim organized by the CERI and the Centre d'Etudes sur les Conflits under the direction of Nathalie Bayon, 24-25 March 2003. The contemporary trends that are under discussion here should be considered alongside the work of Gérard Noiriel on the tyranny of the national and of national identification.

Bibliography

Albert, M., Jacobson, D. and Lapid, Y. (2001), *Identities, Borders, Orders. Rethinking International Relations Theory, Borderlines*, vol. 18, University of Minnesota Press, Minneapolis.

Albrecht, H. J. (1997), 'Ethnic minorities and crime – the construction of foreigners' crime in the Federal Republic of Germany', in Palidda, S. (ed.), *Délit d'immigration, COST A2 Migrations*, Commission Européenne, Brussels, pp. 83-102.

Albrecht, H. J. (1997), 'Minorities, Crime, and Criminal Justice in the Federal Republic of Germany', in Marshall, I. H. (ed.), *Minorities, Migrants, and Crime*, Sage Publications, London.

Allison, G. T. (1999) *Essence of Decision, Explaining the Cuban Missiles*, Crisis, Longman, London.

Althusser, L. (1993), *Ecrits sur la psychanalyse: Freud, Lacan*, Stock, Paris.

Anderson, M. (1996), *Frontiers, State Formation in the Modern World*, Polity Press: London.

Anderson, M. and Bort, E. (1996), *Boundaries and identities: the eastern frontier of the EU*, University of Edinburgh, Edinburgh.

Anderson, M., Den Boer, M., Cullen P., Gilmore, W., Raab, C. and Walker, N. (1996) *Policing the European Union*, Clarendon Studies Press, Oxford University Press, Oxford.

Andreas, P. (2000), *Border Games. Policing the US-Mexico Divide*, Ithaca: Cornell University Press.

Appadurai, A. (1996), *Modernity at large: cultural dimensions of globalization*, Public worlds, vol. 1, University of Minnesota Press, Minneapolis.

Appadurai, A. (1998), 'Dead Certainty: Ethnic Violence in the Era of Globalization', *Public Culture*, **10**(2), pp. 225-247.

Appadurai, A. (2001) *Globalization*, Duke University Press: Durham, NC.

Badie B. and Wihtol de Wenden, C. (1994), *Le défi migratoire, questions de relations internationales*, Presses de la FNSP, Paris.

Badie, B. (1995), *La fin des territoires, Essai sur le désordre international et l'utilité sociale du respect*, Fayard, Paris.

Badie, B. (1999), *Un monde sans souveraineté, Les Etats entre ruse et responsabilité*, Fayard, Paris.

Badie, B. and Smouts, M.-C., (1995), *Le retournement du monde, sociologie de la scène internationale*, Presses de la FNSP/Dalloz, (2e éd.), Paris.

Balibar, E. (2001), *Nous, citoyens d'Europe? Les frontières, l'État, le peuple*, La Découverte, Paris.

Bank, R. (2000), in Bommes, M. and Geddes, A. (eds), *Immigration and Welfare: Challenging the Borders of the Welfare State*, Routledge, London.

Barbagli, M. (1998), *Immigrazione et criminalità in Italia*, Il Mulino, Bologna.

Bauman, Z. (1976), *Towards a Critical Sociology: An Essay on Common Sense and Emancipation, Routledge Direct Editions*, Routledge and Kegan Paul, London, Boston.

Bauman, Z. (1982), *Memories of Class: The Pre-History and after-Life of Class, International Library of Sociology*, Routledge and Paul Kegan, London and Boston.

Bauman, Z. (1998), *Freedom, Concepts in Social Thought*, University of Minnesota Press, Minneapolis.

Bauman, Z. (1998), *Globalisation. The human consequences*, Polity Press, Cambridge.

Bauman, Z. (1999), *Le coût humain de la mondialisation*, Hachette, Paris.

Bauman, Z. (2000), *Liquid Modernity*, Polity Press, Cambridge.

Bauman, Z. (2001), 'Wars of the Globalization Era', *European Journal of Social Theory*, **4**(1), pp. 11-28.

Bayley, D. H. (1975), 'The Police and Political Development in Europe', in Tilly Charles (ed.), *The Formation of National States in Europe*, Princeton University Press, Princeton.

Beaud, S. and Masclet, O. (2002), 'Un passage à l'acte improbable? Notes de recherche sur la trajectoire sociale de Zacarias Moussaoui', *French Politics, Culture and Society*, **20**(2).

Beck, U. (1992), *Risk Society, Towards a New Modernity*, Sage, London.

Beck, U. (1999), *What is Globalization?*, Polity Press, Cambridge.

Berger, P. and Luckmann, T. (1967), *The Social Construction of Reality. A Treatise in the Sociology of Knowledge*, Allen Lane, New York.

Bigo, D. (1992), 'Les Attentats De 1986 En France: Un Cas De Violence Transnationale Et Ses Implications', *Cultures & Conflits*, **4**.

Bigo, D. (1992), *L'Europe des polices et de la sécurité intérieure*, Complexe, Bruxelles.

Bigo, D. (1995), 'Terrorisme, Drogue, Immigration: Les Nouvelles Figures De L'insécurité En Europe (Terrorism, Drugs and Immigration: The New Faces of Insecurity in Europe)', *Revue internationale d'Action communautaire*, **70**, pp. 43-59.

Bigo, D. (1996), *Polices en réseaux. L'expérience européenne*, Presses de Sciences Po, Paris.

Bigo, D. (1997), 'La recherche proactive et la gestion du risque', *Déviance et Société*, **21**(4).

Bigo, D. (1998), 'Sécurité et immigration: vers une gouvernementalité par l'inquiétude?', *Cultures & Conflits*, **31/32**, pp. 13-38.

Bigo, D. (1998), 'L'Europe de la sécurité intérieure: penser autrement la sécurité' in Le Gloannec, A.-M., *Entre Union et Nations: l'Etat en Europe*, Presses de Sciences Po, Paris.

Bigo, D. (2000), 'Polices post-communistes: une transformation inachevée? ', *Les Cahiers De La Sécurité Intérieure*, **41**, IHESI, Paris.

Bigo, D. (2000), 'When Two Becomes One: Internal and External Securitizations in Europe', in Kelstrup, M. and Williams, M. C. (eds), *International Relations Theory and the Politics of European Integration*, Routledge, London.

Bigo, D. (2001), *The Möbius Ribbon of Internal and External Security*, in Albert, M., Jacobson, D. and Lapid, Y. (eds), *Identities, Borders, Orders*, University of Minnesota Press: Minneapolis, pp. 91-116.

Bigo, D. (2002), 'Security and Immigration: Towards a Governmentality of Unease', *Alternatives/Cultures & Conflits*, **27**, pp. 63-92.

Bigo, D. (2004), 'The Globalisation of (In)security and the Ban-Opticon', *Traces: a Multilingual Series of Cultural Theory*, **4**, University of Hong Kong Press.

Bigo, D. and Guild, E. (eds) (2002), 'De Tampere à Séville: bilan de la sécurité européenne', *Cultures & Conflits*, **45**.

Bigo, D. and Guild, E. (eds) (2002), 'De Tampere à Séville: bilan de la sécurité européenne', *Cultures & Conflits*, **46**.

Boer, M. den (ed.) (1997), *The Implementation of Schengen: First the Widening, Now the Deepening*, European Institute of Public Administration, Maastricht.

Bommes, M. and Geddes, A. (2000), *Immigration and Welfare: Challenging the Borders of the Welfare State*, Routledge, London.

Bonelli, L. (2001), 'Les Renseignements généraux et les violences urbaines', *Actes de la Recherche en Sciences Sociales*, **136-137**, pp. 95-103.

Bonelli, L. (2004), 'Formation, conservation et reconversion de dispositions anti-subversives. L'exemple des renseignement généraux', in Tissot, S. (ed.), *Reconversions militantes*, Presses universitaires de Limoges, Limoges.

Bordas-Charon, Jeannine and Tulard, H. (1962), *Inventaire de la série BA des Archives de la Préfecture de police (cartons Ba 1BA 80)*, Impr. Municipale: Paris.

Bourdieu, P. (1979), *La distinction*, Editions de Minuit, Paris.

Bourdieu, P. (1984), 'L'opinion publique n'existe pas', in, Bourdieu, P., *Questions de sociologie*, Editions de Minuit, Paris, pp. 222-235.

Bourdieu, P. (1994), *Raisons pratiques: sur la théorie de l'action*, Seuil, Paris.

Bourdieu, P. (1997), 'L'architecte de l'euro passe aux aveux', *Le monde diplomatique*, September.

Bourdieu, P. (ed.) (2000), 'L'immigrant comme shebollet', in, *Contre-feux 2. Pour Un Mouvement Social Européen*, Liber/Raison d'agir, Paris.

Bourdieu, P. (2000), *Propos Sur Le Champ Politique*, Presses Universitaires de Lyon, Lyon.

Bourdieu, P., Chamboredon, J. C. and Passeron, J. C. (1983), *Le métier de sociologue*, Mouton, Paris.

Bourgois, P. (1995), *In Search of Respect. Selling Crack in El Barrio*, Cambridge University Press, Cambridge.

Bousquet, R. (1998), *Insécurité: les nouveaux risques*, L'Harmattan, Paris.

Bovenkerk, F. (1993), 'Crime and the Multi-Ethnic Society: A View from Europe', *Crime, Law and Social Change*, **3**, pp. 271-280.

Brochet, C. (1995), '*J-2: les frontières tombent...pas les contrôles*', 24 March 1995, *l'Argus de la presse*, Paris.

Brown, C. (2001), 'Borders and Identity in International Political Theory', in Albert, M., Jacobson, D. and Lapid, Y. (eds), *Identities, Borders, Orders*, University of Minnesota Press, Minneapolis, pp. 117-136.

Busch, H. (1995), *Grenzenlose Polizei? Neue Grenzen und polizeiliche Zusammenarbeit in Europa*, Westfälisches dampfboot Verlag, Münster.

Butterwegge, C. (1996), 'Mass Media, Immigrants, and Racism in Germany. A Contribution to an Ongoing Debate', *Communications*, **2**, pp. 203-220.

Buzan, B. (1991), *People States and Fear. An Agenda for International Security Studies in the Post-Cold War Era*, Lynne Rienner, Boulder/Col.

Carlier, J.-Y. (1997), *Who is a Refugee?*, Kluwer Law International, The Hague/London.

Castel, R. (1999), *Les métamorphoses de la question sociale. Une chronique du salariat*, Gallimard, Paris.

Castells, M. (1996), *The Information Age*, 3 volumes. Vol. 1 (1996), *The Rise of the Network Society*, vol. 2 (1997), *The Power of Identity*, vol. 3 (1998), *End of Millennium*, Blackwell, Oxford.

Castles, S., Booth, H. and Wallace, T. (1984), *Here for Good, Western Europe's New Ethnic Minorities*, Pluto Press, London/Sydney.

CEPII (1999), *L'économie mondiale 2000*, La Découverte, Paris.

Césari, J. (1998), *Musulmans et républicains. Les jeunes, l'islam et la France*, Complexe, Bruxelles.

Ceyhan, A. (1994), 'Le communautarisme et la question de la reconnaissance (Communitarianism and the Problem of Recognition)', *Cultures & Conflits*, **12**, pp. 169-84.

Ceyhan, A. (1997), 'Etats-Unis: frontière(s) contrôlée(s), identité(s) sécurisée(s)', *Cultures & Conflits*, **26/27**, pp. 203-254.

Ceyhan, A. (1997), 'Migrants as a Threat: A Comparative Analysis of Securitarian Rhetoric in France and in the US', *ISA Conference*, Toronto.

Ceyhan, A. (2001), 'La fin de l'en-dehors. Les nouvelles constructions discursives de l'ennemi intérieur en Californie', *Cultures & Conflits*, **43**, pp. 3-11.

Ceyhan, A. and Tsoukala, A. (1997), 'Contrôle de l'immigration: mythes et réalités', *Cultures & Conflits*, **26/27**, pp. 9-14.

Ceyhan, A. and Tsoukala, A. (2002), 'The securitization of Migration in Western Countries', *Alternatives/Cultures & Conflits*, **27**, pp. 21-33.

Ceyhan, A. and Peries, G. (2001), 'L'ennemi intérieur: une construction politique et discursive', *Cultures & Conflits*, **43**, pp. 61-90.

Cholewinski, R. (1997), *Migrant Workers in International Human Rights Law: Their Protection in Countries of Employment*, Clarendon Press, Oxford.

Christie, N. (2003), *L'industrie de la punition. Prison et politique pénale en Occident*, Autrement, Paris.

CIREFI (1994), *9 février 1994, Mesures pratiques de coopération entre services chargés des contrôles aux frontières*, Bruxelles, Ronéoté, 122 p.

Citrin, J. et al. (1997), 'Public Opinion toward Immigration Reform: The Role of Economic Motivations', *The Journal of Politics*, **3**, pp. 858-881.

Colvin M. and Spencer M. (2000), 'The Schengen Information System. A Human Rights Audit. A Justice Report', Justice.

Courtovic, I. (1994), 'To nomiko kathestos ton metanaston ergaton stin Ellada [The legal status of migrant workers in Greece]', in *Marangopoulos Foundation for Human Rights, The Protection of the Rights of Migrant Workers and their Families*, Estia, Athens, pp. 182-193.

Crowley, J. (1998), 'The National Dimension of Citizenship', in Marshall, T. H. (ed.), *Citizenship Studies*, pp. 165-178.

Crowley, J. (1999), 'The Politics of Belonging: Some Theoretical Considerations', in, Geddes, A. and Favell, A., *The Politics of Belonging: Migrants and Minorities in Contemporary Europe*, Ashgate, Aldershot, pp. 15-41.

Crowley, J. (2001), 'Differential Free Movement and the Sociology of the "Internal Border"', in Guild, E. and Harlow, C. (eds), *Implementing Amsterdam. Immigration and Asylum Rights in EC Law*, Hart, Oxford, pp. 13-33.

Crowley, J. (2001), 'The Political Participation of Ethnic Minorities', *International Political Science Review*, **22**(1), pp. 99-121.

Crowley, J. (2002), 'Locating Europe', in Guild, E., Gronedijk, C. and Miderhoud, P. (eds), *In Search of Europe's Borders*, Kluwer, Dordrecht.

Cultures & Conflicts (1997) 'Contrôles: frontières identités. Les enjeux autour de l'immigration et de l'asile (Controls: Frontiers-Identities. Stakes of Immigration and Asylum)', *Cultures & Conflits*, **26/27**.

Dal Lago, A. (1997), 'The Impact of Migration on Receiving Societies. Some Ethnographic Remarks', in Palidda, S. (ed.), *Délit d'immigration, COST A2 Migrations*, Commission Européenne, Brussels.

Dal Lago, A. (1999), *Non-Persone. L'esclusione dei migranti in una società globale*, Feltrinelli, Milano.

Dandeker, C. (1990), *Surveillance, Power and Modernity. Bureaucracy and Discipline from 1700 to the Present Days*, Polity Press, Cambridge.

Day, A. J. (1987), *Border and territorial disputes*, Keesing's, London.

De Certeau, M. (1981), 'Californie, un théâtre de passants', *Autrement*, **31**, pp. 10-22.

De Jongh, R. (1984), 'FNV'ers aan het woord over buitenlandse werknemers', *Centrum voor Onderzoek van Maatschappelijke Tegenstellingen Faculteit der Sociale Wteneschappen*, Rijksuniversiteit te Leiden.

Deleuze, G. (1986), *Foucault*, Editions de Minuit, Collection Critique, Paris.

Deleuze, G. and Guattari, F. (1986), *Nomadology: The War Machine*, Semiotext(e), *Foreign Agents Series*, New York.

Deleuze, G. and Guattari, F. (1973), *L'anti-Œdipe. Capitalisme et schizophrénie*, Éditions de Minuit, Paris.

Den Boer, M. (1996), 'Immigrants, Asylum Seekers and Criminalisation: The Interaction between Criminal Justice Policy and Criminology', paper presented at the Round Table *Un nouveau champ de sécurité en Europe*, CERI/CNRS, Paris.

Den Boer, M. (1998), 'Crime et immigration dans l'Union européenne', *Cultures & Conflits*, n° 31-32, pp. 101-123.

Derrida, J. (1994), *Politiques de l'amitié*, Galilée, Paris.

Dezalay, Y. (1998), 'Regionalism, Globalisation, and "Professional Society": Between State, Law and the Market for Professional Services', in Coleman, W. and Underhill, G. (eds), *Regionalism & Global Economic Integration*, Routledge, London, pp. 197-222.

Direction des Affaires Criminelles et des Grâces (2000), *Rapport au Garde des Sceaux sur la politique pénale menée en 1999*, Ministère de la Justice, Paris.

Donzelot, J. (1984), *L'invention du social. Essai sur le déclin des passions politiques*, Fayard, Paris.

Edelman, M. (1987), *The Symbolic Uses of Politics*, Urbana, University of Illinois Press.

Edelman, M. (1988), *Constructing the Political Spectacle*, University of Chicago Press, Chicago.

Edelman, M. (1991), *Pièces et règles du jeu politique*, Seuil, Paris.

Ericson, R. V. and Haggerty, K. D. (1997), *Policing the Risk Society*, University of Toronto Press, Toronto.

Ericson, R. V. and Stehr, N. (2000), *Governing Modern Societies*, The Green College Thematic Lecture Series, University of Toronto Press, Toronto.

Espenshade, T. J. and Hempstead, K. (1996), 'Contemporary American Attitudes toward US Immigration', *International Migration Review*, **30**(2), pp. 535-570.

Ewald, F. (1996), *Histoire de l'État providence*, Folio, Paris.

Foucault, M. (1969), *L'archéologie du savoir*, NRF Gallimard, Paris.

Foucault, M. (1975), *Surveiller et Punir. Naissance de la prison*, Gallimard, Paris.

Foucault, M. (1977), *Discipline and Punish: The Birth of the Prison*, Pantheon Books, New-York.

Foucault, M. (1989), *Sécurité, territoire et population. Résume des cours*, Julliard, Paris.

Foucault, M. (1994), *Dits Et Ecrits: 1954-1988*, Gallimard, Paris.

Foucault, M. (1997), *Il faut défendre la société. Cours au Collège de France, 1976*, Gallimard/Seuil, Paris.

Foucault, M. (1998), *Les anormaux. Cours au Collège de France, 1975*, Gallimard/Seuil, Paris.

Foucault, M. and Kriegel, B. (1975), *I, Pierre Rivière, Having Slaughtered My Mother, My Sister, and My Brother ...: A Case of Parricide in the 19th Century*, Pantheon Books, New-York.

Foucault, M. and Gordon, C. (1980), *Power/Knowledge: Selected Interviews and Other Writings, 1972-1977*, Harvester Press, Hassocks.

Foucher, Michel, (1988), *Fronts et frontières: un tour du monde géopolitique*, Fayard, Paris.

Fransman, L. (1998), *British Nationality Law*, Butterworths, London.

Fullerton, M., Sik, E. and Toth, J. (1995), 'Refugees and Migrants: Hungary at a Crossroads', Institute for Political Sciences of the Hungarian Academy of Sciences, Budapest.

Gambier, D. and Vernieres, M. (1998), *L'emploi en France*, La Découverte, Paris.

Ganster, P., Sweedler, A., Scott, J. and Eberwein, W.-D. (1997), *Borders and Border Regions in Europe and North America*, Institute for Regional Studies of the California, San Diego.

Garland, D. (1998), 'Les contradictions de la "société punitive": le cas britannique', *Actes de la Recherche en Sciences, Sociales*, **124**.

Garland, D. (2001), *The Culture of Control: Crime and Social Order in Contemporary Society*, University of Chicago Press, Chicago.

Gatti, U., Malfatti, D. and Verde, A. (1997), 'Minorities, Crime, and Criminal Justice in Italy', in Marshall, T. H. (ed.), *Minorities, Migrants and Crime*, Sage Publications, London, pp. 110-129.

Geddes, A. (2000), 'Denying Access: Asylum Seekers and Welfare Benefits in the UK', in Bommes, M. and Geddes, A. (eds), *Immigration and Welfare Challenging the Borders of the Welfare State*, Routledge, London, pp. 134-147.

Giddens, A. (1987), *The Nation State and violence, contemporary critique of historical materialism*, UCLA, Los Angeles.

Goldblatt, D., Held, D., McGrew, A. and Perraton, J. (1997), 'Economic globalization and the Nation-State: Shifting Balances of Power', *Alternatives*, **22**(3).

Goodwin-Gil, G. (1978), *The Refugee in International Law*, OUP, Oxford.

Gordon, C. and Gordon, G. (1988), *Immigration Law and procedure. Practice and Strategies*, Matthew Bender, New York.

Gregory, F. (1998), 'Policing Transition in Europe: The Role of EUROPOL and the Problem of Organized Crime', *Innovation*, **3**, pp. 287-305.

Groenedijk, K., Guild, E. and Minderhoud, P. (2003), *In search of Europe's borders, Immigration and Asylum Law and Policy in Europe*, vol. 5, Kluwer Law International, The Hague.

Groenendijk, K. and Hampsink, R. (1995), 'Temporary Employment of Migrants in Europe', *Reeks, Recht & Samenleving*, GNI, Nijmegen.

Groenendijk, K., Guild, E. and Barzilay, R. (1998), *Security of Residence of Long Term Migrants: A Comparative Study of Law and Practice in European Countries*, Council of Europe, Strasbourg.

Groenendijk, K., Guild, E. and Barzilay, R. (2001), *The Legal Status of Third Country Nationals Who Are Long-Term Residents in a Member State of the European Union*, European Commission, Brussels.

Guild, E. (1999), 'The Impetus to Harmonise: Asylum Policy in the European Union', in Nicholson, F. and Twomey, P. (eds), *Refugee Rights and Realities*, CUP, Cambridge, pp. 313-335.

Guild, E. (2000), 'Adjudicating Schengen: National Judicial Control in France', *European Journal of Migration and Law*, 1, **4**, pp. 419-39.

Guild, E. (2000), 'Entry into the UK: The Changing Nature of National Borders', *I&NL&P*, **14**(4), pp. 227-238.

Guild, E. and Minderhoud, P. E. (2001), *Security of Residence and Expulsion: Protection of Aliens in Europe, Immigration and Asylum Law and Policy in Europe*, vol. 1, Kluwer Law International, The Hague.

Guild, E. and Niessen, J. (1996), *The Developing Immigration and Asylum Policies of the European Union*, Kluwer Law International, The Hague/London.

Gulbenkian, P. and Badoux, T. (1993), *Immigration Law and Business in Europe*, European Immigration Lawyers Group, Chichester.

Hall, S. (1996), *Questions of Cultural Identity*, Sage, London.

Hanagan, M. (1998), 'Labor History and the New Migration History: A Review Essay', *International Labor and Working Class History*, **54**, pp. 57-79.

Hantrais, L. (1999), 'What is a Family or Family Life in the European Union?', in Guild, E. (ed.), *The Legal Framework and Social Consequences of Free Movement of Persons in the European Union*, Kluwer Law International, The Hague/London.

Hardt, M. and Negri, A. (2001), *Empire*, Harvard University Press, Cambridge.

Hathaway, J. (1991), *The Law of Refugee Status*, Butterworths, Toronto.

Heisler, M. (2001), 'Now and then, here and there', in Albert, M., Jacobson, D. and Lapid, Y. (eds), *Identities, Borders, Orders*, University of Minnesota Press, Minneapolis, pp. 225-247.

Held, D. (1996), 'Cosmopolitan Democracy and the Global Order: Reflections on the 200th Anniversary of Kant's Perpetual Peace', *Alternatives*, **20**(4), pp. 415-29.

Held, D. (1991), 'Democracy, the Nation-State and the Global System', *Econcomy and Society*, **20**(2), pp. 138-172.

Held, D. (1992), 'Democracy and Globalization', *Alternatives*, **16**(2), pp. 201-208.

Held, D. (2002), 'Globalization, Corporate Practice and Cosmopolitan Social Standards', *Contemporary Political Theory*, **1**(1), pp. 59-78.

Hirschman, A. (1970), *Exit, Voice and Loyalty*, Harvard University Press, Cambridge.

Hirschman, A. (1990), *Deux siècles de rhétoriques réactionnaires*, Fayard, Paris.

Hirst, P. and Thompson, G. (1996), *Globalisation in question: the international economy and the possibility of governance*, Polity Press, Cambridge.

Huntington, S. P. (1993), 'The Clash of Civilizations?', *Foreign Affairs*, **72**(3), pp. 22-49.

Huntington, S. P. (1997), *Le choc des civilisations*, Jacob, Paris.

Hurwitz, A. (1999), 'The 1990 Dublin Convention: A Comprehensive Assessment', *International Journal of Refugee Law*, **11**(4), pp. 646-677.

Huysmans, J. (1995), 'Migrants as a security problem: dangers of securitizing societal issues', in, Miles, R. and Thränhardt, D. (eds), *Migration and European Integration. The Dynamics of Inclusion and Exclusion*, Pinter, London, pp. 53-72.

Huysmans, J. (1997), 'European Identity and Migration Policies: Socio-economic and Security Questions in a Process of Europeanization', in Cederman, L.-E. (ed.), *Constructing Europe's Identity Issues and Tradeoffs*, The Central European University, Political Science Working Papers no. 9, Budapest.

ISPAC (1996), *Migration and Crime*, ISPAC, Milano.

Jackson, J. (1997), *The World Trading System*, MIT Press, Cambridge.

Jacobson, D. (1996), *Rights across borders: Immigration and the decline of citizenship*, John Hopkins University Press, Baltimore.

Join-Lambert, M.-T. (ed.) (1997), *Politiques sociales*, Presses de Sciences-Po/Dalloz, Paris.

Kagan, R. (2003), *Of Paradise and Power: America and Europe in the New World Order*, Knopf, New York.

Karydis, V. (1996), *I eglimatikotita ton metanaston stin Ellada [The crime involvement of migrants in Greece]*, Papazissis, Athens.

Kastoryano, Riva (dir.) (1998), *Quelle identité pour l'Europe? Le multiculturalisme à l'épreuve*, Presses de la FNSP, Paris.

Kelstrup, M. and Williams, M. C. (2000), *International relations theory and the politics of European integration, power, security and community*, Routledge, London.

Kennett, W. (1996), 'The European Community and the General Agreement on Trade in Services', in Emiliou, N. and O'Keeffe, D. (eds), *The European Union and World Trade Law After the GATT Uruguay Round.*, John Wiley & Sons, Chichester.

Khosrokhavar, F. (2003), *Les nouveaux martyrs d'Allah*, Flammarion, Paris.

Kiehl, M. and Werner, H. (1998), 'The Labour Market Situation of EU and of Third Country Nationals in the European Union', *Institut fur Arbeitsmarkt-und Berufsforschung, Nurnberg*, **32**, IAB Labour Market Research Topics, Nurnberg.

Koslowski, R. (1998), 'Personal Security, State Sovereignty and the Deepening and Widening of European Cooperation in Justice and Home Affairs', Conference Paper presented at the Conference, *Dilemmas of Immigration Control in a Globalizing World*, of the European Forum on International Migrations, MIG/59, European University Institute, Florence.

Lahav, G. (1998), 'Immigration and the State: the Devolution and Privatization of Immigration Control in the EU', *Journal of Ethnic and Migration Studies*, **24**(4), pp. 675-694.

Laudon, K. (1986), *The Dossier Society. Value Choices in the Design of National Information System*, Columbia University Press, New York.

Lavenex, S. (1998), 'Asylum, Immigration and Central-Eastern Europe: Challenges to EU Enlargement', *European Foreign Affairs Review*, **3**(2), pp. 275-294.

Lessana, C. (1998), 'Loi Debré: la fabrique de l'immigré', *Cultures & Conflits*, **31/32**.

Lester, R. (1973), *World without Borders*, Vintage books, New-York.

Leveau, R. (1994), 'Les jeunes issus de l'immigration maghrébine', in Badie, B. and De Wenden, C. (eds), *Le défi migratoire, questions de relations internationales*, Presses de la FNSP, Paris.

Leveau, R. (1989), 'Réflexions sur le non-passage au terrorisme dans l'immigration maghrébine en France', *Etudes polémologiques*, **49**, pp. 141-156.

Levin, K., 'The Free Movement of Workers', *CLMRev*, **64/65**, pp. 300-325.

Lipschutz, R. (2000), *After Authority, War, Peace and Global Politics in the 21st Century*, State University Press, Albany.

Lyon, D. (1994), *The Electronic Eye*, Polity Press, Cambridge.

Maneri, M. (1997), 'Les médias dans le processus de construction sociale de la criminalité des immigrés. Le cas italien', in Palidda, S. (ed.), *Délit d'immigration, COST A2 Migrations*. Commission Européenne, Brussels, pp. 51-72.

Mariani, P. (2001), 'Law, Order, and Neoliberalism', *Social Justice*, **28**(3), pp. 1-152.

Marx, G. T (1988), 'La société de sécurité maximale', *Déviance et société*, **2**.

Marx, G. T. (1994), 'The Declining Signification of Traditional Borders and the Appearance of New Borders in an Age of High Technology', Paper for the conference on *Georg Simmel Between Modernity and Post modernity*, Ludwig Maximiliams-Universität, Munchen.

Mathiesen, T. (1997), 'The viewer society: Michel Foucault's Panopticon Revisited', *Theoretical Criminology*, **1/2**, pp. 215-234.

Mead, G. H. (1963), *L'esprit, le soi et la société*, Presses Universitaires de France, Paris.

Minderhoud, P. (1999), 'Asylum Seekers and Access to Social Security: Recent Developments in the Netherlands, United Kingdom, Germany and Belgium', in Bloch, A. and Levy, C. (eds), *Refugees, Citizenship and Social Policy in Europe*, MacMillan, Houndmills, pp. 132-148.

Mukherjee, N. (1996), 'Exporting Labour Services and Market Access Commitments under GATS in the World Trade Organisation', *Journal of World Trade*, **30**(5), pp. 20-41.

Naylor, R. T. (1995), 'From Cold War to Crime War: The Search for a New "National Security"', *Transnational Organized Crime*, **4**, pp. 37-56.

Newman, D. (2001), 'Boundaries, borders, and barriers: changing geographic perspectives on territorial lines', in Albert, M., Jacobson, D. and Lapid, Y. (eds), *Identities, Borders, Orders*, University of Minnesota Press, Minneapolis, pp. 137-151.

Noiriel, G. (1993), *La tyrannie du national: le droit d'asile en Europe 1793-1993*, Calmann-Lévy, Paris.

Noiriel, G. (1996), *The French Melting-Pot: Immigration, Citizenship and National Identity*, University of Minneapolis Press, Minneapolis.

Noiriel, G. (2001), *Etat, nation et immigration. Vers une histoire du pouvoir*, Belin, Paris.

Noll, G. (1997), 'The Non-Admission and Return of Protection Seekers in Germany', *International Journal of Refugee Law*, **9**(3), pp. 415-452.

Noll, G. (2001), 'Formalism vs. Empiricism: Some Reflections on the Dublin Convention on the Occasion of Recent European Case Law', *Nordic Journal of International Law*, **70**(1/2), pp. 161-182.

Noll, G. and Vedsted-Hansen, J. (1999), 'Non-Communitarians: Refugee and Asylum Policies', in Alston, P. (ed.), *The EU and Human Rights*, OUP, Oxford, pp. 359-410.

Nolutshungu, S. C. (ed.) (1996), *Margins of insecurity, minorities and international security*, University of Rochester press, Rochester.

Oakeshott, M. (1975), *On the Character of a Modern European State, On Human Conduct*, Oxford University Press, Oxford.

Ohlemacher, T. (1994), 'Public Opinion and Violence Against Foreigners in the Reunified Germany', *Zeitschrift für Soziologie*, 3, pp. 222-236.

Palidda, S. (1993), 'L'anamorphose De L'etat-Nation: Le Cas Italien (Anamorphosis of the National State: The Italian Case)', *Cahiers internationaux de Sociologie*, 93, pp. 269-98.

Palidda, S. (1997), 'La construction sociale de la déviance et de la criminalité parmi les immigrés. Le cas italien', in Palidda, S. (ed.), *Délit d'immigration, COST A2 Migrations*. Commission Européenne, Brussels, pp. 231-266.

Palidda, S. (1999), 'La criminalisation des migrants', *Actes de la recherche en sciences sociales*, 129, pp. 39-49.

Peers, S. (2000), *EU Justice and Home Affairs Law*, Longman, Harlow.

Peers, S. (2001), 'Key Legislative Developments on Migration in the European Union', *EJML*, 3(2), pp. 231-255.

Perrot, M., Foucault, M. and Agulhon, M. (1980), *L'impossible Prison: Recherches Sur Le Système Pénitentiaire Au XIXe Siècle, L'univers Historique*, Seuil, Paris.

Plender, R. (1997), *Basic Documents on International Migration Law*, Martinus Nijhoff, The Hague.

Prescott, J. R. V. (1987) *Political Frontiers and Boundaries*, London. Brown.

Preuss-Laussignotte, S. (2000), *Les fichiers des étrangers au cœur des nouvelles politiques de sécurité*, unpublished PhD. Thesis, University of Paris X-Nanterre.

Rattansi, A. and Westwood, S. (1994), *Racism modernity identity on the western front*, Polity press, Oxford.

Rea, A. (ed.) (1998), *Immigration et racisme en Europe*, Complexe, Bruxelles.

Remedios, E. (1998), 'Benefits, Immigrants and Asylum Seekers – a Review', *I&NL&P*, 12(3), pp. 188-196.

Roché, S. (2001), *La délinquance des jeunes*, Seuil, Paris.

Rogin, M. (1997), 'La répression politique aux Etats-Unis', *Actes de la recherche en sciences sociales*, 120, pp 32-44.

Rosenau, J. N. (1990), *Turbulence in World Politics, A Theory of Change and Continuity*, Princeton University Press, Princeton, N.J.

Ruggie, J. (1992), 'Territoriality and Beyond: Problematizing Modernity in International Relations', *International Organization*, 472, pp. 139-174.

Ruggie, J. (1998), *Constructing the World Polity. Essays on International Institutionalization*, Routledge, London.

Salt, J. and Kitching, R. (1990), 'Labour Migration and the Work Permit System in the United Kingdom', *International Migration*, 28(3), pp. 267-294.

Salt, J., Singleton, A. and Hogarth, J. (1994), *Europe's International Migrants: Data Sources, Patterns and Trends*, HMSO, London.

Sassen, S. (1995), 'Immigration and Local Labor Markets', in, Portes, A. (ed.), *The Economic Sociology of Immigration: Essays in Networks, Ethnicity, and Enterpreneurship*, Russell Sage Foundation, New-York, pp. 87-127.

Sayad, A. (1999), 'Immigration et "pensée d'Etat"', *Actes de la recherche en sciences sociales*, 129, pp. 5-14.

Sayad, A. (1999), *La double absence. Des illusions de l'émigré aux souffrances de l'immigré*, Seuil, Paris.

Schlesinger, P. and Tumber, H. (1994), *Reporting Crime. The Media Politics of Criminal Justice*, Clarendon Press, Oxford.

Schmitt, C. (1972), *La notion de politique et théorie du partisan*, Calmann-Lévy, Paris.

Schneider, A. and Ingram, H. (1993), 'Social Construction of Target Populations for Politics and Policy', *American Political Science Review*, **67**(2), pp. 334-347.

Sellin, T. (1984), *Conflits de culture et criminalité*, Pedone, Paris.

Sheptycki, J. W. E. (2002), *In Search of Transnational Policing: Towards a Sociology of Global Policing*, *Advances in Criminology*, Ashgate, Aldershot.

Sheptycki, J. W. E. (dir), (2000), *Issues in Transnational Policing*, Routledge, London.

Simmel, G. (1964), 'The Stranger', in, Wolf, K. H. (ed.), *The Sociology of Simmel*, The Free Press, New York.

Solomos, J. and Back, L. (1996), *Racism and society*, Macmillan, London.

Soysal, Y. (1994), *Limits of Citizenship. Migrants and Post national Membership in Europe*, University of Chicago Press Chicago.

Spinellis, C. *et al.* (1996), 'Recent Immigration and Protection of Migrants' Human Rights in Greece', *Chroniques*, September, pp. 119-154.

Stern, B. and Hoekman, N. (1987), 'Negotiations on Services', *The World Economy*, **10**.

Strange, S. (1996), *Retreat of the State: The Diffusion of Power in the World Economy*, Cambridge University Press, Cambridge.

Syndicat de la Magistrature (2002), *Vos papiers. Que faire face à la police?*, Esprit Frappeur, Paris.

Taylor, C. (1992), *Multiculturalism and "The Politics of Recognition"*, Princeton University Press, Princeton, NJ.

Tilley, C. and Tilley, C. (1998), *Work under Capitalism*, Westview, Boulder.

Tilly, C. (1975), *The formation of national states in Western Europe*, Princeton University Press, Princeton.

Torpey, J. (2001), *The Invention of the Passport*, Cambridge University Press, London.

Torpey, J. and Marrus, M. (1985), *The Unwanted: European Refugees in the 20th Century*, Oxford University Press, Oxford.

Tournier, P. (1997), 'La délinquance des étrangers en France – analyse des statistiques pénales', in Palidda, S. (ed.), *Délit d'immigration, COST A2 Migrations,* Commission Européenne, pp. 133-162.

Tournier, P., 'La Délinquance Des étrangers En France – Analyse Des Statistiques Pénales', in, Palidda, S., *Délit D'immigration, Cost A2 Migrations*, Commission Européenne, Brussels, pp. 133-162.

Triandafyllidou, A. (1997), 'Racists? Us? Are you joking? The Discourse of Social Exclusion of Immigrants in Greece and Italy', *Non Military Aspects of Security in Southern Europe: Migration, Employment and Labour Market*, Institute of International Economic Relations et Regional Network on Southern European Societies, Santorini.

Triandafyllidou, A. (1999), 'Nation and Immigration: a Study of the Italian Press Discourse', *Social Identities*, **1**, pp. 65-88.

Trombadori, D. and Foucault, M. (1981), *Colloqui Con Foucault, Discorsi: 1*, 10/17, Salerno.

Tsoukala, A. (1997), 'Le contrôle de l'immigration en Grèce dans les années quatre-vingt-dix', *Cultures & Conflits*, **26/27**, pp. 51-72.

Tsoukala, A. (1999), 'Le discours grec sur la criminalité des immigrés', *Hommes & Migrations*, **1218**, pp. 77-89.

Tsoukala, A. (1999), 'The perception of the "other" and the integration of immigrants in Greece', in Geddes, A. and Favell, A. (eds), *The Politics of Belonging: Migrants and Minorities in Contemporary Europe*, Ashgate, Aldershot, pp. 109-124.

274 *Controlling Frontiers*

Tsoukala, A. (2002), 'Le traitement médiatique de la criminalité étrangère en Europe', *Déviance et société*, **26**(1), pp. 61-82.
van der Klaauw, J. (1998), 'The Dublin Convention: A Difficult Start', in den Boer, M. (ed.), *Schengen's Final Days?*, EIPA, Maastricht, pp. 77-92.
Van Dijk, T. (1993), *Elite Discourse and Racism*, Sage Publications, Newbury Park, London.
van Hoof, F. (1998), 'International Human Rights Obligations of Companies and Domestic Courts: An Unlikely Combination', in Castermans-Holeman, M., van Hoof, F. and Smith, J. (eds), *The Role of the National State in the 21st Century, Human Rights, International Organisations and Foreign Policy, Essays in Honour of Peter Baehr*, Kluwer Law International, London/Boston/The Hague, pp. 135-150.
Van Outrive, L., Renault, G. and Vanderborght, J. (1996), 'La collaboration policière en Europe', *Déviances et sociétés*, **20**(2).
Wacquant, L. (1999), 'Des ennemis commodes', *Actes de la recherche en sciences sociales*, **129**, pp. 63-67.
Wacquant, L. (1999), *Les prisons de la misère*, Raisons d'agir, Paris.
Waever, O. (1997), *Concepts of Security*, Copenhagen Institute for Political Science, University of Copenhagen, Copenhagen.
Walker, R. B. J. (1993), *Inside-outside, international relations as political theory*, Cambridge University Press, Cambridge studies in international relations, Cambridge.
Wayne, C., Martin, P. and Hollifield, J. (eds) (1994), *Controlling Immigration*, Stanford University Press, Stanford.
Weber, M. (1947), *The Theory of Social and Economic Organization*, Parsons, T. (ed.), Free Press, Glencose.
Weil, P. (1991), *La France et ses étrangers*, Presses de la FNSP, Paris.
Wieviorka, M. (1998), 'Un nouveau paradigme de la violence?', *Cultures & Conflits*, **29/30**.
Wilson, J. Q. and Kelling, G. (1982), 'Broken Windows: The Police and Neighborhood Safety', *The Atlantic Monthly*, March 1982, Boston.
Winterbourne, D., Shah, P. and Doebbler, C. (1996), 'Refugees and Safe Countries of Origin: Appeals, Judicial Review and Human Rights', *I&NL&P*, **10**(4), pp. 123-135.
Wyatt-Walker, A. (1998), 'Globalisation, Corporate Identity and EU Technology Policy', in Coleman, W. and Underhill, G. (eds), *Regulation and Global Economic Integration*, Routledge, London, pp. 141-157.
Zielonka, J. (2002), *Europe unbound: enlarging and reshaping the boundaries of the European Union*, Routledge, London.

Index